LIFELINES

SUSTAINABLE INFRASTRUCTURE SERIES

LIFELINES

The Resilient Infrastructure Opportunity

Stéphane Hallegatte
Jun Rentschler
Julie Rozenberg

WORLD BANK GROUP

1818 H Street NW, Washington, DC 20433
Telephone: 202-473-1000; Internet: www.worldbank.org

1 2 3 4 22 21 20 19

ISBN (paper): 978-1-4648-1430-3
ISBN (electronic): 978-1-4648-1431-0
DOI: 10.1596/978-1-4648-1430-3
Cover design and graphs: Brad Amburn, Brad Amburn Creative, LLC

Library of Congress Cataloging-in-Publication Data has been requested

Contents

Boxes

Figures

Maps

Photo

Tables

Foreword

Resilient infrastructure is about people. It is about the households and communities for whom infrastructure is a lifeline to better health, better education, and a better livelihood. It affects people's well-being, their economic prospects, and their quality of life.

Resilient infrastructure, is in part, about bridges that can withstand more frequent or stronger floods, water pipes that can resist earthquakes, or electric poles that are sturdier in the face of more intense hurricanes. And it is also about making sure people will not lose their jobs because they cannot get to work, that they can get urgent medical care, and that their children can get to school.

In developing countries, infrastructure disruptions are an everyday concern. When infrastructure fails, it undermines businesses, job creation, and economic development. With rapidly growing populations and a changing climate increasing the frequency and intensity of natural hazards, the need to adapt and invest in resilience should be an urgent priority.

Disruption to infrastructure costs households and firms in low- and middle-income countries at least $390 billion a year, and the indirect effects place a further toll on households, businesses, and communities. It is typically caused by poor maintenance, mismanagement, and the natural hazards that are increasing due to climate change.

But there is good news. Around the world, there are many examples of investments that make infrastructure more resilient and more economically robust.

This report assesses, for the first time, the cost of infrastructure disruptions to low- and middle-income countries and the economic benefits of investing in resilient infrastructure. It examines four essential infrastructure systems: power, water and sanitation, transport, and telecommunications. And the report lays out a framework for understanding the ability of infrastructure systems to function and meet users' needs during and after natural shocks.

We find that the extra cost of building resilience into these systems is only 3 percent of overall investment needs. Thanks to fewer disruptions and reduced economic impacts, the overall net benefit of investing in the resilience of infrastructure in developing countries would be $4.2 trillion over the lifetime of new infrastructure. That is a $4 benefit for each dollar invested in resilience.

Finally, with a range of clearly defined recommendations, the report lays out how to unlock this $4.2 trillion opportunity. Rather than just spending more, the focus is on spending better. The message for infrastructure investors, governments, development banks, and the private sector is this: Invest in regulations and planning, in the early stages of project design, and in maintenance. Doing so can significantly outweigh the costs of repairs or reconstruction after a disaster strikes.

There is no time to waste. With a rapidly changing climate, and large investments in infrastructure taking place in many countries, business as usual over the next decade would cost $1 trillion more. By getting it right, however, we can provide the critical infrastructure services—lifelines—that will spur sustained and resilient economic development.

Kristalina Georgieva
Chief Executive Officer
The World Bank

Acknowledgments

The *Lifelines* report was prepared by a team led by Stéphane Hallegatte, with Jun Rentschler and Julie Rozenberg. It benefited from contributions from multiple teams working on different sectors and topics. The power sector analysis was led by Claire Nicolas, with a team composed of Christopher Arderne, Diana Cubas, Mark Deinert, Eriko Ichikawa, Elco Koks, Ji Li, Samuel Oguah, Albertine Potter van Loon, and Amy Schweikert. The water sector analysis was led by Zhimin Mao, working with Laura Bonzanigo, Xi Hu, Elco Koks, Weeho Lim, Raghav Pant, Patrick Ray, Clementine Stip, Jacob Tracy, and Conrad Zorn. The transport sector analysis was led by Julie Rozenberg, with Xavier Espinet Alegre, Charles Fox, Stuart Fraser, Jim Hall, Elco Koks, Mercedeh Tariverdi, Michalis Vousdoukas, and Conrad Zorn. The telecommunication analysis was contributed by Himmat Sandhu and Siddhartha Raja. The analysis of firm and household surveys was led by Jun Rentschler, with Paolo Avner, Johannes Braese, Alvina Erman, Nick Jones, Martin Kornejew, Sadick Nassoro, Marguerite Obolensky, Samet Sahin, and Eugene Tan. Shinji Ayuha, Célian Colon, Etienne Raffi Kechichian, Maryia Markhvida, Nah Yoon Shin, Shoko Takemoto, and Brian Walsh contributed to the sections on resilient industries and supply chains. Sanae Sasamori and Naho Shibuya contributed to the sections on public-private partnerships. The team at Miyamoto International provided important insights into the engineering solutions to build resilience.

As World Bank Group peer reviewers, Greg Browder, Marianne Fay, Vivien Foster, Hideaki Hamada, Helen Martin, Shomik Mehndiratta, Artessa Saldivar-Sali, Alanna Simpson, and Vladimir Stenek provided invaluable comments and suggestions. Thanks also to external advisors: Carter Brandon, Jim Hall, Guillaume Prudent-Richard, Adam Rose, and Yasuyuki Todo.

Suggestions, comments, and data were provided by Anjali Acharya, Charles Baubion, Andrii Berdnyk, Moussa Blimpo, Marga Cantada, Debabrata Chattopadhyay, Ashraf Dewan, Mirtha Escobar, Charles Esser, Scott Ferguson, Matias Herrera Dappe, Martin Humphreys, Marie Hyland, Oscar Ishizawa, Asif Islam, Brenden Jongman, Denis Jordy, Balázs Józsa, Shefali Khanna, Brian Kinuthia, Shweta Kulkarni, Mathijs van Ledden, Jia Jun Lee, Richard MacGeorge, Justice Tei Mensah, Jared Mercadante, Brian Min, Alice Mortlock, Sumati Rajput, Steven Rubinyi, Jason Russ, Peter Sanfey, Guillermo Siercke, Ben Stewart, Shen Sun, Janna Tenzing, Joshua Wimpey, Davida Wood, and Fan Zhang.

Susan Graham of the World Bank Group's Publishing Unit was the production editor. Editorial services were provided by Sabra Ledent, Laura Wallace, Nick Paul, Devan Kreisberg, Inge Pakulski, and Elizabeth Forsyth. Brad Amburn designed the cover and created the graphs. The team also thanks Aziz Gökdemir and Jewel McFadden for their help in preparing the report for production. Visibility and launch of the report were supported by Ferzina Banaji, with Uwimana Basaninyenzi, Joana Lopes, Camila Perez, Mehreen Arshad Sheikh, and Gerardo Spatuzzi.

The team thanks Julie Dana, manager of the Global Facility for Disaster Reduction and Recovery (GFDRR), and Luis Tineo for their support in the development of this project.

Finally, the team acknowledges the generous support of the Japan–World Bank Program for Mainstreaming Disaster Risk Management in Developing Countries, the Climate Change Group of the World Bank under the leadership of John Roome and Bernice Van Bronkhorst, and the World Bank Sustainable Development Practice Group led by Laura Tuck.

Abbreviations

AMI	advanced metering infrastructure
APEC	Asia-Pacific Economic Cooperation
DEM	digital elevation model
EAD	expected annual damage
ESG	environmental, social, and governance (principles)
GDP	gross domestic product
GFDRR	Global Facility for Disaster Reduction and Recovery
ICT	information and communication technology
IPCC	Intergovernmental Panel on Climate Change
ISO	International Organization for Standardization
LPI	Logistics Performance Index
OECD	Organisation for Economic Co-operation and Development
PGA	peak ground acceleration
PPP	public-private partnership
RUC	road user cost
UNISDR	United Nations Office for Disaster Risk Reduction
WEF	World Economic Forum
WGI	*Worldwide Governance Indicators* (World Bank report)
WMO	World Meteorological Organization

Overview

From serving our most basic needs to enabling our most ambitious ventures in trade or technology, infrastructure services support our well-being and development. Reliable water, sanitation, energy, transport, and telecommunication services are universally considered to be essential for raising the quality of life of people. Access to basic infrastructure services is also a central factor in the productivity of firms and thus of entire economies, making it a key enabler of economic development. And in this time of rapid climate change and intensifying natural disasters, infrastructure systems are under pressure to deliver resilient and reliable services.

By one estimate, governments in low- and middle-income countries around the world are investing around $1 trillion—between 3.4 percent and 5 percent of gross domestic product (GDP)—in infrastructure every year (Fay et al. 2019).[1] Still, the quality and adequacy of infrastructure services vary widely across countries. Millions of people, especially in fast-growing cities in low- and middle-income countries, are facing the consequences of substandard infrastructure, often at a significant cost. Underfunding and poor maintenance are some of the key factors resulting in unreliable electricity grids, inadequate water and sanitation systems, and overstrained transport networks.

Natural hazards magnify the challenges faced by these already-strained and fragile systems. Urban flooding, for instance, is a reality for people around the world—from Amman, Buenos Aires, and Dar es Salaam to Jakarta and Mumbai. Often exacerbated by poor drainage systems, these floods cause frequent disruptions in transport and energy networks, which in turn affect telecommunications and other essential services. The lack of resilient sanitation systems also means that floods often spread dangerous waterborne diseases.

The disruption of infrastructure services is especially severe when considering more extreme natural shocks. For example, earthquakes damage port infrastructure and slow down local economies, as occurred in Kobe in 1995. Hurricanes wipe out electricity transmission and distribution systems, cutting people's access to electricity for months, as occurred in Puerto Rico in 2017. In these examples, many people who did not experience direct damage from the disaster still experienced impacts from infrastructure disruptions.

This report, *Lifelines: The Resilient Infrastructure Opportunity,* explores the resilience of four essential infrastructure systems: power, water and sanitation, transport, and telecommunications. All of these systems provide critical services for the well-being of households and the productivity of firms, yet they are particularly vulnerable to natural hazards because they are organized in complex networks through which even small local shocks can propagate quickly. Making them more resilient—that is, better able to deliver the services people and firms need during and after natural shocks—is critical, not only to avoid costly damage but also to minimize the wide-ranging consequences of natural disasters for the livelihoods and well-being of people.

Building on a wide range of case studies, global empirical analyses, and modeling exercises, this report arrives at three main messages:

- *The lack of resilient infrastructure is harming people and firms.* Natural disasters cause direct damage to power generation and transport infrastructure, costing about $18 billion a year in low- and middle-income countries. This damage is straining public budgets and reducing the attractiveness of these sectors for private investors. But natural hazards not only damage assets, they also disrupt infrastructure services, with significant impacts on firms and people. Altogether, infrastructure disruptions impose costs between $391 billion and $647 billion a year on households and firms in low- and middle-income countries. These disruptions have a wide range of causes, including poor maintenance, mismanagement, and underfunding. But case studies suggest that natural hazards typically explain 10 percent to 70 percent of the disruptions, depending on the sector and the region.
- *Investing in more resilient infrastructure is robust, profitable, and urgent.* In low- and middle-income countries, designs for more resilient assets in the power, water and sanitation, and transport sectors would cost between $11 billion and $65 billion a year by 2030—an incremental cost of around 3 percent compared with overall investment needs. And these costs can be reduced by looking at *services*, not just *assets*, and making infrastructure service *users*—households and supply chains—better able to manage disruptions. This report finds that investing $1 in more resilient infrastructure is beneficial in 96 percent of thousands of scenarios exploring possible future socioeconomic and climate trends. In the median scenario, the net benefit of investing in more resilient infrastructure in low- and middle-income countries is $4.2 trillion, with $4 in benefit for each $1 invested. Climate change makes action on resilience even more necessary and attractive: on average, it doubles the net benefits from resilience. And because large investments in infrastructure are currently being made in low- and middle-income countries, the median cost of one decade of inaction is $1 trillion.
- *Good infrastructure management is the necessary basis for resilient infrastructure, but targeted actions are also needed.* Unfortunately, no single intervention will make infrastructure systems resilient. Instead, a range of coordinated actions will be required. The first recommendation is for countries to get the basics right—proper planning, operation, and maintenance of their assets—which can both increase resilience and save costs. However, good design and management alone are not enough to make infrastructure resilient, especially against rare and high-intensity hazards and long-term trends like climate change. To address these issues, this report offers four additional recommendations: define institutional mandates and strategies for infrastructure resilience; introduce resilience in the regulations and incentive systems of infrastructure sectors, users, and supply chains; improve decision making through data, tools, and skills; and provide appropriate financing—especially for risk-informed master plans, asset design, and preparedness. Actions on these issues can be highly cost-effective and transformational, but they can nevertheless be challenging to fund in many poor countries, making them priorities for support from the international community.

INFRASTRUCTURE DISRUPTIONS ARE A DRAG ON PEOPLE AND ECONOMIES

This report begins by investigating how infrastructure disruptions—regardless of their origin—affect people and firms. The frequency of these disruptions is generally closely linked to the level of economic development, as shown in figure O.1 using GDP per capita as a proxy and electricity and water outages from the World Bank's Enterprise Surveys. Disruptions cost people both indirectly, through their effects on the productivity of firms, and directly, through their effects on households' consumption and well-being.

Infrastructure disruptions cost firms more than $300 billion per year

Unreliable infrastructure systems affect firms through various impacts (table O.1). Most visible are the direct impacts: a firm relying on water to cool a machine must halt production during a dryout; a restaurant with an electric

FIGURE O.1 Poorer countries are hit hardest by inadequate infrastructure

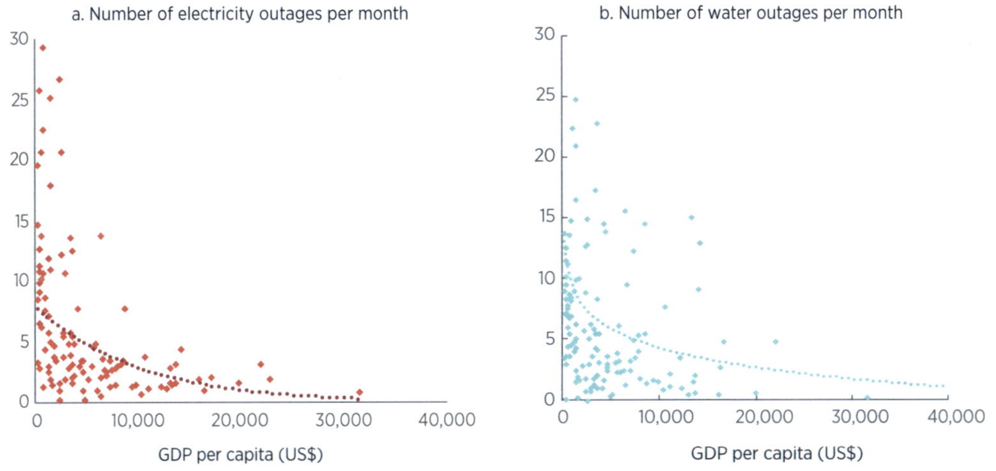

Source: Rentschler, Kornejew, et al. 2019, based on the World Bank's Enterprise Surveys.
Note: Panels a and b show the latest available survey data for 137 countries, but none older than 2009. Panel a only shows countries with up to 30 outages a month. Eight countries (all with GDP per capita below $9,000) report between 30 and 95 outages a month.

TABLE O.1 Disrupted infrastructure services have multiple impacts on firms

Sector	Direct impacts	Coping costs	Indirect impacts
Power	• **Reduced utilization rates ($38 billion a year)** • **Sales losses ($82 billion a year)**	• **Generator investment ($6 billion a year)** • **Generator operation costs ($59 billion a year)**	• Higher barriers to market entry and lower investment • Less competition and innovation due to lack of small and new firms • Bias toward labor-intensive production • Inability to provide on-demand services and goods • Diminished competitiveness in international markets
Water	• **Reduced utilization rates ($6 billion a year)** • Sales losses	• Investment in alternative water sources (reservoirs, wells)	
Transport	• **Reduced utilization rates ($107 billion a year)** • Sales losses • Delayed supplies and deliveries	• Increased inventory • More expensive location choices, for example, in proximity to clients or ports	
Telecommunications	• Reduced utilization rates • Sales losses	• Expensive location choices close to fast Internet	

Source: Rentschler, Kornejew, et al. 2019.
Note: Highlighted in bold are the impacts for which original estimates are presented in this section. Estimates cover low- and middle-income countries.

stove cannot cook meals without power. Disruptions leave production capacity unused, reduce firms' sales, and delay the supply and delivery of goods. Firms also incur costs for coping with unreliable infrastructure, such as for backup power generation or water storage. The indirect impacts of disruptions are less immediate. They include effects on the long-term investment and strategic decisions of firms and on the composition, competition, and innovation of industries. Together, these effects figure in an economy's ability to generate wealth and in its international competitiveness (for details, see Braese, Rentschler, and Hallegatte 2019).

Using a set of microdata on about 143,000 firms, it is possible to estimate the monetary costs of infrastructure disruption for firms in 137 low- and middle-income countries, representing 78 percent of the world population (map O.1).[2] These data are used to assess the impact of infrastructure disruptions on the capacity utilization rates of firms—that is, to compare the actual output of firms with the maximum output they can achieve using all of their available resources—which is a good metric for firms' performance.

The data reveal utilization losses from power, water, and transport disruptions of $151 billion a year. (Unfortunately, a similar estimate for telecommunications is not possible because of a lack of data.) In addition, firm data reveal sales losses from electricity outages of $82 billion a year and additional costs of self-generating electricity of $65 billion a year. Although these figures highlight the significance of unreliable infrastructure, they constitute lower-bound estimates of the global costs of outages because neither all countries nor all types of impacts are covered in this analysis.

Infrastructure disruptions' direct impacts on people are worth at least $90 billion per year

Unreliable infrastructure services negatively affect the welfare of households. Frequent power outages limit the ability of households to engage in productive, educational, and recreational activities (Lenz et al. 2017). In South Asia, Zhang (2019) finds that long power outages are associated with a decrease in both per capita income and women's labor force participation, probably because the lack of electricity is associated with an increase in the time needed for domestic work (figure O.2). Studies also identify a strong and consistent relationship between water outages and health impacts. In the Democratic Republic of Congo, suspected cholera incidence rates increased 155 percent after one day of water disruption, compared with the incidence rate following optimal water provision (Jeandron et al. 2015).

Infrastructure disruptions have many impacts on households, and estimating the global cost is difficult (table O.2). For this analysis, lower and upper bounds were established for power and water outages, based on studies assessing the willingness of households to pay to prevent such outages (see details in Obolensky et al. 2019). For power outages, the estimates range between 0.002 percent and 0.15 percent of GDP a year for low- and middle-income countries, which corresponds to between $2.3 billion and $190 billion.[3] In total, water interruptions are estimated to cost between 0.11 percent and 0.19 percent of GDP each year, which corresponds to a range of from $88 billion to $153 billion. Waterborne diseases stemming from an intermittent water supply are estimated to cause medical treatment costs and lost incomes between $3 billion and $6 billion a year. However, these results are highly uncertain because of differences in methodologies and contexts. Similar assessments of the transport and telecommunications sectors were not possible due to data constraints.

Natural shocks are among the leading causes of infrastructure disruptions

Taken together, the cost of infrastructure disruptions ranges from $391 billion to $647 billion in the low- and middle-income countries for which data are available and for the types

MAP O.1 **Africa and South Asia bear the highest losses from unreliable infrastructure**

a. Countrywide average utilization rate losses from disruptions in electricity, water, and transport infrastructure

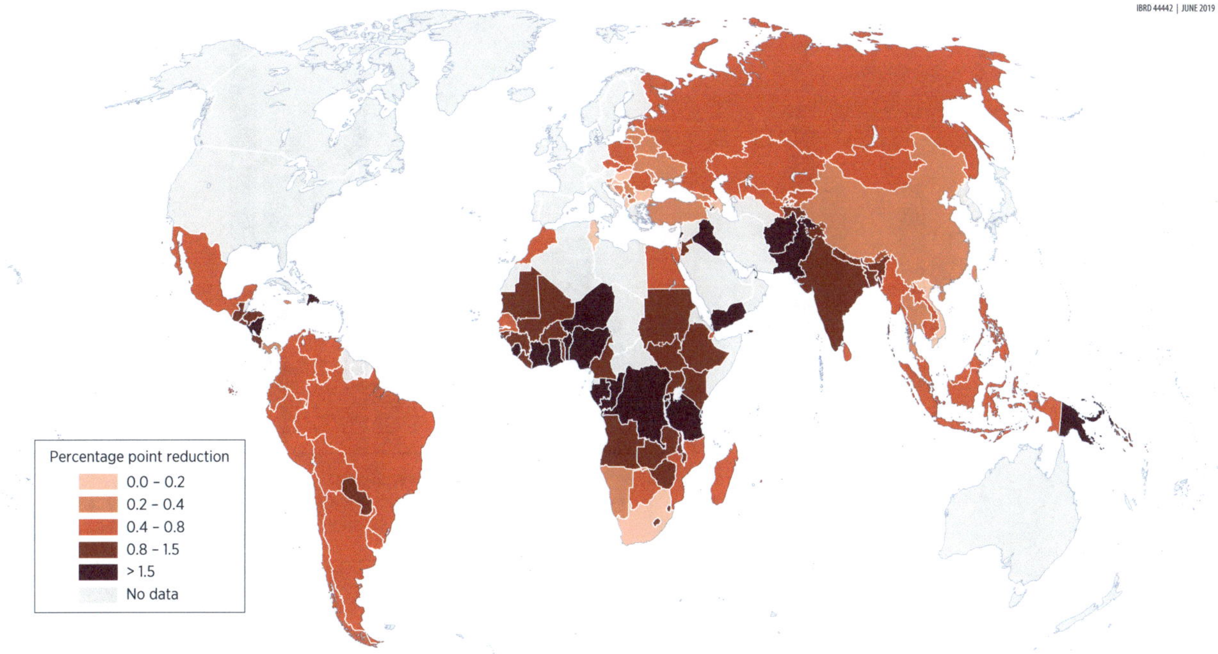

b. Additional costs of firms' backup electricity generation as % of GDP, including up-front investments and additional operating costs

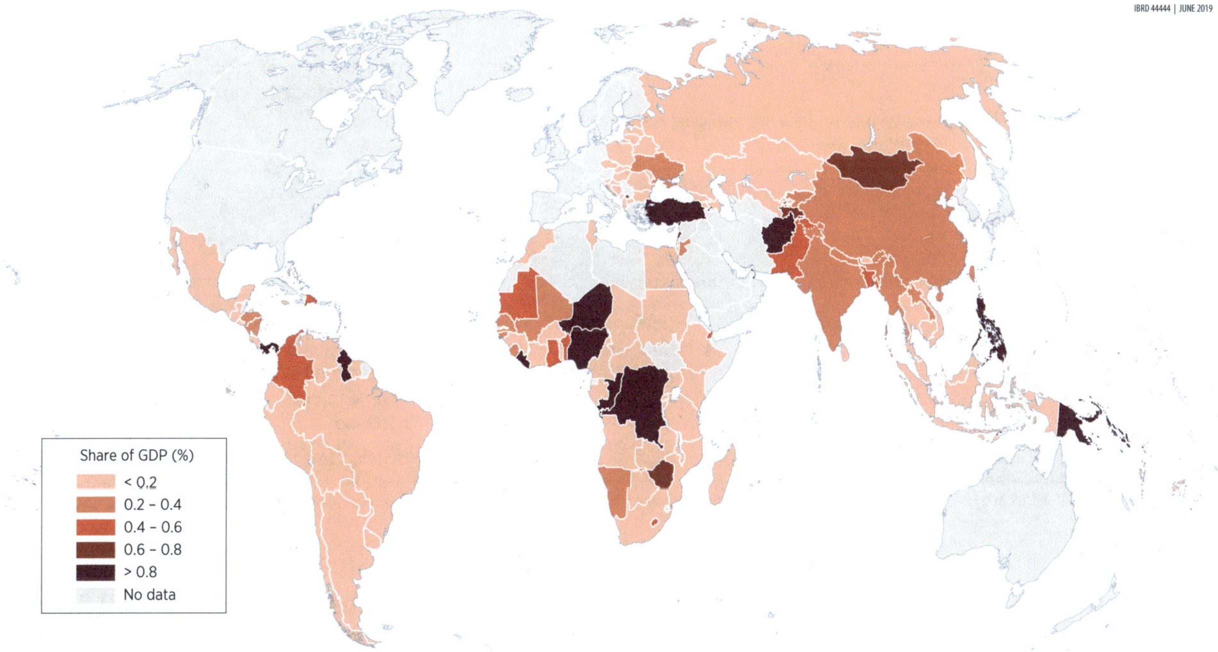

Source: Rentschler, Kornejew, et al. 2019.

FIGURE O.2 Reliable access to electricity has more favorable effects on income and social outcomes than access alone in Bangladesh, India, and Pakistan

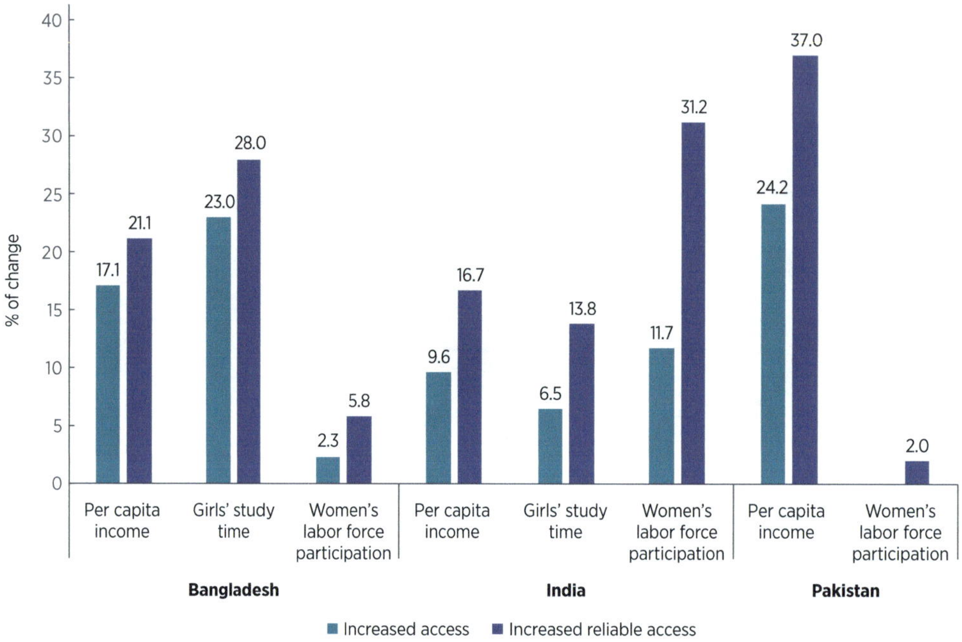

Source: Zhang 2019.
Note: Estimates are based on household surveys in Bangladesh, India, and Pakistan.

TABLE O.2 Disrupted infrastructure services have multiple impacts on households

Sector	Direct impacts	Coping costs	Indirect and health impacts
Power	• Diminished well-being • Lower productivity of family firms	• Generator investments • Generator operation costs	• Higher mortality and morbidity (lack of access to health care, air-conditioning during heat waves, or heat during cold spells)
	Willingness to pay to prevent outages: between $2.3 billion and $190 billion a year		
Water	• Diminished well-being and loss of time	• Investment in alternative water sources (reservoirs, wells, water bottles)	• Higher incidence of diarrhea, cholera, and other diseases
	Willingness to pay to prevent outages: between $88 billion and $153 billion a year		**Medical costs and missed income: between $3 billion and $6 billion a year**
Transport	• Greater congestion and loss of time • Higher fuel costs	• Higher cost of alternative transport modes	• Air pollution and health impacts • Constrained access to jobs, markets, services • People forced to live close to jobs, possibly on bad land
Telecommunications	• Diminished well-being		• Inability to call emergency services

Note: Highlighted in bold are the impacts for which original estimates are presented in this section. Estimates cover low- and middle-income countries.

of impacts that can be quantified. Even though these estimates are incomplete, they highlight the substantial costs that unreliable infrastructure impose on people in low- and middle-income countries. But what role do natural hazards play in these disruptions? While it is impossible to answer this question globally and for all sectors, many case studies document the role of natural hazards in infrastructure disruptions.

FIGURE O.3 Natural shocks explain a significant fraction of power outages

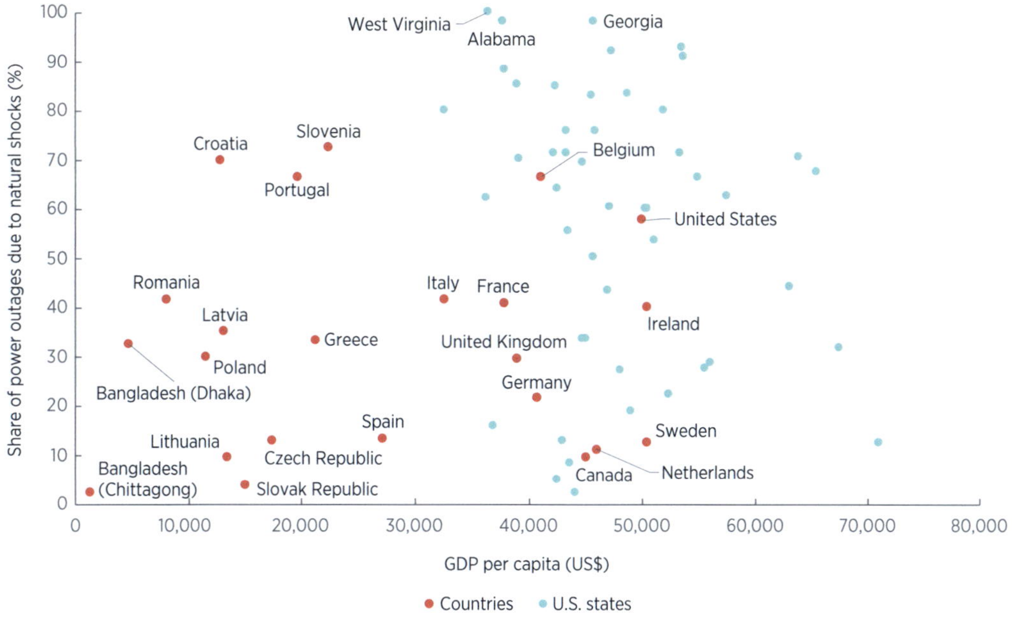

Source: Rentschler, Obolensky, and Kornejew 2019.

In the power sector, natural hazards—in particular, storms—are a major cause of electricity supply disruptions, as shown in figure O.3. In Belgium, Croatia, Portugal, Slovenia, and the United States, they are responsible for more than 50 percent of all outages. By contrast, in Bangladesh, natural shocks account for a smaller share of power outages—not because energy systems are more resilient, but because system failures and nonnatural factors are so frequent that energy users experience daily outages. But this figure also underestimates the role of natural hazards because outages caused by natural hazards tend to be longer and geographically larger than other outages. In Europe between 2010 and 2017, natural hazard–induced outages lasted 409 minutes on average, making them almost four times as long as outages caused by nonnatural causes. And in Bangladesh in 2007, Tropical Storm Sidr caused the largest outage in national history: all 26 power plants tripped and failed, leaving customers without power for up to a week (Rentschler, Obolensky and Kornejew 2019).

In many low- and middle-income countries, natural shocks are responsible for a small fraction of power outages, although this does not mean that resilience is not an issue. Indeed, power systems are more vulnerable to natural shocks in poorer countries than in richer countries, and natural hazards can be responsible for a large number of disruptions. In the power sector, aging equipment, a lack of maintenance, rapid expansion of the grid, and insufficient generation capacity are all factors that reduce the reliability of service in general, while also increasing vulnerability to natural shocks. For example, storms of the same intensity are more likely to cause outages in Bangladesh than in the United States (figure O.4). On a day with average wind speeds exceeding 35 kilometers per hour, electricity users in Bangladesh are 11 times more likely to experience a blackout than U.S. consumers. As a result of this vulnerability, in 2013 in Chittagong, Bangladesh, users experienced about 16 power outages due to storms alone. This number corresponds to only 4 percent of all outages experienced, yet it is already

FIGURE O.4 The vulnerability of the power network to wind is much higher in Bangladesh than in the United States

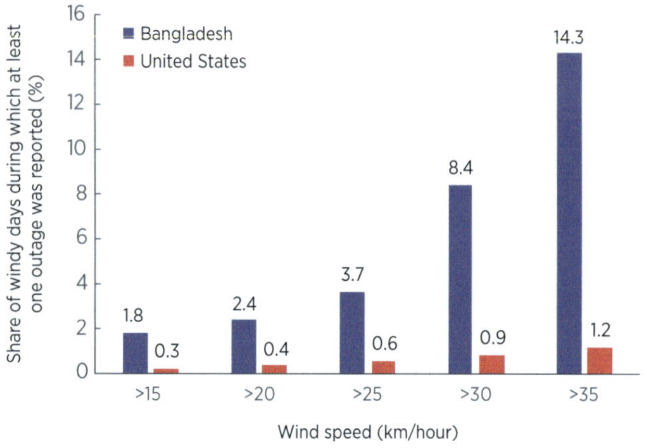

Source: Rentschler, Obolensky, and Kornejew 2019.
Note: Windy days are defined using different thresholds for recorded daily wind speeds. Wind speeds are obtained from the global ERA5 climate reanalysis model, which tends to underrepresent the highest local wind speeds.

more than 15 times higher than the average number of outages experienced by consumers in New York City.

In the transport sector, floods and other hazards disrupt traffic and cause congestion, taking a toll on people and firms in rich and poor countries alike. In Kampala, the impacts of floods on urban transport reduce people's access to a health care facility, according to an analysis undertaken for this report (Rentschler, Braese, et al. 2019) (figure O.5). A network analysis estimates that the mean travel time by car to a hospital from nearly all locations in Inner Kampala is less than 30 minutes. However, during a 10-year flood, disruption of the road network can increase travel times significantly, and about a third of persons living in

FIGURE O.5 Floods in Kampala severely restrict people's access to health care facilities

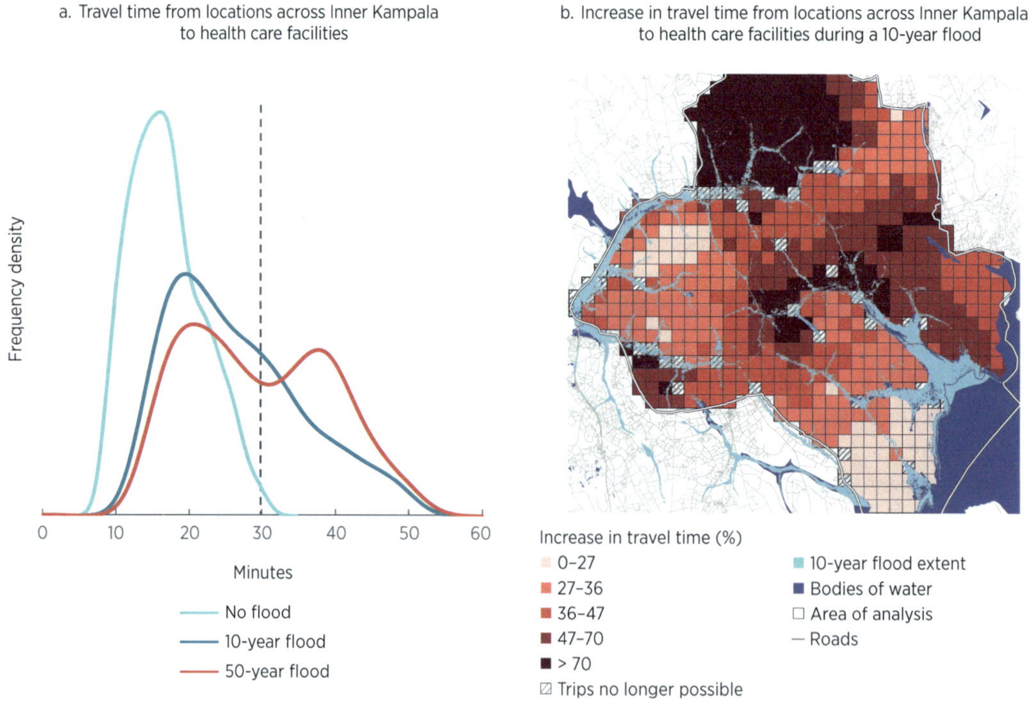

Source: Rentschler, Braese, et al. 2019.
Note: In panel a, the vertical line denotes the "golden hour" (the window of time that maximizes survival of a major health emergency), assuming that ambulances complete a return trip starting at a hospital. The curves show frequency densities that represent the distribution of travel times from all locations. The 10-year flood is the flood of a magnitude that occurs on average once every 10 years.

Inner Kampala would no longer be able to reach health facilities within the "golden hour"—a rule of thumb referring to the window of time that maximizes the likelihood of survival after a severe medical incident.

Such flood-related transport disruptions are costly for firms. The same network analysis estimates travel times between some 400 firms as a proxy for the impact of floods on interfirm connectivity and local supply chains. A moderate flood in Kampala increases the average travel time between firms by 54 percent. A significant number of firms are affected even more severely, with more than a quarter of firms facing an increase in average travel time of between 100 percent and 350 percent. As roads are flooded, people are unable to reach their workplace, and firms wait in vain for supplies, miss their deliveries, and lose sales.

In the water sector, assets and services are also affected by natural hazards, even in the absence of physical damage to assets. The severe landslides that occurred in Lima in March 2017, interrupted the water supply for four days, as the city's river filled with mud. The main water treatment plant could not handle the resulting turbidity and had to shut down (Stip et al. 2019).

In the telecommunications sector, in December 2006, the Great Hengchun Earthquake on the island of Taiwan, China, and in the Luzon Strait was one of the severest examples of disruptions to the submarine cable systems on which international communications networks depend. Submarine landslides caused 19 breaks in seven cable systems, requiring repairs that were carried out over 49 days. Meanwhile, traffic was quickly rerouted using undamaged infrastructure, but the pressures on it resulted in a lower quality of service and delays. Internet connectivity in the region was seriously affected, and financial services and the airlines and shipping industries were significantly hurt (Sandhu and Raja 2019).

Although it is agreed that disruptions from natural hazards represent a significant cost for firms and households, local studies are needed to provide a detailed assessment. To support such an assessment, a survey was developed and piloted in Tanzania for a sample of 800 firms across the country. It found that Tanzanian firms are incurring utilization losses of \$668 million a year from power and water outages and transport disruptions, which is equivalent to 1.8 percent of the country's GDP (figure O.6). Power alone is responsible for losses of \$216 million a year, and 47 percent of these losses are solely due to power outages that can be attributed to rain and floods (equivalent to \$101 million, or 0.3 percent of GDP). As for transport disruptions, about 46 percent of utilization losses stem from disruptions caused by rain and floods (equivalent to \$150 million, or 0.4 percent of GDP). But the survey does not find that rain and floods have a significant impact on the incidence of water supply disruptions.

In addition to these disruptions, natural hazards cause direct damage to infrastructure assets. This damage is critical, given that it burdens public infrastructure budgets and detracts from the attractiveness of the infrastructure sector for private investors. Based on a global risk assessment performed for this report,

FIGURE O.6 Tanzanian firms report large losses from infrastructure disruptions

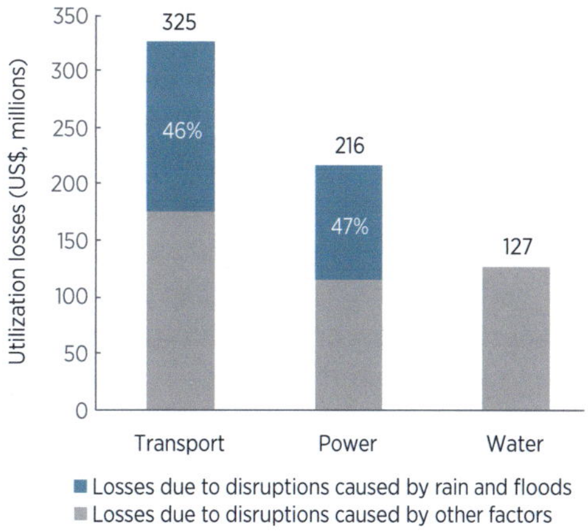

Source: Rentschler, Braese, et al. 2019.

power generation and transport infrastructure incur losses of $30 billion a year on average from natural hazards (about $15 billion each), with low- and middle-income countries shouldering about $18 billion of the total amount (Koks et al. 2019; Nicolas et al. 2019).

Although these numbers remain manageable on average and at the global level, losses can reach high values after extreme events. In some vulnerable countries, they are high enough to impede the provision of universal access to infrastructure services.

The severity of natural disasters is usually measured by the asset losses they provoke (Munich Re 2019; Swiss Re 2019). But the secondary consequences of direct asset losses on economic activities and output can often explain a large share of total disaster impacts, especially when infrastructure systems are affected (Hallegatte 2013; Hallegatte and Vogt-Schilb 2016). For example, Rose, Oladosu, and Liao (2007) estimate the total cost of a two-week blackout in Los Angeles at $2.8 billion—that is, 13 percent of the total economic activity during the two weeks. Colon, Hallegatte, and Rozenberg (2019) find that in Tanzania, the macroeconomic impact of a flood disruption in the transport sector increases nonlinearly with the duration of the disruption. A four-week disruption is, on average, 23 times costlier for households than a two-week disruption. Comprehensive risk assessments need to account for these secondary impacts and look beyond asset losses to inform disaster risk management investments and policies properly and to guide decision making on infrastructure design and operation.

FIGURE O.7 The resilience of infrastructure should be considered at several overlapping and complementary levels

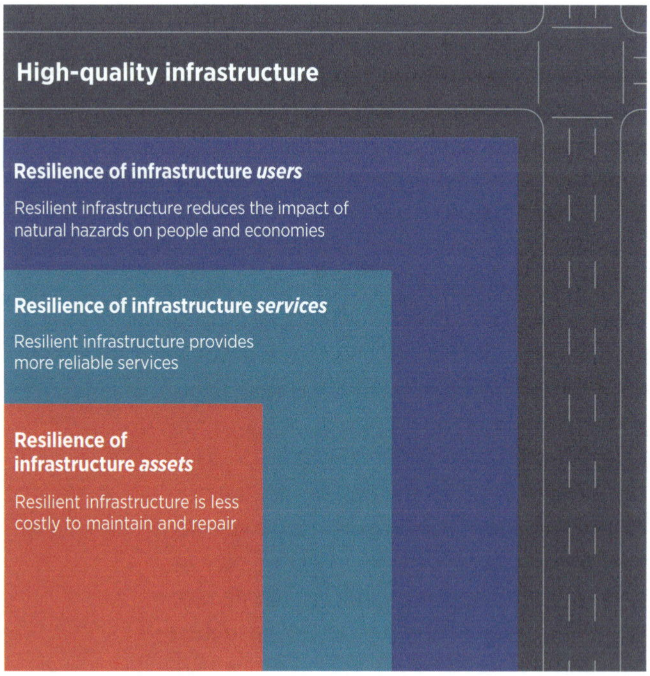

MORE RESILIENT INFRASTRUCTURE ASSETS PAY FOR THEMSELVES

The resilience of infrastructure has three levels (figure O.7):

- *Resilience of infrastructure assets.* In the narrowest sense, resilient infrastructure refers to assets such as roads, bridges, cellphone towers, and power lines that can withstand external shocks, especially natural hazards. Here, the benefit of more resilient infrastructure is that it reduces the life-cycle cost of assets.
- *Resilience of infrastructure services.* Infrastructure systems are interconnected networks, and the resilience of individual assets is a poor proxy for the resilience of services provided at the network level. For infrastructure, a systemic approach to resilience is preferable. At this level, the benefit of more resilient infrastructure is that it provides more reliable services.
- *Resilience of infrastructure users.* Eventually, what matters is the resilience of users. Infrastructure disruptions can be catastrophic or benign, depending on whether users—including people and supply chains—can cope with them. At this level, the benefit of more resilient infrastructure is that it

reduces the total impact of natural hazards on people and economies.

The resilience of infrastructure is one of the many determinants of high-quality infrastructure. However, integrating resilience in the design and implementation of infrastructure investments not only helps to manage natural shocks but also complements the cost-effectiveness and quality of infrastructure services more generally.

Building more resilient infrastructure assets in exposed areas is cost-effective

The additional up-front cost of more resilient infrastructure assets ranges from negative to a doubling of the construction cost, depending on the asset and the hazard. Interventions to make assets more resilient include using alternative materials, digging deeper foundations, elevating assets, building flood protection around the asset, or adding redundant components.

How much would it cost to implement these technical solutions? This report tackles this question with an analysis that begins with the estimates by Rozenberg and Fay (2019) of how much low- and middle-income countries would have to spend on infrastructure to achieve their development goals. The analysis then asks how much those estimates would change if infrastructure systems were designed and built in a more resilient manner (using one set of technical options from Miyamoto International 2019). Note that the solutions assessed here do not guarantee that assets cannot be damaged by natural hazards and do not include all possible options to reduce risks. Many high-income countries like Japan implement technical solutions that go beyond—and are more expensive than—the set of solutions considered in this analysis.

Overall, the incremental cost of building the resilience of infrastructure assets in low- and middle-income countries is small, provided the right data, risk models, and decision-making methods are available. Improving the resilience of only the assets that are exposed to hazards would increase investment needs in power, water and sanitation, and transport by between \$11 billion and \$65 billion a year (figure O.8). Although not negligible, this range represents only 3 percent of infrastructure investment needs and less than 0.1 percent of the GDP of low- and middle-income countries. It would, therefore, not affect the current affordability challenges that countries face.

FIGURE O.8 The incremental cost of increasing the resilience of future infrastructure investments depends on the spending scenario but remains limited in all cases

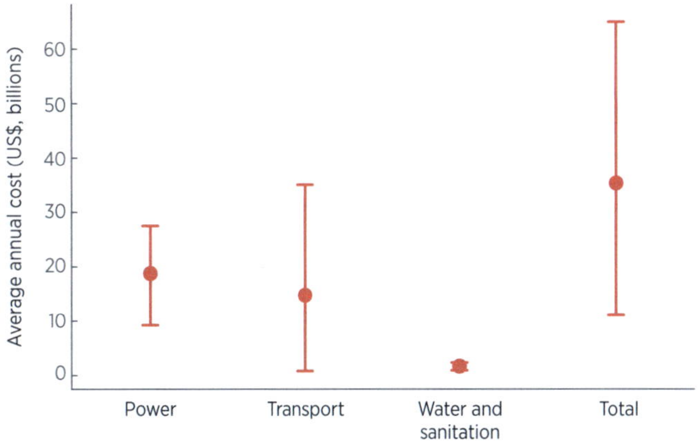

Source: Hallegatte et al. 2019.
Note: This figure shows the incremental annual capital cost for more resilient infrastructure for 2015–30. The range comes primarily from the uncertainty on how much will be invested on infrastructure during the period (and on the technologies chosen).

However, making infrastructure more resilient by strengthening assets is realistic only if the appropriate data on the spatial distribution of natural hazards are available. Without information on which locations are exposed to hazards, strengthening the whole system would cost 10 times more, between \$120 billion and \$670 billion, which suggests that the value of hazards data is orders of magnitude higher than the cost of producing the information.

What are the returns on investments for making exposed infrastructure more resilient to natural disasters? The uncertainty pertaining to the cost of infrastructure resilience and the benefits in terms of both avoided repairs and disruptions for households and firms make it difficult to provide one single estimate for the benefit-cost ratio of strengthening exposed infrastructure assets. However, a set of 3,000 scenarios (which covers the uncertainty of all parameters of the analysis) can be used to explore the costs and benefits of making infrastructure more resilient.

The analysis shows that, despite the uncertainty, investing in more resilient infrastructure is clearly a cost-effective and robust choice. The benefit-cost ratio is higher than 1 in 96 percent of the scenarios, larger than 2 in 77 percent of them, and higher than 6 in 25 percent of them (Hallegatte et al. 2019). The net present value of these investments, over the lifetime of new infrastructure assets, exceeds $2 trillion in 75 percent of the scenarios and $4.2 trillion in half of them. Moreover, climate change makes the strengthening of infrastructure assets even more important. Without climate change, the median benefit-cost ratio would be equal to 2, but it doubles when climate change is considered.

The urgency of investing in better infrastructure is also evident. With massive investment in infrastructure taking place in low- and middle-income countries, the stock of low-resilience assets is growing rapidly, increasing future costs

FIGURE O.9 Belgium's and Morocco's transport systems can absorb much larger road disruptions than Madagascar's

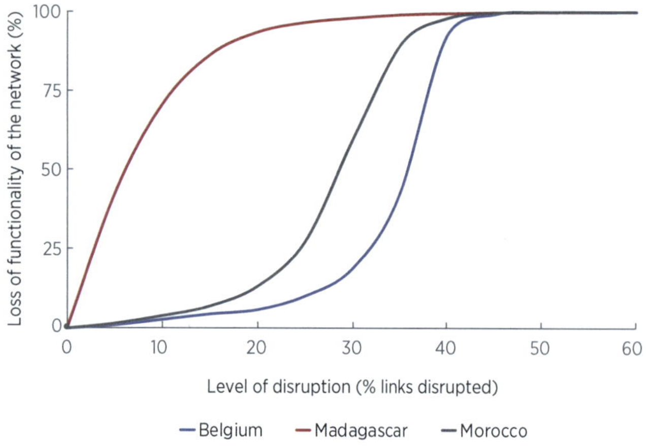

Source: Rozenberg et al. 2019b.

of natural hazards and climate change. In 93 percent of the scenarios, it is costly to delay action from 2020 to 2030—and the median cost of a decade of inaction is $1 trillion.

From resilient infrastructure assets to resilient infrastructure services

Making assets more resistant is not the only option for building resilience. Expansion of the analysis from infrastructure *assets* to infrastructure *services* reveals that the cost of resilience can be reduced further by working at the network and system level—looking at criticality, redundancy, diversification, and nature-based solutions as additional options.

To illustrate the role of networks in infrastructure system resilience, a study conducted for this report quantifies *the resilience of transport networks,* defined as the ratio of the loss of functionality to the loss of assets (Rozenberg et al. 2019b). A resilient road network, such as the one in Belgium or Morocco, can lose many assets (such as road segments) without losing much functionality, whereas fragile networks with little redundancy, such as the one in Madagascar, become disfunctional even with slight damage (figure O.9). Similar approaches can be mobilized in water systems, where the typical methodology consists of mapping all components of a network and assessing the conditions under which they would fail, what the effects of those failures would be, and how they would affect service delivery.

Network effects create opportunities to strengthen the resilience of services and users at a limited cost, either by strengthening critical assets or by building in redundancy only where there are choke points (Rozenberg et al. 2019a). For transmission and distribution networks, for example, resilience is often built up through redundancy, which does not necessarily mean doubling or tripling key components of the network. A more effective approach is usually to create "ringed" or meshed networks that have multiple supply points for various nodes in the grid.

Diversification and decentralization also offer opportunities for more resilient services. The use of power generation with differentiated vulnerabilities (for example, hydropower, which is vulnerable to drought, versus solar and wind, which are vulnerable to strong winds) makes it more likely that a system will be able to maintain a minimum level of service. Multimodal transport systems that rely on nonmotorized modes and public transit are more resilient than systems that rely on private vehicles only. Distributed power systems using solar and batteries can harden a grid and make it more resilient. Minigrids and microgrids, because they do not rely on long-distance transmission wires, can provide useful backup generation in case of grid failure. During Hurricane Sandy, the Co-Op City microgrid in New York City was successfully decoupled from the main grid, and it supported consumers during outages in the wider network (Strahl et al. 2016).

Combining green and gray infrastructure can provide lower-cost, more resilient, and more sustainable infrastructure solutions (Browder et al. 2019). In New York City, 90 percent of water is from well-protected wilderness watersheds, making New York's water treatment process simpler than that of other U.S. cities (National Research Council 2000). According to Beck et al. (2018), without coral reefs the annual damage from coastal flooding would double worldwide. They estimate that Cuba, Indonesia, Malaysia, Mexico, and the Philippines benefit the most from their reefs, with annual savings of more than $400 million for each country. In Colombo, preserving the wetland system was found to be a cost-effective solution to reducing flooding in the city, even when accounting for land development constraints (Browder et al. 2019).

Limits to what is achievable in terms of strengthening also need to be considered. No infrastructure asset or system can be designed to cope with all possible hazards. And great uncertainty surrounds the probability and intensity of the most extreme events. As a result, infrastructure systems have to be stress-tested against a range of events to minimize the risk of catastrophic failures (Kalra et al. 2014). Such stress tests have two goals: (1) identify low-cost options that can reduce the vulnerability of infrastructure systems to extreme events, even quite unlikely ones, and (2) prepare for failure in terms of managing infrastructure systems (such as how to recover from a major failure) and in terms of supporting users (such as how to minimize impacts on hospitals). Running scenarios of failures is the first and most critical step in defining contingency plans.

Finally, sometimes the best way to make an infrastructure resilient is not to build it. Nicholls et al. (2019) find that coastal protection against storm surges and a rise in sea level would make economic sense only for about 22–32 percent of the world's coastlines through the 21st century. Thus, some communities may have to retreat gradually or use lower-cost or nature-based approaches to coastal defense. These communities are mostly in low-density areas where the costs of protection are too high to be affordable. In those areas, the best approach to resilience may be *not* to build new infrastructure. This approach, however, has to be complemented by a consistent strategy to manage retreat, while maintaining livelihoods and community ties.

From resilient infrastructure services to resilient users and economies

In some cases, it can be easier and cheaper to manage service interruptions than to prevent them. This report explores the role of the users of infrastructure services and how their actions can contribute to more resilient infrastructure systems.

Often, a first option for building resilience is to reduce demand by improving efficiency. In the face of growing populations and increasingly scarce water resources, a water utility can use demand management to reduce stress on the city's water supply. A recent example is Cape Town, which had to take drastic measures

MAP O.2 Investment priorities for Tanzania's transport network will depend on its supply chains

a. Impacts of disruption on households' consumption

b. Impacts of disruption on international clients

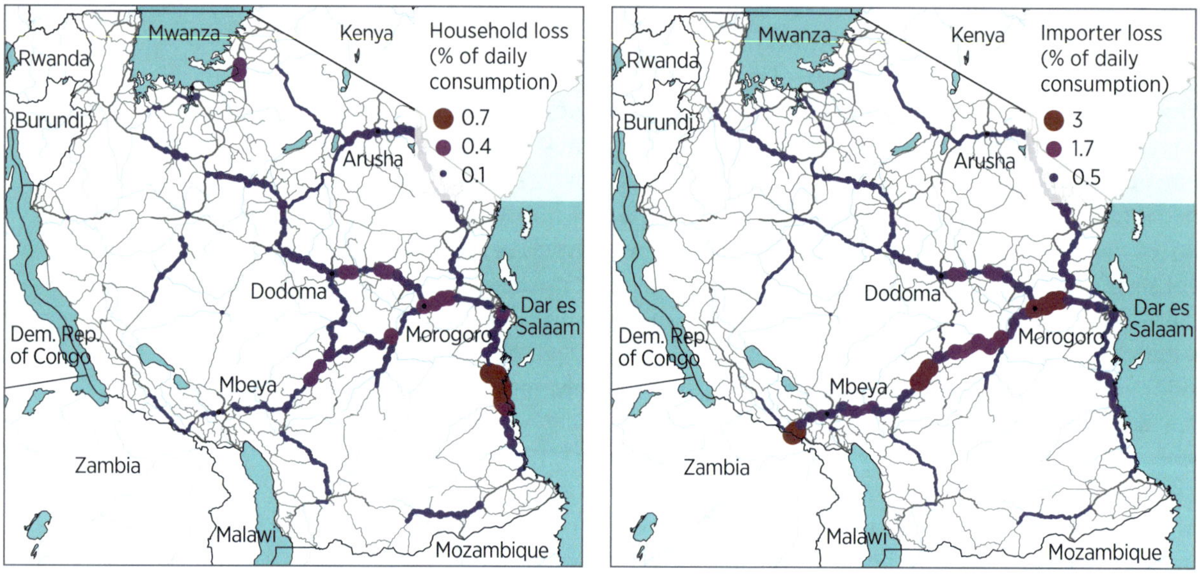

Source: Colon, Hallegatte, and Rozenberg 2019.
Note: The width of the line overlaying a given road is proportional to the impacts that a one-week disruption of that road would trigger. Impacts, measured in percentage of daily consumption, represent exceptional expenditures due to costlier transport and missed consumption due to shortages. Panel a shows these impacts for products consumed by households, and panel b shows these impacts for international buyers.

to avoid reaching "Day 0"—the day the city would run out of water. The demand management measures implemented by the city were extremely successful, reducing use by 40 percent between 2015 and 2018 and preventing what could have been a major socioeconomic crisis.

Understanding the needs and capacities of users helps utilities to target better where to invest and what part of the network to strengthen. A power distribution line to a hospital or a flood shelter is likely more important during and after an emergency than the average power line in a country. To investigate how criticality depends on users and supply chains, a study undertaken for this report combines a transport and a supply chain model to investigate the criticality of the transport network in Tanzania (Colon, Hallegatte, and Rozenberg 2019). Map O.2 shows the most critical assets in the transport sector for two supply chains and reveals that investment priorities for strengthening assets depend on which supply chains are considered most vulnerable or most important. For example, segments of the coastal trunk road, located about 200 km south of Dar-es-Salaam, are critical for domestic consumption but rather irrelevant for international trade. For trade, the road east of Morogoro appears as a priority. This segment accommodates large freight flows between the port of Dar es Salaam and landlocked countries, such as the Democratic Republic of Congo and Zambia.

When preventing disruptions is not possible or not affordable, firms have many options for improving their own resilience to disruptions. Larger inventories will protect them against transport issues. Generators and batteries will help them manage short power outages. Maintaining a diversity of suppliers, from both local and distant locations, is another powerful safeguard, especially against long disruptions. However, holding large inventories and managing multiple suppliers are financial burdens that involve significant transaction costs, making them most relevant for large firms. Because a static supply chain will never be able to cope with a large-scale disaster and associated disruptions, adaptability is critical and should be embedded in business continuity plans (Christopher and Peck 2004; Sheffi 2005).

MAKING INFRASTRUCTURE MORE RESILIENT REQUIRES A CONSISTENT STRATEGY

In many countries, infrastructure disruptions are the symptoms of chronic shortcomings. Power outages occur every day, water supply is unreliable or unsafe, and congestion makes travel slow and unpredictable. In many places, these disruptions occur simply because infrastructure systems are not designed to keep up with ever-rising demand or because system failures are the result of poor asset management or maintenance. While natural hazards can exacerbate these issues, the majority of these disruptions reflect more fundamental challenges related to infrastructure design and management. This means that, to make infrastructure systems resilient, the first step is to make them reliable in normal conditions through appropriate infrastructure design, operation, maintenance, and financing.

Recommendation 1: Get the basics right

Underperforming infrastructure systems are explained largely by poor management and governance, according to a recent analysis of countries across the world (Kornejew, Rentschler, and Hallegatte 2019). Using the World Bank's Logistic Performance Index as a proxy, figure O.10 shows how the performance of the transport system depends on public spending on roads. Performance increases rapidly with spending per capita, but only if the quality of governance improves in parallel (dark blue line). If the quality of governance remains unchanged (light blue line), increased spending only yields marginal improvements in transport system performance and is not cost-effective. Similar analyses yield similar findings for power and water systems.

FIGURE O.10 Spending more improves the reliability of the transport system, but only if governance improves as well

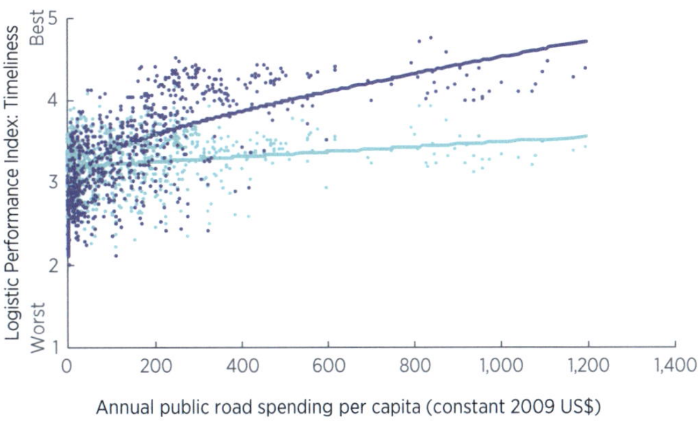

Source: Kornejew, Rentschler, and Hallegatte 2019.

Thus, poor governance of infrastructure systems is the first obstacle that needs to be tackled. If infrastructure is to be resilient to natural shocks, countries first need to get the basics right for infrastructure management, with the following three priority actions.

Action 1.1: Introduce and enforce regulations, construction codes, and procurement rules

Well-designed regulations, codes, and procurement rules are the simplest approach to enhancing the quality of infrastructure services, including their reliability and resilience. Effective enforcement in the infrastructure sector requires a robust legal framework, but also strong regulatory agencies to monitor construction, service quality, and performance and to reward or penalize service providers for their performance. Currently, many regulators lack the resources and capacity to enforce the existing construction codes.

Action 1.2: Create systems for appropriate infrastructure operation, maintenance, and postincident response

Improving maintenance and operations is a no-regret option (it generates benefits whatever happens in the future) for boosting the resilience of infrastructure assets while reducing overall costs. An analysis of member countries of the Organisation for Economic Co-operation and Development performed for this report suggests that each additional $1 spent on road maintenance saves $1.5 in new investments, making better maintenance a very cost-effective option (Kornejew, Rentschler, and Hallegatte 2019). An important tool for this purpose is infrastructure asset management systems, which include an inventory of all assets and their condition, as well as all of the strategic, financial, and technical aspects of the management of infrastructure assets across their life cycle. Such tools help to move toward an evidence-based and preventive maintenance schedule and away from a reactive patch-by-patch approach to maintenance.

Action 1.3: Provide appropriate funding and financing for infrastructure planning, construction, and maintenance

The quality of infrastructure services depends on many factors, from good planning to good maintenance, but each of these comes at a cost (figure O.11). If resources are insufficient to meet the need for any of these factors, the quality of infrastructure services is likely to suffer. Even if investment spending is appropriate, insufficient resources for planning, designing, or maintaining assets would result in low quality and reliability. Dedicated funds and budgetary allocations can be used to ensure that enough resources are available to meet different needs, especially for maintenance.

Implementing these three basic measures would contribute to more reliable infrastructure systems and establish a basic capacity to cope with natural hazards and climate change. But they would not be sufficient to achieve more ambitious objectives regarding resilience. Without targeted actions to strengthen resilience, infrastructure assets will not be able to cope with rarer events, such as hurricanes, river floods, or earthquakes. And without specific actions on climate change, these assets run the risk of being designed for the wrong climate and environmental conditions. To build resilience to these evolving natural hazards, it is necessary to tackle four additional obstacles that are specific to the resilience challenge.

Recommendation 2: Build institutions for resilience

Political economy challenges and coordination failures impede the creation of a resilient infrastructure ecosystem. Governments, therefore, need to play a coordinating role (OECD 2019), with the following three priority actions.

Action 2.1: Implement a whole-of-government approach to infrastructure resilience, building on existing regulatory systems

Analysts agree that governments play a key role in ensuring the resilience of critical infrastructure and that they should adopt a whole-of-government approach (Renn 2008; Wiener and Rogers 2002; World Bank 2013). A common solution to improve the coordination of risk

FIGURE O.11 High-quality infrastructure requires providing for multiple funding needs

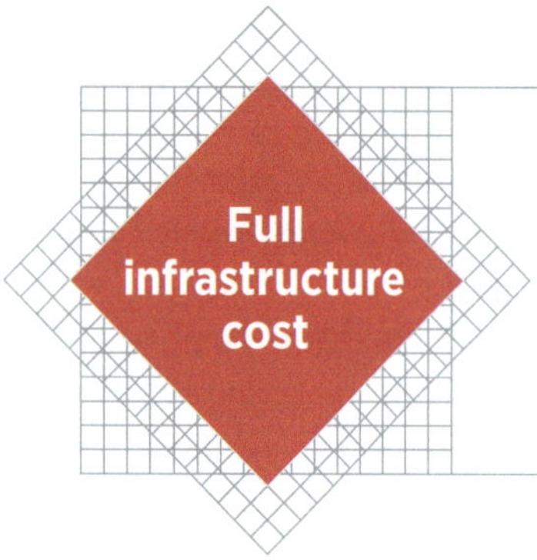

Cost to regulators and government

- Master planning, and regulation design and enforcement
- Data and model development, research, training, and education

Life-cycle cost to (public or private) infrastructure service providers

- Project design and preparation
- Up-front investment cost
- Operational, maintenance, and repair costs
- Decommissioning

management across risks and across systems is to place an existing (or new) multiministry body in charge of information exchange, coordination, and possibly even implementation of risk management measures for infrastructure.

Action 2.2: Identify critical infrastructure and define acceptable and intolerable risk levels

Criticality analyses are an important tool for identifying the most important infrastructure assets and their vulnerability. Once the critical infrastructure assets and systems have been identified, governments need to define risk levels that are acceptable or intolerable. Each infrastructure sector can use these risk levels to design its own regulations and measures, ensuring consistency across systems. Definition of these risk levels needs to consider the local context, especially the resources that are available, and requires an open and participatory approach to ensure that risk management does not become an obstacle to development.

Action 2.3: Ensure equitable access to resilient infrastructure

Decisions regarding resilience cannot be driven by economic considerations alone. The strengthening of infrastructure resilience should be guided by a more complete assessment of the potential risks and impacts of disruptions, especially for vulnerable and marginalized population groups. New approaches enable more comprehensive assessments of spatial priorities. For example, estimates of *well-being losses* or *socioeconomic resilience* provide a balanced assessment of the impacts of natural disasters on poor and rich households (Hallegatte et al. 2016; Walsh and Hallegatte 2019).

Recommendation 3: Include resilience in regulations and incentives

A third obstacle to more resilient infrastructure is that public and private decision makers tend to have few incentives to avoid disruptions. Too often, they only consider lower repair costs when deciding on investments in resilience; they rarely consider the full social cost of infrastructure disruptions. Therefore, governments need to include resilience in a consistent set of regulations and financial incentives to align the interests of infrastructure service providers with the interests of the public (figure O.12), with the following three priority actions.

Action 3.1: Consider resilience objectives in master plans, standards, and regulations and adjust them regularly to account for climate change

Standards and regulations need to account for a range of factors, including climate conditions, geophysical hazards, environmental and socioeconomic trends, local construction practices, and policy priorities. They also need to be revised more regularly than is the case today to consider climate change and other long-term trends (Vallejo and Mullan 2017). In addition, governments can use regulations to strengthen the resilience of specific users of infrastructure services, not just providers. For example, hospitals could be required to maintain backup generators, batteries, and water tanks. And firms could be required to prepare business continuity plans to minimize the economic cost of disasters and infrastructure disruptions.

Action 3.2: Create financial incentives for service providers to promote resilient infrastructure services

Rewards and penalties can be used as incentives for service providers to go beyond the mandatory standards and implement cost-effective solutions to improve resilience (Pardina and Schiro 2018). The Australian Energy Regulator established the Service Target Performance Incentive Scheme, which includes penalties and rewards calibrated according to how willing consumers are to pay for improved service. Another example is payment-for-ecosystem-services schemes, which promote the use of nature-based solutions to increase resilience. In Brazil, water users pay a fee to the local water company that local watershed committees use for watershed maintenance and reforestation (Browder et al. 2019).

FIGURE O.12 Creating the right incentives for infrastructure service providers requires a consistent set of regulations and financial incentives

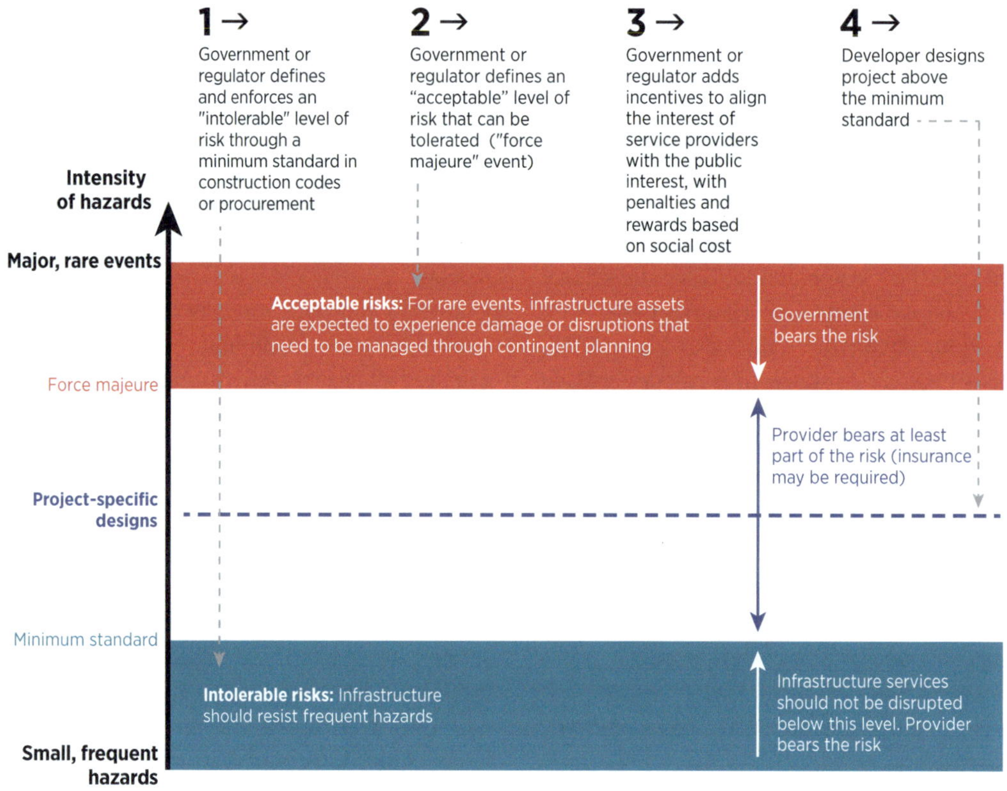

Action 3.3: Ensure that infrastructure regulations are consistent with risk-informed land use plans and guide development toward safer areas

Since infrastructure investments influence spatial development patterns, they can influence people's exposure to natural hazards. To ensure that new infrastructure contributes to the resilience of users, regulations should be aligned with risk-informed land use and urbanization plans. And the choice of infrastructure localizations needs to account for the potential investments that a new infrastructure asset will attract and the implications for resilience. Even better, infrastructure localization choices can be used to support the implementation of land use planning and promote low-risk spatial development.

Recommendation 4: Improve decision making

Even if regulators and providers of infrastructure services have the right incentives to build more resilient infrastructure systems, they often lack access to data and tools, as well as the skills and competencies they need to make good decisions. Governments, therefore, need to help all stakeholders to improve their decision making, with the following three priority actions.

Action 4.1: Invest in freely accessible natural hazard and climate change data

Investments in risk data and models (such as hydrological models, maps of flood hazards, digital elevation models, and inventories of infrastructure assets) can have extremely high returns by improving the design and maintenance of infrastructure assets. Producing digital elevation models for all urban areas in low- and middle-income countries would cost between $50 million and $400 million in total and make it possible to perform in-depth risk assessments for all new infrastructure assets, informing hundreds of billions in investments per year. However, such data have public goods characteristics that discourage private actors from investing in them and require public support. To be useful, risk and infrastructure data must be made available (and affordable) to infrastructure service providers and users. While privacy and security concerns can make it necessary to restrict access, it is preferable to make open access the default situation for hazard and infrastructure data and to create processes to restrict access for data proven to be too sensitive.

Action 4.2: Make robust decisions and minimize the potential for regret and catastrophic failures

Often, large uncertainties make it impossible to design "optimal" systems or assets. An alternative is to seek *robust* designs that yield good results across a wide range of futures, preferences, and worldviews, even if they may not be optimal for any particular future. Decision makers can identify robust strategies through systematic stress-testing of possible options for a variety of hazards and threats—even highly unlikely ones—to ensure that the residual vulnerabilities are acceptable and manageable. These stress tests can help to capture low-cost opportunities to build resilience to low-probability, high-consequence events and prevent catastrophic failures. They can also support the development of contingency plans for service providers and business continuity plans for users.

Action 4.3: Build the skills needed to use data and models and mobilize the know-how of the private sector

Even if infrastructure risk data and models are available to all those seeking to improve infrastructure resilience, their appropriate use requires skills that are not always available. Universities and research centers need to be supported so that they can offer training, develop new methodologies (or adapt them to the local context), and advise policy and decision makers. When public sector expertise is insufficient, bringing in the private sector—through direct procurement or public-private partnerships—can be a solution.

Recommendation 5: Provide financing

The fifth obstacle is linked to affordability and financing constraints. Increasing resilience can increase various components of the life-cycle cost of infrastructure, including the costs borne by the government or regulators or the costs borne by infrastructure providers (figure O.11).

At times, these costs can lead to *affordability* challenges, when resilience increases the full life-cycle cost of an asset or system. Solutions might include either an increase in funding (financed through higher taxes, user fees, or transfers) or a trade-off between the resilience and quantity of infrastructure services (such as fewer but safer roads). But more often, making infrastructure more resilient increases only the costs of design, construction, or maintenance, while decreasing other costs such as repairs, so that the overall life-cycle cost is reduced. The challenge in that case is linked to *financing*—that is, transforming annual revenues or budgets into the resources needed at each stage of the infrastructure project life cycle, with the following three priority actions.

Action 5.1: Provide adequate funding to include risk assessments in master plans and early project design

Even though hundreds of billions of dollars are invested in infrastructure every year, it remains difficult to mobilize resources for infrastructure-sector regulations, risk-informed master plans, infrastructure risk assessment, or early-stage project design. More resources tend to become available when infrastructure projects are mature, but at this stage most strategic decisions have already been made, and most low-cost options to increase resilience are no longer available (such as changing the location of an asset or even the nature of the project). Supporting and funding these activities is highly cost-effective and can be transformational, especially in poorer countries, making them a priority for international aid and cooperation (World Bank 2018). Dedicated organizations and project preparation facilities, such as the Global Facility for Disaster Reduction and Recovery or the Global Infrastructure Facility, are already active in these domains, but they remain small compared with the magnitude of the needs.

Action 5.2: Develop a government-wide financial protection strategy and contingency plans

In the aftermath of a disaster, governments are typically required to raise significant financing for response and recovery measures. Several instruments are available to do so, including reserve funds or budget reallocation, contingent credit, or insurance or risk transfers. The choice of financial instruments is determined by the risks that need to be covered, the cost of the instrument, the speed of disbursement, and the transparency and predictability of the resources (Clarke and Dercon 2016; World Bank 2017). After a disaster, however, the availability of financial resources is only half of the story; just as important is the ability to deliver resources effectively and rapidly to where they are needed, including to the firms and households that are affected by infrastructure disruptions, even if they are not affected directly by the disaster. Financial instruments therefore need to be combined with contingency plans and flexible delivery mechanisms—if possible, building on existing instruments, such as social protection systems.

Action 5.3: Promote transparency to better inform investors and decision makers

One way to ensure that resilient infrastructure projects are adequately financed is to inform investors and decision makers about the risks associated with projects. Multiple international, regional, and national initiatives are seeking to make the physical risks associated with investments and assets more transparent. Examples include the work of the Task Force for Climate-Related Financial Disclosure, which recommends that firms and investors report on physical risks and how they are managed. To contribute to this trend, the World Bank Group is committed to developing a resilience rating system to inform investors about the resilience of their infrastructure investments and help them to select the most resilient projects.

In sum, as illustrated by these five recommendations and 15 actions (table O.3), no single measure can make infrastructure systems resilient. Instead, governments need to define and implement a consistent strategy—in partnership with all stakeholders, such as utilities, investors, business associations, and citizen organizations—to tackle the many obstacles to more resilient infrastructure systems. One common feature of these recommendations is a focus on the early stages of infrastructure system development—the design of regulations, the production of hazards data and master plans, or the initial stages of new infrastructure asset design. These early stages are when small investments can significantly improve the overall resilience of infrastructure systems and generate very large benefits. In poor countries, however, mobilizing resources to invest in these actions may be challenging, which makes targeted support from the international community necessary, transformational, and highly cost-effective.

Although these recommendations are aimed at making infrastructure more resilient,

TABLE O.3 Five recommendations to address the five obstacles to resilient infrastructure

Recommendation	Actions
1: Get the basics right	1.1: Introduce and enforce regulations, construction codes, and procurement rules 1.2: Create systems for appropriate infrastructure operation, maintenance, and postincident response 1.3: Provide appropriate funding and financing for infrastructure planning, construction, and maintenance
2: Build institutions for resilience	2.1: Implement a whole-of-government approach to resilient infrastructure, building on existing regulatory systems 2.2: Identify critical infrastructure and define acceptable and intolerable risk levels 2.3: Ensure equitable access to resilient infrastructure
3: Create regulations and incentives for resilience	3.1: Consider resilience objectives in master plans, standards, and regulations and adjust them regularly to account for climate change 3.2: Create economic incentives for service providers to offer resilient infrastructure assets and services 3.3: Ensure that infrastructure regulations are consistent with risk-informed land use plans and guide development toward safer areas
4: Improve decision making	4.1: Invest in freely accessible natural hazard and climate change data 4.2: Make robust decisions and minimize the potential for regret and catastrophic failures 4.3: Build the skills needed to use data and models and mobilize the know-how of the private sector
5: Provide financing	5.1: Provide adequate funding to include risk assessments in master plans and early project design 5.2: Develop a government-wide financial protection strategy and contingency plans 5.3: Promote transparency to better inform investors and decision makers

most of them tackle market or government failures that are responsible not only for less resilient infrastructure but also for less efficient, less inclusive, and costlier infrastructure. As a result, taking these actions will contribute to more than infrastructure resilience and help create more productive, livable, and inclusive societies.

NOTES

1. In this report, all dollar amounts are U.S. dollars, unless otherwise indicated.
2. The data set covers 137 countries representing 80 percent of the GDP of low- and middle-income countries, or 32 percent of global GDP. Due to data limitations, the exact country coverage varies for different analyses. For details, refer to chapter 2 and Rentschler, Kornejew, et al. (2019).
3. The estimates summarized in this paragraph cover up to 137 low- and middle-income countries, although the exact country coverage varies across infrastructure sectors due to data constraints. For details, refer to chapter 3 and Obolensky et al. (2019).

REFERENCES

Beck, M. W., I. J. Losada, P. Menéndez, B. G. Reguero, P. Díaz-Simal, and F. Fernández. 2018. "The Global Flood Protection Savings Provided by Coral Reefs." *Nature Communications* 9 (1): 2186. https://doi.org/10.1038/s41467-018-04568-z.

Braese, J., J. Rentschler, and S. Hallegatte. 2019. "Resilient Infrastructure for Thriving Firms: A

Review of the Evidence." Background paper for this report, World Bank, Washington, DC.

Browder, G., S. Ozment, I. Rehberger Bescos, T. Gartner, and G.-M. Lange. 2019. *Integrating Green and Gray: Creating the Next Generation Infrastructure*. Washington, DC: World Bank and World Resources Institute.

Christopher, M., and H. Peck. 2004. "Building the Resilient Supply Chain." *International Journal of Logistics Management* 15 (2): 1–14. https://doi.org/10.1108/09574090410700275.

Clarke, D., and S. Dercon. 2016. *Dull Disasters? How Planning Ahead Will Make a Difference*. Oxford: Oxford University Press.

Colon, C., S. Hallegatte, and J. Rozenberg. 2019. "Transportation and Supply Chain Resilience in the United Republic of Tanzania." Background paper for this report, World Bank, Washington, DC.

Fay, M., I. L. Hyoung, H. Sungmin, M. Mastruzzi, and M. Cho. 2019. "Hitting the Trillion Mark: A Look at How Much Countries Are Spending on Infrastructure." Policy Research Working Paper 8730, World Bank, Washington, DC.

Hallegatte, S. 2013. "Modeling the Roles of Heterogeneity, Substitution, and Inventories in the Assessment of Natural Disaster Economic Costs." *Risk Analysis* 34 (1): 152–67. https://doi.org/10.1111/risa.12090.

Hallegatte, S., J. Rozenberg, C. Fox, C. Nicolas, and J. Rentschler. 2019. "Strengthening New Infrastructure Assets—A Cost-Benefit Analysis." Background paper for this report, World Bank, Washington, DC.

Hallegatte, S., and A. Vogt-Schilb. 2016. "Are Losses from Natural Disasters More Than Just Asset Losses? The Role of Capital Aggregation, Sector Interactions, and Investment Behaviors." Policy Research Working Paper 7885, World Bank, Washington, DC.

Hallegatte, S., A. Vogt-Schilb, M. Bangalore, and J. Rozenberg. 2016. *Unbreakable: Building the Resilience of the Poor in the Face of Natural Disasters*. Washington, DC: World Bank. https://doi.org/10.1596/978-1-4648-1003-9.

Jeandron, A., J. M. Saidi, A. Kapama, M. Burhole, F. Birembano, T. Vandevelde, A. Gasparrini, B. Armstrong, S. Cairncross, and J. H. J. Ensink. 2015. "Water Supply Interruptions and Suspected Cholera Incidence: A Time-Series Regression in the Democratic Republic of the Congo." *PLoS Medicine* 12 (10): 1–16. https://doi.org/10.1371/journal.pmed.1001893.

Kalra, N. S. Hallegatte, R. Lempert, C. Brown, A. Fozzard, S. Gill, and A. Shah. 2014. "Agreeing on Robust Decisions: New Processes for Decision Making under Deep Uncertainty." Policy Research Working Paper 6906, World Bank, Washington, DC. https://doi.org/doi:10.1596/1813-9450-6906.

Koks, E., J. Rozenberg, C. Zorn, M. Tariverdi, M. Vousdoukas, S. A. Fraser, J. Hall, and S. Hallegatte. 2019. "A Global Multi-Hazard Risk Analysis of Road and Railway Infrastructure Assets." Forthcoming in *Nature Sustainability*.

Kornejew, M., J. Rentschler, and S. Hallegatte. 2019. "Well Spent: How Governance Determines the Effectiveness of Infrastructure Investments." Background paper for this report, World Bank, Washington, DC.

Lenz, L., A. Munyehirwe, J. Peters, and M. Sievert. 2017. "Does Large Scale Infrastructure Investment Alleviate Poverty? Impacts of Rwanda's Electricity Access Roll-Out Program #555." *World Development* 89 (January): 88–110.

Miyamoto International. 2019. "Overview of Engineering Options for Increasing Infrastructure Resilience." Background paper for this report, World Bank, Washington, DC.

Munich Re. 2019. "Natural Catastrophe Review 2018." Munich Re, January 8. https://www.munichre.com/en/media-relations/publications/press-releases/2019/2019-01-08-press-release/index.html.

National Research Council. 2000. *Watershed Management for Potable Water Supply: Assessing the New York City Strategy*. Washington, DC: National Academies Press.

Nicolas, C., J. Rentschler, A. Potter van Loon, S. Oguah, S. Schweikert, M. Deinert, E. Koks, C. Arderne, D. Cubas, J. Li, and E. Ichikawa. 2019. "Stronger Power: Improving Power Sector Resilience to Natural Disasters." Sector note for this report, World Bank, Washington, DC.

Nicholls, R. J., J. Hinkel, D. Lincke, and T. van der Pol. 2019. "Global Investment Costs for Coastal Defense through the 21st Century." Policy Research Working Paper 8745, World Bank, Washington, DC.

Obolensky, M., A. Erman, J. Rozenberg, P. Avner, J. Rentschler, and S. Hallegatte. 2019. "Infrastructure Disruptions: Impacts on Households." Background paper for this report, World Bank, Washington, DC.

OECD (Organisation for Economic Co-operation and Development). 2019. *Good Governance for*

Critical Infrastructure Resilience. OECD Review of Risk Management Practices. Paris: OECD.

Pardina, M. R., and J. Schiro. 2018. "Taking Stock of Economic Regulation of Power Utilities in the Developing World: A Literature Review." Policy Research Working Paper 8461, World Bank, Washington, DC.

Renn, O. 2008. "White Paper on Risk Governance: Toward an Integrative Framework." In *Global Risk Governance*, edited by O. Renn and K. D. Walker, 3–73. Stuttgart: Springer.

Rentschler, J., J. Braese, N. Jones, and P. Avner. 2019. "Three Feet Under: The Impacts of Flooding on Urban Jobs, Connectivity, and Infrastructure." Background paper for this report, World Bank, Washington, DC.

Rentschler, J., M. Kornejew, S. Hallegatte, M. Obolensky, and J. Braese. 2019 "Underutilized Potential: The Business Costs of Unreliable Infrastructure in Developing Countries." Background paper for this report, World Bank, Washington, DC.

Rentschler, J., M. Obolensky, and M. Kornejew. 2019. "Candle in the Wind? Energy System Resilience to Natural Shocks." Background paper for this report, World Bank, Washington, DC.

Rose, A., G. Oladosu, and S. Y. Liao. 2007. "Business Interruption Impacts of a Terrorist Attack on the Electric Power System of Los Angeles: Customer Resilience to a Total Blackout." *Risk Analysis* 27 (3): 513–31. https://doi.org/10.1111/j.1539-6924.2007.00912.x.

Rozenberg, J., and M. Fay. 2019. *Beyond the Gap: How Countries Can Afford the Infrastructure They Need While Protecting the Planet*. Washington, DC: World Bank.

Rozenberg, J., X. Espinet Alegre, P. Avner, C. Fox, S. Hallegatte, E. Koks, J. Rentschler, and M. Tariverdi. 2019a. "From a Rocky Road to Smooth Sailing: Building Transport Resilience to Natural Disasters." Sector note for this report, World Bank, Washington, DC.

Rozenberg, J., C. Fox, M. Tariverdi, E. Koks, and S. Hallegatte. 2019b. "Road Show: Comparing Road Network Resilience around the World." Background paper for this report, World Bank, Washington, DC.

Sandhu, H. S., and S. Raja. 2019. "No Broken Link: The Vulnerability of Telecommunication Infrastructure to Natural Hazards." Sector note for this report, World Bank, Washington, DC.

Sheffi, Y. 2005. *The Resilient Enterprise: Overcoming Vulnerability for Competitive Advantage*. Cambridge, MA: MIT Press.

Stip, C., Z. Mao, L. Bonzanigo, G. Browder, and J. Tracy. 2019. "Water Infrastructure Resilience: Examples of Dams, Wastewater Treatment Plants, and Water Supply and Sanitation Systems." Sector note for this report, World Bank, Washington, DC.

Strahl, J., M. Bebrin, E. Paris, and D. Jones. 2016. "Beyond the Buzzwords: Making the Specific Case for Community Resilience Microgrids." ACEEE Summer Study on Energy Efficiency in Buildings, American Council for an Energy-Efficient Economy, Washington, DC.

Swiss Re. 2019. "Preliminary Sigma Estimates for 2018: Global Insured Losses of USD 79 Billion Are Fourth Highest on Sigma Records." Swiss Re, December 18. https://www.swissre.com/media/news-releases/nr_20181218_sigma_estimates_for_2018.html.

Vallejo, L. and M. Mullan. 2017. Climate-Resilient Infrastructure: Getting the Policies Right." OECD Environment Working Papers, No. 121, OECD Publishing, Paris.

Walsh, B., and S. Hallegatte. 2019. "Measuring Natural Risks in the Philippines." Policy Research Working Paper 8723, World Bank, Washington, DC.

Wiener, J. B., and M. D. Rogers. 2002. "Comparing Precaution in the United States and Europe." *Journal of Risk Research* 5 (4): 317–49.

World Bank. 2013. *World Development Report 2014: Risk and Opportunity—Managing Risk for Development*. Washington, DC: World Bank. https://doi.org/10.1596/978-0-8213-9903-3.

———. 2017. *Sovereign Catastrophe Risk Pools: World Bank Technical Contribution to the G20*. Washington, DC: World Bank. https://openknowledge.worldbank.org/handle/10986/28311.

———. 2018. *Strategic Use of Climate Finance to Maximize Climate Action*. Washington, DC: World Bank. https://openknowledge.worldbank.org/handle/10986/30475.

Zhang, F. 2019. *In the Dark: How Much Do Power Sector Distortions Cost South Asia*? South Asia Development Forum. Washington, DC: World Bank. https://doi.org/doi:10.1596/978-1-4648-1154-8.

Resilient Infrastructure: A Lifeline for Sustainable Development 1

In Dar es Salaam, frequent urban flooding disrupts the city's entire economy, even beyond the directly affected flood zones. As roads become flooded, all traffic, including public transport, comes to a near standstill. People are unable to reach their workplaces, supply chains are interrupted, deliveries are missed, and sales are lost. The supply of electricity is often affected as well, resulting in power outages and halting economic activity. Because these incidents occur so frequently, businesses have to invest in expensive coping measures, ranging from buying diesel generators to keeping expensive backup inventories and contracting with backup suppliers. Overall, the lack of reliable transport and electricity systems is a defining factor of the urban economy of Dar es Salaam, influencing the investment and risk-taking behavior of everyone who lives and works there.

But Dar es Salaam is by no means an exception. Cities and countries around the world are facing the challenging consequences of substandard infrastructure, often at a significant cost to people and firms. Worldwide, 940 million people still lack access to modern electricity, let alone modern telecommunications services; 2.1 billion have no access to safe drinking water; 4.5 billion lack adequate sanitation facilities; 1 billion live more than 2 kilometers away from an all-season road; and uncounted numbers are unable to access work and educational opportunities because transport services remain either unavailable or unaffordable.

Simply being connected to infrastructure networks does not guarantee reliable services. Many people and businesses experience frequent power outages, intermittent water supply, congested or regularly disrupted transport, or unreliable communication. In the areas of transport, water, electricity, and infrastructure more generally, low- and middle-income countries tend to experience more disruptions and have less reliable infrastructure than richer countries, with large differences across countries, even at similar income levels (figure 1.1).

There is ample evidence that natural hazards affect the functioning of infrastructure systems in poor and rich countries alike. Floods like those in Mozambique in 2019 destroy roads and isolate entire communities or regularly paralyze public transit systems, as they do in Dar es Salam every rainy season. Earthquakes like the one in San Francisco in 1989 damage bridges, slowing down local economies. Hurricanes wipe out electricity transmission and distribution systems, cutting people's access to electricity for months, as the 2017 storm in Puerto Rico did. Moreover, in the next decades, many factors—including climate

FIGURE 1.1 Poorer countries experience more infrastructure disruptions

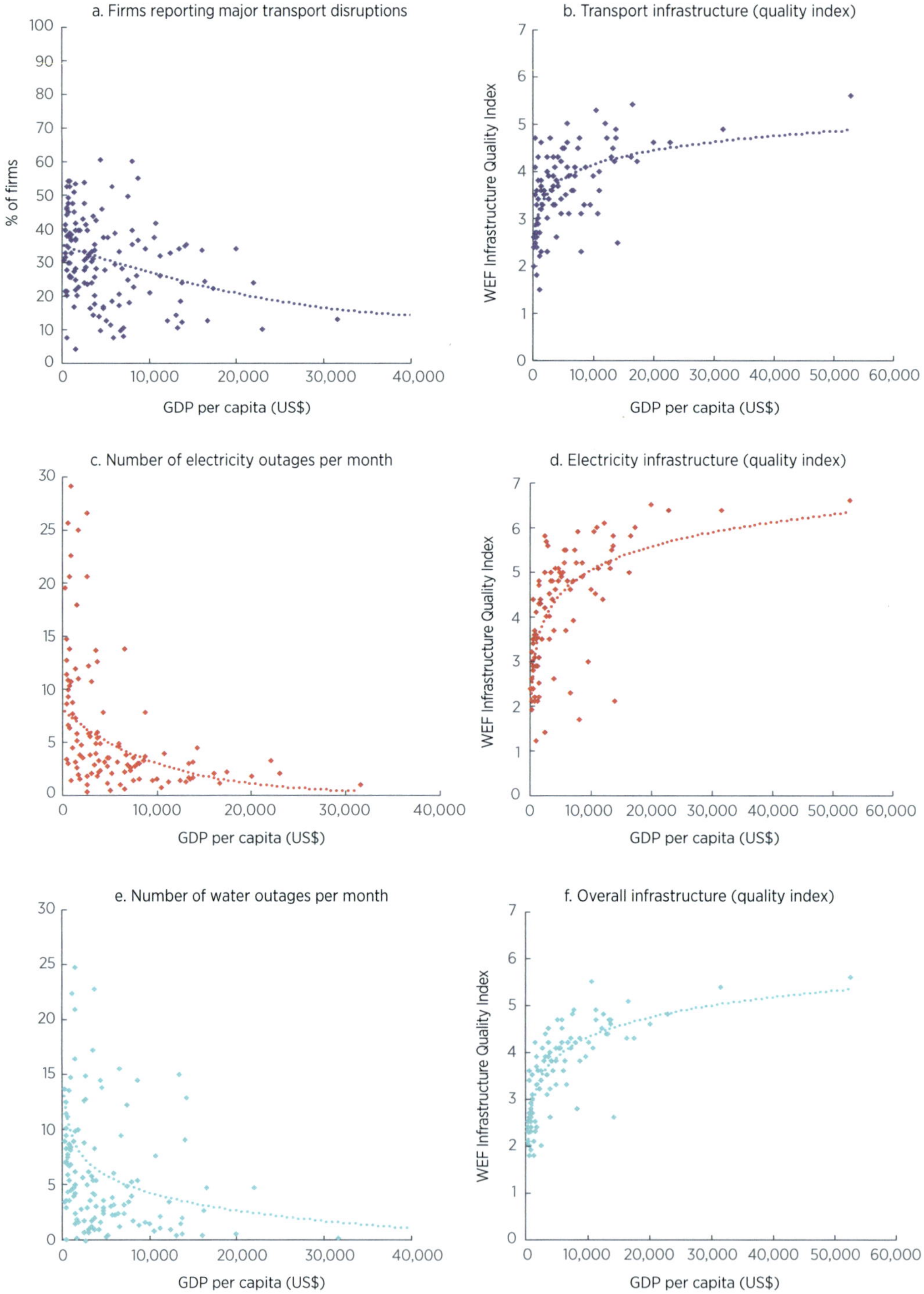

Source: Rentschler et al. 2019, based on data from the World Bank's Enterprise Surveys (panels a, c, and e), and the Infrastructure Quality Index in the Global Competitiveness Index of the World Economic Forum (panels b, d, and f).
Note: Panel c only shows countries with up to 30 electricity outages a month. Eight countries (all with GDP per capita below $9,000) report between 30 and 95 outages a month.

BOX 1.1 Resilience is central to achieving many international objectives

In the last decade, a series of international agreements have made resilience a central objective for development.

These agreements include the Sendai Declaration and the Sendai Framework for Disaster Risk Reduction 2015–2030, which seeks "the substantial reduction of disaster risk and losses in lives, livelihoods, and health and in the economic, physical, social, cultural, and environmental assets of persons, businesses, communities, and countries." This goal is translated into multiple targets for 2030, such as reducing mortality and direct economic loss in relation to global GDP and increasing the availability of and access to multihazard early warning systems and disaster risk information and assessments.

The Paris Agreement was approved in December 2015 at the 21st Conference of the Parties of the United Nations Framework Convention on Climate Change. It includes many objectives and decisions for supporting more resilient development. In particular, Article 7 establishes "the global goal on adaptation of enhancing adaptive capacity, strengthening resilience, and reducing vulnerability to climate change, with a view to contributing to sustainable development."

The United Nations' Sustainable Development Goals also relate to disaster risk. Target 1.5, for example, aims "by 2030, [to] build the resilience of the poor and those in vulnerable situations and reduce their exposure and vulnerability to climate-related extreme events and other economic, social, and environmental shocks and disasters." Target 13.1 aims to "strengthen resilience and adaptive capacity to climate-related hazards and natural disasters in all countries." The targets for food security and urban development are also relevant to reducing disaster risks.

change, population and economic growth, and urbanization—will magnify many of these threats (IPCC 2012, 2014).

When disasters affect infrastructure services, even the households and companies not directly affected by the shocks experience impacts. People are sometimes left without electricity or water for weeks or more. They are also affected indirectly through impacts on businesses—such as reduced productivity and competitiveness—which in turn affect their ability to provide the jobs, incomes, and goods and services on which people depend. At the macro level, infrastructure disruptions add to the already large impacts of natural disasters on people's assets and livelihoods, thereby threatening the achievement of many international objectives (box 1.1) (Hallegatte et al. 2016).

How are low- and middle-income countries responding? By one estimate, governments in these countries are investing around $1 trillion—or between 3.4 percent and 5 percent of their gross domestic product (GDP)—in infrastructure (Fay et al. 2019). Much more will be invested in the next decades. In low- and middle-income countries alone, it is estimated that new infrastructure could cost between 2 percent and 8 percent of GDP a year to 2030, or from $640 billion to $2.7 trillion a year (Rozenberg and Fay 2019).

However, as countries continue to build their stock of infrastructure assets at a rapid pace, they will have to emphasize the quality of investments. Ensuring that infrastructure services are reliable is critical for making large investments worthwhile. Infrastructure investments that do not meet these criteria are bound to fail to deliver—not only financially but also in their ability to contribute to sustainable socioeconomic development.

OBJECTIVES OF THIS REPORT

This report explores the *resilience of infrastructure*—that is, the ability of infrastructure to provide the services users need during and after a natural shock. While natural hazards are only one of the causes of infrastructure disruptions, resilience is still an essential dimension of the overall reliability of infrastructure systems.

"Resilience" here is used in a broader sense than the traditional definition in ecology, which refers to the ability of systems to recover and bounce back. Boosting resilience, using this broad definition, can be achieved in many ways, including:

- Reducing the exposure of infrastructure assets to natural hazards, such as by building energy assets outside floodplains
- Reducing the vulnerability of assets, such as by making roads able to cope with heavy precipitation or bridges able to resist strong wind
- Designing infrastructure systems so they are able to deliver services, even if some of their components have been damaged or destroyed
- Ensuring that infrastructure systems do not fail catastrophically, can recover quickly, and be repaired efficiently if damaged
- Making the users of infrastructure services better able to cope with service disruptions, such as by installing batteries or generators in hospitals or ensuring that firms rely on multiple suppliers.

Building on a wide range of case studies, global empirical analyses, and modeling exercises, the report explores how natural hazards and climate change reduce the reliability of infrastructure services—and in the process not only diminish their socioeconomic and development benefits but also make people and firms less resilient. The report also identifies technical solutions and policies for (a) building the resilience of infrastructure services; (b) improving their reliability and quality; (c) strengthening the resilience of infrastructure users; (d) maximizing development benefits; and (e) reducing the impacts of climate change.

This report focuses primarily on four infrastructure systems that are essential to economic activity and people's well-being:

- *Power systems,* including the generation, transmission, and distribution of electricity
- *Water and sanitation systems,* focusing on water utilities (large-scale water storage, hydropower, and irrigation systems are considered, but are not the focus of the analysis)
- *Transport systems,* looking at multiple modes (including road, rail, waterways, and airports) and considering multiple scales (including urban transit and rural access)
- *Telecommunications,* including telephones and Internet connections.

These systems share two characteristics that make them worthy of in-depth investigation. First, they provide critical services for the well-being of households and the productivity of firms and are thus often referred to as "lifelines" or "critical infrastructure systems." Their importance is clear over the short term, because they provide what are often considered basic services, and over the long term, because their reliability and quality are often considered a prerequisite for modern, productive economies.

Second, these systems—from transport systems to electricity grids—are organized in networks, with direct implications for their vulnerability to natural hazards. For example, a localized shock can propagate very quickly through these networks, affecting households or firms located even in a safe area. A network also creates some very specific challenges, in that the vulnerability of one infrastructure asset can be a poor proxy for the network's ability to perform during or after a shock. Only a network-wide, system-wide view can provide a reliable assessment of vulnerability and resilience, but doing so brings significant data and methodological challenges. For this reason, the report also describes existing or new tools, data sets, and models, with examples of applications in specific case studies to demonstrate what is possible and to offer a toolbox not only for investigating infrastructure resilience but also for identifying the most promising interventions.

Other systems sometimes described as "infrastructure"—such as buildings, schools, or hospitals—are not discussed at length in this report. This is because they are not organized primarily as networks, even though the lines are sometimes blurred (for example, when an ensemble of regional hospitals collaborates to respond better to a shock).

STRUCTURE OF THE REPORT

This report is organized into three parts. Part I establishes the scale of the problem, quantifies the total cost of infrastructure disruptions, and explores the role of natural hazards and climate change in these disruptions. It also demonstrates the adverse effects that a lack of resilient infrastructure has on households and firms, and how this lack may contribute to poverty and poor health. Part II identifies viable and affordable solutions to make infrastructure systems and their users more resilient and provides estimates of the costs and benefits of more resilient infrastructure systems. Part III proposes concrete steps for the development of more resilient infrastructure, including policy measures to ensure that the report's suggested solutions can be implemented in practice.

REFERENCES

Fay, M., S. Han, H. I. Lee, M. Mastruzzi, and M. Cho. 2019. "Hitting the Trillion Mark: A Look at How Much Countries Are Spending on Infrastructure." Policy Research Working Paper 8730, World Bank, Washington, DC.

Hallegatte, S., A. Vogt-Schilb, M. Bangalore, and J. Rozenberg. 2016. *Unbreakable: Building the Resilience of the Poor in the Face of Natural Disasters*. Washington, DC: World Bank. https://doi.org/10.1596/978-1-4648-1003-9.

IPCC (Intergovernmental Panel on Climate Change). 2012. *Special Report on Managing the Risks of Extreme Events and Disasters to Advance Climate Change Adaptation: Summary for Policymakers—A Report of Working Groups I and II of the IPCC.* Geneva: IPCC.

———. 2014. *Climate Change 2014: Synthesis Report: Contribution of Working Groups I, II, and III to the Fifth Assessment Report of the Intergovernmental Panel on Climate Change.* Geneva: IPCC.

Rentschler, J., M. Kornejew, S. Hallegatte, M. Obolensky, and J. Braese. 2019. "Underutilized Potential: The Business Costs of Unreliable Infrastructure in Developing Countries." Background paper for this report, World Bank, Washington, DC.

Rozenberg, J., and M. Fay. 2019. *Beyond the Gap: How Countries Can Afford the Infrastructure They Need While Protecting the Planet.* Washington, DC: World Bank.

PART I

A Diagnosis: A Lack of Resilient Infrastructure Is Harming People and Firms

How are natural shocks, infrastructure systems, economic activities, and human well-being interconnected? To visualize these interactions, figure PI.1 provides a framework for part I of this report. It illustrates the channels through which natural hazards and shocks eventually affect people and firms via their impacts on infrastructure systems. The direct impacts of natural shocks on firms and people are an important topic that has been discussed in past studies (for example, Hallegatte et al. 2016). This report focuses on how natural shocks affect infrastructure systems, which in turn affect firms and people.

Part I begins with chapters 2 and 3, which analyze the effects and costs of unreliable infrastructure on firms and households—whether disruptions are provoked by natural shocks or other causes, such as technical failures (the white arrows in figure PI.1). Both chapters explore the high cost of infrastructure disruptions on people, either directly through their impacts on health and well-being or indirectly through their impacts on firms, jobs, and income.

FIGURE PI.1 A framework for analyzing how natural shocks affect people and firms through their impact on infrastructure systems

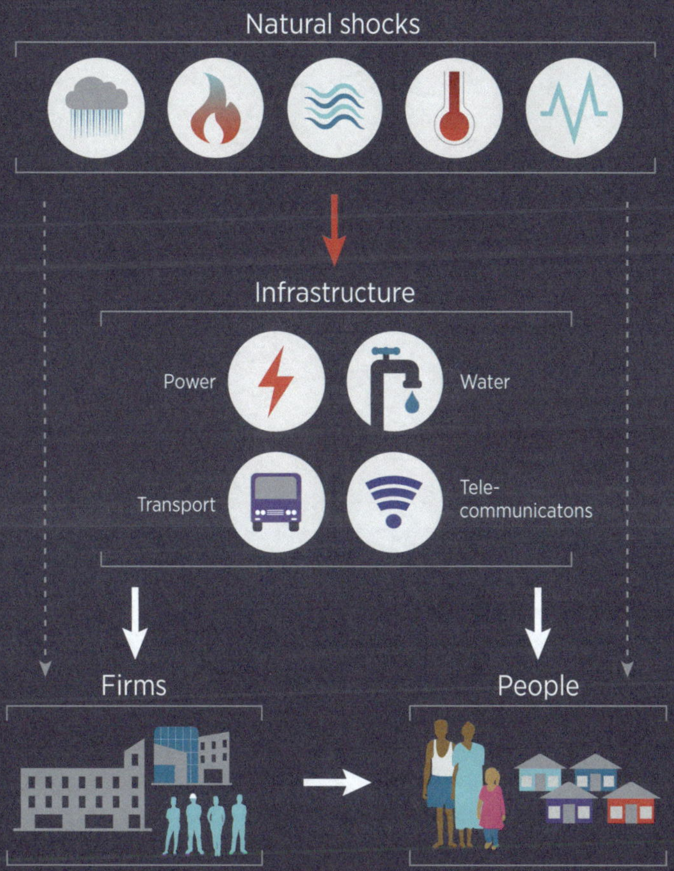

Note: The dashed arrows represent the direct impacts of natural hazards on firms and people, effects that are treated elsewhere—see, for example, Hallegatte et al. (2016). This report focuses on the impact of natural shocks on infrastructure systems (red arrow) and how this impact, in turn, affects firms and people (white arrows).

Then chapter 4 examines the impact of natural shocks—floods, storms, earthquakes, and droughts—on infrastructure systems (the red arrow in figure PI.1). It shows that natural hazards account for a significant fraction of infrastructure service disruptions, at least in electricity and transport, and create large needs for reconstruction. Finally, chapter 5 provides a review of evidence from household and firm surveys and modeling exercises, which detail how infrastructure system disruptions and damages magnify the macroeconomic cost of natural disasters and the impacts on people's well-being.

REFERENCE

Hallegatte, S., A. Vogt-Schilb, M. Bangalore, and J. Rozenberg. 2016. *Unbreakable: Building the Resilience of the Poor in the Face of Natural Disasters*. Washington, DC: World Bank. https://doi.org/10.1596/978-1-4648-1003-9.

Infrastructure Disruptions Are a Barrier to Thriving Firms | 2

Lack of access to infrastructure services can have severe economic consequences. Just as bad, however, can be the lack of reliability in infrastructure services: being connected to the electricity grid is of little use if the power is out. This chapter offers an overview of the real costs that infrastructure disruptions impose on firms and the resulting damages at the macro level.

Unreliable infrastructure systems affect firms through three key channels:

- *Direct impacts.* These impacts are the most visible, immediate consequences of infrastructure disruptions. For example, a firm relying on water to cool a machine cannot manufacture products during a drought; likewise, a restaurant with an electric stove cannot cook meals without power. Infrastructure disruptions interrupt firms' activities, force them to operate at less than full production capacity, reduce their sales, and cause delays in the supply and delivery of goods.
- *Coping costs.* For example, a backup power generator reduces the direct impacts of blackouts but has high operating costs and requires an up-front purchase that prohibits alternative, more productive investments.
- *Indirect impacts.* These impacts are less visible and less immediate; they affect firms' investment decisions, influence what products can and cannot be produced, and influence the composition and innovativeness of an industry. For example, a firm is less likely to upgrade its machinery to more productive technology if frequent blackouts force it to revert regularly to manual production.

Together, these impacts take a big toll on an economy's ability to generate wealth and maintain international competitiveness. But how high is this toll? What are the real costs that infrastructure disruptions impose on firms, and what are the resulting damages at the macroeconomic level?

This chapter addresses these questions by looking at the impacts of disruptions in key infrastructure sectors (table 2.1). It presents estimates of the monetary costs of outages based on a set of microdata for more than 143,000 firms from the World Bank's Enterprise Surveys. This data set covers 137 countries, representing 78 percent of the world's population and 80 percent of the gross domestic product (GDP) of low- and middle-income countries. However, the various estimates reported in this chapter often use subsets of

TABLE 2.1 Disrupted infrastructure services have multiple impacts on firms

Sector	Direct impacts	Coping costs	Indirect impacts
Power	• **Reduced utilization rates ($38 billion a year)** • **Sales losses ($82 billion a year)**	• **Generator investment ($6 billion a year)** • **Generator operation costs ($59 billion a year)**	• Higher barriers to market entry and lower investment • Less competition and innovation due to lack of small and new firms • Bias toward labor-intensive production • Inability to provide on-demand services and goods • Diminished competitiveness in international markets
Water	• **Reduced utilization rates ($6 billion a year)** • Sales losses	• Investment in alternative water sources (reservoirs, wells)	
Transport	• **Reduced utilization rates ($107 billion a year)** • Sales losses • Delayed supplies and deliveries	• Increased inventory • More expensive location choices in proximity to, for example, clients or ports	
Telecommunications	• Reduced utilization rates • Sales losses	• Expensive location choices close to fast Internet	

Source: Rentschler, Kornejew, et al. 2019.
Note: Bolded are the impact channels for which original estimates are presented in this section, based on the World Bank's Enterprise Surveys of 143,000 firms in 137 countries, representing 78 percent of the world's population and 80 percent of the GDP of low- and middle-income countries.

the full sample, due to missing data in some countries.

The analysis, detailed in a technical background study for this report by Rentschler, Kornejew, et al. (2019), estimates that annual losses due to disruptions are substantial in low- and middle-income countries (summarized in table 2.1). Utilization rate losses due to power, water, and transport disruptions amount to $151 billion a year, sales losses from electricity outages amount to $82 billion a year, and the additional costs of self-generating electricity amount to $65 billion a year. At a total cost of about $300 billion a year, these figures highlight the significance of unreliable infrastructure. These are lower-bound estimates of the global costs of outages because neither all countries nor all impact channels are covered by this analysis. To address these gaps, this chapter also relies on examples from the extensive literature on this topic (Braese, Rentschler, and Hallegatte 2019).

INFRASTRUCTURE SERVICES ENABLE FIRMS TO THRIVE

The availability of infrastructure systems is a key factor of production that determines the competitiveness of firms and thus of entire economies. In a prominent paper on the "competitive advantage of nations," Porter (1990) argues that the ability of a country to host high-performing firms is supported by a wide range of factors—including the availability of reliable and efficient infrastructure systems.

The importance of infrastructure for economic growth has been confirmed by a wide range of studies, reviewed by Braese, Rentschler, and Hallegatte (2019). For example, Calderón and Servén (2014) review the theoretical and empirical literature on infrastructure and growth and conclude that, overall, the literature finds that infrastructure development has positive effects on income growth and even distributive equity. Bom and Ligthart (2014) conduct a meta regression of 68 quantitative studies, predominantly in high-income economies, to quantify the impact of public infrastructure capital on GDP. Their assessment suggests that on average a 1 percent increase in public infrastructure capital is associated with a 0.1 percent increase in GDP.

The same positive impact of infrastructure investments emerges from studies investigating individual countries at different income levels. A prominent study by Aschauer (1989) finds that public investment in U.S. infrastructure has a significant positive effect on total factor productivity (TFP). In particular, investments in "core" infrastructure—such as transport, electricity, gas, water, and sanitation—have the strongest explanatory power for productivity. In a 30-year-long panel of South African manufacturing firms, Fedderke and Bogetić (2009) find that investments in different types of transport, telecommunications, and power generation infrastructure have positive and significant impacts on measures of productivity, output, and growth.

Many more studies focus on the firm-level benefits of the four critical infrastructure sectors studied in this report. Electricity infrastructure has been shown to benefit both small enterprises and industrial firms. Evidence from Indonesia and South Africa shows that electrification resulted in increased employment (especially among women), incentivized the formation of new small and medium firms, and enhanced productivity (Dinkelman 2011; Kassem 2018). Transport infrastructure has been found to yield similar benefits by creating employment, increasing productivity, lowering production costs, and allowing firms to reduce inventory holdings (Duranton and Turner 2012; Ghani, Goswami, and Kerr 2016; Gibbons et al. 2017; Volpe Martincus and Blyde 2012; Wan and Zhang 2018). Information and communications technology infrastructure has also been shown to generate growth through higher productivity and innovation. For instance, in an analysis of 45 countries in Sub-Saharan Africa from 1990 to 2014, Albiman and Sulong (2016) find significant positive effects of mobile phones, the Internet, and telephone lines on economic growth. As with other types of infrastructure, the underlying effect channels are increases in firm-level productivity and innovation activities (Paunov and Rollo 2015, 2016; Polák 2017).

Overall, this rich evidence base highlights why infrastructure disruptions are so detrimental to firms. As firms rely on infrastructure services to operate effectively and compete internationally, the disruptions and lack of reliability have significant adverse impacts on the performance of firms.

INFRASTRUCTURE DISRUPTIONS HAVE DIRECT AND REAL COSTS FOR FIRMS

Frequent disruptions of electricity, water, or transport infrastructure often mean that firms are unable to utilize all of their available production capacity. Capacity utilization is a common measure of the effectiveness with which a firm converts its resources into output. A firm that is frequently forced to halt production—for example, because of power outages or input shortages caused by transport disruptions or upstream production stops—will be operating below its full capacity.

This section presents estimates of the impacts of electricity, water, and transport disruptions using a pooled data set of firms from low- and middle-income countries. This data set is based on the World Bank's Enterprise Surveys, which provide harmonized firm-level data on the operating conditions experienced by businesses worldwide. As part of the survey, firms report on their capacity utilization rate and on the quality of water and electricity infrastructure, including the average monthly frequency and duration of service disruptions. Firms also report transport disruptions using a subjective ordinal scale. These data allow exploration of how infrastructure disruptions affect firms' performance, controlling for a range of other factors.[1] (Unfortunately, the survey does not include information on disruptions in telecommunications.)

The results show that the annual losses due to disruptions in low- and middle-income countries are substantial (table 2.1). For the 118 countries for which data are available, unreliable power, water, and transport infrastructure leads to utilization losses of $151 billion a year, which is equivalent to 0.59 percent of the sample GDP (see map 2.1).[2] These utilization rate losses can be separated into the

MAP 2.1 Firms in low- and middle-income countries are incurring high utilization rate losses due to infrastructure disruptions

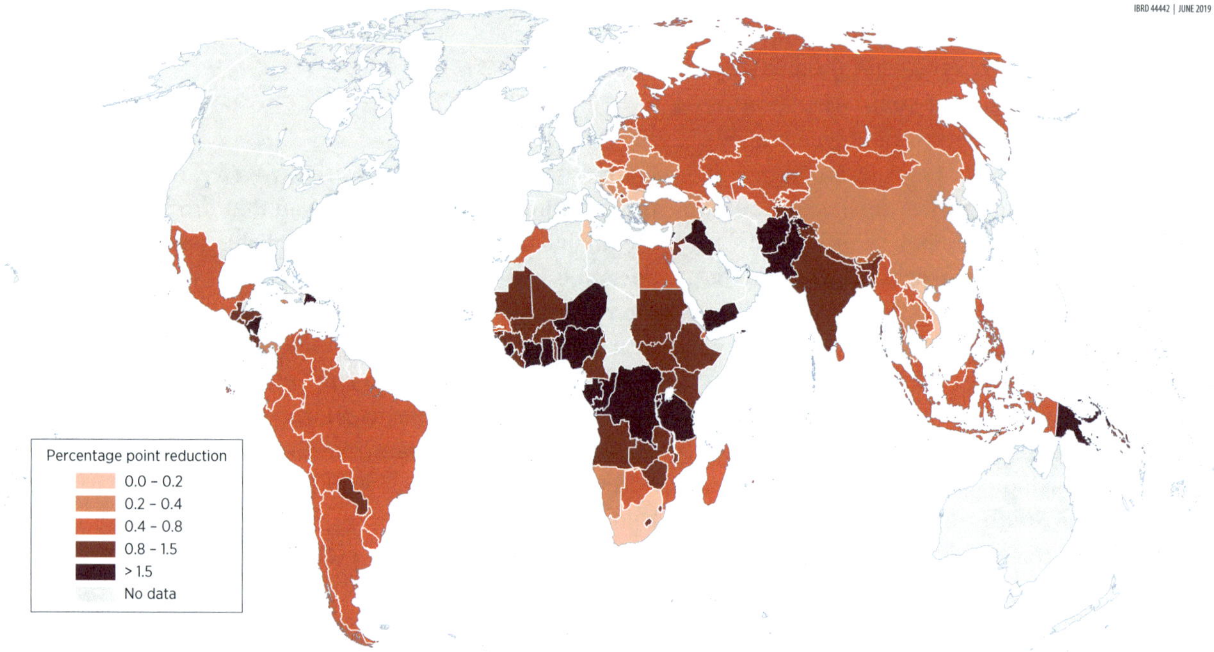

Source: Rentschler, Kornejew, et al. 2019.
Note: Map shows countrywide average utilization rate losses from electricity, water, and transport infrastructure disruptions.

three types of infrastructure covered by the Enterprise Surveys (figure 2.1). The results show that most utilization losses are caused by disruptions in transport infrastructure, accounting for losses of $107 billion annually, or 0.42 percent of sample GDP. Disruptions in the electricity supply account for $38 billion, and water disruptions cause utilization rate losses of $6 billion a year.

Strikingly, some countries, especially low-incomes ones, face very high utilization rate losses from unreliable power and water infrastructure (figure 2.2, panels a and b). By contrast, most middle-income countries are barely affected because of their much more reliable power and water systems. Transport disruptions show a different pattern. Although poorer countries still tend to incur higher transport-related utilization losses, the losses remain significant even for middle-income countries. This persistence of transport losses in richer countries and areas can explain their large contribution to the overall loss figure and suggests that the damage that unreliable transport infrastructure inflicts on an economy is hard to eliminate.

Of course, firms are vulnerable not only to disruptions that directly affect their facilities, but also to disruptions in their wider region. For example, even if a firm is not directly affected by infrastructure breakdowns (for example, by experiencing a power outage onsite), it may still be forced to stop production as interruptions along the supply chain bring input supply or output demand to a halt.

To assess this issue, Rentschler, Kornejew, et al. (2019) estimate how the utilization rates of individual firms are affected indirectly by infrastructure disruptions, proxied by region-level (instead of firm-level) disruptions. The results

FIGURE 2.1 For all critical infrastructure sectors, poorer countries experience the highest utilization rate losses due to disruptions

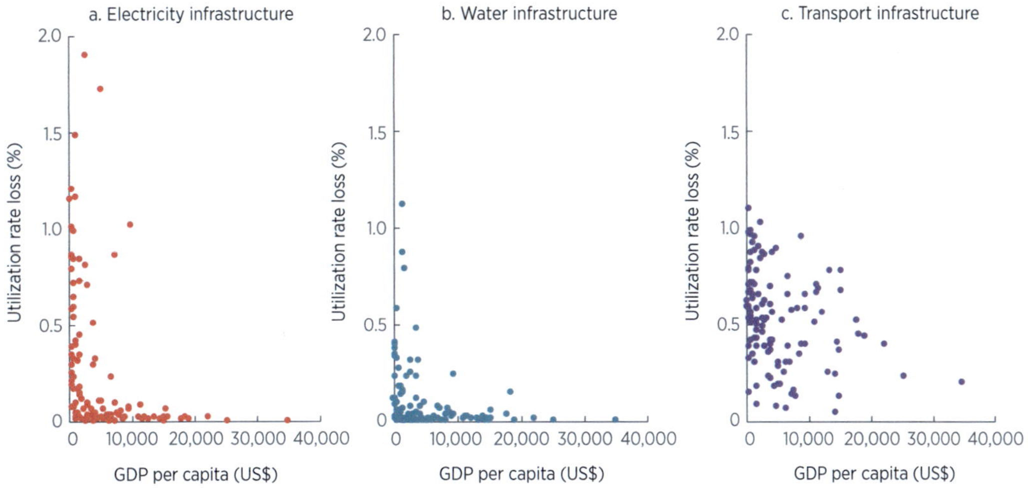

Source: Rentschler, Kornejew, et al. 2019.
Note: Data points represent 118 countries.

FIGURE 2.2 In the most affected countries, utilization rate losses are a significant share of GDP

Top 15 countries with greatest utilization rate losses, by type of infrastructure disruption

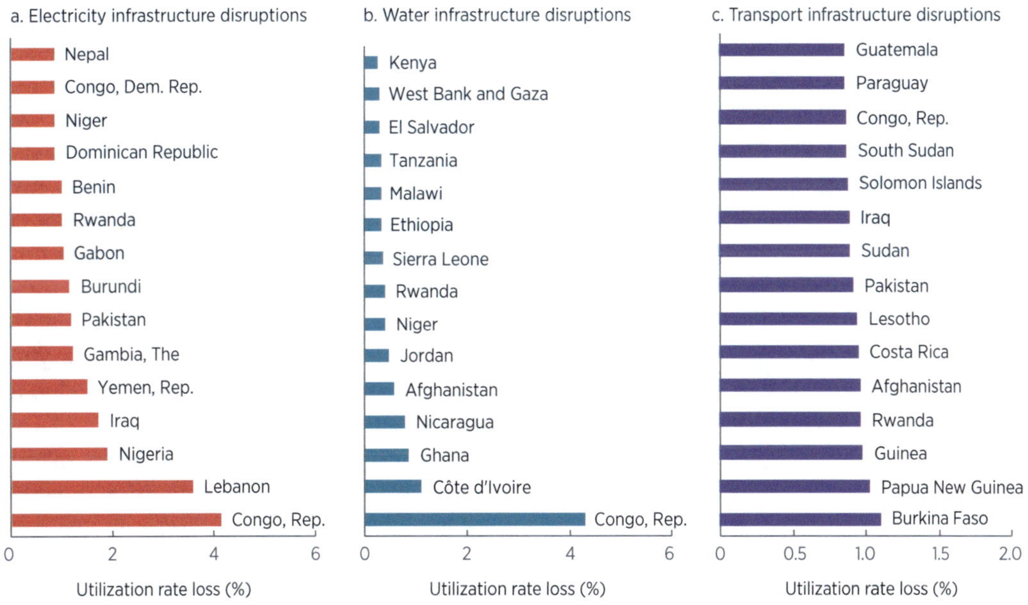

Source: Rentschler, Kornejew, et al. 2019.

suggest that the regional effects of infrastructure disruptions are significant. For water and transport, but not power, the regional effects may be as important as, or even more important than, the direct firm-level impacts. In fact, for water disruptions (and depending on model specifications), the indirect losses can exceed the direct losses by a ratio of 3 to 1. Although

MAP 2.2 Power outages are causing large sales losses in low- and middle-income countries, especially in Africa

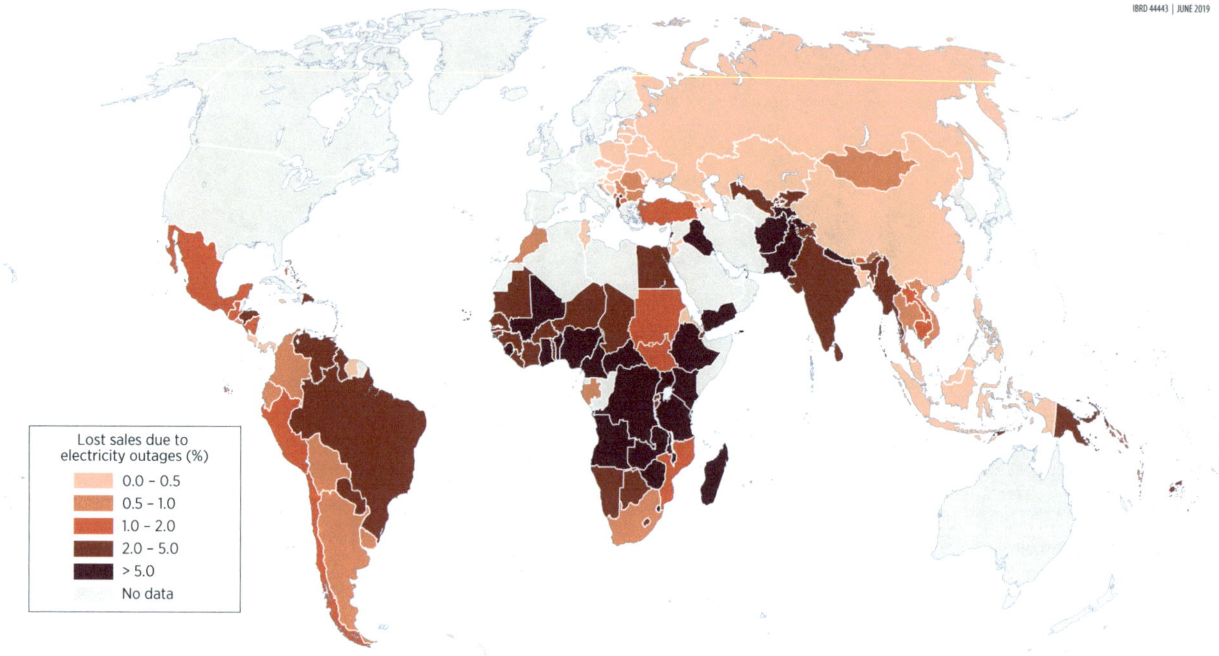

Source: Rentschler, Kornejew, et al. 2019.
Note: Map shows average sales losses reported by firms, as country-level averages.

regional disruption levels provide only an imperfect measure of indirect effects, it is evident that considering just the direct impacts of infrastructure disruptions misses a large part of the economic cost.

FIGURE 2.3 More frequent power outages tend to result in larger sales losses

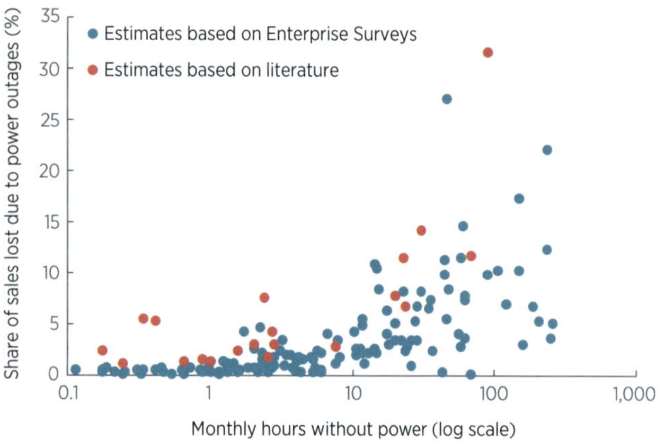

Source: Rentschler, Kornejew, et al. 2019, based on the World Bank's Enterprise Surveys.

With regard to sales, the World Bank's Enterprise Surveys also collect self-reported data on sales losses due to power outages for more than 80,000 firms from 122 mostly low- and middle-income countries (although the same data are not available for transport and water supply disruptions). The data show that power outages in these countries are causing sales losses of $81.6 billion a year (map 2.2)—or more than twice the value of capacity utilization losses (table 2.1). And because a significant fraction of firms (about 15 percent) did not report their sales, the sales loss figure is likely to be a conservative estimate. These results correlate closely with those from other studies (see Braese, Rentschler, and Hallegatte 2019), which find that firms located in countries with frequent power outages tend to incur large sales losses. Power outages are particularly hard on sales if they average more than 10 hours a month (figure 2.3).

Across countries, firms exhibit varying capacities to deal with electricity disruptions. Take the case of the 15 countries for which firms on average report the highest shares of sales lost from outages. As figure 2.4 shows, although all of these countries suffer significant power outages of more than 10 hours a month, at this high level of outages, the sales losses are no longer clearly related to electricity downtime. This finding indicates that the relationship is mediated by other factors that determine firms' vulnerability to electricity network disruptions, such as the sectoral distribution of firms, competition, and the energy intensity of production. Moreover, the extent to which firms are affected by power outages is determined by their coping strategies, which are discussed later in this chapter.

Water supply infrastructure also plays an important role in production. In agriculture, the relationship between water availability—determined by weather and irrigation technology—and agricultural production is clearly established (Damania et al. 2017). Iimi (2011) finds that if all water supply disruptions could be halted in Europe and Central Asia, firms would on average be able to reduce their costs by 0.5 percent. This effect would likely be significantly larger in low- and middle-income countries with less reliable water infrastructure. Indeed, Islam and Hyland (2018), using Enterprise Survey data for 103 countries, find that water supply disruptions have adverse impacts on firms in low- and lower-middle-income countries, but not in upper-middle- and higher-income countries. In the first group, an additional water outage incident would lead to sales losses of about 8.2 percent for the average manufacturing firm.

Traffic congestion also causes significant economic losses and has been shown to have a negative effect on economic growth (Sweet 2011). The evidence suggests that firms reliant on high-skilled labor, specialized inputs, and geographically distributed markets are especially sensitive to congestion because it interferes with their access to these production factors (Weisbrod, Vary, and Treyz 2003). Sweet (2013) finds that in 88 U.S. metropolitan areas, a 1 percent increase in congestion—measured by daily traffic per freeway lane—not only affects economic growth but also leads to a decrease in productivity growth per worker of up to 0.033 percent. Using a panel similar in geographic scope, Jin and Rafferty (2017) find that an increase in congestion growth of 1 percent—here measured by an index of traffic delays—causes a decrease in employment growth of 0.08 percent.

Traffic disruptions and congestion have negative productivity effects in low- and middle-income countries as well. Based on a survey of commuters in Kumasi, Ghana, congestion has been estimated to result in an average loss of

FIGURE 2.4 Size of sales losses depends on more than the length of outages

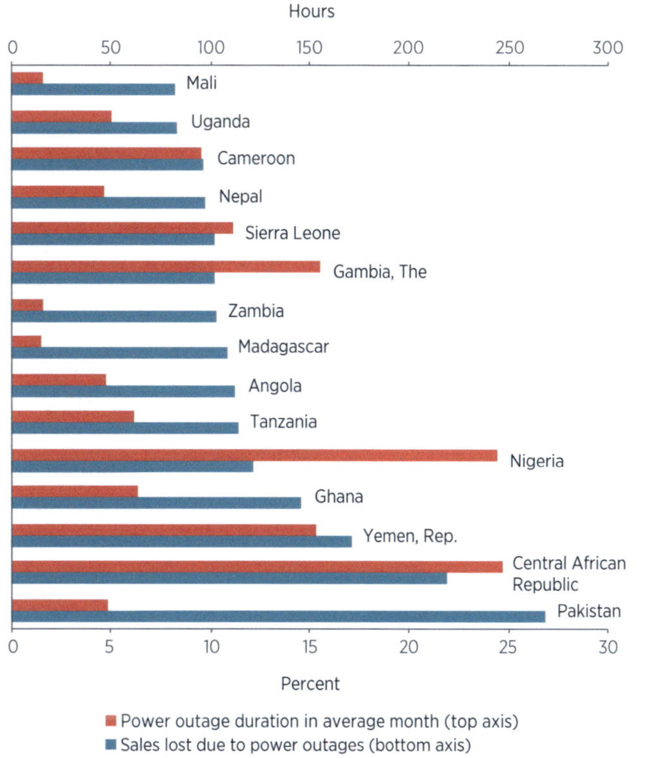

Source: Rentschler, Kornejew, et al. 2019.
Note: Figure shows the top 15 countries with the largest estimated sales losses due to power outages.

daily productive hours of 9 percent per worker (Harriet, Poku, and Emmanuel 2013). In the Greater Cairo Metropolitan Area in the Arab Republic of Egypt, traffic congestion was accounting for direct costs of $5.1 billion a year as of 2010, a number that is only expected to increase (World Bank 2013). For a range of Sub-Saharan African cities, Rentschler, Braese, et al. (2019) show that urban flooding can be an important driver of disrupted traffic flows, thus reducing the connectivity between firms and supply chains (chapter 5).

Telecommunications and the Internet have become essential to many types of economic activities, and telecommunications outages can present firms with large costs. Although the global annual costs are not available, many high-visibility events show the magnitude of the potential impacts, especially in businesses that operate in real time and rely on data or online sales. For example, when Delta Airlines experienced a five-hour interruption in one of its Atlanta data centers in 2016, some 2,000 flights were grounded over the course of three days, costing the company an estimated $150 million (Sverdlik 2016). Small events can also be costly. Based on a survey of 49 organizations in 16 sectors, the Ponemon Institute (2016) has estimated the average cost of a data center outage at more than $700,000, with the highest cost reaching more than $2 million. It is no surprise that vulnerabilities are the highest in financial services, telecommunication services, health care, and e-commerce.

Internet disruptions affect not only individual companies but also entire countries. In fact, for many countries, their entire access to the Internet depends on one or two submarine cables that are vulnerable to both natural and human-made hazards, ranging from earthquakes to fishing equipment and attacks. Disruptions of these cables or associated landing stations can be very expensive. For example, a fault in all landing points in Australia would entail a direct cost (for cable repair) estimated at $2.2 million, and an indirect economic cost of $3.2 billion, mostly from the loss of international Internet traffic. In addition, the loss of an Internet connection in Australia would cut off the Internet connection in Papua New Guinea. By contrast, in Canada, the economic costs would be zero because alternative overland connectivity is available to the United States (APEC 2013).

FIRMS EMPLOY COSTLY MEASURES TO COPE WITH UNRELIABILITY

Self-generation of electricity

Firms that are, or expect to be, heavily affected by infrastructure disruptions can take measures to minimize the impact on their operations. Although these actions reduce the costs of an additional disruptive event, they come with their own costs as well. Such coping costs, which can take various forms, are yet another aspect of the effects of unreliable infrastructure.

Self-generating electricity is a ubiquitous albeit costly strategy to adapt to frequent power outages. Facing frequent electricity outages, firms often choose to operate their own backup generator, usually powered by diesel. These generators enable firms to bridge power outages, but they also require firms to purchase, install, maintain, and operate costly machinery. Generators tend, then, to be less affordable for smaller firms with limited cash reserves. As a result, generator ownership is significantly higher among large firms (figure 2.5, panel a) for a panel of firms in low- and middle-income countries and in countries with an unreliable electricity supply (figure 2.5, panel b).

In addition to high up-front investments, operational costs also make self-generation significantly more expensive than conventional grid supply (Adenikinju 2003; Farquharson, Jaramillo, and Samaras 2018). For example, Steinbuks and Foster (2010) find for 25 African countries that self-generation is on average three times more expensive than national electricity tariffs.

An analysis conducted for this report estimates the installed self-generation capacity and

FIGURE 2.5 Generator ownership is more common for large firms and in countries with many power outages

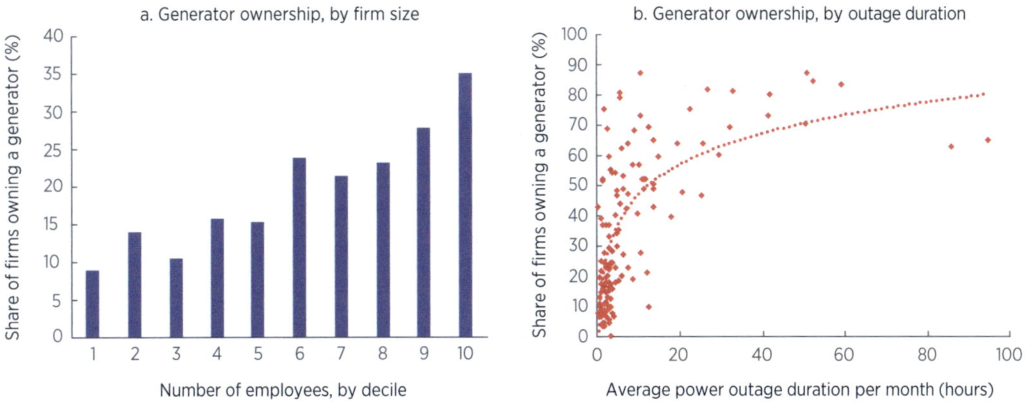

Source: Rentschler, Kornejew, et al. 2019.

the total annual cost of self-generation in the industrial sectors of 129 low- and middle-income countries for which the required data are available (Rentschler, Kornejew, et al. 2019). These estimates yield the costs of backup electricity generation, accounting for both the annualized up-front investment and the operational costs.

Overall, the estimates suggest that the costs of backup generation are substantial.[3] Total up-front investments in backup generation amount to about $6 billion a year in low- and middle-income countries. The annual operating costs of generators are estimated to add around $59 billion a year to total electricity costs for firms in low- and middle-income countries.

Thus, because power is unreliable, firms in the industrial sector spend an estimated additional $65 billion a year on backup self-generation, corresponding to 0.28 percent of GDP of the 129 countries considered in this analysis—with Africa bearing the highest costs (map 2.3).

This large sum, however, does not capture the full opportunity costs incurred by firms operating power generators. Although generators can mitigate short-term losses, they are also linked to lower longer-term productivity because of the higher marginal costs that limit investments in other input factors (Mensah 2016). Furthermore, backup generation using diesel generators significantly increases emissions of air pollutants such as fine inhalable particulates and carbon dioxide, thereby producing indirect costs in the form of health impacts or climate change (Farquharson, Jaramillo, and Samaras 2018).

Measures to conserve and reuse water

Many firms rely on a dependable water supply for their operations. When outages occur, firms can take measures to cope and decrease their reliance on the usual supply, often at significant costs. Efforts to conserve water, such as through automated control systems, allow firms to use less water in their operations and also reduce stress on the water network (Rose and Krausmann 2013). The recycling and reuse of water within a firm can serve similar purposes. Such options appear to make sense even in the absence of disruptions, but the low cost of water may make them uneconomical until unreliability reaches a high level. These measures lessen the impact of disruptions on firms, but do not make them independent of the water grid and will not help in case of sustained outages. Then, more costly options that eliminate firms' reliance on the water grid can

MAP 2.3 Additional costs of backup electricity generation are substantial in low- and middle-income countries

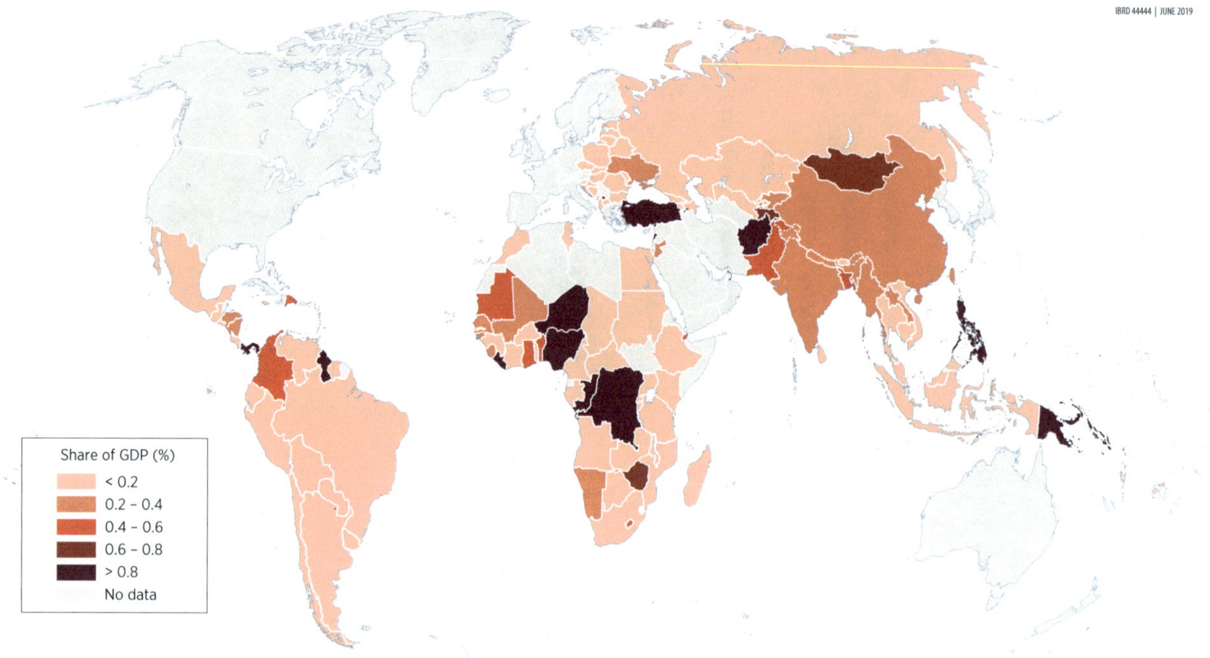

Source: Rentschler, Kornejew, et al. 2019.
Note: Map shows the cost of backup electricity generation as a percentage of GDP, including up-front investments and additional operating costs.

be used, including adopting technologies that give access to underground, river, or lake water or installing water storage facilities (Kajitani and Tatano 2009).

Adapting to transport disruptions

Many studies in rich and poor countries show that transport infrastructure has a significant impact on firms' location choices (see Arauzo-Carod, Liviano-Solis, and Manjón-Antolín 2010). Other types of infrastructure affect location choices as well. For example, Kim and Cho (2017) find that in the rural United States, the availability of broadband connectivity significantly increases the chance that a firm will choose a rural location. As a result of this influence of infrastructure reliability on location choice, firms may incur higher costs for real estate or face other difficulties such as lack of proximity to the labor force. In addition, regions with poor infrastructure quality are bound to be less attractive to businesses, which has implications for local economic activity and employment.

Having to increase an inventory to shield it from low-quality transport infrastructure or transport disruptions is costly for a firm. This adaptation measure comes with significant coping costs in the form of the opportunity costs of capital bound in the inventory, the costs of storage, and the possible depreciation of stored goods. In a cross-country analysis, a decrease in an infrastructure quality indicator of 1 standard deviation increases raw material inventories by 11–37 percent (Guasch and Kogan 2003). The importance of this effect is also evident at the micro level in East Africa, as confirmed in an analysis of firms in Burundi, Kenya, Rwanda, Tanzania, and Uganda (Iimi, Humphrey, and Melibaeva 2015).

UNRELIABLE INFRASTRUCTURE LEADS TO LOWER PRODUCTIVITY

Clearly, the indirect impacts of infrastructure disruptions are harder to quantify than the direct effects just described. It is not easy to observe the influence of unreliable infrastructure on firm behavior and industry dynamics at one moment in time because that influence continually and often subtly alters firms' decisions. Nevertheless, ample evidence exists of its importance, especially for firm productivity. Although the analysis for this report considers power, water, and transport infrastructure, most of the literature revolves around the indirect impacts of disruptions in electricity supply.

In Africa and Asia, power outages have been shown to affect firms' productivity significantly. A study based on a firm panel of 23 African countries estimates that a 1 percent increase in electricity outages would account for a loss in firms' TFP of 3.5 percent on average (Mensah 2018). A similar study for 14 countries in Sub-Saharan Africa estimates that a 1 percent increase in electricity outages would result in productivity losses of between 1 and 3.5 percent (figure 2.6; Mensah 2016). Considering absolute rather than relative effects, Bbaale (2018) shows that one additional power outage in a typical month reduces productivity by 0.1–0.2 percentage point on average in 26 African countries. Similarly, Zhang (2019) finds that manufacturing firms in Bangladesh would suffer TFP losses of 3–4 percent from an increase in load shedding by 10 percent. In India, electricity deficits decrease the TFP of manufacturing firms by about 2 percent (Allcott, Collard-Wexler, and O'Connell 2016).

The complexity of indirect impacts is highlighted by the relationship between the impact of electricity disruptions and intensity of power usage. Disaggregating the impact of outages on productivity shows that firms with very low and very high power usage intensities suffer the most productivity losses from electricity disruptions. Intuitively, firms with low electricity intensity adopt costly coping mechanisms to a lesser degree and are therefore harder hit by disruptions, whereas firms with high power intensity do invest in adaptation measures, but they also must contend with the high costs of self-generation, thus leading to greater losses (Gurara and Tessema 2018; Ramachandran, Shah, and Moss 2018).

FIGURE 2.6 Increased power outages result in lower firm productivity in African countries

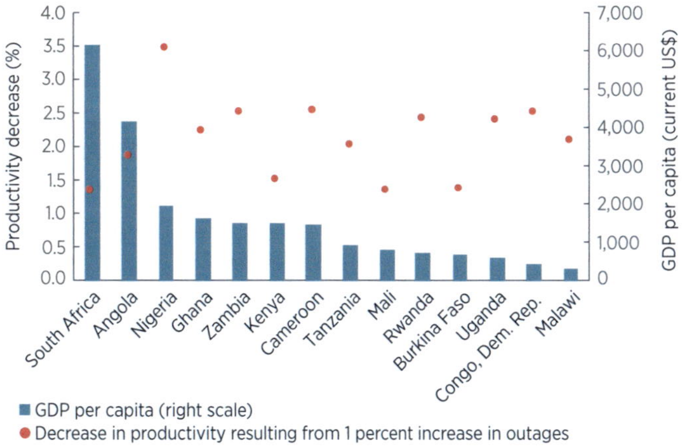

Source: Mensah 2016.
Note: The left scale (dots) shows the percentage decrease in productivity resulting from a 1 percent increase in outages. The right scale (bars) shows GDP per capita of the countries analyzed (in current US$).

The burden of unreliable infrastructure services is particularly large for small firms, which often are the economic foundation of people's livelihoods in low- and middle-income countries. For them, it is harder to deal with the higher operational costs resulting from outages because they have weaker financial security or less diversified income sources. Small firms in India, for example, are disproportionately affected by outages, and so they face production costs that are higher by 0.29 percent of revenue for every percentage point increase in electricity shortages (Zhang 2019). Such higher operational costs then affect firms' investment decisions and their productivity. In Indonesia, the negative effect of electricity unreliability on firm productivity is more than 50 percent larger for smaller manufacturing firms than for bigger ones (Poczter 2017). Furthermore, unreliable power networks can drastically increase the initial investments required to start a business. In Nigeria, small firms have to spend between 10 and 30 percent of their start-up costs on power self-generation (Adenikinju 2003, 2008).

Such large start-up costs and the prospect of disproportionally high operational costs have dire consequences for entrepreneurship. An analysis of Enterprise Survey data for 23 African countries finds that power outages diminish the probability that individuals will start their own business by 32 percent, an effect that rises to 44 percent when considering only the nonfarm sector (Mensah 2018). This lack of start-ups reduces competition and leads to efficiency losses. Alby, Dethier, and Straub (2013) analyze Enterprise Survey data for 77 countries and find that energy-intensive sectors such as the chemical and textile industries have a significantly lower share of small firms in countries with frequent outages.

The unreliability of infrastructure can also reduce firm efficiency and lead to inefficient resource allocation at the national level. Because most new technology relies on electricity, power outages reduce the adoption of innovative means of production. Capital is thus directed toward more labor-intensive operations, which can be less productive. As a result, national economies are stuck in inefficient sectoral allocations and miss out on certain high-growth sectors. For example, the provision of on-demand goods and services is complicated or not possible because of unreliable infrastructure, and low power reliability makes it impossible for countries to host large data centers (World Bank 2019).

The overall effect of these inefficiencies from unreliable infrastructure can also mean that firms must struggle to compete in international markets. In 23 African countries, a 1 percentage point increase in power outage frequency reduces the average firm's share of sales from exports by 0.12 percent (World Bank 2019). The inefficiency costs borne by individual firms translate into disadvantages for entire sectors and economies. Higher costs, lower productivity, a lack of entrepreneurship and innovation, and the absence of high-growth sectors all negatively affect the chances of a country finding success in increasingly internationalized markets.

Eventually, the impacts of outages on firms are passed on to people—workers and consumers—in the form of loss of income or well-being. Workers may carry the burden through lower employment and lower wages. A study of 23 African countries estimates that a 1 percentage point increase in outages reduces the employment of low-skilled workers by 1.1 percent and of high-skilled workers by 0.35 percent (World Bank 2019). For a sample of 21 countries in Africa, Mensah (2018) finds that living in a community with frequent electricity outages reduces the probability of being employed by 35–41 percent on average. Rentschler and Kornejew (2017) find that when manufacturing firms in Indonesia lack access to reliable electricity, they switch to less efficient fuels and pass the higher prices down their supply chains to consumers and other firms. And households are also affected directly by infrastructure disruptions, as discussed in the next chapter.

NOTES

1. For the full methodology of this and the following analyses, see the work on firms and infrastructure published as a background paper for this report by Rentschler, Kornejew, et al. (2019).
2. All monetary estimates have been converted to real 2018 U.S. dollars.
3. These estimates are based on a review of the literature on self-generation, which suggests an annualized capital cost approximation of \$0.032 per kilowatt-hour of self-generated electricity (ESMAP 2007) and an approximate price markup factor of 2 over the national electricity tariff (Steinbuks and Foster 2010). Estimates of self-generated electricity in the industrial sector are based on estimates from the Enterprise

Surveys of electricity consumption by the industrial sector and self-reported shares of backup generation. See Rentschler, Kornejew, et al. (2019) for details.

REFERENCES

Adenikinju, A. F. 2003. "Electric Infrastructure Failures in Nigeria: A Survey-Based Analysis of the Costs and Adjustment Responses." *Energy Policy* 31 (14): 1519–30. https://doi.org/https://doi.org/10.1016/S0301-4215(02)00208-2.

———. 2008. "Efficiency of the Energy Sector and Its Impact on the Competitiveness of the Nigerian Economy." *International Association for Energy Economics* (Fourth Quarter): 27–31.

Albiman, M. M., and Z. Sulong. 2016. "The Role of ICT Use to the Economic Growth in Sub-Saharan African Region (SSA)." *Journal of Science and Technology Policy Management* 7 (3): 306–29. https://doi.org/10.1108/JSTPM-06-2016-0010.

Alby, P., J.-J. Dethier, and S. Straub. 2013. "Firms Operating under Electricity Constraints in Developing Countries." *World Bank Economic Review* 27 (1): 109–32. https://doi.org/10.1093/wber/lhs018.

Allcott, H., A. Collard-Wexler, and S. D. O'Connell. 2016. "How Do Electricity Shortages Affect Industry? Evidence from India." *American Economic Review* 106 (3): 587–624. http://www.aeaweb.org/articles?id=10.1257/aer.20140389.

APEC (Asia-Pacific Economic Cooperation). 2013. "Economic Impact of Submarine Cable Disruptions." Report APEC#213-SE-01.2, APEC, Singapore. http://publications.apec.org/Publications/2013/02/Economic-Impact-of-Submarine-Cable-Disruptions.

Arauzo-Carod, J.-M., D. Liviano-Solis, and M. Manjón-Antolín. 2010. "Empirical Studies in Industrial Location: An Assessment of Their Methods and Results." *Journal of Regional Science* 50 (3): 685–711. https://doi.org/10.1111/j.1467-9787.2009.00625.x.

Aschauer, D. A. 1989. "Is Public Expenditure Productive?" *Journal of Monetary Economics* 23 (2): 177–200. https://doi.org/10.1016/0304-3932(89)90047-0.

Bbaale, E. 2018. "Infrastructure Quality and Firm Productivity in Africa." *World Journal of Entrepreneurship, Management, and Sustainable Development* 14 (4): 367–84. https://doi.org/10.1108/WJEMSD-11-2017-0091.

Bom, P. R. D., and J. E. Ligthart. 2014. "What Have We Learned from Three Decades of Research on the Productivity of Public Capital?" *Journal of Economic Surveys* 28 (5): 889–916. https://doi.org/10.1111/joes.12037.

Braese, J., J. Rentschler, and S. Hallegatte. 2019. "Resilient Infrastructure for Thriving Firms: A Review of the Evidence." Background paper for this report, World Bank, Washington, DC.

Calderón, C., and L. Servén. 2014. "Infrastructure, Growth, and Inequality: An Overview." Policy Research Working Paper 7034, World Bank, Washington, DC.

Damania, R., S. Desbureaux, M. Hyland, A. Islam, S. Moore, A.-S. Rodella, J. Russ, and E. Zaveri. 2017. *Uncharted Waters: The New Economics of Water Scarcity and Variability*. Washington, DC: World Bank. https://doi.org/10.1596/978-1-4648-1179-1.

Dinkelman, T. 2011. "The Effects of Rural Electrification on Employment: New Evidence from South Africa." *American Economic Review* 101 (7): 3078–108. https://doi.org/10.1257/aer.101.7.3078.

Duranton, G., and M. A. Turner. 2012. "Urban Growth and Transportation." *Review of Economic Studies* 79 (4): 1407–40. https://doi.org/10.1093/restud/rds010.

ESMAP (Energy Sector Management Assistance Program). 2007. *Technical and Economic Assessment of Off-Grid, Mini-Grid, and Grid Electrification Technologies*. Washington, DC: World Bank.

Farquharson, D., P. Jaramillo, and C. Samaras. 2018. "Sustainability Implications of Electricity Outages in Sub-Saharan Africa." *Nature Sustainability* 1 (10): 589–97. https://doi.org/10.1038/s41893-018-0151-8.

Fedderke, J. W., and Ž. Bogetić. 2009. "Infrastructure and Growth in South Africa: Direct and Indirect Productivity Impacts of 19 Infrastructure Measures." *World Development* 37 (9): 1522–39. https://doi.org/10.1016/J.WORLDDEV.2009.01.008.

Ghani, E., A. G. Goswami, and W. R. Kerr. 2016. "Highway to Success: The Impact of the Golden Quadrilateral Project for the Location and Performance of Indian Manufacturing." *Economic Journal* 126 (591): 317–57. https://doi.org/10.1111/ecoj.12207.

Gibbons, S., T. Lyytik, H. Overman, and R. Sanchis-Guarner. 2017. "New Road Infrastructure: The Effects on Firms." *Journal of Urban Economics* 110 (March): 35–50.

Guasch, J. L., and J. Kogan. 2003. "Just-in-Case Inventories: A Cross-Country Analysis." Policy Research Working Paper 3012, World Bank, Washington, DC.

Gurara, D., and D. Tessema. 2018. "Losing to Blackouts: Evidence from Firm Level Data." IMF

Working Paper 18(159), International Monetary Fund, Washington, DC. https://doi.org/10.1177/00220345740530061001.

Harriet, T., K. Poku, and A. K. Emmanuel. 2013. "An Assessment of Traffic Congestion and Its Effect on Productivity in Urban Ghana." *International Journal of Business and Social Science* 4 (3): 10–20.

Iimi, A. 2011. "Effects of Improving Infrastructure Quality on Business Costs: Evidence from Firm-Level Data in Eastern Europe and Central Asia." *Developing Economies* 49 (2): 121–47. https://doi.org/10.1111/j.1746-1049.2011.00126.x.

Iimi, A., R. M. Humphrey, and S. Melibaeva. 2015. "Firm Inventory Behavior in East Africa." Policy Research Working Paper 7280, World Bank, Washington, DC. https://doi.org/10.1596/1813-9450-7280.

Islam, A., and M. Hyland. 2018. "The Drivers and Impacts of Water Infrastructure Reliability: A Global Analysis of Manufacturing Firms." Working Paper 8637, World Bank, Washington, DC. http://www.worldbank.org/research.

Jin, J., and P. Rafferty. 2017. "Does Congestion Negatively Affect Income Growth and Employment Growth? Empirical Evidence from US Metropolitan Regions." *Transport Policy* 55 (C): 1–8. https://doi.org/https://doi.org/10.1016/j.tranpol.2016.12.003.

Kajitani, Y., and H. Tatano. 2009. "Estimation of Lifeline Resilience Factors Based on Surveys of Japanese Industries." *Earthquake Spectra* 25 (4): 755–76. https://doi.org/10.1193/1.3240354.

Kassem, D. 2018. "Does Electrification Cause Industrial Development? Grid Expansion and Firm Turnover in Indonesia." Job Market Paper, Department of Economics and STIRCED, London School of Economics, London, August.

Kim, K., and Y. Cho. 2017. "Estimation of Power Outage Costs in the Industrial Sector of South Korea." *Energy Policy* 101 (C): 236–45. https://doi.org/10.1016/J.ENPOL.2016.11.048.

Mensah, J. T. 2016. "Bring Back Our Light: Power Outages and Industrial Performance in Sub-Saharan Africa." Paper presented at the Annual Meeting of the Agricultural and Applied Economics Association, Boston, July 31–August 2.

———. 2018. "Jobs! Electricity Shortages and Unemployment in Africa." Policy Research Working Paper WPS 8415, World Bank, Washington, DC (April).

Paunov, C., and V. Rollo. 2015. "Overcoming Obstacles: The Internet's Contribution to Firm Development." *World Bank Economic Review* 29 (Suppl. 1): S192–S204. https://doi.org/10.1093/wber/lhv010.

———. 2016. "Has the Internet Fostered Inclusive Innovation in the Developing World?" *World Development* 78 (February): 587–609. https://doi.org/https://doi.org/10.1016/j.worlddev.2015.10.029.

Poczter, S. 2017. "You Can't Count on Me: The Impact of Electricity Unreliability on Productivity." *Agricultural and Resource Economics Review* 46 (3): 579–602. https://doi.org/10.1017/age.2016.38.

Polák, P. 2017. "The Productivity Paradox: A Meta-Analysis." *Information Economics and Policy* 38 (March): 38–54. https://doi.org/https://doi.org/10.1016/j.infoecopol.2016.11.003.

Ponemon Institute. 2016. "Cost of Data Center Outages." Data Center Performance Benchmarking Series, Traverse City, MI.

Porter, M. 1990. "The Competitive Advantage of Nations." *Harvard Business Review* 90 (2, March-April): 73–95.

Ramachandran, V., M. K. Shah, and T. Moss. 2018. "How Do African Firms Respond to Unreliable Power? Exploring Firm Heterogeneity Using K-Means Clustering." CGD Working Paper 493, Center for Global Development, Washington, DC. https://www.cgdev.org/publication/how-do-african-firms-respond-unreliable-power-exploring-firm-heterogeneity-using-k-means.

Rentschler, J., J. Braese, N. Jones, and P. Avner. 2019. "Three Feet Under: The Impacts of Flooding on Urban Jobs, Connectivity, and Infrastructure." Background paper for this report, World Bank, Washington, DC.

Rentschler, J., and M. Kornejew. 2017. "Energy Price Variation and Competitiveness: Firm Level Evidence from Indonesia." *Energy Economics* 67 (C): 242–54. https://doi.org/https://doi.org/10.1016/j.eneco.2017.08.015.

Rentschler, J., M. Kornejew, S. Hallegatte, M. Obolensky, and J. Braese. 2019. "Underutilized Potential: The Business Costs of Unreliable Infrastructure in Developing Countries." Background paper for this report, World Bank, Washington, DC.

Rose, A., and E. Krausmann. 2013. "An Economic Framework for the Development of a Resilience Index for Business Recovery." *International Journal of Disaster Risk Reduction* 5 (September): 73–83. https://doi.org/https://doi.org/10.1016/j.ijdrr.2013.08.003.

Steinbuks, J., and V. Foster. 2010. "When Do Firms Generate? Evidence on In-House Electricity Supply in Africa." *Energy Economics* 32 (3): 505–14.

https://doi.org/https://doi.org/10.1016/j.eneco.2009.10.012.

Sverdlik, Yevgeniy. 2016. "Delta: Data Center Outage Cost Us $150M." *DataCenterKnowledge*, September 8.

Sweet, M. 2011. "Does Traffic Congestion Slow the Economy?" *Journal of Planning Literature* 26 (4): 391–404. https://doi.org/10.1177/0885412211409754.

———. 2013. "Traffic Congestion's Economic Impacts: Evidence from US Metropolitan Regions." *Urban Studies* 51 (10): 2088–110. https://doi.org/10.1177/0042098013505883.

Volpe Martincus, C., and J. S. Blyde. 2012. *Shaky Roads and Trembling Exports: Assessing the Trade Effects of Domestic Infrastructure Using a Natural Experiment*. Washington, DC: Inter-American Development Bank. http://publications.iadb.org/handle/11319/4650.

Wan, G., and Y. Zhang. 2018. "The Direct and Indirect Effects of Infrastructure on Firm Productivity: Evidence from Chinese Manufacturing." *China Economic Review* 49 (C): 143–53. https://doi.org/https://doi.org/10.1016/j.chieco.2017.04.010.

Weisbrod, G., D. Vary, and G. Treyz. 2003. "Measuring Economic Costs of Urban Traffic Congestion to Business." *Transportation Research Record* 1839 (1) : 98–106. https://doi.org/10.3141/1839-10.

World Bank. 2013. *Cairo Traffic Congestion Study: Final Report*. Washington, DC: World Bank.

———. 2019. *Electricity Uptake for Economic Transformation in Sub-Saharan Africa*. Africa Development Forum. Washington, DC: World Bank.

Zhang, F. 2019. *In the Dark: How Much Do Power Sector Distortions Cost South Asia?* South Asia Development Forum. Washington, DC: World Bank. https://doi.org/doi:10.1596/978-1-4648-1154-8.

3 Infrastructure Disruptions Affect the Health and Well-Being of Households

Infrastructure disruptions and lack of reliability affect people as workers and consumers. But they can also impose direct costs on households through a variety of channels: direct impacts, coping costs, and indirect impacts. Each disruption can have real adverse impacts, including the direct short-term consequence of not having access to electricity, safe water, transport, or communication. For example, power outages can affect cooling and heating (which in turn may have health implications), economic activities and income, children's educational outcomes, social and leisure activities, and regular household tasks such as cooking and cleaning (World Bank 2019).

Some of the negative consequences of unreliable service may materialize only in the long term as a result of the prolonged high frequency of disruptions. For example, households may decide not to invest in food refrigeration or air-conditioning. In these cases, individual outages may not carry a large cost because households give up on some types of energy use, but the long-term costs may be substantial. Households also may be forced to invest in expensive measures to mitigate the impact of outages, such as a diesel generator for a backup electricity supply, a water reservoir for a backup water supply, or a vehicle to compensate for inadequate public transit. Moreover, money spent on backup capacity will not be available for more productive investments that could help people to escape poverty or grow a business.

Infrastructure disruptions have many impacts on households, and estimating the global cost is difficult. This chapter sheds more light on the issue by looking at the impacts of disruptions in the power, water, transport, and telecommunications sectors (table 3.1). It finds that the willingness to pay for power outages ranges between 0.002 percent and 0.15 percent of gross domestic product (GDP) per year for low- and middle-income countries (corresponding to between \$2.3 billion and \$190 billion). For water, the range is between 0.11 percent and 0.19 percent of their GDP per year (corresponding to between \$88 billion and \$153 billion).

INFRASTRUCTURE PROVIDES HOUSEHOLDS WITH ESSENTIAL SERVICES

Infrastructure services not only help households to meet their most basic needs but also enhance their quality of life in many ways. Indeed, many studies have documented the extent to which

TABLE 3.1 Disrupted infrastructure services have multiple impacts on households

Sector	Direct impacts	Coping costs	Indirect and health impacts
Power	• Diminished well-being • Lower productivity of family firms	• Generator investments • Generator operation costs	• Higher mortality and morbidity (lack of access to health care, air-conditioning during heat waves, or heat during cold spells)
	Willingness to pay to prevent outages: between \$2.3 billion and \$190 billion a year		
Water	• Diminished well-being and loss of time	• Investment in alternative water sources (reservoirs, wells, water bottles)	• Higher incidence of diarrhea, cholera, and other diseases
	Willingness to pay to prevent outages: between \$88 billion and \$153 billion a year		**Medical costs and missed income: between \$3 billion and \$6 billion a year**
Transport	• Greater congestion and loss of time • Higher fuel costs	• Higher cost of alternative transport modes	• Air pollution and health impacts • Constrained access to jobs, markets, services • People forced to live close to jobs, possibly on bad land
Telecommunications	• Diminished well-being		• Inability to call emergency services

Source: Based on Obolensky et al. 2019.
Note: The bolded terms in this table are the impact channels for which original estimates are presented in this section. Values are based on willingness-to-pay estimates in a few countries, applied to water and power outages from the World Bank's Enterprise Surveys, covering 143,000 firms in 137 low- and middle-income countries.

households rely on infrastructure services, as reviewed in detail by Obolensky et al. (2019).

Electrification, for instance, has been shown to facilitate entrepreneurship, education, and female empowerment. Not only does it extend the length of an active day through lighting, but it also can free up time, especially for women who can afford labor-saving electric appliances, and have positive impacts on health through refrigeration and the replacement of polluting kerosene lamps. Moreover, electrification may help to alleviate poverty because the poorest bear the largest opportunity costs of not being electrified (Samad and Zhang 2016; Zhang 2019).

Water and sanitation infrastructure has been shown to be particularly critical for good health. Access to in-house water and sanitation services reduces the risk of exposure to germs and the time households spend collecting water and accessing public toilets. For example, in India, the incidence of diarrhea in children was found to be 21 percent lower for households with access to piped water (Jalan and Ravallion 2003). The public health benefits of improved access to sanitation facilities also grow in the long term. In Guatemala, access to improved sanitation facilities was found to increase the average height-for-age of children (Poder and He 2011).

Studies also show that more efficient and reliable transportation infrastructure reduces travel times and transport costs (BenYishay and Tunstall 2011). This reduction in time and costs, in turn, improves access to schools and hospitals in rural areas and can raise productivity and income (Levy 2004). Reduced transport time and costs also enable workers to access more distant employment opportunities (Gannon and Liu 1997) and stimulate economic activity by increasing regional and interregional trade (Roberts et al. 2018; Volpe Martincus and Blyde 2012).

While infrastructure services benefit all people in modern economies, they can also increase the inclusion of disadvantaged population groups, especially women. When modern infrastructure does not exist, women often have to perform time-consuming tasks at the expense of their education and livelihoods. For instance, without a centralized water supply, women carry the burden of collecting water from wells in 72 percent of cases (Birch 2011). As for sanitation, women living in poorly served settlements are typically responsible for disposing of human waste or accompanying children to toilet facilities (Chant 2007). Furthermore, it is now widely reported in a range of settings that women and girls are at particular risk of attack in and around toilet facilities located some distance from their homes (Cornman-Levy et al. 2011; McIlwaine 2013; Sommer et al. 2015).

Overall, the literature provides ample evidence for why the well-being and livelihoods of households depend so critically on the availability of quality infrastructure services. This evidence also explains why a lack of resilience and reliability of infrastructure services has direct adverse effects on the well-being of households.

POWER OUTAGES DIRECTLY REDUCE THE WELL-BEING OF HOUSEHOLDS

In the long run, an unreliable electricity supply has negative effects on household welfare. Frequent outages limit households' ability to engage in productive, educational, and recreational activities during nighttime hours (Lenz et al. 2017). Access to reliable electricity can help to mitigate inequality and promote social inclusion. An unreliable power network increases the time needed for domestic work, mainly performed by women, and largely reduces the benefits from being connected to electricity networks (figure 3.1). In South Asia, Zhang (2019) finds that long power outages are associated with a decrease in women's labor force participation. The persistence of electricity outages can constrain efforts toward economic transformation by reducing opportunities in nonagricultural sectors.

Poor-quality electricity networks also affect public health. During extreme weather events, power outages are common, and they affect health by making it more difficult to access health care and maintain frontline services. After Hurricane Maria hit Puerto Rico, the difficulty in accessing health care was one of the main causes of indirect deaths (Kishore et al. 2018). Power outages also cause indirect health impacts that stem from loss of refrigeration (leading to food-borne diseases and vaccine spoilage, among other things), heat, and higher levels of air pollution due to emissions from backup power generation (Farquharson, Jaramillo, and Samaras 2018).

FIGURE 3.1 Power outages hurt the well-being of households

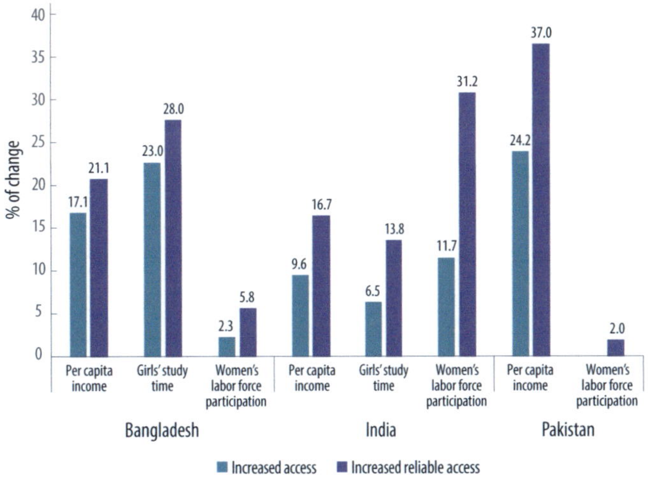

Source: Zhang 2019.
Note: Estimation is based on household surveys in Bangladesh, India, and Pakistan. The effects of electrification on girls' study time and the effects of power outages on women's labor force participation in Pakistan are not estimated because the data are not available.

The total cost of outages has different components, the importance of which depends on the context. In Pakistan, the total annual cost of outages for households adds up to 6.7 percent of a household's annual expenditures (Pasha and Saleem 2013). The largest source of this cost is self-generation, making up 56 percent of the total cost. Other costs include loss of well-being and forgone economic activity due to outages, each of which accounts for 22 percent of the total cost. Disaggregating by income levels reveals a very different picture: for poorer households, monetization of utility loss makes up the largest source of losses—44 percent—because these households usually cannot afford self-generation.

An analysis done for this report offers an estimate of the total well-being cost of power outages in low- and middle-income countries (Obolensky et al. 2019). It suggests that the

FIGURE 3.2 There is large variation in people's willingness to pay to avoid one hour without power

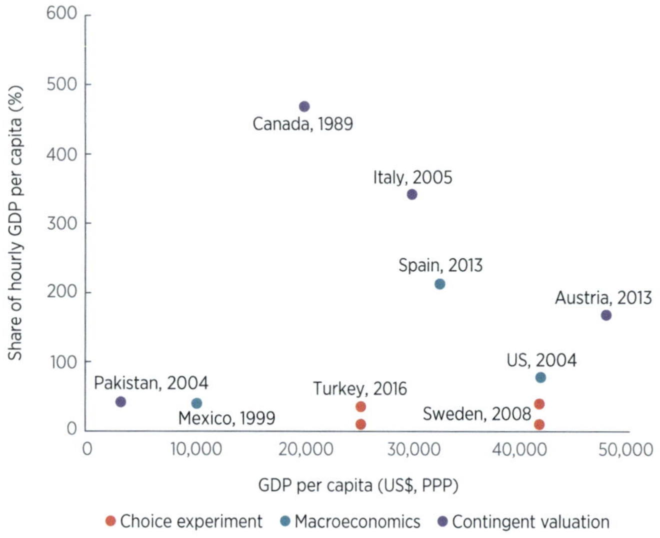

Source: Obolensky et al. 2019.
Note: A country-year is matched to the closest nonmissing value of GDP per capita. See Obolensky et al. (2019) for additional details on the willingness-to-pay estimates.

cost of power outages for households is between 0.002 percent and 0.15 percent of GDP a year for 137 countries, which corresponds to between \$2.3 billion and \$190 billion a year. This estimate is based on several studies that calculate the willingness to pay of households to prevent power outages. This range is so large because of uncertainty regarding the willingness to pay to prevent power outages (figure 3.2). In fact, this value depends on a variety of parameters—wealth of the respondents, quality of the power network, and timing and length of outages. It also depends on the methodology, with contingent valuation methodologies leading to higher estimates than choice experiments.

PEOPLE'S HEALTH AND WELL-BEING SUFFER WHEN THE WATER SUPPLY IS UNRELIABLE

Worldwide, 925 million people have an intermittent water supply—almost half in Southeast Asia—with tremendous impacts on health, as documented by Bivins et al. (2017). Water disruptions cause germs to settle in the water, which increases the risk of the spread of waterborne diseases. Even though these pathogens do not have a strong effect on mortality, they are significant factors in morbidity. Bivins et al. (2017) estimate that an intermittent water supply causes several million infections and diarrhea cases every year in all parts of the world, especially in South Asia and the Western Pacific (figure 3.3). Moreover, the impacts of intermittent water supply are particularly significant in poor households because of their higher dependency on tap water for their own consumption (Ercumen et al. 2015; Jeandron et al. 2015; Nygård et al. 2007).

Case studies of specific water disruptions find consistently that households experiencing water disruption and low water pressure are more at risk of contracting diarrhea (figure 3.4). For instance, several studies have documented widespread diarrhea outbreaks, caused by cholera and *Escherichia coli* infections, in the aftermath of floods (Ahern et al. 2005; Qadri et al. 2005).

FIGURE 3.3 Intermittent water supply poses major health risks in regions around the world

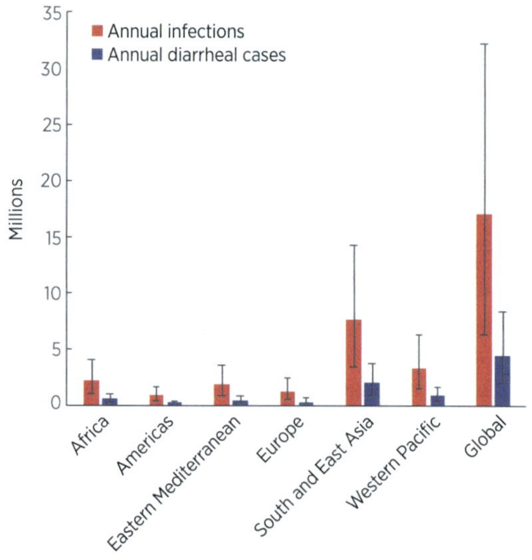

Source: Adapted from Bivins et al. 2017.
Note: This figure shows the impact of an intermittent water supply on health. The black lines represent 95 percent confidence intervals.

Inadequate drainage systems aggravate the situation, especially in overcrowded neighborhoods. In Dar es Salaam, water tends to stagnate and inundate neighborhoods during the rainy season. Hospital records show that the incidence of waterborne illnesses increases significantly during the rainy months when floods are common, and this effect is stronger in neighborhoods with a higher flood risk and poor infrastructure (Picarelli, Jaupart, and Chen 2017). Dwellings situated downstream are the worst affected because sanitary waste overflows when rains cause flooding. Cholera, fungus, skin infections, and diarrhea are a common consequence for members of these households.

The economic cost of the waterborne diseases caused by an intermittent water supply is difficult to determine, but it can be estimated by combining the number of cases of illness caused by an intermittent water supply (figure 3.3) with the estimated costs of treatment plus the estimated costs associated with the loss of productive work for the sick or the caregiver.[1] The financial cost is between $3 billion and $6 billion a year for the low- and middle-income countries covered in this analysis (Obolensky et al. 2019). This relatively limited value stems from the low incomes of the people being affected and does not take into account how being sick affects well-being. It should therefore be considered an underestimate.

When a central water supply is disrupted, people have no choice but to rely on alternative sources of water, which can be 10–100 times more expensive than piped water (Kjellen 2000; UN-Habitat 2003). In most cities, people have to rely on water kiosks, street vendors, or tanker trucks. Some households may be able to use their own well, but energy for pumping can be expensive. In addition to these monetary costs are the value of the time spent fetching water and the fact that such tasks are usually performed by women, reinforcing gender inequality.[2]

Willingness-to-pay estimates suggest a total well-being cost for water outages of between 0.11 percent and 0.19 percent of GDP for 123 countries, which corresponds to $88 billion and $153 billion a year, respectively. Here, the uncertainty is probably larger than what is suggested by this range because available assessments of the willingness to pay to improve water distribution services have been conducted only in high-income countries, where water-related health issues are less prevalent.

FIGURE 3.4 Water disruptions are linked with higher diarrheal risk

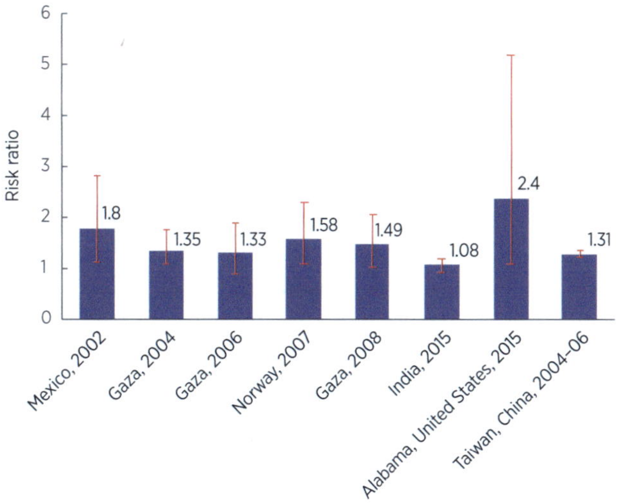

Source: Adapted from Bivins et al. 2017.
Note: This figure compares the risk of contracting diarrhea in households with an intermittent water supply to the risk in households with a reliable water supply. To illustrate, in Mexico, a household with an intermittent water supply is 1.8 times more at risk of contracting diarrhea than a household with a reliable supply.

TRANSPORT DISRUPTIONS LEAD TO LOST TIME, INCOME, AND ACCESS TO SERVICES

Transport disruptions are costly for households because they give rise to longer travel times, wasted fuel, and missed work opportunities. In 2013 drivers in British, French, German, and U.S. metropolitan areas spent on average 36 hours in gridlock (Cebr 2014). The time lost to congestion increases threefold, to 111 hours, when additional planning time is included.[3] According to these estimates, congestion across Germany, the United Kingdom, and the United

States cost almost $450 billion in 2016, or $971 per capita (INRIX Research 2018).

Capital cities in low- and middle-income countries suffer the most from traffic disruptions and congestion because roads and public transit systems in those cities have not kept pace with population growth. In Thailand, drivers lose an average of 56 hours a year to congestion at peak travel times. Indonesia and Colombia are second and third, with 51 and 49 hours, respectively (Cebr 2014).

Transport disruptions can become life-and-death issues when they affect people's ability to reach hospitals and health facilities quickly. Based on a network analysis, Rentschler, Braese, et al. (2019) estimate that the mean travel time to a hospital from nearly all locations in Inner Kampala is less than 30 minutes by car (figure 3.5). However, in the case of a 10-year flood—a flood that occurs on average every 10 years—disruptions of the road network mean that travel times are significantly longer. A common rule of thumb in emergency responses is that the survival rate for life-threatening health incidents drops significantly 60 minutes after an incident—the so-called golden hour (Campbell 2017). Road disruptions from a 10-year flood would mean that, for residents of about a third of Inner Kampala, travel times to a hospital would exceed the golden hour.[4]

In sum, infrastructure disruptions are found to affect households, both indirectly through their effects on firms and consequences on jobs and income and directly through people's health and well-being. Reducing these disruptions should therefore be a policy priority, which in

FIGURE 3.5 Transport disruptions can become life-and-death issues

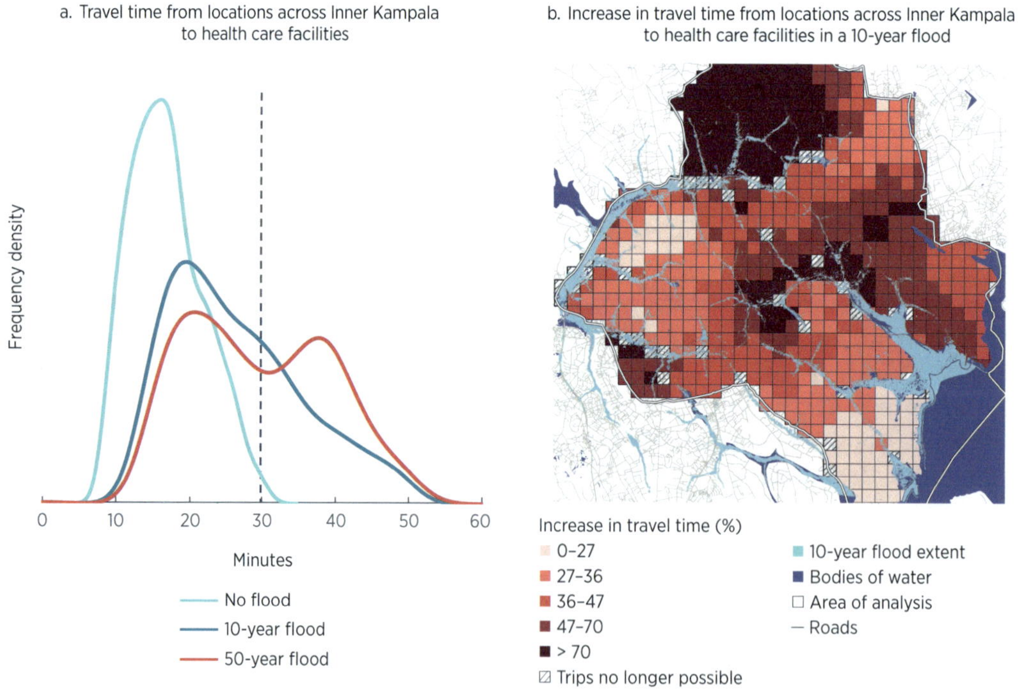

Source: Rentschler, Braese, et al. 2019.
Note: This figure shows the average travel times from inner Kampala to health care facilities during the different flood scenarios. In panel a, the vertical line denotes the "golden hour" (the window of time that maximizes survival of a major health emergency), assuming that ambulances complete a return trip starting at a hospital. Curves show frequency densities that represent the distribution of travel times from all locations.

turn requires a better understanding of their causes. Of particular interest for this report is the role of natural hazards in causing these disruptions, which is the topic of the next chapter.

NOTES

1. Assuming that a diarrheal disease leads to between four and seven days of loss of productive work for the sick or the caregiver and that treatment costs are between $2 and $4 (Rozenberg and Hallegatte 2015).
2. Data on the time spent to fetch water are usually for rural households with no piped connection. No estimate could be identified of the time needed for connected households that experience a water supply outage.
3. Planning time is the time lost due to uncertainty in travel speed because drivers have to leave earlier to make sure they arrive on time (here, at least 95 percent of the time).
4. Assuming that ambulances are based at hospitals and one-way travel time is at least 30 minutes, a round trip would exceed the 60-minute threshold.

REFERENCES

Ahern, M., R. S. Kovats, P. Wilkinson, R. Few, and F. Matthies. 2005. "Global Health Impacts of Floods: Epidemiologic Evidence." *Epidemiologic Reviews* 27 (1): 36–46. https://doi.org/10.1093/epirev/mxi004.

BenYishay, A., and R. Tunstall. 2011. "Impact Evaluation of Infrastructure Investments: The Experience of the Millennium Challenge Corporation." *Journal of Development Effectiveness* 3 (1): 103–30. https://doi.org/10.1080/19439342.2010.545892.

Birch, E. L. 2011. *Design of Healthy Cities for Women: Women's Health and the World's Cities*. Philadelphia: University of Pennsylvania Press.

Bivins, A. W., T. Sumner, E. Kumpel, G. Howard, O. Cumming, I. Ross, K. Nelson, and J. Brown. 2017. "Estimating Infection Risks and the Global Burden of Diarrheal Disease Attributable to Intermittent Water Supply Using QMRA." *Environmental Science and Technology* 51 (13): 7542–51. https://doi.org/10.1021/acs.est.7b01014.

Campbell, J. 2017. *International Trauma Life Support for Emergency Care Providers, Global Edition*. New York: Pearson Education Limited.

Cebr (Centre for Economics and Business Research). 2014. "The Future Economic and Environmental Costs of Gridlock in 2030." Report for INRIX Research, Cebr, London. https://www.ibtta.org/sites/default/files/documents/MAF/Costs-of-Congestion-INRIX-Cebr-Report %283%29.pdf.

Chant, S. 2007. *Gender, Cities, and the Millennium Development Goals in the Global South*. London: London School of Economics. http://www.lse.ac.uk/collections/GenderInstitute.

Cornman-Levy, D., G. R. Dyrness, J. Golden, D. Gouverneur, and J. A. Grisso. 2011. *Transforming Urban Environments. Women's Health and the World's Cities*. Philadelphia: University of Pennsylvania Press.

Ercumen, A., B. F. Arnold, E. Kumpel, Z. Burt, I. Ray, K. Nelson, and J. M. Colford Jr. 2015. "Upgrading a Piped Water Supply from Intermittent to Continuous Delivery and Association with Waterborne Illness: A Matched Cohort Study in Urban India." *PLoS Medicine* 12 (10): e1001892. https://doi.org/10.1371/journal.pmed.1001892.

Farquharson, D., P. Jaramillo, and C. Samaras. 2018. "Sustainability Implications of Electricity Outages in Sub-Saharan Africa." *Nature Sustainability* 1 (10): 589–97. https://doi.org/10.1038/s41893-018-0151-8.

Gannon, C. A., and Z. Liu. 1997. *Poverty and Transport*. Washington, DC: World Bank.

INRIX Research. 2018. "INRIX Global Traffic Scorecard." *INRIX Global Traffic Scorecard*. Kirkland, WA, February. https://media.bizj.us/view/img/10360454/inrix2016trafficscorecarden.pdf.

Jalan, J., and M. Ravallion. 2003. "Does Piped Water Reduce Diarrhea for Children in Rural India?" *Journal of Econometrics* 112 (1): 153–73.

Jeandron, A., J. M. Saidi, A. Kapama, M. Burhole, F. Birembano, T. Vandevelde, A. Gasparrini, B. Armstrong, S. Cairncross, and J. H. J. Ensink. 2015. "Water Supply Interruptions and Suspected Cholera Incidence: A Time-Series Regression in the Democratic Republic of the Congo." *PLoS Medicine* 12 (10): 1–16. https://doi.org/10.1371/journal.pmed.1001893.

Kishore, N., D. Marqués, A. Mahmud, M. V. Kiang, I. Rodriguez, A. Fuller, P. Ebner, C. Sorensen, F. Racy, J. Lemery, L. Maas, J. Leaning, R. Irizarry, S. Balsari, and C. O. Buckee. 2018. "Mortality in Puerto Rico after Hurricane Maria." *New England Journal of Medicine* 379 (2): 162–70. https://doi.org/10.1056/NEJMsa1803972.

Kjellen, M. 2000. "Complementary Water Systems in Dar es Salaam, Tanzania: The Case of Water Vending." *International Journal of Water Resources Development* 16 (1): 143–54. https://doi.org/10.1080/07900620048626.

Lenz, L., A. Munyehirwe, J. Peters, and M. Sievert. 2017. "Does Large-Scale Infrastructure Investment Alleviate Poverty? Impacts of Rwanda's Electricity Access Roll-Out Program." *World Development* 89 (C): 88–110. https://doi.org/10.1016/j.worlddev.2016.08.003.

Levy, H. 2004. "Rural Roads and Poverty Alleviation in Morocco." Working Paper 30817, World Bank, Washington, DC.

McIlwaine, C. 2013. "Urbanization and Gender-Based Violence: Exploring the Paradoxes in the Global South." *Environment and Urbanization* 25 (1): 65–79. https://doi.org/10.1177/0956247813477359.

Nygård, K., E. Wahl, T. Krogh, O. A. Tveit, E. Bøhleng, A. Tverdal, and P. Aavitsland. 2007. "Breaks and Maintenance Work in the Water Distribution Systems and Gastrointestinal Illness: A Cohort Study." *International Journal of Epidemiology* 36 (4): 873–80. https://doi.org/10.1093/ije/dym029.

Obolensky, M., A. Erman, J. Rozenberg, P. Avner, J. Rentschler, and S. Hallegatte. 2019. "Infrastructure Disruptions: Impacts on Households." Background paper for this report, World Bank, Washington, DC.

Pasha, H. A., and W. Saleem. 2013. "The Impact and Cost of Power Load Shedding to Domestic Consumers." *Pakistan Development Review* 52 (4): 355–73.

Picarelli, N., P. Jaupart, and Y. Chen. 2017. "Cholera in Times of Floods: Weather Shocks and Health in Dar es Salaam." IGC Working Paper C-4040-TZA-1, International Growth Centre, London.

Poder, T., and J. He. 2011. "How Can Sanitary Infrastructures Reduce Child Malnutrition and Health Inequalities? Evidence from Guatemala." *Journal of Development Effectiveness* 3 (4): 543–66.

Qadri, F., A. I. Khan, A. S. G. Faruque, Y. A. Begum, F. Chowdhury, G. B. Nair, M. A. Salam, D. A. Sack, and A.-M. Svennerholm. 2005. "Enterotoxigenic Escherichia Coli and Vibrio Cholerae Diarrhea, Bangladesh, 2004." *Emerging Infectious Diseases* 11 (7): 1104–07. https://doi.org/10.3201/eid1107.041266.

Rentschler, J., J. Braese, N. Jones, and P. Avner. 2019. "Three Feet Under: The Impacts of Flooding on Urban Jobs, Connectivity, and Infrastructure." Background paper for this report, World Bank, Washington, DC.

Roberts, M., M. Melecky, T. Bougna, and Y. Xu. 2018. "Transport Corridors and Their Wider Economic Benefits: A Critical Review of the Literature." Policy Research Working Paper 8302, World Bank, Washington, DC, January. https://doi.org/10.1596/1813-9450-8302.

Rozenberg, J., and S. Hallegatte. 2015. "The Impacts of Climate Change on Poverty in 2030 and the Potential from Rapid, Inclusive, and Climate-Informed Development." Policy Research Working Paper 7483, World Bank, Washington, DC.

Samad, H. A., and F. Zhang. 2016. "Benefits of Electrification and the Role of Reliability: Evidence from India." Policy Research Working Paper 7889, World Bank, Washington, DC. http://documents.worldbank.org/curated/en/980911479147772730/Benefits-of-electrification-and-the-role-of-reliability-evidence-from-India.

Sommer, M., S. Ferron, S. Cavill, and S. House. 2015. "Violence, Gender, and WASH: Spurring Action on a Complex, Under-Documented, and Sensitive Topic." *Environment and Urbanization* 27 (1): 105–16. https://doi.org/10.1177/0956247814564528.

UN-Habitat (United Nations Human Settlements). 2003. *Water and Sanitation in the World's Cities: Local Action for Global Goals.* Abingdon-on-Thames: Routledge.

Volpe Martincus, C., and J. S. Blyde. 2012. "Shaky Roads and Trembling Exports: Assessing the Trade Effects of Domestic Infrastructure Using a Natural Experiment." Inter-American Development Bank, Washington, DC. http://publications.iadb.org/handle/11319/4650.

World Bank. 2019. *Electricity Uptake for Economic Transformation in Sub-Saharan Africa.* Africa Development Forum. Washington, DC: World Bank.

Zhang, F. 2019. *In the Dark: How Much Do Power Sector Distortions Cost South Asia?* South Asia Development Forum. Washington, DC: World Bank Group. https://doi.org/doi:10.1596/978-1-4648-1154-8.

Natural Shocks Are a Leading Cause of Infrastructure Disruptions and Damages

4

So far, this report has shown that the cost of infrastructure disruptions ranges from $391 billion to $647 billion in the low- and middle-income countries where data are available and for the types of impacts that can be quantified. Even though these estimates are incomplete, they highlight the substantial costs that unreliable infrastructure imposes on people in low- and middle-income countries. But what role do natural hazards play in these disruptions? While it is impossible to answer this question globally and for all sectors, many case studies do document the importance of natural shocks in causing infrastructure disruptions.

Infrastructure disruptions can have a range of causes. Conceptually, four categories of causes can be distinguished: accidents that are human-made external shocks, system failures during which parts of the functionality of infrastructure systems break down, intentional external attacks, and natural shocks (figure 4.1).

The importance of these types of shocks varies across different types of infrastructure and different countries, and even from year to year. A lack of comprehensive data makes it difficult to estimate accurately the share of infrastructure disruptions that is caused by natural shocks. Nevertheless, from the little data that are available, several general observations are possible:

- *In low-income countries*, the most frequent cause of infrastructure disruptions tends to be system failure. Even under normal operating conditions, systems are inherently fragile, prone to equipment failure, and quick to reach capacity constraints. Even relatively minor external shocks can trigger failures. A lack of resilience to natural shocks is linked closely to a lack of reliability more generally—for example, from a lack of investments in technical upgrades or maintenance.
- *In high-income countries*, natural shocks are a leading cause of infrastructure disruptions. Systems tend to be stable under normal operating conditions, offering reliable services and suffering from relatively few internal system failures. Yet external shocks still affect the functionality of systems, especially when maintenance is neglected.
- *Middle-income countries* tend to be in a transition phase, which implies that the impacts of infrastructure disruptions are particularly large. The reliability and resilience of infrastructure systems may not be keeping up with rapid economic, urban, and demo-

FIGURE 4.1 Classification of causes of infrastructure disruptions

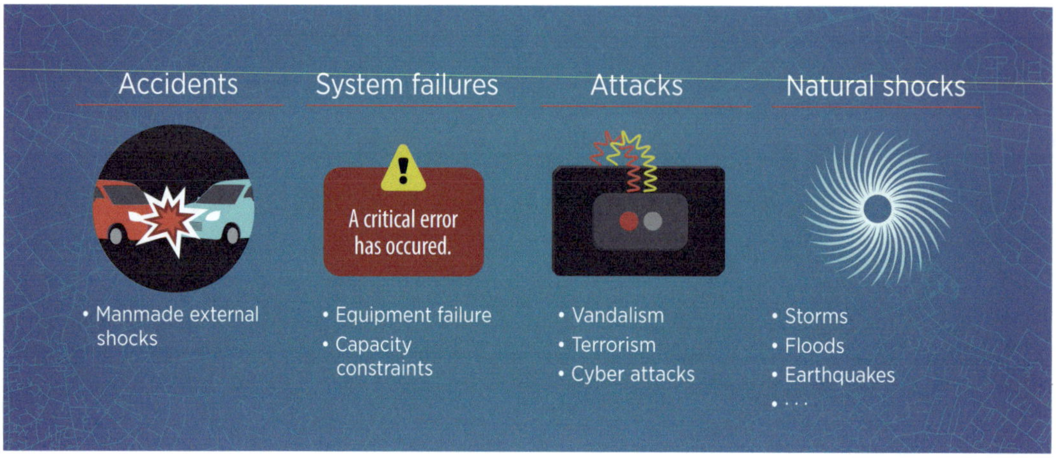

graphic growth, which means that frequent disruptions are causing widespread damage to economic activity and well-being.

This chapter explores these issues in detail, focusing on the role of natural shocks. It also explores the direct damage that natural hazards inflict on infrastructure assets, which translates into repair and maintenance costs. The key findings are that in most countries natural shocks are a significant and often leading cause of infrastructure disruptions. Further, a significant share of power, water, transport, and telecommunications infrastructure is located in areas exposed to natural hazards—and postdisaster repairs are a significant drag on the journey toward universal access to infrastructure services.

THE POWER SECTOR IS HIGHLY VULNERABLE TO NATURAL HAZARDS

In the power sector, analyses conducted for this report find that storms are a major cause of outages worldwide. They contribute to more than 50 percent of outages in Belgium, Croatia, Portugal, Slovenia, and the United States, stemming from damaged transmission networks. Besides, a global risk analysis of power generation infrastructure finds that every year on average about $15 billion in assets are at risk from natural hazards.

Severe weather events—especially storms—are among the main causes of power outages

The high wind speeds produced by storms can disturb the transmission and distribution of electricity when flying debris hits lines or when transmission poles are damaged. Lightning can strike conductors and disconnect lines through short circuits, leading to voltage surges and damaging additional equipment (Panteli and Mancarella 2015). Falling trees are another major source of disruption. Reviewing almost 20 years of power outage data for the United States, Rentschler, Obolensky, and Kornejew (2019) find that states with dense forest cover are especially likely to experience outages during storms.

The share of power outages from natural shocks can vary anywhere from 0 percent to 100 percent—although most country-level estimates fall within the range of 10 percent to 70 percent, according to evidence produced for this report (figure 4.2). Between 2000 and 2017, 55 percent of all recorded power outage events in the United States were caused by natural shocks and 44 percent were caused by nonnatural causes (figure 4.3).[1]

FIGURE 4.2 The share of power outages caused by natural shocks varies significantly across countries

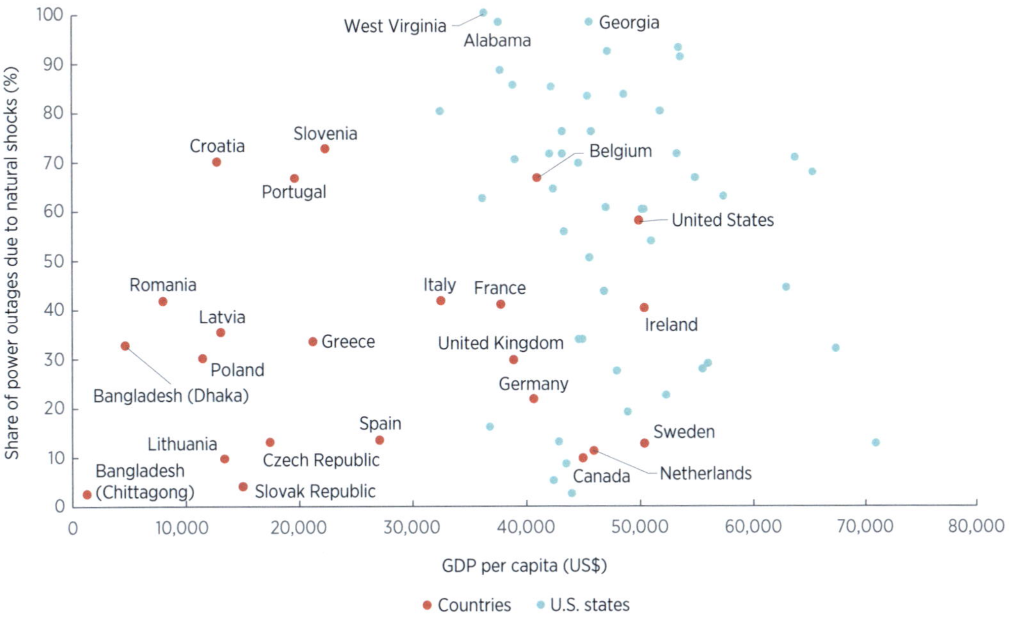

Source: Rentschler, Obolensky, and Kornejew 2019.

As for their duration, in the United States from 2000 to 2017, power outages caused by natural shocks lasted on average 2.5 days. This means that outages due to natural shocks lasted more than twice as long as outages due to nonnatural causes and three times as long as outages due to vandalism. In short, 74 percent of the total recorded outage time between 2000 and 2017 was caused by natural shocks. In Europe between 2010 and 2016, climate-induced outages lasted 409 minutes on average, making them almost four times as long as outages having nonnatural external causes. Over the period, natural shocks were responsible for 37 percent of the total outage duration in the European countries considered.

However, for developing countries such as Bangladesh, natural shocks account for a smaller share of power outages—not because their energy systems are more resilient, but because system failures and nonnatural factors are so frequent that energy users experience daily outages (figure 4.4). In Chittagong, a major coastal city in Bangladesh, storms are estimated to cause as few as 4 percent of all outages (Rentschler, Obolensky, and Kornejew 2019). In Dhaka, the World Bank's Enterprise Surveys suggest that about two outages occur a day on average throughout the year. However, during the storm season in April and May, outages are significantly more frequent (although they do not necessarily occur in the same areas of the city). In other words, a fragile system is vulnerable not only to natural shocks but also to a host of other stressors and shocks that include unmet demand, equipment failure, and accidents.

For most low- and middle-income countries, limited data prevent quantification of the link between power outages and storms. Still, in those countries, a storm is likely to have a more severe impact than in high-income countries. Aging equipment, lack of maintenance, rapid expansion of the grid, and excess demand due

FIGURE 4.3 Power outages from natural shocks last much longer than those from other causes

Total power outage duration in the United States and 26 European countries, by cause

Source: Rentschler, Obolensky, and Kornejew 2019.
Note: The European countries include the EU-28 (without Bulgaria, Denmark, and Hungary) plus Serbia.

to limited power generation capacity are all factors that reduce reliability and increase the vulnerability to natural shocks. However, these factors also mean that energy systems in low-income countries are typically characterized by frequent disruptions. As a result, outages from natural shocks can be expected to account for a smaller share of the overall number of outages than in higher-income countries.

This does not mean that resilience to natural hazards is not an issue in low- and middle-income countries. Power systems are indeed more vulnerable to natural shocks in these countries than in richer countries, and natural hazards can be responsible for a large number of outages. For example, storms of the same intensity are far more likely to cause outages in Bangladesh than in the United States (figure 4.5). Wind speeds exceeding 25 kilometers an hour lead to six times more outages in Bangladesh than in the United States. The gap becomes even wider when the threshold is increased to winds over 35 kilometers an hour. At that point, Bangladeshi consumers are 11 times more likely to experience a blackout than U.S. consumers.

The higher vulnerability of power systems in low- and middle-income countries means that even frequent events have large disruptive impacts. In Bangladesh, severe cyclones damage power plants and power distribution networks. Even relatively frequent storm events, such as the nor'westers occurring each year during April and May, significantly increase the incidence of power outages. These storms, known for their localized but violent gusts and lightning strikes, tend to cause significant damage to power transmission and distribution systems—as illustrated by a recent event in March 2019, after which 6,000 communication towers lost access to power (*Dhaka Tribune* 2019). In fact, these nor'westers appear to be the main cause of storm-induced power outages (figure 4.6).

Natural hazards also damage power generation assets

What about the impact of natural shocks on power generation assets? In an analysis conducted for this report, Nicolas, Koks, et al. (2019) demonstrate the significant exposure of power generation infrastructure to natural hazards. Using the Global Power Plant Database of the World Resources Institute to pinpoint the location of power plants, the study assesses the exposure of plants to a large range of hazards (including cyclones, earthquakes,

FIGURE 4.4 Natural shocks only explain a fraction of power outages in Bangladesh

Number of storm-induced outages in Chittagong and Dhaka, compared with annual average outages from all causes

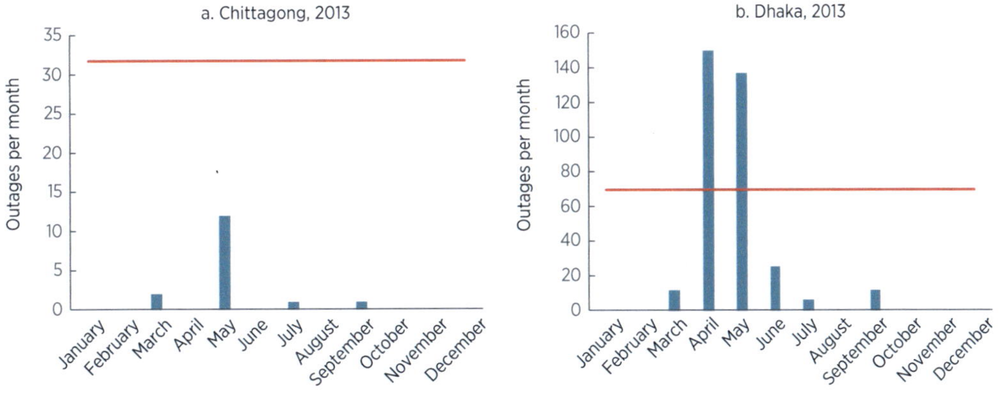

Source: Rentschler, Obolensky, and Kornejew 2019.

floods, extreme heat, droughts, volcanic eruptions, tsunamis, and wildfires).

A power plant is considered exposed if (1) the type of asset is considered vulnerable to a hazard (for example, a wind farm is never considered exposed to drought) and (2) the area where it is located has a "high" hazard level for the relevant hazard in the ThinkHazard! database of the Global Facility for Disaster Reduction and Recovery. The *exposed capacity* in a country is calculated by totaling the capacity of the plants exposed to each hazard and dividing this sum by the total generation capacity in the country. Exposed capacity can exceed 100 percent when power plants are exposed to multiple hazards (such as when a wind farm is exposed to storms and floods).

The study finds that a large fraction of the power generation capacity of many countries is exposed to hazards, often exceeding 100 percent due to the presence of multiple hazards (map 4.1). Floods and coastal floods dominate in most countries, cyclones dominate in most island states as well as Mexico and the United States, and extreme heat and water scarcity dominate in most of northern Africa and Asia.

FIGURE 4.5 The vulnerability of the power network to wind is much higher in Bangladesh than in the United States

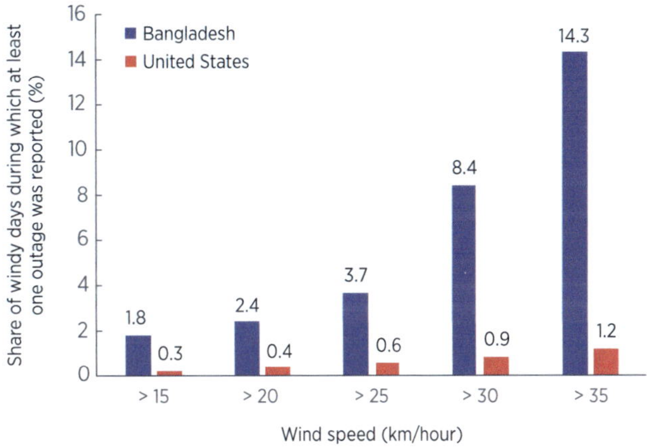

Source: Rentschler, Obolensky, and Kornejew 2019.
Note: Windy days are defined using different thresholds for recorded daily wind speeds. Wind speeds are obtained from the global ERA5 climate reanalysis model, which tends to underrepresent the highest local wind speeds. km = kilometers.

For the most exposed countries, a large share of the generation capacity is exposed to multiple hazards, and the dominant hazards are landslides, tsunamis, and earthquakes (figure 4.7). Earthquakes can inflict severe damage on power infrastructure. In the 2015

FIGURE 4.6 Storm-induced power outages are closely associated with the April–May nor'westers in Bangladesh

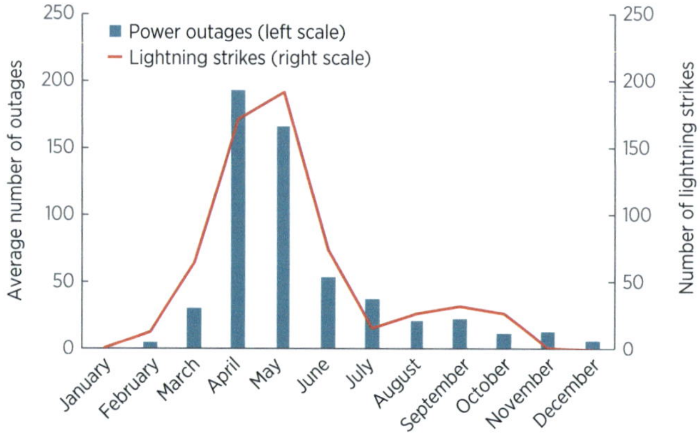

Source: Rentschler, Obolensky, and Kornejew 2019.
Note: Data shown are for 2000–17. Nor'westers are proxied by lightning strikes. Only outages due to natural shocks are included. Monsoon season accounts for the slight increase in outages in September.

earthquake in Nepal, for example, hydropower plants accounting for 34 percent of the country's capacity were damaged (Moss et al. 2015).

Nicolas, Koks, et al. (2019) then repeat the exercise with high-voltage line infrastructure, considering the three most devastating hazards for power lines: earthquakes, cyclones, and wildfires. They find that, as is the case for generation, many countries are exposed to more than one hazard. High-voltage infrastructure in countries such as Japan, Mexico, Mozambique, Nepal, and New Zealand is heavily exposed to various natural hazards. Notwithstanding, most of the Middle East and South Asia face between 70 percent and 120 percent high-voltage line exposure.

The exposure of power generation to droughts is an overlooked risk that is, nevertheless, increasing. Indeed, the vast majority of the world's electricity generation relies on either hydropower or thermoelectric power, both of which are among the most water-intensive sources of electricity (Nicolas, Rentschler, et al. 2019). Almost half of all global thermal power plant capacity is located in areas of water scar-

MAP 4.1 Global exposure of power generation to multiple hazards

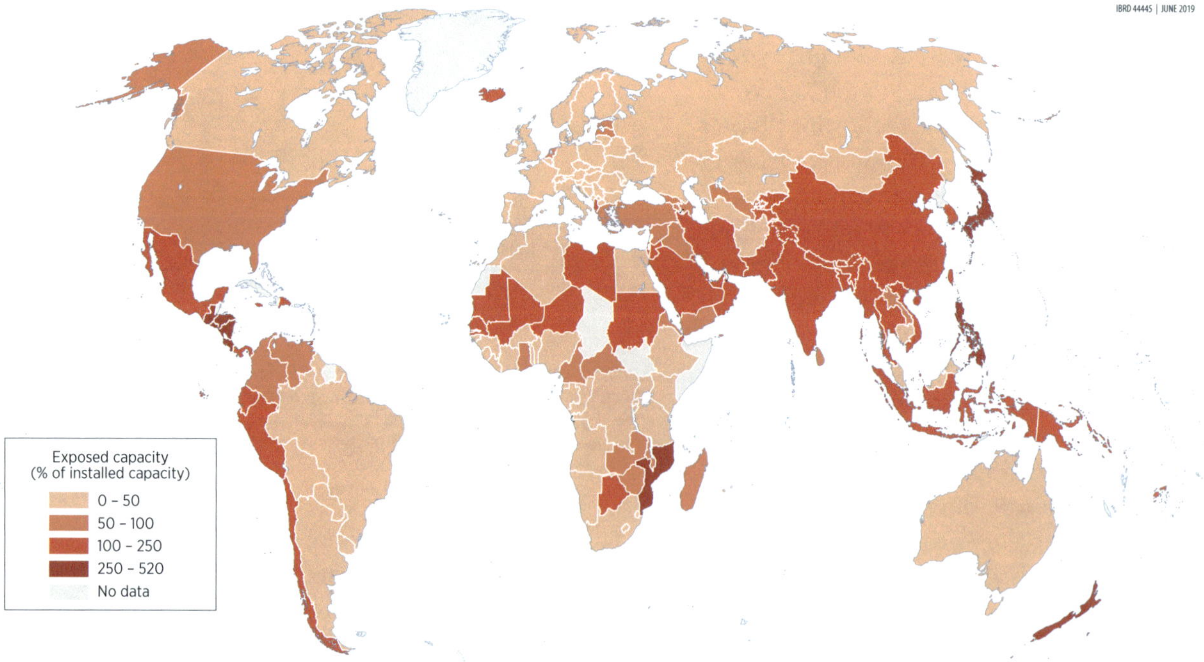

Source: Nicolas, Koks, et al. 2019.
Note: Map 4.1 shows the total exposed capacity for all hazards divided by the total installed capacity in each country. The value may exceed 100 percent because one power plant could be exposed to more than one hazard. Power plants are considered to be exposed to a hazard when they are in an area in which the hazard level is "high" in the ThinkHazard! database. The following hazards are considered: coastal flooding, earthquakes, floods, water scarcity, cyclones, volcanic eruptions, tsunamis, extreme heat, and wildfires.

FIGURE 4.7 Economies with the highest exposed generation capacity to multiple hazards

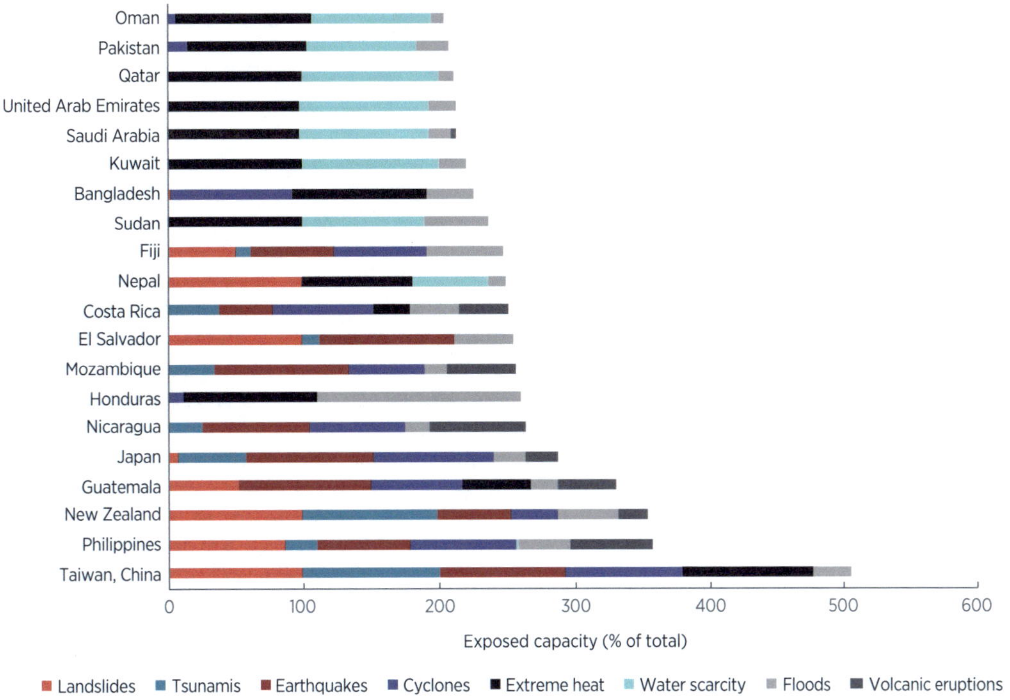

Source: Nicolas, Koks, et al. 2019.
Note: The index represents the total exposed capacity for all hazards divided by the total installed capacity in the country. The value can exceed 100 percent, because one power plant could be exposed to more than one hazard.

city, and 11 percent of hydroelectric capacity is located in such areas (Kressig et al. 2018; Wang, Schleifer, and Zhong 2017). In India, 40 percent of thermal power plants are located in severely water-stressed areas. And between 2011 and 2016, 14 of the 20 largest plants were forced to cease generating power at least once because of a water shortage, resulting in revenue losses of $1.4 billion (Luo, Krishnan, and Sen 2018).

Often, hydropower generation installations rely on a specific streamflow to function, but that streamflow cannot be maintained with low water availability (U.S. Department of Homeland Security and U.S. Department of Energy 2017). Van Vliet et al. (2016) quantify the relationship between water scarcity and power generation at the global level between 1981 and 2010. They find that droughts and warm years reduce the utilization rates for hydropower by 5.2 percent and thermoelectric power by 3.8 percent from the rates in an average year.

Based on the global exposure analysis, Nicolas, Koks, et al. (2019) then estimate the expected annual damages (or repair costs) by considering the types of generation infrastructure, hazard intensities, building standards used in the country, fragility curves, and infrastructure investment costs, using data from Miyamoto International (2019) and Schweikert et al. (2019). Damages are assessed only for the most frequently recorded and costliest disasters—cyclones, earthquakes, surface flooding, river flooding, and coastal flooding—based on the hazard data summarized in box 4.1.[2]

The study finds that the total global expected annual damage (EAD) from all hazards totals about $15 billion, or around 0.2 percent of the global value of the power generation infrastructure. For low- and middle-income coun-

BOX 4.1 Exposure analysis of infrastructure assets is based on various hazard data sets

Tropical cyclones. Tropical cyclones are represented by global cyclone hazard maps generated for the *UNISDR Global Assessment Report 2015* (Cardona et al. 2015). These maps show the distribution of cyclone wind speeds (peak wind speed of 3-second gusts in kilometers per hour) for five return periods between 50 and 1,000 years. The maps are an output of probabilistic cyclone analysis, based on perturbation of historical cyclone tracks and wind-field modeling. Note that tropical cyclones are referred to as hurricanes in the Atlantic, Caribbean Sea, and central and northeast Pacific; they are referred to as typhoons in the northwest Pacific.

Inland floods. River flooding (caused by rivers overtopping their banks) and surface flooding (caused by extreme local rainfall) are represented by the Fathom Global pluvial and fluvial flood hazard data set (Sampson et al. 2015). This is a 3-arcsecond (~90 meters) resolution gridded data set showing the distribution of maximum expected water depth in meters. The hazard maps are for 10 return periods (5 to 1,000 years). This analysis applies the "undefended" flood hazard maps, which do not consider the effects of flood protection on inundation. The flood design standards for road and rail are implemented from the FLOPROS database (Scussolini et al. 2016).

Coastal floods. Coastal inundation maps are generated using the hydrological model LISFLOOD-FP (Bates, Horritt, and Fewtrell 2010). Topographic information at 3-inch horizontal resolution is available from the MERIT-DEM model (Yamazaki et al. 2017). Inundation simulations take place at 90-meter resolution. More details on inundation modeling can be found in Vousdoukas et al. (2016). Flood simulations are forced by extreme sea levels obtained from wave and storm surge reanalysis, combined with tidal information (Vousdoukas et al. 2018). Waves are simulated using the WAVEWATCH-III model (Tolman 2009), and storm surges are simulated using the DFLOW-FM model (Muis et al. 2016).

Earthquakes. Ground shaking hazard is represented by the global earthquake hazard maps produced for the *UNISDR Global Assessment Report 2015* (Cardona et al. 2015). These maps present the expected severity of ground shaking as peak ground acceleration (PGA in centimeters per square second), for five return periods between 250 and 2,475 years. The hazard maps are an output of probabilistic seismic hazard analysis with global coverage. Because state of practice in situ testing for assessing liquefaction potential is not feasible at the global scale, the geospatial prediction models of Zhu, Baise, and Thompson (2017) are adopted. Liquefaction susceptibility is computed at a 1.2-kilometer grid resolution based on a global data set (Worden et al. 2017).

Source: Koks et al. 2019.

tries, expected annual damages are $10 billion. In some countries, annual losses exceed 1 percent of the installed generation capital value (map 4.2, panel a). Globally, losses are driven mainly by thermal plants for cyclones and by hydropower plants for earthquakes. Map 4.2, panel b, shows the resulting expected annual generation losses, which can represent up to 5 percent of the total generation in some countries. Those losses have been calculated considering not only the expected damage for each plant but also an estimate of the restoration time in each country. Countries with the highest production risks are those with power systems that often are already under tight constraints in terms of generation capacity.

Several climate change–induced phenomena are likely to increase power sector risk.

MAP 4.2 Some low- and middle-income countries face high annual damage and generation losses

Multihazard risk indicator for damage and lost production

a. Expected annual damage to power plants (% of total capital value)

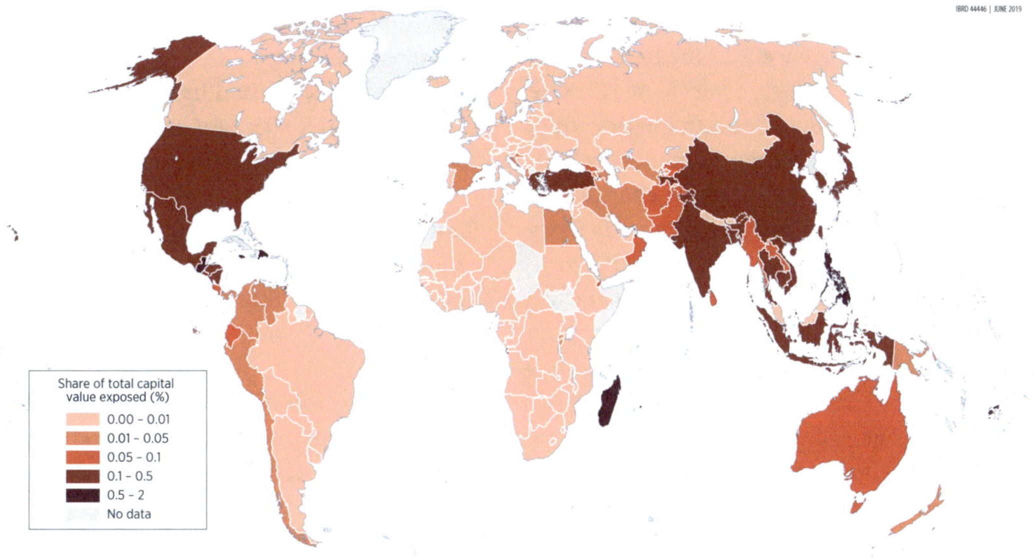

b. Expected annual generation losses (% of total potential production)

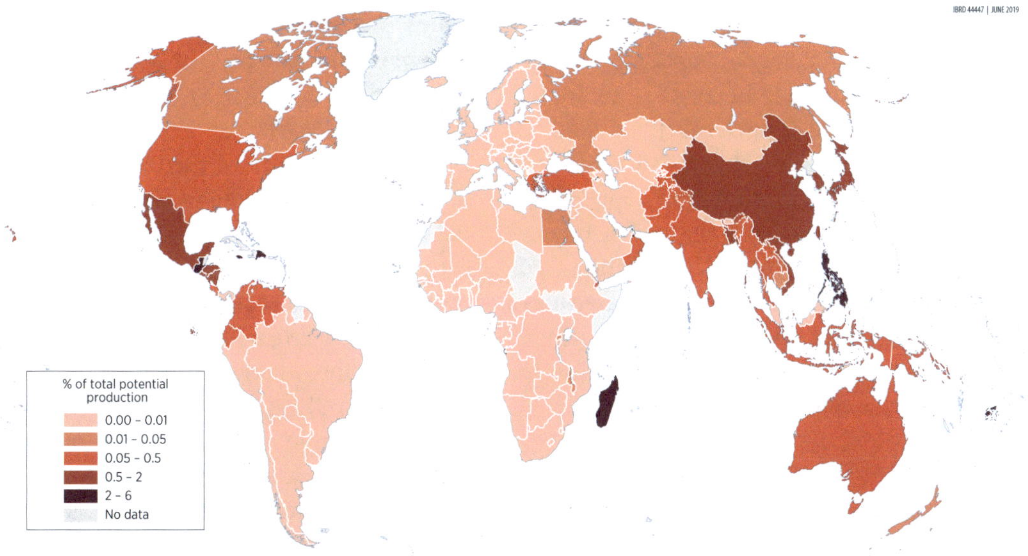

Source: Nicolas, Koks, et al. 2019.
Note: Panel a shows the expected annual damage divided by installed capital values in the country. Panel b shows the expected lost generation (in megawatt-hours) divided by the total potential generation of the country.

With more frequent droughts and higher temperatures, the efficiency of nuclear and thermal power plants is likely to decrease. Research suggests that a 1°C temperature increase could reduce power output by 0.45 percent to 0.8 percent (Mideksa and Kallbekken 2010). At the same time, these events will affect substation equipment and the current rating of cables and lines. They are also likely to increase system stress, because of the increased demand for air-conditioning.

In most regions, wind speed is likely to increase with climate change, and atmospheric icing (which negatively affects the performance of wind turbines) is likely to decrease. Climate change will also affect flood frequency, river flows, and evaporation, with implications for dam safety. In addition, climate change will increase temperature, reducing the efficiency of photovoltaic systems, which could drop by about 0.5 percent for every temperature increase of 1°C (Patt, Pfenninger, and Lilliestam 2013). Another impact of higher temperatures could be increased transmission losses, because of the increased resistance of power lines.

Finally, climate change–induced sea-level rise may require power plant relocation. Sea-level rise will be responsible not only for increased flooding of coastal assets but also, combined with higher wind speeds, for more corrosion of these assets due to saltwater sprays. A study of potential impacts of climate change on the Bangladeshi power sector found that around a third of power plants should be relocated by 2030 to avoid inundations caused by sea-level rise (Khan, Alam, and Alam 2013). Another 30 percent of Bangladesh power plants will likely be affected by the increased salinity of cooling water and increased frequency of flooding, while the northern region power plants will probably see a decrease in output because of droughts.

WATER SYSTEMS ARE PARTICULARLY VULNERABLE TO CLIMATE CHANGE AND CAN CONTRIBUTE TO MANAGING FLOODS AND DROUGHTS

Water systems consist of reservoirs, groundwater pumps, and transmission lines. They provide different services, like bulk water provision, standard water supply and sanitation services, irrigation, and drainage. In addition to supplying water—whether to cities, industry, or farms—water infrastructure is central to reducing natural hazard risks related to floods and droughts. This infrastructure includes multipurpose reservoirs, river embankments, stormwater drains, and coastal dikes, among others.

A global analysis of the exposure of all water infrastructure to natural hazards was impossible because of a lack of global data on water sector assets. However, two partial assessments were possible: (1) a crude global assessment of large dams, looking at their exposure to the two main natural hazards: high river inflows and earthquakes(Stip et al. 2019); and (2) a case study of China's wastewater treatment plants (WWTPs) to understand the level of risks faced by this critical water infrastructure for river floods and earthquakes (Hu et al. 2019). The case study is based on a data set of 1,346 WWTPs in China that includes the location of assets and the size of the population dependent on each asset.

Dams are critical for reducing downstream floods, but they can also create disasters if they collapse due to high river inflows

Dams' reservoirs can be used for multiple purposes, depending on the context. These potential purposes include providing hydropower, supplying water for cities or irrigation, and reducing downstream flood risks. Dams are built with concrete spillways that release excess flows back into the river downstream from the dam. The spillways are built with a specific design discharge to accommodate maximum flows, typically ranging from 500-year to 10,000-year or maximum probable discharges. If the discharge exceeds the spillway capacity, then water flows over the dam itself, which creates an emergency. If the dam is made from earth, rock, or both, then the chances of dam collapse become quite high; if the dam is made of concrete, then the chances of dam collapse are lower, but it is still an emergency situation.

If a dam collapses, it may have catastrophic impacts on downstream communities. In

Henan Province, China, in 1975, the extreme rainfall produced by Typhoon Nina was beyond the design criteria of the Banqiao Reservoir-Dam. When exposed to such high levels of rainfall, the dam failed, killing tens of thousands of people, with estimates reaching up to 171,000.

Spillway design standards are usually based on the risk to downstream communities as well as historical hydrological records. For example, a dam immediately upstream from a city typically has higher standards than a dam in a rural area. However, over time the downstream populations may grow or a country's risk tolerance may change, and thus there is a need to increase the spillway capacity and take additional measures to ensure the structural integrity of the dam.

The exposure analysis in this report is based on the Global Reservoir and Dams Dataset (Version 1.01), which contains 6,862 records of reservoirs and associated dams with a cumulative storage capacity of 6,179 cubic kilometers. These only represent 20 percent of the dams registered by the International Commission on Large Dams, which lists more than 33,000 large dams. The Global Reservoir and Dams Dataset is thus limited and likely biased toward the high-income world; however, it is the only georeferenced record of dams (Lehner et al. 2019) and was used for this exercise.

The level of exposure of dams to high river inflows—which could increase the chances of exceeding spillway capacity and possible dam collapse—is difficult to assess at a global level. In this exercise, the "river flood risk" information from the ThinkHazard! database (2019) was used as an indirect proxy for considering river flows into a reservoir. If a dam is in an area classified as having a "high river flood risk," this risk should indirectly and imprecisely correlate with high river flows. The ThinkHazard! database does not take future climate change into account, but rather relies on historical data. Of the 6,862 dam sites in the Global Reservoir and Dams Dataset, 15 percent are in areas of high river flood risk, representing around 21 percent of the total global capacity. The actual risk of dam collapse depends on the design capacity of the spillway and the construction quality of the dam.

Until recently, climate change and its impacts on hydrological flows have not been considered in dam design. However, this is changing quickly, and the latest example is the *Hydropower Sector Climate Resilience Guide* (IHA 2019), which was prepared under the auspices of the International Hydropower Association, with technical and financial support from the World Bank and other international donors. The risks associated with underdesigning for future climates are multifold: dams will not be able to provide reliable services to users—be it supplying water or power to cities or supplying irrigation water for agriculture—or help to mitigate flood and drought risks. Cervigni et al. (2015) stress how uncertainties about the future climate create a barrier to optimal dam design (box 4.2).

Water and wastewater treatment plants often face flood hazards, as they are typically in the lowest part of the network

Wastewater collection systems typically work by gravity to reduce energy costs, and treatment plants are generally located in low-lying flood-prone areas adjacent to the rivers, deltas, or lakes into which they discharge. For wastewater systems with a combined sanitary and storm drainage network, heavy precipitation can often overload the capacity of the network, resulting in combined sewer overflows of untreated sewage into the environment. Constructing combined sewer overflow retention basins to store water temporarily and then convey it back to the treatment plant is one option that some cities are pursuing, but this approach is very expensive and only accessible to the richest cities. The case study on China conducted for this report finds that climate change will significantly increase the

BOX 4.2 In hydropower, climate change adaptation is impaired by uncertainties

Climate change will alter the amount of water available for important productive uses, such as hydropower and irrigation. But as illustrated by a study of Africa, different climate models lead to different results—with some projecting an increase in available water and others projecting a decrease, making long-term planning particularly challenging (Cervigni et al. 2015). In the central and southern Africa basins (Congo, Orange, and Zambezi), depending on the climate scenarios considered, the power and water sectors could underperform in many scenarios and overperform in others. In economic terms, the impacts of climate change include lost revenue from underperforming hydropower or irrigation infrastructure in drier climate futures and, by contrast, the opportunity cost of not taking advantage of an abundance of exploitable water resources in wetter climate futures.

In simulations of the economic performance of infrastructure in the climate scenario at the end of the range, the deviations from the results expected under a historical climate are dramatic. In hydropower (figure B4.2.1), dry scenarios lead to revenue losses on the order of 10–60 percent of baseline values, with the Nile (Equatorial Lakes region), Senegal, and Zambezi basins being most affected. Wet scenarios result in potential revenue increases on the order of 20–140 percent, with the Eastern Nile, Niger, and Volta basins having the largest gains. In some wetter climate futures, infrastructure could perform better than expected because, for a given installed capacity, more hydropower or more crops could be produced with the extra water. However, many of the corresponding gains could be only potential ones, because power systems would have been planned in anticipation of lower than actual generation from hydropower. As a result, the transmission lines and power trading agreements needed to bring the extra hydropower to market may simply not be available. Without them, the gains from more abundant water might not be realized.

FIGURE B4.2.1 Large changes in Africa's hydropower revenues can be expected from climate change from 2015 to 2050

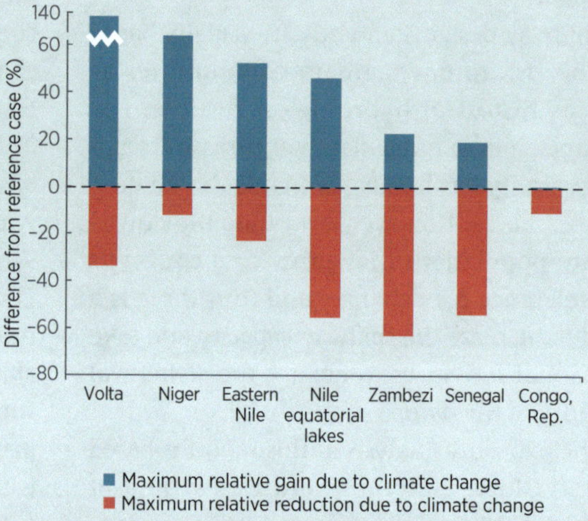

Source: Cervigni et al. 2015.
Note: The bars reflect the range of economic outcomes across all climate futures for each basin—that is, the highest increase (blue bars) and highest decrease (red bars) of hydropower revenues (discounted at 3%), relative to the no-climate-change reference case. The outlier bar corresponding to the Volta Basin has been trimmed to avoid distorting the scale of the chart and skewing the values for the other basins. Estimates reflect the range, but not the distribution, of economic outcomes across all climate futures. Each basin's results reflect the best and worst scenarios for that basin alone rather than the best and worst scenarios across all basins.

exposure of Chinese WWTPs to floods, even over the short term, with large potential impacts on users (Hu et al. 2019). The sign of this effect is consistent in 10 out of the 11 climate models considered, although the magnitude of the impacts varies across models. For an event with a 30-year return period under a scenario of moderate climate change, 35 percent of the WWTPs (472 out of 1,346 plants) supplying 176 million people could experience significantly higher flood risk by 2035. By 2055, the number of exposed people could rise by up to 208 million from the present number.

Dams and wastewater treatment plants are also exposed and vulnerable to earthquakes

Overtopping of dams can have large negative consequences, whereas dam collapses caused by earthquakes can be catastrophic—possibly triggering rapid flooding with many human casualties. In Japan, central China, the U.S. West Coast, Southern Europe, and the Middle East, dams and reservoirs face the highest seismic risk (map 4.3) (Stip et al. 2019). About 2 percent of the dams considered in this study face very high peak ground acceleration (PGA) levels, with a return period of 2,475 years.[3] High-income countries have the largest number of dam sites exposed to earthquakes. However, upper-middle-income countries have the largest capacity of dams exposed to the risk of seismic shaking. This finding is probably a reflection of the higher concentration of dams in richer economies and the large number of mega-dams in middle-income countries, particularly in Brazil and China.

For China, Hu et al. (2019) find that earthquakes also pose a significant risk to wastewater treatment operations. In an earthquake event with a return period of 250 years in China, 31 WWTPs are exposed to ground shaking of medium severity. More than half of these plants are also in areas with high liquefaction susceptibility, indicating their high vulnerability. Spatially, the western regions of mainland China and the surroundings of Beijing are prone to the highest seismic risks.[4]

Dams and WWTPs are not the only water assets that are exposed and vulnerable to natural hazards, so the analysis described here considers only part of the vulnerability of the water system to climate change and natural hazards. That vulnerability arises as well from pumping stations or control centers subject to

MAP 4.3 Dams and reservoirs face a high seismic risk

Peak ground acceleration faced by dam sites for a 2,500-year earthquake event

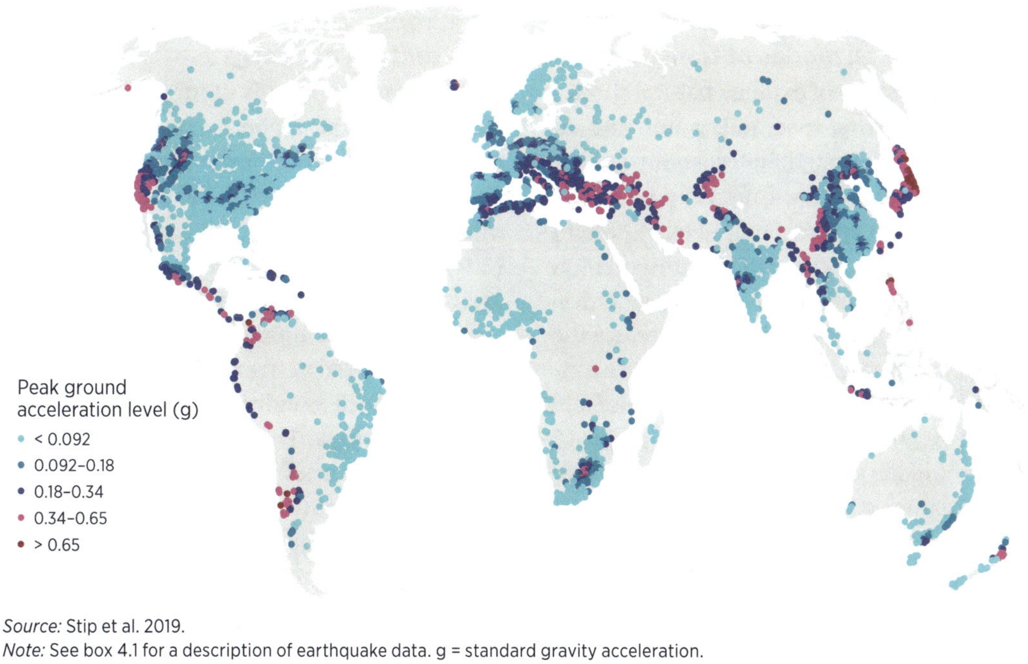

Source: Stip et al. 2019.
Note: See box 4.1 for a description of earthquake data. g = standard gravity acceleration.

collapse or flooding. In addition, a significant part of damage to water systems is caused by breaking or leaking pipes from ground liquefaction, landslides, and fault crossings (Kakderi and Argyroudis 2014). Furthermore, growing water scarcity in many parts of the world will make it even more challenging to provide water for many competing uses (Damania et al. 2017). Although some studies show promise in identifying vulnerable sections of water infrastructure (such as Bagriacik et al. 2018), they rely on high-quality data describing the existing network, which limits their applicability to low- and middle-income countries.

NATURAL HAZARDS FREQUENTLY DISRUPT AND EXTENSIVELY DAMAGE TRANSPORT INFRASTRUCTURE

In the transport sector, weather events cause accidents, congestion, and delays. An analysis conducted for this report also finds that natural hazards cost about $15 billion a year on average in direct damage to global transport infrastructure.

Variations in the weather cause frequent disruptions in all modes of transport

Even in the absence of extreme natural shocks, weather can disrupt road, rail, water, and air transport. In the United States, about 16 percent of flight delays are caused by relatively minor weather events and only about 4 percent by extreme weather (Bureau of Transportation Statistics 2018). And a survey of the empirical literature finds that precipitation increases the frequency of road accidents and increases congestion by reducing vehicle speeds (Koetse and Rietveld 2009). In the United States, about 15 percent of road traffic congestion is attributed to bad weather (Cambridge Systematics Institute and Texas Transportation Institute 2005). Such effects are not limited to road networks; in Finland, 60 percent of freight train delays between 2008 and 2010 were related to winter weather (Ludvigsen and Klæboe 2014).

Meanwhile, warm summers with low precipitation can affect inland waterway transport: in northwestern Europe, the dry summer of 2013 resulted in low water levels and losses of €480 million stemming from the inoperability of some large vessels and a shift to other forms of transport (Jonkeren et al. 2014).

Transport disruptions are costly. In the European Union, the total costs of the influence of extreme weather events on the transport system are an estimated €2.5 billion a year. Of these costs, about 72 percent are attributed to roads, 14 percent to air travel, and 12 percent to the rail sector. The remaining 2 percent are related, in descending order of magnitude, to maritime transport, inland waterways, and intermodal freight transport (Enei et al. 2011). Looking at the next four decades in the European Union and using the same methodology, Doll, Klug, and Enei (2014) expect the road transport costs arising from extreme weather events to increase by 7 percent. Higher flood risks and less predictable winters could increase rail traffic costs by up to 80 percent.

Natural hazards are responsible for large repair and maintenance costs in road and rail networks

How do natural hazards fit in? A new analysis conducted for this report demonstrates the significant exposure of transport infrastructure to natural hazards. With a resolution that is unprecedented on a global scale, Koks et al. (2019) combine data on road and rail network assets with information on the most significant types of natural hazards. This global study assesses damaged network infrastructure at the asset level, such as individual road segments or bridge structures. The road and railway data used in this analysis are based on open-access data from OpenStreetMap, which, thanks to voluntary contributors, is a comprehensive data set (Barrington-Leigh and Millard-Ball 2017; Meijer et al. 2018).

The exposure and risk of road and railway assets are assessed for the most frequently recorded and costliest disasters: tropical cyclones, earthquakes, surface flooding, river flooding, and coastal flooding (see box 4.1 for hazard data sources). An asset is considered to be exposed only when the probability of occurrence of the hazardous event exceeds the assumed design protection standards of the asset. In this way, countries' different resilience standards can be incorporated in the analysis.

This analysis finds that about 27 percent of all global road and railway assets are exposed to at least one hazard, and about 7.5 percent of assets are exposed to a 100-year flood event. Road and rail networks are most exposed to surface flooding, followed by tropical cyclones, river flooding, and earthquakes (figure 4.8). For earthquakes and surface flooding, richer countries with more assets are proportionally

FIGURE 4.8 Global exposure of transport infrastructure to multiple natural hazards

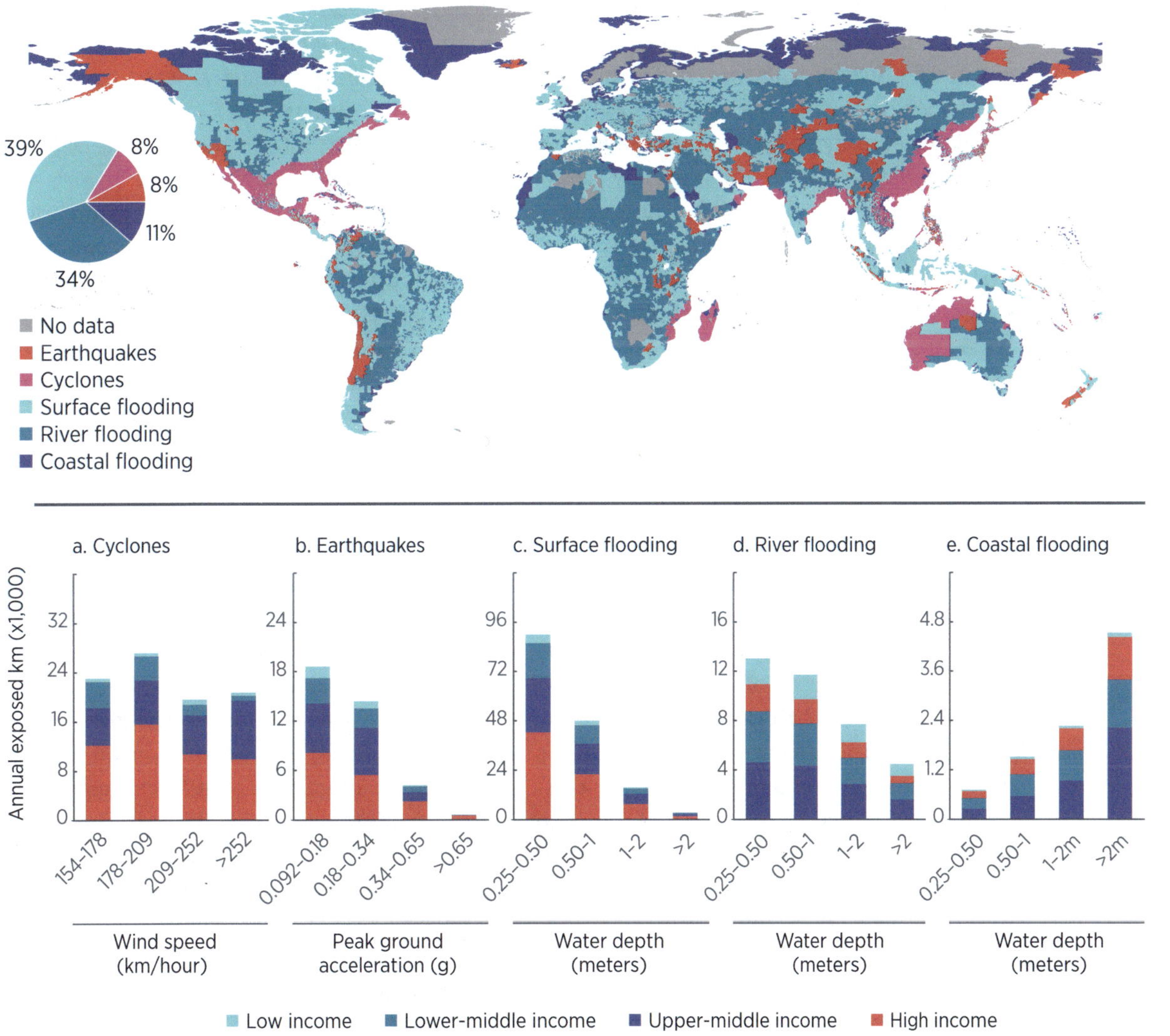

Source: Koks et al. 2019.

Note: Map shows the hazard causing the highest transport infrastructure exposure in each region. The accompanying pie chart indicates the percentage of land area with the highest exposure to each hazard. Panels a to e present the exposure of the four country income groups to each hazard type and intensity. g = standard gravity acceleration; km = kilometers.

more exposed. But for river and coastal flooding, high-income countries have fewer kilometers exposed because of their higher flood protection standards. For tropical cyclones and earthquakes, the large share of exposed infrastructure in upper-middle- and high-income countries is related predominantly to the geographic distribution of the hazards.

The resulting total global expected annual damage from all hazards ranges from $3.1 billion to $22 billion, with a mean EAD of $14.6 billion, depending on various assumptions about construction and reconstruction costs and other uncertainties. Considering only low- and middle-income countries, the mean EAD is $8 billion on average across scenarios. Of the global damage, about 73 percent is caused by surface and river flooding, followed by coastal floods (16 percent), earthquakes (7 percent), and tropical cyclones (4 percent) (Koks et al. 2019). The results are driven mainly by primary roads, which experience the highest relative damage, and by tertiary roads, which represent the greatest cumulative length.

But expected annual losses can hide the fact that rare events cause devastating damage. Although earthquakes represent only 7 percent of total annual losses, ground shaking or soil liquefaction can severely affect the functionality of transport infrastructure. Roads and railroads can be blocked by fault ruptures, collapsed buildings, or landslides; tunnels may collapse; embankments can be displaced by soil liquefaction; and bridges can collapse or become unstable (Argyroudis and Kaynia 2014). In the 1995 earthquake in Kobe, accessibility as measured by the length of the open network dropped by 86 percent directly after the shock for highways and by 71 percent for railways (Chang and Nojima 2001).

Another interesting finding of Koks et al. (2019) is that as the wealth of countries increases, the damage to their transport infrastructure first rises and then falls. This bell-shaped relationship between income and EAD, as shown in figure 4.9, is caused by two key dynamics facing in opposite directions. At first, states accumulate infrastructure as gross domestic product (GDP) increases, but this expansion is at the expense of higher disaster exposure and greater damage. After they reach a given level of income (in the middle-income category), they have enough resources to prioritize higher resilience. Thus they reduce the exposure and vulnerability of their infrastructure through investments in more rigorous design standards for transport assets and in flood protection.

In absolute terms, losses are the largest in big and wealthy countries, which is not surprising. However, when EAD is considered in relation to GDP, infrastructure value, or infrastructure length, it appears that lower- and middle-income countries are often more severely affected (figure 4.10). In small island developing states, for example, the annual damage relative to the total infrastructure value is more than double the global average.

At the global level, expected annual damages are small compared to the budget required for maintaining reliable transport networks (0.2 percent to 1.5 percent). However, our results reveal geographic disparities in exposure and risk, and for several countries and regions, investing in transport asset resilience should be a priority (Rozenberg et al. 2019).

Climate change will intensify the impacts of natural hazards on transport infrastructure. For example, in Mozambique, Kwiatkowski et al. (2019) find that the risk of river flooding to bridges under current conditions amounts to $200 million a year (1.5 percent of Mozambique's GDP) and could reach up to $400 million by 2050 in the worst-case climate change scenario.

Zooming in on urban flooding and road networks

Urban flooding is a major cause of transport disruptions in cities across the world, and these

FIGURE 4.9 Transport infrastructure damage first increases with income growth and then decreases

Expected annual damage (EAD) per hazard, by country income group

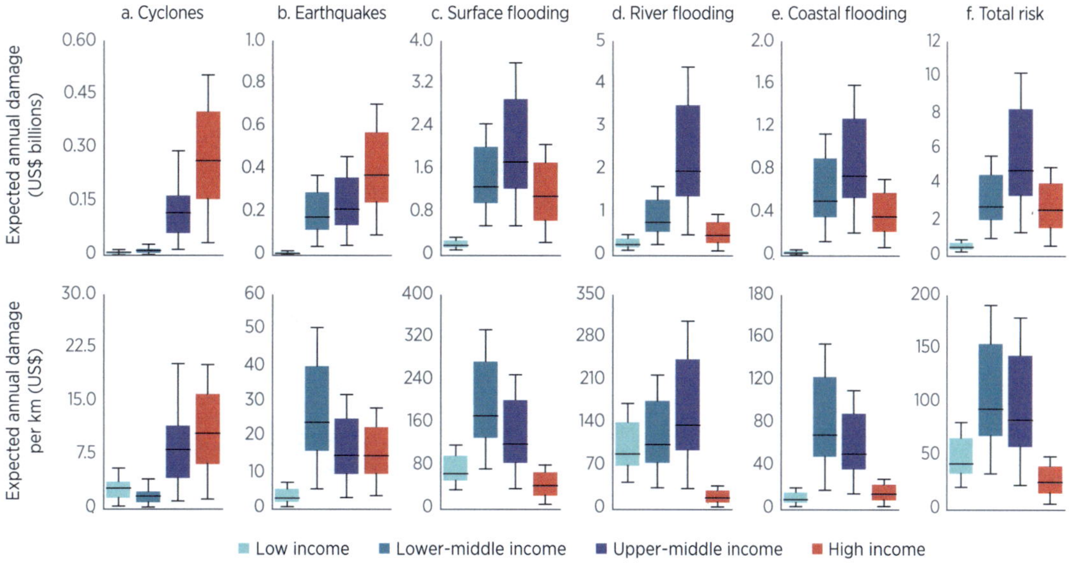

Source: Koks et al. 2019.
Note: Graphs show the expected annual damage (EAD) in absolute terms (top row) and per kilometer (km) of road (bottom row).

FIGURE 4.10 Low- and middle-income countries bear the highest damage costs relative to their GDP

Multihazard risk in expected annual damage (EAD), by country

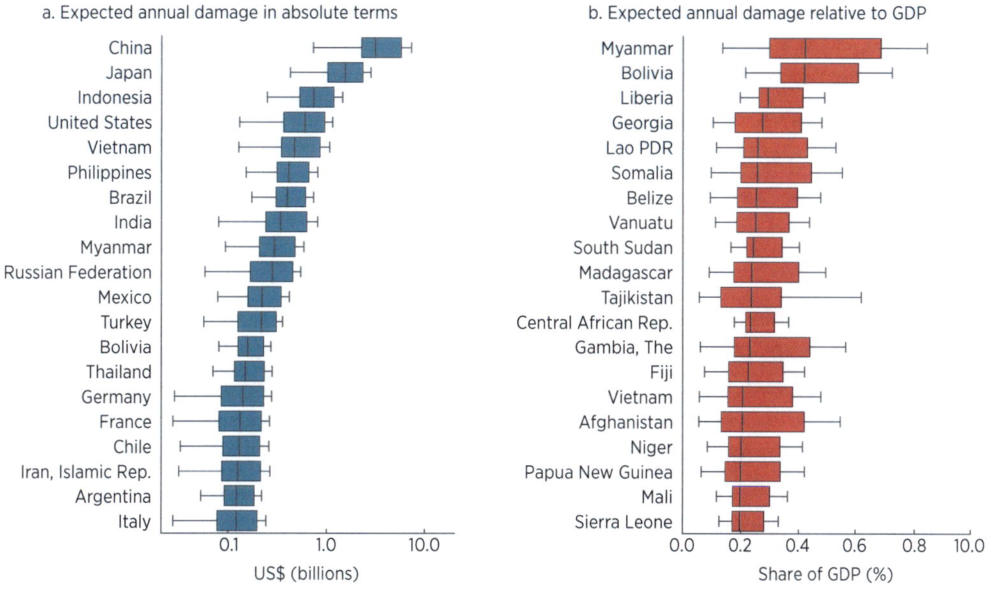

Source: Koks et al. 2019.
Note: Panel a presents the 20 countries that have the highest multihazard EAD in absolute terms. Panel b presents the 20 countries that have the highest multihazard EAD relative to the country's GDP.

MAP 4.4 Flooded segments of the road network (50-year return period), Inner Kampala

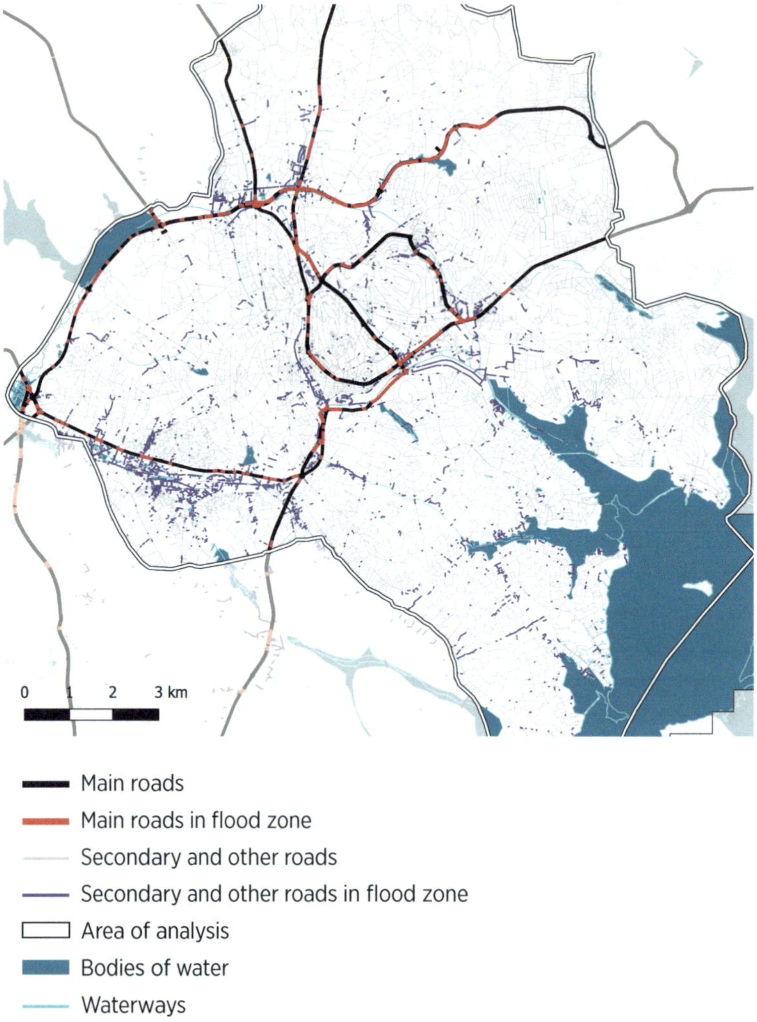

Source: Rentschler et al. 2019.

disruptions extend well beyond just the flood zone. From Buenos Aires to Dar es Salaam, Amman, Dhaka, and Jakarta, urban flooding is a frequent and devastating occurrence, especially in low- and middle-income countries.

Open-source road network data reveal how exposed urban road networks are to flooding. For example, Rentschler et al. (2019) estimate that in Inner Kampala, about 4 percent of all roads are affected by a flood with a return period of 50 years. Primary roads (such as motorways) are disproportionally located in flood zones (map 4.4). In a 50-year flood, an estimated 10 percent (11 kilometers) of all primary roads in Inner Kampala are flooded, and 8 percent of all primary roads are flooded at a depth of more than 15 centimeters, thereby preventing passage of most conventional cars.[5] However, only 3 percent (45 kilometers) of residential roads are directly affected.

In Dar es Salaam, the bus rapid transit lanes, the bus depot, and the port access road are highly exposed to flooding by rainfall events with intensities as low as 4–6 millimeters per hour over a 24-hour period, which currently occur every 2–10 years (ICF 2019). By 2050, all segments of Dar es Salaam's bus rapid transit system will be exposed to routine flooding by events on the order of 4–6 millimeters an hour. Climate change will likely increase the frequency and intensity of rainfall events and thus lead to more frequent flooding.

The story is much the same in other African cities—such as Bamako and Kigali—where a significant share of roads is affected by a flood depth of more than 15 centimeters in an event with a 50-year return period (figure 4.11). Just as in Kampala, primary roads in Bamako and Kigali are disproportionally affected by flooding. This high exposure of primary roads suggests that urban floods have significant indirect effects on the wider urban economy because they affect the linkages even between nonflooded areas. Indeed, infrastructure disruptions are by no means limited to certain low-income neighborhoods—infrastructure systems are networks that transmit the disruptions from urban flooding across wide areas. Chapter 3 of this report reveals how flooding in a few locations of Kampala's road network can affect households' access to health care across the entire city.

FIGURE 4.11 Urban flooding affects a significant share of the road networks in Bamako, Dar es Salaam, Kampala, and Kigali

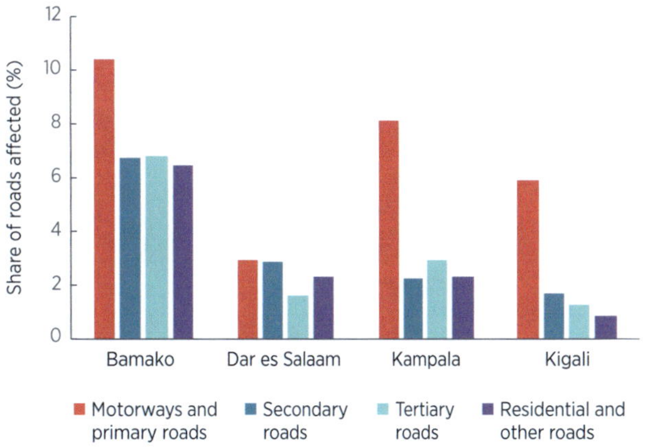

Source: Rentschler et al. 2019.
Note: Figure shows the percentage of roads affected by a flood depth of more than 15 centimeters in an event with a 50-year return period.

WHEN NATURAL SHOCKS DISRUPT TELECOMMUNICATIONS SYSTEMS, WHOLE COUNTRIES CAN GO OFFLINE

Telecommunications infrastructure, if dense enough, has a certain level of resilience built into its structure; but like other critical infrastructure, points of failure exist that are vulnerable to acute and chronic natural hazards. The core telecommunications infrastructure and information and communication technology (ICT) making up global networks can be categorized as

- Submarine cables
- Landing stations for submarine cables
- Terrestrial cables—underground and overland
- Internet exchange points and other data centers
- Wireless transmission infrastructure—towers and antennas.

Table 4.1 depicts the impacts of various climatic events on telecommunications infrastructure based on studies commissioned by public sector agencies in the United Kingdom, the United States, and academia. As seen in the table, acute events have a significant impact on almost all forms of infrastructure, with earthquakes (high intensity) the most destructive across the spectrum of infrastructure.

Data centers and landing stations are particularly vulnerable to flooding because of the large quantities of ICT equipment involved in their operations. As a result, submarine cable landing stations are the most vulnerable to a rise in sea level—one of the most direct impacts of long-term climate change.

Analyzing the climate risks to different types of ICT infrastructure using the broadband value chain can improve our understanding of the impacts of damage to each type of asset. The broadband value chain comprises three broad segments:

TABLE 4.1 Climatic events and their impacts on telecommunications infrastructure

Infrastructure	Inland and coastal floods	Earthquakes	Tsunamis	Sea-level rise	High temperatures	Water scarcity	High winds and storms
Submarine cable (deep sea)	L	H	M	L	L	L	L
Submarine cable (near shore)	L	H	H	L	L	L	L
Landing station	H	H	H	H	L	L	L
Terrestrial cables (underground)	M	H	L	L	L	L	L
Terrestrial cables (overland)	L	M	L	L	L	L	M
Data centers	H	M	L	L	M	M	L
Wireless transmission antennas	L	M	L	L	L	L	H

Source: Adapted from Adams et al. 2014; Dawson et al. 2018; Fu, Horrocks, and Winnie 2016; and U.S. Department of Homeland Security 2017.
Note: L = low; M = medium; H = high.

- *First mile.* International Internet connectivity through submarine cables or terrestrial cross-border links
- *Middle mile.* Domestic connectivity infrastructure linking sources of first-mile connectivity to population centers—mostly cables running along existing connectivity routes (transport and energy)
- *Last mile.* Infrastructure connecting individuals and premises to telecommunications networks—fiber or cable to the home from local cabinets, mobile towers, or Wifi transmitters.

First-mile infrastructure is critical—and the most vulnerable to earthquakes, tsunamis, and landslides

First-mile infrastructure corresponds to more than 370 submarine cable systems that connect to terrestrial networks through landing stations in almost all coastal and island countries. These cable systems—the main arteries of the global Internet—carry the world's information, including virtually all international financial transactions. Although the number and frequency of faults in submarine cable systems are low, the parts of the world prone to seismic activity keep their submarine cable repair teams fairly busy. For example, off the coast of eastern China, and particularly between Taiwan, China, and mainland China, frequent undersea earthquakes result in almost one cable break a week (Brandon 2013). The presence of a highly active port contributes to more frequent cable breaks, mostly from dropped or dragging anchors hitting the submarine cables on the sea floor.

Submarine cable systems are most at risk from earthquakes and landslides on the seabed (table 4.1). This vulnerability also extends to landing stations, but modern construction techniques have improved the resilience of the buildings housing them. That said, coastal flooding and tsunamis can cause great damage to landing stations, whereas the offshore cables themselves may remain protected. The great Hengchun Earthquake on the island of Taiwan, China, and in the Luzon Strait in December 2006 was one of the severest examples of the disruption of submarine cable systems. Submarine landslides triggered by the earthquakes and the subsequent turbulent currents traveled more than 300 kilometers, causing 19 breaks in seven cable systems. Some of the damaged cables were at depths of 4,000 meters. Repairs were carried out by 11 vessels over 49 days.

The Internet connectivity of China; Japan; the Philippines; Singapore; Taiwan, China; and Vietnam was seriously affected, with all countries losing a portion of their international capacity. Financial services, airlines, and shipping industries were significantly affected, and commerce in Taiwan, China, in general, came to a halt. Traffic was rerouted rapidly using undamaged infrastructure, but the pressure on them resulted in lower-quality service, delays, and failures in those cable systems because of overloading. Following the earthquake, a survey was conducted in China to estimate the impact of the disruption, and the results were staggering. It found that 97 percent of Chinese Internet users faced issues visiting foreign websites, and 57 percent felt that their life and work were affected (APEC Secretariat 2013).

Middle-mile infrastructure can be protected by redundancy

The middle mile of broadband networks consists of telecommunications infrastructure connecting population centers within a country, similar to road highways. These connectivity routes, which can connect internationally across terrestrial borders, are part of the global Internet. Countries with well-developed telecommunications sectors have dense middle-mile networks, with a larger number of routes and carriers per route. Unlike electricity, the transmission routes carry two-way traffic. Therefore, a break at one point of the network does not necessarily mean everything downstream is unconnected. Large parts of the network can be revived by using the alternate routes available, perhaps even originating downstream from the failure point.

The primary risks to middle-mile infrastructure—areal and underground cables—are earthquakes, landslides, and strong winds. Underground infrastructure is also at risk from flooding. Infrastructure that runs along coastlines is perhaps most at risk because of exposure to multiple hazards.

Last-mile infrastructure is most exposed, but can be recovered quickly

The infrastructure most prevalent in last-mile access—poles and antennas—is physically quite resilient and can withstand significant climatic pressures. For example, mobile antennas can withstand winds of up to 250 kilometers an hour, and terrestrial cables are either underground in ducts or on wooden and metal poles in urban centers. However, falling trees or dislodged debris can cause failures and are unavoidable in these situations. Therefore, investments to ensure timely recovery of services in the event of a disaster may be more effective than investments in protecting the exposed last-mile assets.

Data centers are also vulnerable to climatic conditions and extreme events

Another important element of the digital ecosystem—and now a core digital infrastructure—are the data centers that host the various websites, services, and applications used globally. According to a survey by the Ponemon Institute (2016) covering 63 data centers, between 10 percent and 12 percent of data center outages are attributable to weather conditions.

In January 2015, thousands of residents of Perth, found themselves suddenly disconnected from the Internet. The Internet service provider had suffered cooling system failures in part of its data center. Under normal circumstances, the failure may not have led to network outages, but because the second-hottest day of the summer that year had led to fears of server failure, the Internet service provider shut down the servers affected by the failed cooling system. Although annoying and cumbersome for residential customers, the economic impact of a loss of connectivity is felt almost immediately by businesses. Simple tasks such as paying for goods with a credit card become impossible without Internet connectivity.

Climate change can have far-reaching impacts on telecommunications through chronic changes, particularly because cooling is a core requirement of data centers, which are the foundation of the Internet. Rising temperatures and lowering water tables will make cooling increasingly challenging at industrial scales. The Uptime Institute, which tracks data center trends, estimates that today telecommunications companies can spend almost 80 percent of the cost of running their server on cooling them.

INFRASTRUCTURE SOMETIMES CREATES OR INCREASES NATURAL RISKS

Not only are infrastructure assets exposed to risks, but they also create risks and can increase exposure. Sometimes, infrastructure directly creates a hazard, such as when electricity transmission and distributional lines trigger wildfires. In California in 2007, San Diego Gas and Electric was found liable for $2 billion in damages from three fires that led to two deaths and the destruction of 1,300 homes (Daniels 2017). Large reservoirs can increase the frequency of earthquakes in areas of high seismic activity and can cause earthquakes to happen in areas that were thought to be seismically inactive. Sometimes, infrastructure magnifies natural risks through so-called natech disasters (technological disasters triggered by a natural hazard). For example, the Fukushima nuclear accident in Japan in 2011 was a technological accident provoked by an earthquake and tsunami. At times, infrastructure may not influence the hazard itself but may increase the exposure to the hazard. An example is the development of transport, energy, or water infrastructure that attracts people and investment to risky areas.

Urban infrastructure and air-conditioning worsen heat waves

Heat waves are already a big threat to well-being and health in cities, and this threat will drastically increase with climate change. Extreme heat waves in cities lead to worse air quality and numerous heat-related health issues and even death, especially among vulnerable groups such as children and the elderly. Today, the impact of such events is significant: in a 2015 heat wave in Delhi, more than 2,000 deaths were recorded. It is estimated that more than 350 cities and more than 200 million people are regularly exposed to extreme heat, defined as a three-day period with average maximum temperature of at least 35°C. By 2050, the number of affected people will increase by 700 percent, to 1.6 billion, in more than 970 cities (Viguié et al. 2019).

Urban infrastructure contributes to heat waves through the urban heat island effect and air-conditioning systems. In the urban heat island effect, cities are warmer than their surrounding areas because they consist of built-up surfaces that absorb heat (map 4.5). The transportation infrastructure necessary for the functioning of cities, such as paved roads, contributes to this effect. To cope with high temperature levels, residents and businesses resort to air-conditioning to maintain cool interiors. Air-conditioning systems, however, usually emit warm air to the outside and thus further increase the overall urban heat island effect.

Heat waves stress infrastructure, especially by increasing the demand for electricity. In a case study of Paris, Viguié et al. (2019) simulate the effect of more frequent and hotter heat waves on air-conditioning. To maintain a temperature of 23°C in all buildings, they project an average increase in final energy consumption of 1.134 terawatt-hours a year. During a heat wave, the additional energy consumption from cooling corresponds to 81 percent of the current average daily electricity consumption for offices and housing in Paris. Such additional demand represents a significant challenge and can lead to outages, especially in places where power systems are underdimensioned and struggle to keep pace with growing energy consumption.

MAP 4.5 Simulation of air temperature in the streets of Greater Paris at 4 a.m., after nine days of a heat wave similar to that of 2003

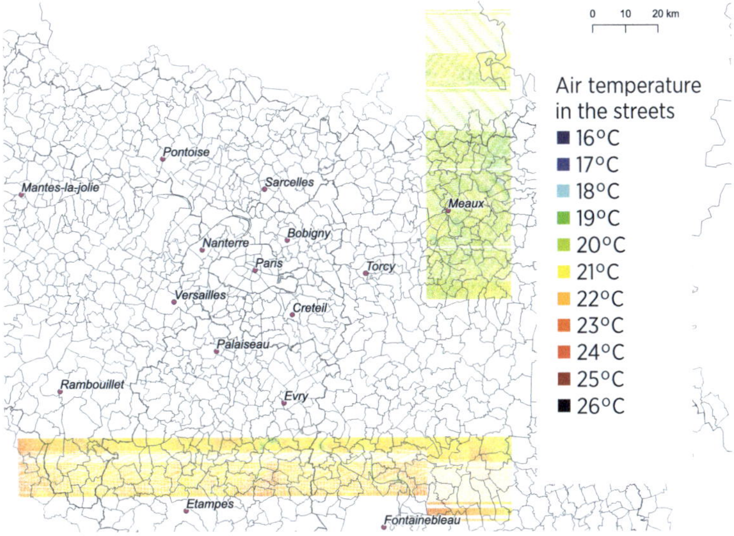

Source: Viguié et al. 2019.
Note: The urban heat island effect is clearly visible, with a 6°C temperature difference between the center of Paris and the countryside.

Infrastructure system interdependencies can amplify the impacts of a shock

Although it is important to understand how specific shocks influence certain infrastructure systems, such analyses done in isolation are likely to underestimate an event's actual impact, because infrastructure systems are interconnected. These connections, or interdependencies, can be classified as physical, cyber, geographical, and logical. Physical interdependency describes a system that is materially dependent on another system. Cyber interdependency refers to a system that is reliant on functioning information infrastructure. Geographical interdependency describes an environment that can simultaneously alter local systems. Finally, logical interdependency can be used to classify all other connections between two or more systems that cannot be described as being physical, cyber, or geographical (Rinaldi, Peerenboom, and Kelly 2001).

In the event of a shock, disruptions in one infrastructure system can thus translate into disruptions in dependent systems and cause a cascading effect that greatly amplifies the impact of the original event (Kadri, Birregah, and Châtelet 2014). Such domino effects are difficult to anticipate because they consist of the interactions of several highly complex systems, each of which is difficult to understand individually. Several approaches can be taken to modeling interdependent infrastructure systems differing in scope, complexity, and data requirements, but typically they are more useful for depicting the nature and direction of interdependencies than for accurately quantifying these relationships (Barker and Santos 2010; Ouyang 2014). In power grids, for example, critical infrastructure interdependencies link electricity infrastructure to transport, water supply, and ICT infrastructure, and the provision of oil and gas. Disruptions in any of these components can cause outages in all of the other systems and render restoration after a shock difficult. This again highlights the need for coordination among different actors in preparation and recovery activities (Wender, Morgan, and Holmes 2017).

This chapter has presented new analysis on the exposure of infrastructure networks and the damages they face due to natural disasters and climate change. However, the impacts of disasters go way beyond the direct damages to the infrastructure assets and can propagate to regions and economic actors that were not hit directly. This is the subject of the next chapter of this report.

NOTES

1. The cause of the remaining 1 percent of outage events is unknown.
2. Extreme heat days and droughts are also high-frequency events, but their impact is mostly on service continuity during the event and very rarely affects the integrity of the asset.
3. Normally, the return period for maximum design earthquake is 10,000. However, since the global data set only has return periods up to 2,475 years, this was taken as the basis for assessment and should still indicate the approximate earthquake hazard level.
4. The analysis looks at PGA hazard maps for return periods of 250, 475, 950, 1,500, and 2,475 years.
5. Technically, flood depths of up to 20 centimeters may be safe for most vehicles to navigate. However, in practice—and confirmed anecdotally—drivers cannot gauge exact water depths and thus need to avoid submerged roads.

REFERENCES

Adams, P., J. Steeves, B. Ashe, J. Firth, and B. Rabb. 2014. "Climate Risks Study for Telecommunications and Data Center Services." Report for the General Services Administration, Washington, DC.

APEC (Asia-Pacific Economic Cooperation) Secretariat. 2013. "Economic Impact of Submarine Cable Disruptions." APEC#213-SE-01.2, APEC Secretariat, Singapore.

Argyroudis, S., and A. M. Kaynia. 2014. "Fragility Functions of Highway and Railway Infrastructure." In *SYNER-G: Typology Definition and Fragility Functions for Physical Elements at Seismic Risk—Buildings, Lifelines, Transportation Networks, and Critical Facilities,* edited by K. Pitilakis, H. Crowley, and A. M. Kaynia, 299–326. Dordrecht: Springer Netherlands.

Bagriacik, A., R. A. Davidson, M. W. Hughes, B. A. Bradley, and M. Cubrinovski. 2018. "Comparison of Statistical and Machine Learning Approaches to Modeling Earthquake Damage to Water Pipelines." *Soil Dynamics and Earthquakes Engineering* 112 (September): 76–88.

Barker, K., and J. R. Santos. 2010. "A Risk-Based Approach for Identifying Key Economic and Infrastructure Systems." *Risk Analysis* 30 (6): 962–74.

Barrington-Leigh, C., and A. Millard-Ball. 2017. "The World's User-Generated Road Map Is More Than 80% Complete." *PLoS One* 12 (8): e0180698.

Bates, P. D., M. S. Horritt, and T. J. Fewtrell. 2010. "A Simple Inertial Formulation of the Shallow Water Equations for Efficient Two-Dimensional Flood Inundation Modelling." *Journal of Hydrology* 387 (1-2): 33–45.

Brandon, J. 2013. "Protecting the Cables That Wire Our World." *Popular Mechanics,* March 15.

Bureau of Transportation Statistics. 2018. "Understanding the Reporting of Causes of Flight Delays and Cancellations." Bureau of Transportation Statistics, Washington, DC, March 29.

Cambridge Systematics Institute and Texas Transportation Institute. 2005. *Traffic Congestion and Reliability: Trends and Advanced Strategies for Congestion Mitigation.* Medford, MA: Cambridge Systematics Institute; College Station, TX: Texas Transportation Institute.

Cardona, O. D., G. A. Bernal, M. G. Ordaz, M. A. Salgado-Gálvez, S. K. Singh, M. G. Mora, and C. P. Villegas. 2015. "Update on the Probabilistic Modelling of Natural Risks at Global Level: Global Risk Model—Global Earthquake and Tropical Cyclone Hazard Assessment; Disaster Risk Assessment at Country Level for Earthquakes, Tropical Cyclones (Wind and Storm Surge), Floods, Tsunami, and Volcanic Eruptions." Background paper for GAR15, CIMNE and INGENIAR Consortium, Barcelona and Bogotá.

Cervigni, R., R. Liden, J. E. Neumann, and K. M. Strzepek. 2015. *Enhancing the Climate Resilience of Africa's Infrastructure: The Power and Water Sectors.* Washington, DC: World Bank.

Chang, S. E., and N. Nojima. 2001. "Measuring Post-Disaster Transportation System Performance: The 1995 Kobe Earthquake in Comparative Perspective." *Transportation Research Part A: Policy and Practice* 35 (6): 475–94.

Damania, R., S. Desbureaux, M. Hyland, A. Islam, S. Moore, A.-S. Rodella, J. Russ, and E. Zaveri.

2017. *Uncharted Waters: The New Economics of Water Scarcity and Variability.* Washington, DC: World Bank.

Daniels, J. 2017. "Southern California Utilities Shut Off Power in 'Extremely' Windy Weather to Prevent Wildfires." CNBC, December 13.

Dawson, R. J., D. Thompson, D. Johns, R. Wood, G. Darch, L. Chapman, P. N. Hughes, G. V. R. Watson, K. Paulson, S. Bell, S. N. Gosling, W. Powrie, and J. W. Hall. 2018. "A Systems Framework for National Assessment of Climate Risks to Infrastructure." *Philosophical Transactions of the Royal Society A: Mathematical, Physical, and Engineering Sciences* 376 (2121): 20170298.

Dhaka Tribune. 2019. "Nor'wester Knocks out 6,000 Cell Towers." April 1. http://www.dhakatribune.com/bangladesh/nation/2019/04/01/nor-wester-knocks-out-6-000-cell-towers.

Doll, C., S. Klug, and R. Enei. 2014. "Large and Small Numbers: Options for Quantifying the Costs of Extremes on Transport Now and in 40 Years." *Natural Hazards* 72 (1): 211–39.

Enei, R., C. Doll, S. Klug, I. Partzsch, N. Sedlacek, J. Kiel, N. Nesterova, L. Rudzikaite, A. Papanikolaou, and V. Mitsakis. 2011. *Vulnerability of Transport Systems: Main Report.* Karlsruhe: Fraunhofer-Institute for Systems and Innovation Research.

Fu, G., L. Horrocks, and S. Winnie. 2016. "Exploring Impact of Climate Change on UK's ICT Infrastructure." *Infrastructure Asset Management* 3 (1): 42–52.

Hu, X., R. Pant, C. Zorn, W. Lim, E. Koks, and Z. Mao. 2019. "Methodology and Findings for the Exposure Analysis of the Chinese Wastewater Sector to Flooding and Earthquakes Hazards." Background paper for this report, World Bank, Washington, DC.

ICF (Investment Climate Facility). 2019. "Strategic Assessment of the Climate Resilience of Dar es Salaam Transport Infrastructure." ICF, African Development Bank, Abidjan.

IHA (International Hydropower Association). 2019. *Hydropower Sector Climate Resilience Guide.* London: IHA.

Jonkeren, O., P. Rietveld, J. van Ommeren, and A. te Linde. 2014. "Climate Change and Economic Consequences for Inland Waterway Transport in Europe." *Regional Environmental Change* 14 (3): 953–65.

Kadri, F., B. Birregah, and E. Châtelet. 2014. "The Impact of Natural Disasters on Critical Infrastructures: A Domino Effect-Based Study." *Journal of Homeland Security and Emergency Management* 11 (2): 217–41.

Kakderi, K., and S. Argyroudis. 2014. "Fragility Functions of Water and Waste-Water Systems." In *SYNER-G: Typology Definition and Fragility Functions for Physical Elements at Seismic Risk—Buildings, Lifelines, Transportation Networks, and Critical Facilities,* edited by K. Pitilakis, H. Crowley, and A. M. Kaynia, 221–58. Dordrecht: Springer Netherlands.

Khan, I., F. Alam, and Q. Alam. 2013. "The Global Climate Change and Its Effect on Power Generation in Bangladesh." *Energy Policy* 61 (October): 1460–70.

Koks, E., J. Rozenberg, C. Zorn, M. Tariverdi, M. Vousdoukas, S. A. Fraser, J. Hall, and S. Hallegatte. 2019. "A Global Multi-Hazard Risk Analysis of Road and Railway Infrastructure Assets." Forthcoming in *Nature Sustainability.*

Koetse, M. J., and P. Rietveld. 2009. "The Impact of Climate Change and Weather on Transport: An Overview of Empirical Findings." *Transportation Research Part D: Transport and Environment* 14 (3): 205–21.

Kressig, A., L. Byers, J. Friedrich, T. Luo, and C. McCormick. 2018. "Water Stress Threatens Nearly Half the World's Thermal Power Plant Capacity." World Resources Institute (blog), April 11. https://www.wri.org/blog/2018/04/water-stress-threatens-nearly-half-world-s-thermal-power-plant-capacity.

Kwiatkowski, K., Y. Qiao, S. Young, E. Bell, and R. Medina. 2019. "Quantifying Risk of Flood-Induced Bridge Failure in Mozambique Considering Climate Variability." University of New Hampshire.

Lehner, B., C. R. Liermann, C. Revenga, C. Vörösmarty, B. Fekete, P. Crouzet, P. Döll, M. Endejan, K. Frenken, J. Magome, C. Nilsson, J. Robertson, R. Rödel, N. Sindorf, and D. Wisser. 2019. "Global Reservoir and Dam (GRanD) Database. Technical Documentation." Global Water System Project, Bonn.

Ludvigsen, J., and R. Klæboe. 2014. "Extreme Weather Impacts on Freight Railways in Europe." *Natural Hazards* 70 (1): 767–87.

Luo, T., D. Krishnan, and S. Sen. 2018. "Parched Power: Water Demands, Risks, and Opportunities for India's Power Sector." World Resources Institute, Washington, DC.

Meijer, J. R., M. A. J. Huijbregts, K. C. G. J. Schotten, and A. M. Schipper. 2018. "Global Patterns of Current and Future Road Infrastructure." *Environmental Research Letters* 13 (6): 064006.

Mideksa, T. K., and S. Kallbekken. 2010. "The Impact of Climate Change on the Electricity Market: A Review." *Energy Policy* 38 (7): 3579–85.

Miyamoto International. 2019. "Overview of Engineering Options for Increasing Infrastructure Resilience." World Bank, Washington, DC.

Moss, R. E. S., E. M. Thompson, D. S. Kieffer, B. Tiwari, Y. M. A. Hashash, I. Acharya, B. R. Adhikari, D. Asimaki, K. B. Clahan, B. D. Collins, S. Dahal, R. W. Jobson, D. Khadka, A. McDonald, C. L. Madugo, B. Mason, M. Pehlivan, D. Rayamajhi, and S. Uprety. 2015. "Geotechnical Effects of the 2015 Magnitude 7.8 Gorkha, Nepal, Earthquake and Aftershocks." *Seismological Research Letters* 86 (6): 1514–23.

Muis, S., M. Verlaan, H. C. Winsemius, J. C. J. H. Aerts, and P. J. Ward. 2016. "A Global Reanalysis of Storm Surges and Extreme Sea Levels." *Nature Communications* 7 (11969).

Nicolas, C., E. Koks, A. Potter van Loon, C. Arderne, C. Zorn, and S. Hallegatte. 2019. "Global Power Sector Exposure and Risk Assessment to Natural Disasters." Background paper for this report, World Bank, Washington, DC.

Nicolas, C., J. Rentschler, A. Potter van Loon, S. Oguah, S. Schweikert, M. Deinert, E. Koks, C. Arderne, D. Cubas, J. Li, and E. Ichikawa. 2019. "Stronger Power: Improving Power Sector Resilience to Natural Disasters." Sector note for this report, World Bank, Washington, DC.

Ouyang, M. 2014. "Review on Modeling and Simulation of Interdependent Critical Infrastructure Systems." *Reliability Engineering and System Safety* 121 (January): 43–60.

Panteli, M., and P. Mancarella 2015. "Influence of Extreme Weather and Climate Change on the Resilience of Power Systems: Impacts and Possible Mitigation Strategies." *Electric Power Systems Research* 127 (October): 259–70.

Patt, A., S. Pfenninger, and J. Lilliestam. 2013. "Vulnerability of Solar Energy Infrastructure and Output to Climate Change." *Climatic Change* 121 (1): 93–102. http://dx.doi.org/10.1007/s10584-013-0887-0.

Ponemon Institute. 2016. "Cost of Data Center Outages." Ponemon Institute, Traverse City, MI.

Rentschler, J., M. Obolensky, and M. Kornejew. 2019. "Candle in the Wind? Energy System Resilience to Natural Shocks." Background paper for this report, World Bank, Washington, DC.

Rentschler, J., J. Braese, N. Jones, and P. Avner. 2019. "Three Feet Under: The Impacts of Flooding on Urban Jobs, Connectivity, and Infrastructure." Background paper for this report, World Bank, Washington, DC.

Rinaldi, S. M., J. P. Peerenboom, and T. K. Kelly 2001. "Identifying, Understanding, and Analyzing Critical Infrastructure Interdependencies." *IEEE Control Systems Magazine* 21 (6): 11–25.

Rozenberg, J., X. Espinet Alegre, P. Avner, C. Fox, S. Hallegatte, E. Koks, J. Rentschler, and M. Tariverdi. 2019. "From a Rocky Road to Smooth Sailing: Building Transport Resilience to Natural Disasters." Sector note for this report, World Bank, Washington, DC.

Sampson, C. C., A. M. Smith, P. B. Bates, J. C. Neal, L. Alfieri, and J. E. Freer. 2015. "A High-Resolution Global Flood Hazard Model." *Water Resources Research* 51 (9): 7358–81.

Schweikert, A. E., L. Nield, E. Otto, and M. Deinert. 2019. "Resilience and Critical Power System Infrastructure: Lessons Learned from Natural Disasters and Future Research Needs." Background paper for this report, World Bank, Washington, DC.

Scussolini, P., J. C. J. H. Aerts, B. Jongman, L. M. Bouwer, H. C. Winsemius, H. De Moel, and P. J. Ward. 2016. "FLOPROS: An Evolving Global Database of Flood Protection Standards." *Natural Hazards and Earth System Sciences* 16 (May 3): 1049–61.

Stip, C., Z. Mao, L. Bonzanigo, G. Browder, and J. Tracy. 2019. "The Resilience of Water Infrastructure: Examples from Dams, Wastewater Treatment Plants, and Water Supply and Sanitation Systems." Sector note for this report, World Bank, Washington, DC.

Tolman, H. L. 2009. "User Manual and System Documentation of WAVEWATCH III TM Version 3.14." Technical Note, MMAB Contribution 276, U.S. Department of Commerce, National Oceanic and Atmospheric Administration, National Weather Service, National Centers for Environmental Prediction, Camp Springs, MD.

U.S. Department of Homeland Security. 2017. "Threats to Undersea Cable Communications." Public-Private Analytic Exchange Program, Washington, DC, September.

U.S. Department of Homeland Security and U.S. Department of Energy. 2017. "Dams and Energy Sectors Interdependence Study: An Update to the 2011 Study." U.S Department of Homeland Security and U.S. Department of Energy, Washington, DC.

Van Vliet, M. T. H., J. Sheffield, D. Wiberg, and E. F. Wood. 2016. "Impacts of Recent Drought and

Warm Years on Water Resources and Electricity Supply Worldwide." *Environmental Research Letters* 11 (12): 124021.

Viguié, V., A. Lemonsu, S. Hallegatte, A.-L. Beaulant, C. Marchadier, V. Masson, G. Pigeon, and J.-L. Salagnac. 2019. "Early Adaptation to Heat Waves and Future Reduction of Air-Conditioning Energy Use in Cities." Unpublished manuscript.

Vousdoukas, M. I., L. Mentaschi, E. Voukouvalas, M. Verlaan, S. Jevrejeva, L. P. Jackson, and L. Feyen. 2018. "Global Probabilistic Projections of Extreme Sea Levels Show Intensification of Coastal Flood Hazard." *Nature Communications* 9 (1): 2360.

Vousdoukas, M. I., E. Voukouvalas, L. Mentaschi, F. Dottori, A. Giardino, D. Bouziotas, A. Bianchi, P. Salamon, and L. Feyen. 2016. "Developments in Large-Scale Coastal Flood Hazard Mapping." *Natural Hazards and Earth System Sciences* 16 (8): 1841–53.

Wang, J., L. Schleifer, and L. Zhong. 2017. "No Water, No Power." World Resources Institute (blog), June 29. https://www.wri.org/blog/2017/06/no-water-no-power.

Wender, B. A., M. G. Morgan, and K. J. Holmes 2017. "Enhancing the Resilience of Electricity Systems." *Engineering* 3 (5): 580–82.

Worden, C. B., D. J. Wald, J. Sanborn, and E. M. Thompson. 2017. "Development of an Open-Source Hybrid Global Vs30 Model." Seismological Society of America Annual Meeting, Pasadena, CA, April 21–23.

Yamazaki, D., D. Ikeshima, R. Tawatari, T. Yamaguchi, F. O'Loughlin, J. C. Neal, C. C. Sampson, S. Kanae, and P. D. Bates. 2017. "A High-Accuracy Map of Global Terrain Elevations." *Geophysical Research Letters* 44 (1): 5844–53.

Zhu, J., L. G. Baise, and E. M. Thompson. 2017. "An Updated Geospatial Liquefaction Model for Global Application." *Bulletin of the Seismological Society of America* 107 (3): 1365–85.

From Micro to Macro: Local Disruptions Translate into Macroeconomic Impacts 5

The severity of natural disasters is usually measured by the asset losses they provoke (Munich Re 2019; Swiss Re 2018). However, for many reasons such a metric is insufficient. The same loss can have very different impacts, depending on who is affected and their ability to cope with and recover from the loss (Hallegatte et al. 2016). But even without considering distributional impacts, asset losses do not capture the full macroeconomic impact of a disaster.

As shown by Hallegatte and Vogt-Schilb (2016), $1 in asset loss can translate into more than $1 in output or consumption loss, especially if infrastructure assets are damaged. The reason? Complementarities among assets in the economic system mean that the loss of one asset reduces the productivity of other assets (for example, the loss of a road makes a factory less productive because workers cannot access it or goods cannot be delivered to or from it). These effects have been well identified theoretically (Baqaee and Farhi 2017).

The secondary effects of direct asset losses on economic activities and output often represent a large share of total disaster losses. Simulations suggest that a major earthquake on the Hayward fault—a seismic fault line near San Francisco—could generate almost $40 billion in indirect losses and a drop in employment of 36,700 employee-years, in addition to $115 billion in asset losses (box 5.1). Disasters can even reduce output without destroying any assets. In 2010 the eruption of the Eyjafjallajökull Volcano in Iceland disrupted air transport, leading to a global supply disruption of low-volume, high-value goods (such as electronic components) and perishable goods (such as food and flowers) (BBC 2010). Similar indirect impacts affect households as well. When McCarty and Smith (2005) investigated the impact of the 2004 hurricane season on households in Florida, they found that among the 21 percent of households forced to move after the disaster, 50 percent had to do so because of the disruption of utilities such as water supply; only 37 percent had to move because of structural damage to their homes.

Various modeling studies have estimated the macroeconomic impact of disaster-related infrastructure disruptions—see, for example, Cho et al. (2001); Gordon, Richardson, and Davis (1998); Kroll et al. (1991); Rose and Wei (2013); and Tsuchiya, Tatano, and Okada (2007). By simulating the reduction in the quality of services delivered by the disrupted infrastructure, these studies were able to estimate the production losses in various sectors of an economy and evaluate the macroeconomic losses using

BOX 5.1 When natural shocks affect firms, people suffer

By destroying assets and infrastructure, earthquakes also destroy people's jobs and economic opportunities. These effects are then transmitted across sectors and supply chains. A study analyzing the likely consequences of a major earthquake in the San Francisco Bay Area in California finds that the direct and indirect consequences of such an event can be devastating. For example, a major earthquake in the Hayward fault (moment-magnitude 7.2) can result in direct losses—losses associated with the cost of asset repair—valued on average at $115 billion, or 15 percent of the Bay Area's gross domestic product (GDP). The majority of the damages (56 percent) occur in the housing sector, followed by educational services, health care, and social assistance (7 percent); and manufacturing (6 percent).

Critically, the study finds that damage to infrastructure and buildings in the private sector also causes significant indirect losses—mainly in the form of lower production as a result of damage to productive capital, supply constraints, and changes in demand. The average losses in value added total $39 billion, or an additional 5 percent of the Bay Area's GDP.

These losses accumulate over a recovery period of 10 years, but they are concentrated mainly in the first months and years following a major shock. The industries suffering the largest absolute reduction in their value added are professional and business services (37 percent of total indirect losses), followed by finance, insurance, and real estate (33 percent); and educational services, health care, and social assistance (18 percent). However, the most vulnerable sectors in relative terms (largest losses relative to their annual value added) are service industries such as repair and maintenance services and personal and laundry services, whose losses total 74 percent of their annual value added. Some economic sectors are expected to increase their production as a result of reconstruction demand, most notably the construction industry, with an average value-added increase of $11 billion during the recovery period.

These changes in production in turn affect employment and labor income across the Bay Area. The average drop in employment is 36,700 employee-years over the recovery period, with an initial drop of 8.7 percent of overall employment. The top industries affected by unemployment are the service industries—in particular, education, health care, and social assistance (15,000 employee-years); professional and business services (8,900 employee-years); and other services (8,700 employee-years). The effects on unemployment are felt all across the Bay Area (not just where the asset losses are concentrated) because employment is related to the economic health of the entire region. Overall, this study illustrates that it is essential to account for the indirect consequences of infrastructure disruption caused by natural disasters when quantifying the long-term impacts of disasters on households and individuals.

Source: Markhvida et al. 2019.

input-output or general equilibrium models. Such studies show that the impact of a disaster can spread far beyond the businesses directly affected. Through input shortages, many more firms suffer losses in production and sales, resulting in reductions in workers' incomes and a drop in demand up the supply chain. Rose and Wei (2013) investigate the impact of a 90-day disruption at the twin seaports of Beaumont and Port Arthur, Texas, and find that such indirect losses alone could reduce regional gross output by as much as $13 billion.

In another study, Rose and Liao (2005) demonstrate how a major earthquake disrupting the Portland water supply system would change the composition of economic activity in the affected regions. Several studies model the effect of blackouts on economic activity by tracing the initial impacts, such as damage to equipment and lost sales, through to further damage resulting from economic interdependencies (Anderson, Santos, and Haimes 2007; Rose, Oladosu, and Liao 2007). These impacts, like those for disrupted transport infrastructure, include effects on firms up and down the supply chain (through the cancellation of orders and lack of inputs), lower income for workers resulting in decreased consumption, and lower investments because of the lower profitability of affected firms. Rose, Oladosu, and Liao (2007) estimate the total cost of a two-week blackout in Los Angeles at $2.8 billion, or 13 percent of the city's total economic activity over that period. This figure is, however, relatively limited, thanks to multiple "resilience factors." For example, some firms are able to find a substitute for electricity or to reschedule production.

A SURVEY CONFIRMS THE COST OF NATURAL HAZARDS FOR FIRMS THROUGH INFRASTRUCTURE DISRUPTIONS

Although it is agreed that disruptions from natural hazards represent a significant cost for firms and households, local studies are needed to provide a detailed assessment. But such surveys are rare—and almost nonexistent in low- and middle-income countries—making it difficult for governments to assess the full economic losses after a disaster or to identify and prioritize investments in more resilient infrastructure. To address this gap, a dedicated questionnaire for firms was developed for this report, with the objective of providing insights on several key questions:

- What is the direct damage to firms from natural shocks (such as destroyed or damaged assets)?
- What are the indirect impacts of disrupted infrastructure (such as on workers and jobs)?
- What are the impacts on supply chains (suppliers, clients, and end users)?
- What adaptation strategies do firms use, and what are their associated costs (such as additional inventories, generators, own water sources, and tanks)?

The pilot survey was conducted in Tanzania for a sample of 800 firms, representing a wide range of economic sectors. By comparing disruption levels during the dry and the rainy seasons, the survey was able to identify the role of flooding in firm-level losses.

Overall, Tanzanian firms are incurring utilization losses of $670 million a year (or 1.8 percent of the country's GDP) from power and water outages and transport disruptions (figure 5.1).[1] Power alone is responsible for $216 million a year in losses. Of these losses, 47 percent ($101 million, or 0.3 percent of GDP) are solely due to power outages caused by rain and floods. The remaining 53 percent of utilization losses are due to baseline power outages associated with causes other than rain and flooding (such as load shedding or equipment failures).

FIGURE 5.1 Tanzanian firms report large losses from infrastructure disruptions

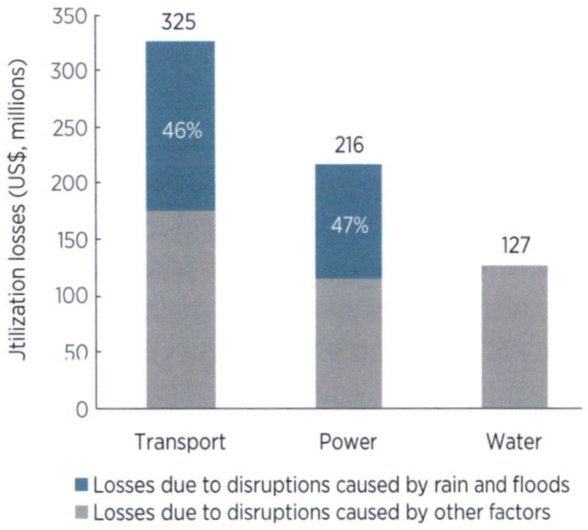

Source: Based on Rentschler, Kornejew, et al. 2019.

FIGURE 5.2 Floods in Kampala cause transport disruptions and congestion

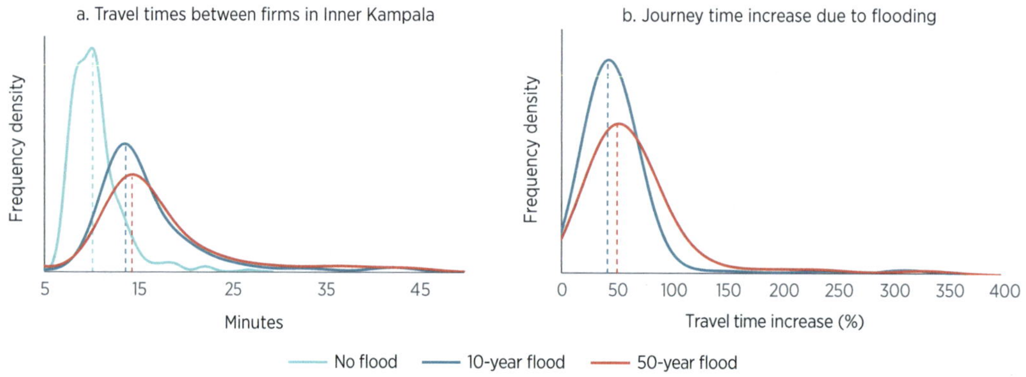

Source: Rentschler, Braese, et al. 2019.
Note: Curves show frequency densities that represent the distribution of all firm-to-firm travel times. Panel a shows the travel times between 400 firms surveyed in Kampala during road network disruptions due to urban flooding with 10- and 50-year return periods. Panel b shows the percentage increase in average travel times due to road network disruptions from urban flooding.

For transport disruptions, about 46 percent of utilization losses ($150 million, or 0.4 percent of GDP) are due to disruptions caused by rain and floods. But the survey does not find that rain and floods have a significant impact on the incidence of water supply disruptions.

Evidence from Kampala illustrates why floods have such significant impacts on firms, even though relatively few are flooded directly. By blocking road segments throughout the city, floods significantly reduce the connectivity between firms and thus the ease with which goods and services can be moved between them. For Kampala, Rentschler, Braese, et al. (2019) estimate that a moderate flood increases average travel times between firms by 54 percent. Many firms are affected even more severely: more than a quarter of firms would face an increase in average travel time of from 100 to 350 percent (figure 5.2). The prospect of such delays means that many firms will avoid undertaking trips altogether, resulting in missed deliveries and halted production. In fact, just a few flooded intersections can affect firms and their supply chains, and thus overall economic activity. These results also indicate that it does not take an extreme event to disrupt supply chains significantly.

CONSEQUENCES SPREAD THROUGH DOMESTIC AND INTERNATIONAL SUPPLY CHAINS

What about the role of supply chains? The Tanzania survey also confirms the vital role of these chains. When firms were asked why they cannot deliver on time to their clients, the most important factor cited by about a third of all firms was delays in their supply chain (figure 5.3). Interdependencies within and across supply chains can magnify the economic costs of a disaster. If a producer is hit by a disaster and forced to interrupt its operations, customers may rapidly fall short of supply, leading to disruptions that may spread further down the chain.[2]

These effects are also observed in international supply chains. In 2011 Thailand was affected by the largest floods in 70 years. The country's car manufacturing then fell by 50–80 percent. Strikingly, Toyota had the largest production loss of all carmakers, even though none of its plants were inundated. Its profit loss, which amounted to over $1.35 billion, was triggered by the disruption of critical suppliers in the flooded areas, which were unable to supply Toyota's assembly lines (Haraguchi and Lall 2015). Suppliers of damaged firms also may face sales losses, putting their finances at risk.

Supply chain effects can cross borders and have worldwide consequences. For example, a consequence of the 2011 floods in Thailand was a 30 percent decrease in the global production of hard disk drives (HDDs) in the six months after the floods, causing a price spike of between 50 and 100 percent (Haraguchi and Lall 2015). This loss was caused not only by the flooding of HDD manufacturers in Thailand, but also by the disruption of producers around the world because of the missing parts from Thailand (Chee Wai and Wongsurawat 2012). Similarly, the 2011 Great Eastern Japan Earthquake and the tsunami that followed were of global economic significance because their impacts spread well beyond the borders of Japan (Boehm, Flaaen, and Pandalai-Nayar 2015; World Economic Forum 2012).

The supply chain amplification of disasters has also been documented statistically beyond these specific case studies. Barrot and Sauvagnat (2016) find that the sales of U.S. firms affected by a natural disaster drop by about 5 percent, and the sales by their clients—even if not directly affected by the disaster—also fall by 3 percent up to 4 months after the event. Kashiwagi, Matous, and Todo (2018) find that when the ripple effects of natural disasters spread along supply chains within regions, the large firms tend to be able to switch suppliers quickly, thereby containing the spread internationally. However, studies also show that—similar to the negative effects of disruptions—the positive effects of postdisaster reconstruction subsidies can also propagate through supply chains (Kashiwagi 2019; Kashiwagi and Todo 2019). Moreover, having a geographically diverse range of suppliers and clients can alleviate the indirect impacts of a disaster and accelerate recovery (Kashiwagi, Matous, and Todo 2018; Todo, Nakajima, and Matous 2015).

The risk of a wide-ranging spread of disruptions along supply chains are a by-product of the offshoring and outsourcing strategies of the past decades. These corporate decisions have led to an unprecedented globalization and complexity of supply chains, resulting in firms becoming more specialized and interdependent (Baldwin and Lopez-Gonzalez 2015). Although only a few firms will experience a disaster directly, most firms are likely to be exposed to the indirect ripple effects of disasters. In other words, supply chains globalize local disasters and generate systemic risks (Colon et al. 2017). These risks are particularly hard to evaluate because firms often lack a full understanding of their own supply chains. Firms usually know their direct suppliers, but they often struggle to keep track of their subsuppliers, from which about half of supply disruptions seem to originate (Business Continuity Institute 2014). Supply chain managers have to deal with uncertainties, unknowns, and interdependent risks, making decision-making processes particularly complex (Doroudi et al. 2018).

Measures that firms commonly take to reduce costs and increase competitiveness can also aggravate their supply chain risks. For example, reducing inventories and streamlin-

FIGURE 5.3 Supply chain disruptions are the main reason for delivery delays

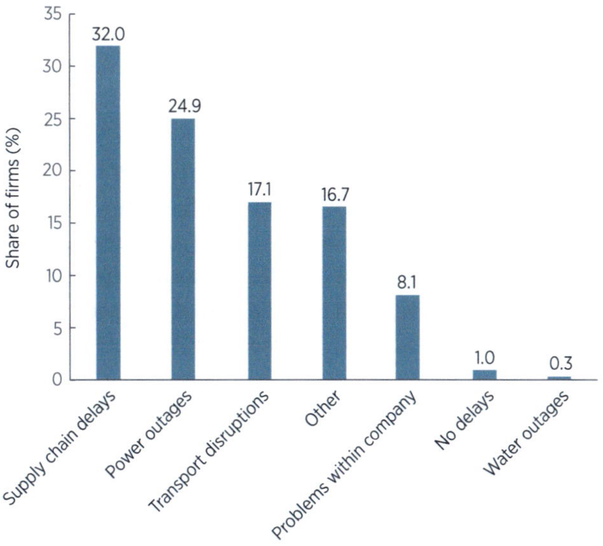

Source: World Bank staff.

ing the supplier base are effective cost-cutting measures that can be adapted to deal with frequent and lower-impact risks. However, firms with low inventories and concentrated suppliers are more exposed to low-probability and high-impact disasters because these strategies reduce flexibility and backup capacity (Stecke and Kumar 2009). Similarly, custom-made supplies may help firms to offer innovative and distinctive products, but they increase the domino effect when a disaster hits because they cannot be easily replaced by other suppliers (Barrot and Sauvagnat 2016).

SUPPLY CHAIN SIMULATIONS ENABLE BETTER MEASUREMENT OF THE MACROECONOMIC IMPACTS OF DISASTERS

So how do supply chains and transport disruptions interact? The answer is key for assessing the resilience of an economy. To shed more light on this issue, a new supply chain model was developed for this report to evaluate the impacts of transport disruptions on supply chains and household consumption in Tanzania (Colon, Hallegatte, and Rozenberg 2019). It builds on Hallegatte (2013) and Henriet, Hallegatte, and Tabourier (2012).

The model maps the domestic and international supply chains of Tanzania onto its transport network, using subnational and trade data (map 5.1, panel a). Firm-level data on coping strategies from the dedicated survey are used to calibrate the model, including the level of reserve inventories or the number of suppliers. The data clearly indicate that supply chains connect firms not only across sectors but also across the country and across borders. Physically, these connections take the form of freight flows on the road network between the main cities. Flows are particularly large around Dar es Salaam and its port, which acts as a trade hub for shipments

MAP 5.1 Mapping Tanzania's supply chains onto its transport network (panel a) reveals the impact of transport disruptions on Tanzanian households (panel b)

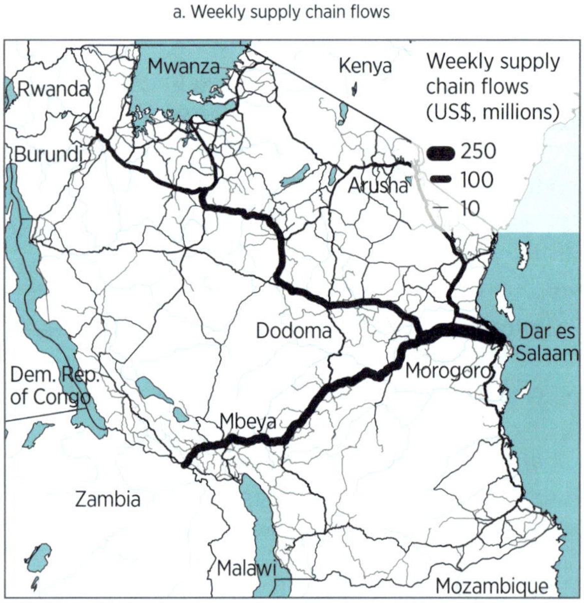

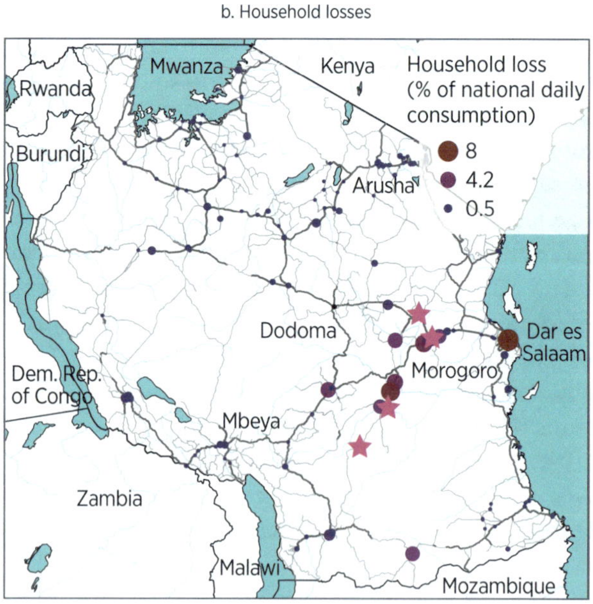

Source: Colon, Hallegatte, and Rozenberg 2019.
Note: Panel a maps weekly supply chain flows onto the road network. The width of the black lines is proportional to the monetary value of the flow. The widest lines are in the Dar es Salaam region and amount to $260 million a week. Panel b simulates the indirect impact of the 2016 Morogoro flood. The pink stars indicate the locations of disrupted roads. The size and color of the bubbles represent household losses, shown as a percentage of national daily household consumption.

to and from neighboring landlocked countries (including Burundi, the Democratic Republic of Congo, Malawi, Rwanda, Uganda, and Zambia). In monetary terms, these freight flows account for about 20 percent of the total flows. Exports and imports by Tanzanian firms also primarily transit through the port of Dar es Salaam, accounting for another 20 percent.

The model can be used to assess the consequences of a flood that in the spring of 2016 affected the Morogoro region, about 200 kilometers west of Dar es Salaam. Disruptions were long enough—about a month—to induce shortages in local supply chains (map 5.1, panel b). Overall, the estimated indirect costs for households amount to about 0.5 percent of annual consumption, mostly because of shortages in three of the largest sectors in Tanzania: agriculture, food (processed food and food-related services), and wholesale and retail trade. Figure 5.4 depicts how these impacts evolve through time and ripple across these sectors. First, consumption losses pile up during the flood. Blocked shipments of agricultural products trigger production delays in the food sector and induce product unavailability for wholesalers and retailers. After the flood, losses remain sizable for another two weeks. In the flooded area, production recovery in agriculture and the food sectors is slowed down by missing inputs from wholesalers and retailers. Particularly important is the fact that impacts on households spread, with significant consequences far from the location of floods, such as around Dar es Salam (map 5.1, panel b).

Applying this model allows disasters of different magnitudes and locations to be simulated, revealing useful insights. For example, simulating similar transport disruptions that vary in duration shows that the macroeconomic impact increases nonlinearly with the duration of the disruption. A four-week disruption is on average 23 times costlier for households than a two-week disruption. This result highlights the large benefit of responding rapidly to a disaster and building back quickly, which depend on the systems in place for road system maintenance

FIGURE 5.4 Long-duration floods trigger disruptions in Tanzania, with cascading impacts on supply chains and households

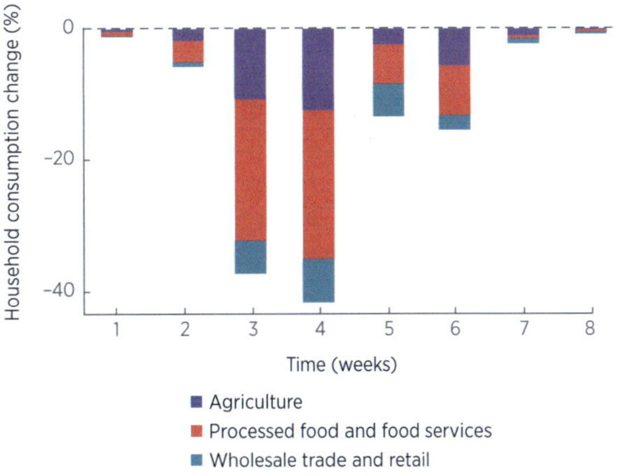

Source: Colon, Hallegatte, and Rozenberg 2019. The flood occurs from week 1 to week 4, but impacts on households continue after the flood is over.

and the availability of financial resources after a disaster (see the discussion in the recommendation chapters in part III).

Sectors also differ in their vulnerability to transport disruption. For example, because agricultural products are primary products, they are less dependent on suppliers, which reduces their vulnerability. Impacts on food products and manufacturing are, by contrast, magnified by supply chain issues. By applying this model, it is possible to assess the most vulnerable firms and municipalities, depending not only on their location but also on their economic structure. It is then possible to target interventions to strengthen the resilience of firms and supply chains where it matters the most, which can be far from where disruptions are the most likely to occur.

Such analyses make it possible to assess the relative importance of individual segments of infrastructure networks for enabling supply chains and to identify the most vulnerable users of infrastructure services. By identifying bottlenecks and vulnerability hotspots, they help to prioritize investments and develop resilience strategies—the topic of the next part of this report.

NOTES

1. See chapter 2 for details on firms' utilization losses due to infrastructure disruptions.
2. These ripple effects can even take place within a factory, if one segment of the production process is impossible and therefore interrupts the entire production.

REFERENCES

Anderson, C. W., J. R. Santos, and Y. Y. Haimes. 2007. "A Risk-Based Input-Output Methodology for Measuring the Effects of the August 2003 Northeast Blackout." *Economic Systems Research* 19 (2): 183–204.

Baldwin, R., and J. Lopez-Gonzalez. 2015. "Supply-Chain Trade: A Portrait of Global Patterns and Several Testable Hypotheses." *World Economy* 38 (11): 1682–721.

Baqaee, D. R., and E. Farhi. 2017. "The Macroeconomic Impact of Microeconomic Shocks: Beyond Hulten's Theorem." 2017 Meeting Paper 479, Society for Economic Dynamics.

Barrot, J.-N., and J. Sauvagnat. 2016. "Input Specificity and the Propagation of Idiosyncratic Shocks in Production Networks." *Quarterly Journal of Economics* 131 (3): 1543–92.

BBC (British Broadcasting Corporation). 2010. "Iceland Volcano: Nissan and BMW Suspend Some Production." *BBC News*, April 20.

Boehm, C., A. Flaaen, and N. Pandalai-Nayar. 2015. "Input Linkages and the Transmission of Shocks: Firm-Level Evidence from the 2011 Tōhoku Earthquake." CES 15-28, Center for Economic Studies, Washington, DC.

Business Continuity Institute. 2014. "Supply Chain Resilience 2014: An International Survey to Consider the Origin, Causes, and Consequences of Supply Chain Disruption." BCI, Caversham, U.K.

Chee Wai, L., and W. Wongsurawat. 2013. "Crisis Management: Western Digital's 46 Day Recovery from the 2011 Flood Disaster in Thailand." *Strategy & Leadership* 41 (1): 34–38.

Cho, S., P. Gordon, J. E. Moore II, H. W. Richardson, M. Shinozuka, and S. Chang. 2001. "Integrating Transportation Network and Regional Economic Models to Estimate the Costs of a Large Urban Earthquake." *Journal of Regional Science* 41 (1): 39–65.

Colon, C., Å. Brännström, E. Rovenskaya, and U. Dieckmann. 2017. "Fragmentation of Production Amplifies Systemic Risks in Supply Chains." Interim Report, International Institute for Applied Systems Analysis (IIASA), Laxenburg, Austria.

Colon, C., S. Hallegatte, and J. Rozenberg. 2019. "Transportation and Supply Chain Resilience in the United Republic of Tanzania." Background paper for this report, World Bank, Washington, DC.

Doroudi, R., R. Azghandi, Z. Feric, O. Mohaddesi, Y. Sun, J. Griffin, O. Ergun, D. Kaeli, P. Sequeira, S. Marsella, and C. Harteveld. 2018. "An Integrated Simulation Framework for Examining Resiliency in Pharmaceutical Supply Chains Considering Human Behaviours." In *Proceedings of the 2018 Winter Simulation Conference*, edited by M. Rabe, A. A. Juan, N. Mustafee, A. Skoogh, S. Jain, and B. Johansson. Piscataway, NJ: IEEE Press.

Gordon, P., H. W. Richardson, and B. Davis. 1998. "Transport-Related Impacts of the Northridge Earthquake." National Emergency Training Center, Emmitsburg, MD.

Hallegatte, S. 2013. "Modeling the Roles of Heterogeneity, Substitution, and Inventories in the Assessment of Natural Disaster Economic Costs." *Risk Analysis* 34 (1): 152–67.

Hallegatte, S., and A. Vogt-Schilb. 2016. "Are Losses from Natural Disasters More Than Just Asset Losses? The Role of Capital Aggregation, Sector Interactions, and Investment Behaviors." Policy Research Working Paper 7885, World Bank, Washington, DC.

Hallegatte, S., A. Vogt-Schilb, M. Bangalore, and J. Rozenberg. 2016. *Unbreakable: Building the Resilience of the Poor in the Face of Natural Disasters*. Washington, DC: World Bank.

Haraguchi, M., and U. Lall. 2015. "Flood Risks and Impacts: A Case Study of Thailand's Floods in 2011 and Research Questions for Supply Chain Decision Making." *International Journal of Disaster Risk Reduction* 14 (3): 256–72.

Henriet, F., S. Hallegatte, and L. Tabourier. 2012. "Firm-Network Characteristics and Economic Robustness to Natural Disasters." *Journal of Economic Dynamics and Control* 36 (1): 150–67.

Kashiwagi, Y. 2019. *Enterprise Resilience to Disasters: Who Needs Public Support?* RIETI Discussion Paper 19-E-029. Tokyo: Research Institute on Economy, Trade, and Industry.

Kashiwagi, Y., P. Matous, and Y. Todo. 2018. "International Propagation of Economic Shocks through Global Supply Chains." WINPEC Working Paper E1810, Waseda Institute of Political Economy, Waseda University, Tokyo.

Kashiwagi, Y., and Y. Todo. 2019. *Propagation of Positive Effects of Post-Disaster Policies through Supply Chains: Evidence from the Great East Japan Earthquake.* RIETI Discussion Paper 19-E-030. Tokyo: Research Institute on Economy, Trade, and Industry.

Kroll, C. A., J. D. Landis, Q. Shen, and S. Stryker. 1991. "Economic Impacts of the Loma Prieta Earthquake: A Focus on Small Businesses." *Berkeley Planning Journal* 5 (1): 38–58.

Markhvida, M., B. Walsh, S. Hallegatte, and J. Baker. 2019. "Well-Being Loss: A Comprehensive Metric for Household Disaster Resilience." EarthArXiv. May 17. doi:10.31223/osf.io/6r93z.

McCarty, C., and S. K. Smith. 2005. "Florida's 2004 Hurricane Season: Local Effects." *Florida Focus* 1 (3): 1–13. Bureau of Economic and Business Research, University of Florida.

Munich Re. 2019. *Natural Catastrophe Review 2018.* Munich: Munich Re.

Rentschler, J., J. Braese, N. Jones, and P. Avner. 2019. "Three Feet Under: The Impact of Flooding on Urban Jobs, Connectivity, and Infrastructure." Background paper for this report, World Bank, Washington, DC.

Rentschler, J., M. Kornejew, S. Hallegatte, M. Obolensky, and J. Braese. 2019. "Underutilized Potential: The Business Costs of Unreliable Infrastructure in Developing Countries." Background paper for this report, World Bank, Washington, DC.

Rose, A., and S.-Y. Liao. 2005. "Modeling Regional Economic Resilience to Disasters: A Computable General Equilibrium Analysis of Water Service Disruptions." *Journal of Regional Science* 45 (1): 75–112.

Rose, A., G. Oladosu, and S.-Y. Liao. 2007. "Business Interruption Impacts of a Terrorist Attack on the Electric Power System of Los Angeles: Customer Resilience to a Total Blackout." *Risk Analysis* 27 (3): 513–31.

Rose, A., and D. Wei. 2013. "Estimating the Economic Consequences of a Port Shutdown: The Special Role of Resilience." *Economic Systems Research* 25 (2): 212–32.

Stecke, K. E., and S. Kumar. 2009. "Sources of Supply Chain Disruptions, Factors That Breed Vulnerability, and Mitigating Strategies." *Journal of Marketing Channels* 16 (3): 193–226.

Swiss Re. 2018. "Preliminary Sigma Estimates for 2018: Global Insured Losses of USD 79 Billion Are Fourth Highest on Sigma Records." Swiss Re, December 18.

Todo, Y., K. Nakajima, and P. Matous. 2015. "How Do Supply Chain Networks Affect the Resilience of Firms to Natural Disasters? Evidence from the Great East Japan Earthquake." *Journal of Regional Science* 55 (2): 209–29.

Tsuchiya, S., H. Tatano, and N. Okada. 2007. "Economic Loss Assessment Due to Railroad and Highway Disruptions." *Economic Systems Research* 19 (2): 147–62.

World Economic Forum. 2012. *New Models for Addressing Supply Chain and Transport Risk.* Geneva: World Economic Forum.

PART II

A Matter of Design: Resilient Infrastructure Is Cost-Effective

Part I of this report highlights the high costs of infrastructure disruptions and damages—for infrastructure asset owners and governments, for firms, and for households—and the important role that natural hazards and climate change play in these costs. Part II investigates how these costs may be reduced through engineering and planning solutions that can help to make infrastructure more resilient.

It does so by exploring the resilience of infrastructure at three levels (figure PII.1):

1. *Resilience of infrastructure assets.* In the narrowest sense, resilient infrastructure refers to assets such as roads, bridges, and power lines that can withstand external shocks, especially natural ones. Here, the benefit of more resilient infrastructure is a reduction in the life-cycle cost of assets.

2. *Resilience of infrastructure services.* Infrastructure systems are interconnected networks, and the resilience of individual assets is a poor proxy for the resilience of services provided at the network level. For infrastructure, a systemic approach to resilience is preferable. At this level, the benefit of more resilient infrastructure is the provision of more reliable services.

FIGURE PII.1 The resilience of infrastructure needs to be considered at several overlapping and complementary levels

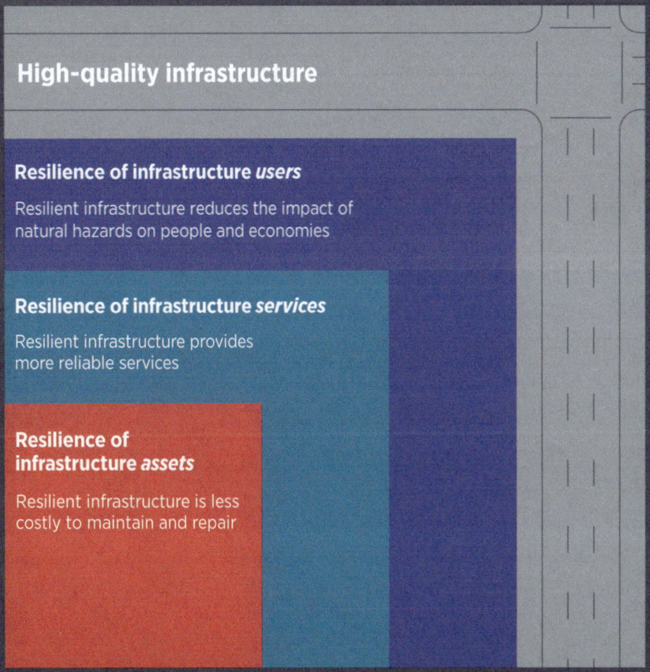

3. *Resilience of infrastructure users.* Eventually, what matters is the resilience of users. Infrastructure disruptions can be catastophic or more benign, depending on whether users—including people and supply chains—can cope with them. At this level, the benefit of more resilient infrastructure is a reduction in the total impact of natural hazards on people and economies.

Resilience is one of the many determinants of high-quality infrastructure. However, integrating resilience into the design and implementation of infrastructure investments not only helps to manage natural shocks but also complements the cost-effectiveness, efficiency, and quality of infrastructure services more generally.

Following this framework, chapter 6 explores how infrastructure assets can be made more resilient (such as stronger bridges and better-designed power transmission systems); provides an estimate of the additional cost of investing in more resilient assets, which is small compared with the cost of the assets; and offers a cost-benefit analysis of key options to increase resilience, which turn out to be cost-efficient. Then chapter 7 expands the analysis to examine the resilience of infrastructure services—demonstrating that the cost of resilience can be reduced by working at the network and system levels and considering nature-based solutions. Finally, chapter 8 explores the role of the users of infrastructure services and how their actions can contribute to more resilient economies and societies (such as through more resilient supply chains and business continuity plans).

More Resilient Infrastructure Assets Are Cost-Effective 6

How do countries increase the resilience of their infrastructure systems? One solution is to build assets that can withstand bigger shocks, such as cell phone towers with deeper foundations and roads with larger culverts. Doing so can prevent damage from natural hazards and generate significant benefits in terms of lower repair costs and maintenance needs over the life cycle of the asset. But to be resilient, assets not only need to be strong; they also need to be well maintained, which requires a steady flow of resources as well as processes and systems.

This chapter discusses the options for enhanced resilience at the asset level. Using a set of scenarios of infrastructure investments developed by Rozenberg and Fay (2019), it also assesses the additional costs of making all new infrastructure assets more resilient in low- and middle-income countries. It finds that the cost of building the resilience of infrastructure assets in these countries is small compared with total infrastructure needs, provided the right data and approaches are available. Building resilience does not affect current affordability challenges and is robust and cost-effective.

THE ADDITIONAL UP-FRONT COST OF MORE RESILIENT ASSETS DEPENDS ON THE ASSET AND THE HAZARD

Interventions to develop more resilient assets include using alternative materials, digging deeper foundations, elevating assets, building flood protection around the asset, or adding redundant components. Deeper foundations for power plants, windmills, or water treatment plants are often needed to protect them against earthquake liquefaction. Better materials for wind turbines, cell phone towers, and transmission and distribution systems can increase their resistance to strong winds and extend their lifetime. Increasing the redundancy of components of water and wastewater treatment plants by adding backup components can improve the performance of plants during earthquakes. Building higher dikes around water treatment plants and nuclear plants is the best option for protecting them against floods.

In a review performed for this report, Miyamoto International (2019) presents a high-level assessment of the costs and benefits of these various technical and engineering options (see Appendix A for an overview of these options and their performance). The additional cost of making assets stronger in the face of natural hazards depends on the hazard and the type of asset. Increasing the flood resilience of a road through bigger drainage pipes or trenches requires a small percentage of the road's construction cost, while increasing the flood resilience of a railway by elevating it requires 50 percent of its costs. Similarly, protecting a hydropower plant against earthquakes by installing the proper anchorage and seismic components requires 20 percent of its construction cost, whereas protecting a hydropower plant against flooding through bigger spillway capacity requires 3 percent of its cost (Miyamoto International 2019). In Puerto Rico, a study of the recovery after Hurricanes Irma and Maria finds that the cost of building back better, when compared with baseline estimates, varies greatly in magnitude, depending on the component and the hazard against which it should be protected. There is a 3–40 percent increase in the cost to upgrade transmission and distribution infrastructure to withstand category 3 hurricanes and a 24–70 percent increase in cost to upgrade to withstand category 4 hurricanes (130 miles per hour sustained wind speeds). When wooden power poles (low wind speed design) are compared with tubular steel poles, for example, the cost may differ by as much as 200 percent (Schweikert et al. 2019).

Some resilience-building interventions can even lower the cost of assets. With advances in construction technology, some low-cost technologies perform better than traditional approaches. Meanwhile, advanced materials and methods are making infrastructure both less expensive and more climate-resilient. One example is modular bridge solutions that encase the deck structure of a bridge in stainless steel. This approach results in a significantly longer design life of up to 100 years with lower maintenance costs—a performance well beyond that achieved with the traditional in situ reinforced concrete. Construction costs are also lower because a standardized formwork (including reinforcement) can be delivered to a site in a container, with deck casting conducted in a single pour, as opposed to the longer times and complex formwork needed for traditional in situ structures (World Bank 2017).

Improved quality control is required to ensure that an asset is actually built and maintained to expected standards. Miyamoto International (2019) estimates that this quality control costs from 1 percent to 5 percent of the value for most assets and hazards, but it can cost up to 15 percent to ensure that drainage systems can cope with earthquake motion and highway systems can cope with flooding. This

BOX 6.1 Infrastructure unit costs vary from country to country

Infrastructure unit costs vary widely across countries and over time. For example, the unit cost of sewage collection and treatment, as examined by Hutton and Varughese (2016), is less than $100 in Guinea, Nepal, and Somalia, but more than $1,000 in Costa Rica, Papua New Guinea, and Sudan. Similar spreads exist for all of the technologies considered for water and sanitation infrastructure. For rural roads, a single surface treatment can cost anywhere from $10,000 per kilometer in the Lao People's Democratic Republic to $65,000 per kilometer in Armenia (World Bank 2018). Unit costs also vary within countries. The unit cost of dikes varies between $6 million and $17 million per meter height and kilometer width for urban areas in the Netherlands, the United Kingdom, and Vietnam (Nicholls et al. 2019).

Many factors can explain these spreads—from variations in the cost of local labor and materials to vast differences in the efficiency of public spending, the prevalence of corruption, and the

(Box continues next page)

BOX 6.1 Infrastructure unit costs vary from country to country *(continued)*

lack of competition in public procurement. In the road sector, for example, collusion can increase the per-kilometer cost of building a road by as much as 40 percent (Messick 2011). In South Africa, the difference between the price charged by a cement cartel during collusive and noncollusive periods was 7.5–9.7 percent. The total savings to South African customers from the breakup of the cartel was from $79 million to $100 million between 2010 and 2013 (World Bank and OECD 2017). In Bangladesh, the introduction of transparent and competitive procurement procedures led to a substantial reduction in electricity prices, whereas in Pakistan, it saved more than Rs 187 million ($3.1 million) for the Karachi Water and Sewerage Board (World Bank and OECD 2017).

Although the lack of efficiency and competition in public procurement can explain a large share of the spread in unit costs, understanding why building infrastructure is far more expensive in some countries than others would require extensive analysis that is beyond the scope of this report.

quality control would accompany the good procurement practices that are key to lower infrastructure construction costs (box 6.1).

THE ADDITIONAL UP-FRONT COST OF MORE RESILIENT ASSETS COULD BE OFFSET BY LOWER MAINTENANCE AND REPAIR COSTS

The decision to invest more up-front in making infrastructure assets more resilient should depend on many criteria, including the current and future exposure of the asset, the consequences of failure compared with the level of risk acceptable to users, and the life-cycle cost savings generated by the higher up-front cost.

More resilient energy systems would reduce life-cycle costs. Schweikert et al. (2019) find that above-ground transmission systems are the energy system component most commonly affected by wind, debris, ice, fires, floods, earthquakes, and landslides. Wires buried below ground are affected by flooding, liquefaction, and landslides, but they are much less vulnerable overall than those above ground. In New Zealand, case studies following the earthquakes in 2010–11 highlight the value of preemptive investment in transmission and distribution infrastructure. According to the estimates, $6 million spent to harden transmission and distribution infrastructure resulted in a $30 million to $50 million reduction in direct asset replacement costs (Kestrel Group 2011). Recently, the World Bank conducted a study analyzing the impact of climate risks on the planned energy system expansion in Bangladesh, a country highly vulnerable to climate change. The analysis determined that accounting for climate change in the design increases capital requirements by $560 million for additional flood protection but could save up to $1.6 billion (Oguah and Khosla 2017).

The use of earthquake-resistant pipes for water supply systems would pay off in areas exposed to earthquakes. A pilot project undertaken in Los Angeles, by the Los Angeles Department of Water and Power revealed the benefits of making up-front improvements (Davis and Castruita 2013). The 1994 Northridge Earthquake caused numerous failures in the network, leading to repair costs of around $41 million. By contrast, the earthquake-resistant ductile iron pipes (ERDIPs) used in Japan have survived many large earthquakes and have sustained several meters of permanent ground deformation. Replacing the old piping system in Los Angeles with ERDIPs increased the total cost of the pilot project by about 20 percent.

IMPROVING MAINTENANCE AND OPERATIONS IS AN OPTION FOR BOOSTING RESILIENCE AND REDUCING COSTS

Improving maintenance and operations is a no-regret option for boosting the resilience of infrastructure assets while reducing overall costs. Rozenberg and Fay (2019) find that, without good maintenance, infrastructure capital costs could increase 50 percent in the transport sector and more than 60 percent in the water sector. An analysis of member countries of the Organisation for Economic Co-operation and Development performed for this report suggests that every additional $1 spent on road maintenance saves on average $1.50 in new investments, making better maintenance a very cost-effective option (Kornejew, Rentschler, and Hallegatte 2019).

There is indeed strong evidence that good maintenance increases the lifetime of assets. In Salzburg, most water pipelines are more than 100 years old, but they suffer very low water losses because of an effective strategic maintenance plan (European Union 2015). In addition, maintenance is critical for ensuring that assets can withstand extreme events. The World Bank (2017) argues that better asset management systems and better maintenance should be the number one priority for small island developing states in order to increase the resilience of their transport systems. The report finds that improved road maintenance could reduce asset losses by 12 percent in Belize and 18 percent in Tonga.

For energy systems, good maintenance of the vegetation on each side of power transmission lines is crucial to reducing vulnerability to strong winds. Such maintenance requires easements of 20–100 meters (figure 6.1). As described in chapter 4, power outages during storms occur especially in areas with forest cover. Indeed, during storms, flying debris and vegetation are the primary causes of pole damage, not the strong winds themselves. Therefore, reinforcing poles is less efficient than

FIGURE 6.1 Clearing vegetation around transmission and subtransmission electricity networks requires an easement

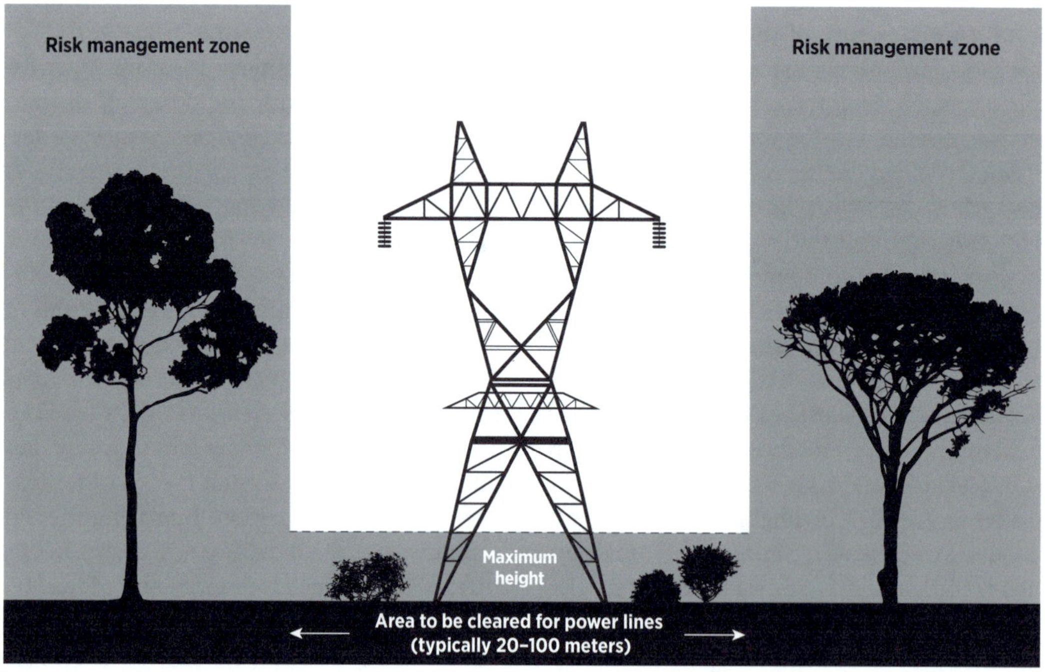

trimming trees. In September 2017, Hurricanes Irma and Maria severely damaged the power grid in Puerto Rico, largely because of trees falling on the transmission lines. As a result, 100 percent of Puerto Rico Electric Power Authority customers lost power for more than a week after the storm, and the slow pace of recovery left many customers in the dark for several months (U.S. Department of Energy 2018).

Good forest maintenance can also prevent wildfires. Wildfires are a unique threat to transmission and distribution infrastructure. Various case studies illustrate that during high-risk conditions (droughts, high temperatures, high winds), curtailments are used to reduce the risk of transmission infrastructure causing a wildfire. The potential risk was illustrated in California in 2007, when San Diego Gas and Electric was found liable for causing three fires that led to three deaths and the destruction of 1,300 homes. The utility ultimately paid out $2 billion in settlements (Daniels 2017). Recent wildfires have put the large utility Pacific Gas and Electric under scrutiny due to $10 billion in liabilities from fires in 2017 and unknown amounts from fires in 2018 (McNeely 2018).

In water supply networks, good maintenance reduces water losses. Lack of maintenance often leads to deterioration of pipes and failure of valves, which in turn leads to physical losses in the distribution system called nonrevenue water. A 2006 study estimates that every year more than 32 billion cubic meters of treated water physically leak from the world's urban water supply systems, with half of these losses in low- and middle-income countries (Kingdom, Liemberger, and Marin 2006). In addition, when maintenance is irregular, a water system is less likely to be inspected and thus well known by technicians, increasing the likelihood that illegal connections will go unnoticed and cause commercial losses (water that is treated and delivered to users but not billed). The same study estimates total losses at 16 billion cubic meters a year globally. In low- and middle-income countries, the estimated loss is $5.8 billion a year, of which $2.6 billion are commercial losses. According to Kingdom, Liemberger, and Marin (2006, 4), it is "not unrealistic to expect that the high levels of physical losses could be reduced by half" through improved leak detection, pipe replacement, and maintenance, thereby saving 8 billion cubic meters of treated water a year. Such programs lead to better-quality services, higher utility revenues, and a positive financial flow that enables future investment in rehabilitation and maintenance, which in turn enhances resilience.

New technology can be deployed to improve maintenance at a low cost. Sensors with telemetry are already being deployed to monitor pressure and flow, minimizing losses and improving system maintenance. The ePulse system was used in Washington, DC, during pipe replacement works. Condition assessment found that 32 kilometers of pipe were in good condition, numerous leaks were located, and $14 million in investments were saved. Miniaturized robots are also being tested for deployment in pipes to identify leaks. Fiber-optic cable can be used to detect very small leaks by measuring variations in the signal in an external fiber, before the leaks develop into larger leaks and burst a pipe.

Finally, regular cleaning of canals and drainage systems is essential for ensuring the reliability of flood protection systems. In many low- and middle-income countries, the current flood protection systems do not deliver the intended protection, because canals and drainage pipes are clogged by solid waste. Long-term solutions have to include solid waste management, but regular cleaning of canals would also increase the efficiency of the system.

THE COST OF INCREASING RESILIENCE DEPENDS ON THE ABILITY TO SPATIALLY TARGET STRENGTHENING

How much do low- and middle-income countries need to spend on infrastructure to achieve their development goals? A new study by Rozenberg and Fay (2019) estimates that it would take between 2 percent and 8 percent of low- and middle-income countries' gross domestic product (GDP), depending on the countries' objectives (in terms of service provision) and spending efficiency (box 6.2). The next question then becomes, by how much would estimates change if infrastructure systems were designed and built in a more resilient

BOX 6.2 Large investments in infrastructure will be necessary to close the service gap

In an effort to shift the debate on infrastructure investment needs away from spending more and toward spending better on the right objectives, a recent study by Rozenberg and Fay (2019) offers a new way forward. They use a systematic approach to estimate the funding needs (capital and operations and maintenance) for closing the service gap in water and sanitation, transport, electricity, irrigation, and flood protection by 2030. (Telecommunications is not included in their analysis because it is mostly privately funded.)

They estimate that new infrastructure could cost low- and middle-income countries between 2 percent and 8 percent of their GDP a year to 2030, depending on the quality and quantity of infrastructure services sought and the spending efficiency achieved to reach this goal (table B6.2.1). Moreover, with the right policies, investments of 4.5 percent of GDP could enable low- and middle-income countries to achieve the infrastructure-related Sustainable Development Goals and stay on track to full decarbonization by the second half of the century.

The ambitious goals and high efficiency of Rozenberg and Fay's "preferred scenario" depend on smart policies and good planning. Countries would take long-term climate goals into account now to avoid expensive stranded assets later; they would combine transport planning with land use planning, resulting in denser cities and cheaper and more reliable public transport; and they would develop reliable railway systems that freight haulers would find attractive. Decentralized technologies, such as minigrids for electricity and water purification systems powered by renewable energy, would be deployed in rural areas.

However, improving services requires much more than capital expenditures. Success will depend on ensuring a steady flow of resources for operations and maintenance. In the preferred scenario, low- and middle-income countries would need to spend 2.7 percent of GDP a year to maintain their existing and new infrastructure, in addition to the 4.5 percent of GDP in new capital (table B6.2.1). Meanwhile, good maintenance generates substantial savings, reducing the total life-cycle cost of transport and water and sanitation infrastructure by more than 50 percent.

TABLE B6.2.1 With the right policies in place, investments of 4.5 percent of GDP in infrastructure may be needed

Infrastructure spending on capital and maintenance needs in low- and middle-income countries between 2015 and 2030, by sector

	Share of GDP (%)		US$ (billions)	
Sector	Capital	Maintenance	Capital	Maintenance
Electricity	2.2	0.6	780	210
Transport	1.3	1.3	420	460
Water and sanitation	0.55	0.75	200	70
Flood protection	0.32	0.07	100	20
Irrigation	0.13	—	50	—
Total	4.5	2.7	1,550	760

Source: Rozenberg and Fay 2019.
Note: — = maintenance costs of irrigation infrastructure are included in the capital costs.

manner, through the technical and engineering solutions identified in Miyamoto International (2019)? These options—listed in Appendix A—have been selected because they are realistic and can make assets more resilient in low- and middle-income countries. However, they are not necessarily the ones that will reduce risk the most, and they do not guarantee that assets cannot be damaged by natural hazards. Many high-income countries, like Japan, implement technical solutions that go beyond—and are more expensive than—the set of solutions considered in this analysis.

Because the incremental costs of making assets more resilient can be significant, it is important to target strengthening to areas where exposure to natural disasters is high. Ideally, infrastructure standards and codes should be asset and localization specific. Road designs should account for the hydrological and hydraulic data and climate model results at the location of the road in order to account for the range of impacts that climate change can have on the probability of flood events in the future. For electricity distribution systems—because they are particularly vulnerable to wind from storms, hurricanes, and typhoons—historical data and model results on wind velocities with hour-level resolution could be used for a geospatial analysis to inform risk and design standards in many regions of the world. Data on water availability for cooling is also central to planning for electricity generation.

The analysis used in this report explores two extreme scenarios in terms of the knowledge on the spatial distribution of natural hazards and the ability to target strengthening to the places exposed to them (Hallegatte et al. 2019). In the first scenario, it is assumed that the location and intensity of the hazard are perfectly known, now and in the future, and that different standards can be applied in different locations, depending on the level of risk. In the second scenario, it is assumed that the hazard is unknown, or is too uncertain to be acted on, and that a uniform standard has to be applied to the full network. In both scenarios, it is assumed that future infrastructure assets are exposed in a similar fashion to the existing infrastructure in each region (in other words, on average, the space available for future infrastructure location is exposed to the same level of hazards as the space already used). Results for these two scenarios are compared here for three infrastructure systems: power, transport, and water and sanitation.

Power

In the power sector, baseline investment needs, assuming current resilience levels, would range from $298 billion to $1 trillion a year in low- and middle-income countries between 2015 and 2030. This depends on energy efficiency and the timing of the transition toward carbon-free power generation (which creates stranded assets, such as coal power plants that need to be decommissioned before the end of their lifetime). In addition, between $106 billion and $282 billion a year would be needed for maintenance. How would those costs increase to make power systems more resilient?

- *Scenario 1.* If only exposed assets are made more resilient to hazards, the incremental cost would rise from $9 billion to $27 billion a year, which represents a 3 percent cost increase on average across the spending range and a 6 percent cost increase in the most expensive case. These investments would reduce the damage risk by a factor of two to three for new infrastructure assets.
- *Scenario 2.* If, instead, all new power assets were made more resilient to wind, floods, and earthquakes, because data on natural hazards are not available, then an additional $96 billion to $296 billion a year would be needed. This is a 30 percent increase in capital cost on average over the spending range and a 10-fold increase compared with that in the scenario for which hazard data are available.

Transport

In the transport sector, baseline investment needs—with current resilience standards—could range from $157 billion to $1.1 trillion a year between 2015 and 2030 in low- and middle-income countries. The exact value would depend on the choice of mode (such as personal cars versus public transit in cities) and on the policies put in place to encourage switching to rail and public transport. In addition, between $550 billion and $700 billion would be needed every year to maintain the existing and new transport infrastructure in low- and middle-income countries by 2030, bringing the total annual spending needs to between $700 billion and $1.8 trillion. How would those costs increase to make transport systems more resilient?

- *Scenario 1.* The incremental cost of making new exposed transport assets more resilient to floods and landslides lies between $860 million and $35 billion. This is a 0.6 percent increase in cost, on average, across the spending range and potentially a 5 percent increase in the most expensive case. These investments would reduce the risk of damage for new infrastructure by a factor of two. According to Koks et al. (2019), these investments would pay for themselves through the lower repair costs for about 60 percent of roads exposed to a 1/100-year flood event (4.5 percent of the network).
- *Scenario 2.* If, instead, all new transport assets were made more resilient to floods and landslides regardless of their exposure, the incremental cost would range from $8 billion to $350 billion a year. This is a 5.5 percent increase in cost, on average, across the spending range, but potentially a 17 percent increase in the most expensive case for many rail investments. Considering the benefit of upgrades to be only the cost of repairs after a disaster, Koks et al. (2019) estimate that the benefit-cost ratio of strengthening all transport infrastructure is less than 1—suggesting that, in the absence of hazard data, it is not cost-effective to strengthen all assets in transport systems.

Water and sanitation

In the water supply and sanitation sector, the cost of providing universal access to safe water and sanitation in low- and middle-income countries by 2030, with the current resilience level, would range from $116 billion to $229 billion a year for capital investments and from $32 billion to $69 billion a year for maintenance. How would those costs increase to make water and sanitation systems more resilient?

- *Scenario 1.* The cost of protecting new exposed water assets would be between $0.9 billion and $2.3 billion a year (assuming that, on average, water and sanitation infrastructure has the same exposure to earthquakes as transport and power assets). These investments would reduce the risk of damage to new infrastructure by 50 percent.
- *Scenario 2.* Instead, if all water assets were made more resilient to floods, an additional $2 billion to $5 billion a year would be required. This estimate represents a 1.1 percent to 2.2 percent increase in capital costs. Increasing the resilience of these assets to earthquakes would require an additional $8 billion to $20 billion a year (or between 5 percent and 9 percent of capital investment needs).

SUMMING UP

Unfortunately, similar estimates were not possible for telecommunications, and these numbers only include low- and middle-income countries. Yet this exercise provides three important insights.

First, there is huge value in knowing the spatial distribution of natural hazards, including climate change. Focusing the strengthening of infrastructure assets on exposed assets reduces total annual costs from between $120 billion and $670 billion to between $11 billion and $65 billion (figure 6.2). The savings from targeting the infrastructure assets most exposed appear to be orders of magnitude larger than the costs of data collection and modeling that would be required to improve knowledge of current and future hazards. Indeed, a global platform like Think Hazard! (Fraser 2017), which compiled most of the hazards data that were used for the risk assessments in this report (see chapter 4), costs a few million dollars to create and maintain. At most, creating high-resolution digital elevation models and hazard maps for all cities in low- and middle-income countries would cost a few hundred million dollars (Croneborg et al. 2015).

Second, the cost of building the resilience of infrastructure assets in low- and middle-income countries is small compared with total infrastructure needs, provided the right data and approaches are available. Increasing the resilience of only the assets exposed to hazards would increase investment needs in power, transport, and water and sanitation by between $11 billion and $65 billion a year. While not negligible, this is only around 3 percent of baseline infrastructure investment needs and less than 0.1 percent of the GDP of low- and middle-income countries. Therefore, making infrastructure more resilient does not affect current affordability challenges for new infrastructure, and it would decrease the risk of damage for new infrastructure by a factor of between two and three.

Third, these investments to increase infrastructure resilience are cost-effective. In transport, where an asset-per-asset cost-benefit analysis is possible, 60 percent of the exposed assets are worth strengthening, even if the only benefits included are the avoided repair costs. However, avoided repairs are far from being the only benefits of strengthened assets (chapters 2, 3, and 5 of this report review the costs associated with disruptions).

What are the returns on investments for making exposed infrastructure more resilient to natural disasters? The uncertainty pertaining to the cost of infrastructure resilience and the benefits in terms of both avoided repairs and disruptions for households and firms make it difficult to provide a single estimate for the benefit-cost ratio of strengthening exposed infrastructure assets. To manage this uncertainty, an analysis performed for this report explores the benefit-cost ratio in 3,000 scenarios (Hallegatte et al. 2019). These scenarios combine uncertainties regarding the cost of the technical options to increase resilience, the current and future exposure of infrastructure assets to natural hazards, the current and future role of natural hazards in infrastructure disruptions, and their full social costs to firms and households. In addition, the analysis considers various assumptions about economic growth, the depreciation rate of the existing infrastructure stock, and the impacts of climate change on natural hazards.

Results suggest that strengthening infrastructure assets exposed to natural hazards is a very robust investment. The benefit-cost ratio is higher than 1 in 96 percent of the scenarios, larger than 2 in 77 percent of them, and higher

FIGURE 6.2 The incremental cost of increasing the resilience of future infrastructure investments is significantly reduced if asset exposure is known

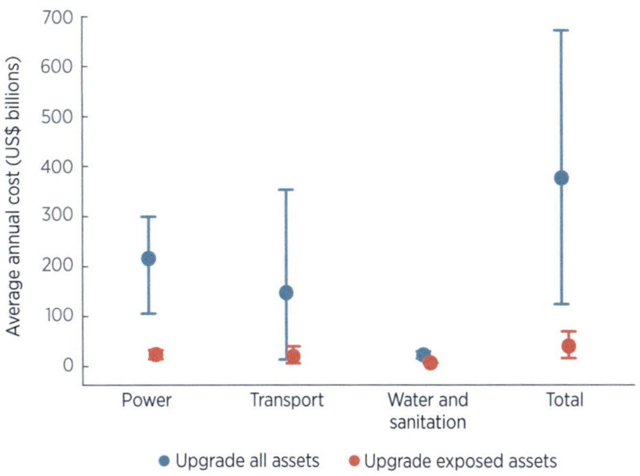

Source: Hallegatte et al. 2019.
Note: "Cost " here is the average annual capital investment cost between 2015 and 2030. The circles represent the median, and the vertical bars represent the full range of possible incremental costs.

FIGURE 6.3 Increasing the resilience of future infrastructure investments is cost-efficient—even more so with climate change

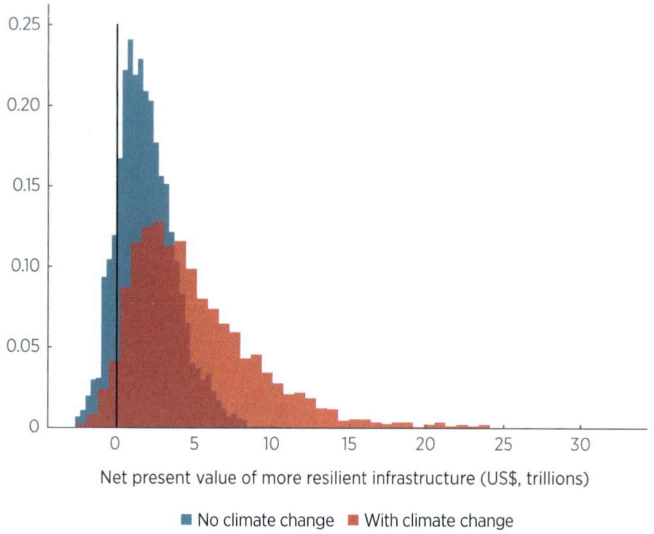

Source: Hallegatte et al. 2019.
Note: A net present value higher than 0 means that benefits are higher than costs.

FIGURE 6.4 The cost of inaction increases rapidly—even more so with climate change

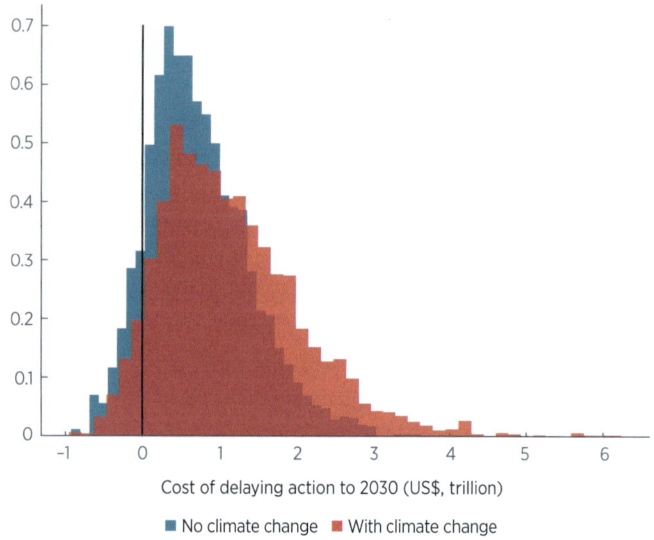

Source: Hallegatte et al. 2019.

than 6 in 25 percent of them (Hallegatte et al. 2019). The net present value of these investments, over the lifetime of new infrastructure assets, exceeds $2 trillion in 75 percent of the scenarios and $4.2 trillion in half of them (figure 6.3). Moreover, climate change makes the strengthening of infrastructure assets even more important. Without climate change, the median benefit-cost ratio would be equal to 2, but it is doubled when climate change is considered.

The 4 percent of scenarios with a benefit-cost ratio below 1—meaning that strengthening new assets is not desirable—are scenarios in which all estimates are consistently biased in the same direction. In other words, the cost of strengthening is at the top of the range, the impact of hazards on infrastructure assets and disruptions is at the bottom of the range, the socioeconomic consequences of disruptions are the lowest, and climate change barely affects natural hazards. Overall, strengthening infrastructure assets seems a very robust and attractive solution: it is very likely to be cost-effective, has a high likelihood of generating very large benefits, and cannot generate massive losses, even in the worst-case scenarios.

The urgency of designing better infrastructure is also evident in the simulations (figure 6.4). In 93 percent of the scenarios, it is costly to delay action from 2020 to 2030. The median cost of delaying action to 2030 is $1.0 trillion. The only scenarios in which delaying action is beneficial are scenarios in which strengthening infrastructure assets has a benefit-cost ratio below, or very close to, 1. Here again, climate change makes action more urgent: climate change almost doubles the median cost of delaying action by 10 years.

This analysis underestimates the desirability of investing in more robust infrastructure assets. The options considered here to strengthen infrastructure assets against natural hazards would also make them more resistant to other types of shocks, such as technical failures. Thus, there are large co-benefits in terms of avoided disruptions, going beyond the hazard-related ones explored here. However, as discussed later in this report, infrastructure owners and operators often bear only a fraction of the social cost of infrastructure disruptions and damages. As a result, their incentive to build resilient assets is largely reduced, unless specific regulations and policies are implemented, a subject covered in more detail in part III of this report.

This chapter has explored how to make infrastructure systems more resilient through more robust assets, leaving aside all system-level instruments to build resilience (or even something as simple as building assets in safer areas). The next chapter explores how looking at systems and services instead of assets opens new ways to build resilience at a low cost.

REFERENCES

Croneborg, L., K. Saito, M. Matera, D. McKeown, and J. van Aardt. 2015. "Digital Elevation Models: A Guidance Note on How Digital Elevation Models Are Created and Used—Includes Key Definitions, Sample Terms of Reference, and How Best to Plan a DEM-Mission." World Bank and Global Facility for Disaster Reduction and Recovery, Washington, DC.

Daniels, J. 2017. "Southern California Utilities Shut Off Power to Prevent Wildfires." CNBC, December 13.

Davis, C. A., and J. Castruita. 2013. "Los Angeles Pilot Project Using Japanese Earthquake Resistant Joint Ductile Iron Pipe." American Water Works Association, Denver.

European Union. 2015. "EU Reference Document Good Practices on Leakage Management." WFD CIS WG PoM: Case Study Document, European Union, Brussels.

Fraser, S. 2017. "Think Hazard! Methodology Report. Version 2.0." World Bank, Washington, DC.

Hallegatte, S., J. Rozenberg, C. Fox, C. Nicolas, and J. Rentschler. "Strengthening New Infrastructure Assets—A Cost-Benefit Analysis." Background paper for this report, World Bank, Washington, DC.

Hutton, G., and M. C. Varughese. 2016. "The Costs of Meeting the 2030 Sustainable Development Goal Targets on Drinking Water, Sanitation, and Hygiene." Water and Sanitation Program Technical Paper, World Bank, Washington, DC.

Kestrel Group. 2011. "Resilience Lessons: Orion's 2010 and 2011 Earthquake Experience: Independent Report." Report for Orion New Zealand Ltd., Kestrel Group, Wellington.

Kingdom, B., R. Liemberger, and P. Marin. 2006. "The Challenge of Reducing Non-Revenue Water in Developing Countries: How the Private Sector Can Help—A Look at Performance-Based Service Contracting." Water Supply and Sanitation Sector Board Discussion Paper 8, World Bank, Washington, DC.

Koks, E., J. Rozenberg, C. Zorn, M. Tariverdi, M. Vousdoukas, S. A. Fraser, J. Hall, and S. Hallegatte. 2019. "A Global Multi-Hazard Risk Analysis of Road and Railway Infrastructure Assets." Forthcoming in *Nature Sustainability*.

Kornejew, M., J. Rentschler, and S. Hallegatte. 2019. "Well Spent: How Governance Determines the Effectiveness of Infrastructure Investments." Background paper for this report, World Bank, Washington, DC.

McNeely, A. 2018. "PG&E Credit Cut to Brink of Junk by Moody's on Wildfire Risk." *Bloomberg News*, November 15.

Messick, R. 2011. "Curbing Fraud, Corruption, and Collusion in the Roads Sector." World Bank, Washington, DC.

Miyamoto International. 2019. "Overview of Engineering Options for Increasing Infrastructure Resilience." Background paper for this report, World Bank, Washington, DC.

Nicholls, R. J., J. Hinkel, D. Lincke, and T. van der Pol. 2019. "Global Investment Costs for Coastal Defense through the 21st Century." Policy Research Working Paper 8745, World Bank, Washington, DC.

Oguah, S., and S. Khosla. 2017. "Disaster Preparedness Offers Big Payoffs for Utilities." Live Wire 2017/84, World Bank, Washington, DC.

Rozenberg, J., and M. Fay. 2019. *Beyond the Gap: How Countries Can Afford the Infrastructure They Need While Protecting the Planet.* Washington, DC: World Bank.

Schweikert, A. E., L. Nield, E. Otto, and M. Deinert. 2019. "Resilience and Critical Power System Infrastructure: Lessons Learned from Natural Disasters and Future Research Needs." Background paper for this report, World Bank, Washington, DC.

U.S. Department of Energy. 2018. "Energy Resilience Solutions for the Puerto Rico Grid." U.S. Department of Energy, Washington, DC.

World Bank. 2017. *Climate and Disaster Resilient Transport in Small Island Developing States: A Call for Action.* Washington, DC: World Bank.

———. 2018. *Road Costs Knowledge System (ROCKS)—Doing Business Update.* Washington, DC: World Bank.

World Bank and OECD (Organisation for Economic Co-operation and Development). 2017. *A Step Ahead: Competition Policy for Shared Prosperity and Inclusive Growth.* Washington, DC: World Bank.

From Resilient Assets to Resilient Infrastructure Services 7

The resilience of infrastructure assets is only a small part of the overall picture of resilience described in this report. Because the cost of disruptions exceeds the cost of repairs, infrastructure *services* offer a better perspective on resilience. For networked infrastructure, a look at services requires a systemic view of both the resilience of the full system, including supporting systems such as ecosystems and wider river basins, and the full cost of failures.

This chapter explores how the high costs of infrastructure disruptions and damages may be reduced by focusing on infrastructure services rather than assets and working at the network and system levels. It finds that countries can increase the resilience of their networks at a cost that is even lower than what chapter 6 suggests. But they must assign priority to the assets that are *critical* to users or the functioning of their economic system. Identification of critical assets allows utilities and planners to hedge against disruptions by strengthening these assets, adding redundant components to the networks to reduce their criticality, developing contingency plans by simulating what happens when they fail, or using network-informed solutions to boost resilience.

Not all assets need to be made more resilient. By looking at the system that supports infrastructure services, it is possible to identify the most critical parts of a network and assess the performance of options that reduce vulnerabilities, from strengthening critical assets to creating redundancy in the system.

USING CRITICALITY ANALYSES TO PRIORITIZE INTERVENTIONS

A simple approach to giving priority to interventions is to assign a level of criticality to assets based on the quantity of services they provide—that is, their capacity. For example, construction standards are often higher for primary roads such as highways and freeways than for tertiary roads that have a much lower volume of traffic. Power generation plants or water reservoirs can also be ranked as a function of their capacity. Although this is a useful first assessment for criticality, it is limited in that it does not include information on the type of service the asset provides (for example, a freeway that provides access to a tourist area is less critical than one that leads to the main port or hospital) or the role that the asset plays in overall network functionality. Sophisticated

BOX 7.1 Network topology and resilience

Infrastructure systems can be represented by an abstract network of nodes and connecting links. A network establishes and maintains connectivity between these nodes to facilitate a flow between them. A flow is the movement of people, goods, material, energy, and services through the system. The vulnerability of the system can therefore be linked to the network connectivity that guarantees an available and functional path between intended origin-destination (O-D) pairs.

The shape of a network contributes to its coping capacity. Because the shape of an infrastructure system network is static in practice (after all, a new road cannot be built in an instant), the network topological attributes are viable indications of its coping capacity in the face of disruptive events. Overall, networks with a higher number of interconnection paths between O-D pairs have a greater redundancy, which generally translates into higher accessibility and lower probability of node isolation. Connectivity and accessibility metrics from graph theory can thus be directly employed to gauge the coping capacity of systems. Connectivity metrics describe basic network characteristics such as the ratio of links to nodes or the maximum possible number of links. Accessibility metrics describe the best possible flow conditions. Such a measure is, for example, the *network diameter,* defined as the maximum distance among all shortest distances between all O-D pairs in the network. Accessibility metrics can also be used to identify critical nodes (or links) in the network. For example, a node that is crossed by many of the shortest paths in the network (a node with the largest *betweenness centrality*) is likely to have higher importance for maintaining the functioning of the network (Kwakkel et al. 2019).

MAP 7.1 The criticality of a link can be measured by the additional road user cost resulting from its disruption

Example from Zambezia Province, Mozambique

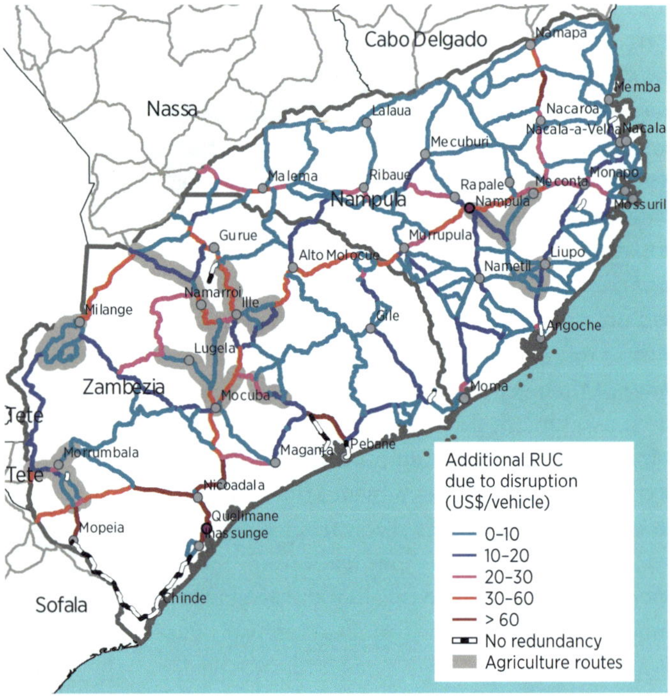

Source: Espinet Alegre et al. 2018.

approaches to prioritizing infrastructure assets model infrastructure systems as a network of nodes and links (box 7.1).

Transport systems

Criticality can be assessed by systematically simulating disruptions in a network and estimating the resulting loss of functionality. Links and nodes can be removed one by one—or several at a time—and the network functionality (such as for transport, travel time, and cost) can be recalculated in the absence of these elements. Doing so enables identification of the most critical links as the ones that lead to the highest loss of functionality when they are removed (map 7.1).

Networks should also be stress-tested against realistic shocks that include multiple simultaneous disruptions (also referred to as *n-p*), not just against shocks to a single component. For example, Kwakkel et al. (2019) test the vulnerability of the Bangladeshi transport network to past flood events by examining the spatial correlation of disruptions. They find that the best solutions for increasing the resilience of the network depend on the set of events that are used for simulating the disruptions. If data on the full distribution of possible events are not available, it may be more robust to invest in improvements that will increase the resilience of the network to a wide range of random events.

These approaches make it possible to measure the *resilience of a network,* defined as the ratio of the loss of functionality to the loss of assets (Rozenberg et al. 2019). A highly resilient transport network can lose many assets (such as road segments) without losing much functionality. Figure 7.1 represents the functionality loss (expressed as isolated trips—that is, when travelers can no longer reach their destination) from the disruption of random transport links as a function of the percentage of links disrupted. It shows that, thanks to their redundancy, the transport networks in Belgium and Morocco exhibit much more resilience than the network in Madagascar. For low levels of disruption (below 20 percent of links), functionality losses are mostly negligible in Belgium, whereas in Madagascar they quickly rise to 80 percent. The key here is that, because Madagascar's network has much less redundancy than Belgium's network (map 7.2), a disruption of critical roads can paralyze the whole network. This type of analysis provides more valuable information than static network metrics because it allows identification of the extreme cases in which even a small number of disrupted links can lead to high functionality loss.

Such criticality analyses can help to identify investments that increase the redundancy of a network and have positive economic returns. In Peru, Rozenberg et al. (2017) show that targeted investments to increase the redundancy of the road network around Carretera Central, a strategic export route for agricultural products, could be justified on the sole basis of the annual user losses from floods and landslides avoided. This measure yields a positive return in almost all possible scenarios, combining uncertainty regarding the intensity, frequency,

FIGURE 7.1 Belgium's and Morocco's transport systems can absorb much larger road disruptions than Madagascar's

Examples of functionality loss in a transport system as a function of the percentage of links disrupted

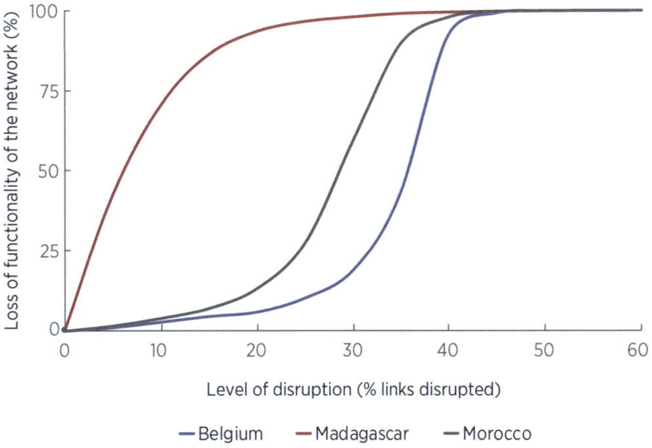

Source: Rozenberg et al. 2019.

MAP 7.2 Belgium's transport network is much denser and offers greater redundancies than Madagascar's

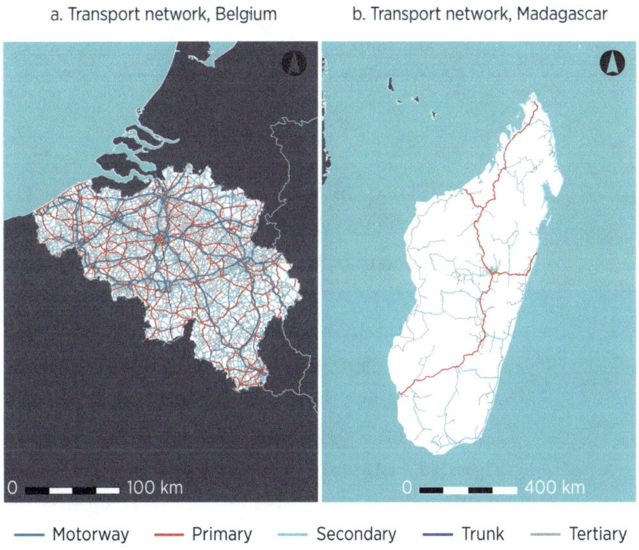

Source: Based on OpenStreetMap data.

and duration of climate-related events; the structural impact of water levels on the road; the amount of traffic to be rerouted when a flood or landslide hits; and the time and total cost of reconstructing a road after a disaster (figure 7.2). In transport, redundancy can also be

FIGURE 7.2 Increased redundancy can have high net benefits, if well targeted

Net benefits of four interventions across hundreds of scenarios, Carretera Central, Peru

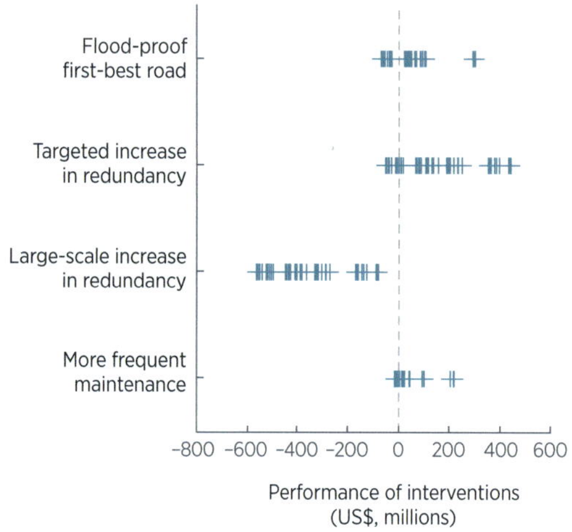

Source: Rozenberg et al. 2017.
Note: The net benefits focus on avoided losses and do not include benefits from interventions regarding reduced road user costs in the absence of disasters. Each cross in this graph is a different scenario, with various assumptions about the intensity, frequency, and duration of climate-related events; the structural impact of water levels on the road; the amount of traffic to be rerouted when a flood or landslide hits; and the time and total cost of reconstructing a road after a disaster.

built through multimodal systems so that users can switch between modes after a disruption.

In Mozambique, Espinet Alegre et al. (2018) prioritize interventions in the rural road network based on a combination of criticality and risk to infrastructure—that is, the expected annual damage based on hazards and vulnerability (map 7.3). They define criticality using not only the loss of functionality if a road is damaged but also information on users, including the poverty and agricultural potential in the province served by the road. They find that in provinces with a high risk of floods and low redundancy, the *direct* benefits of investments in new culverts and stronger bridges are relatively small. However, the *indirect* benefits, expressed in lower expected annual costs for road users due to flood disruptions, are four times larger and justify the investments under most of the scenarios considered.

Power systems

Network resilience can also play a role in power transmission and distribution system planning. Vulnerable or critical parts of the network can be identified using a network analysis with a single-element contingency ($n - 1$), a double-element contingency ($n - 2$), or even a p-element contingency ($n - p$). It is important to understand how the network will behave should 1 to p elements fail, as the criticality of the remaining nodes changes when the most critical node is removed (Carlotto and Grzybowski 2014). Unfortunately, because of the complexity of power flow analysis models, even the $n - 2$ contingency analysis is often very difficult to perform. Thus, an $n - p$ contingency analysis at the system level is often not possible, and studying how the system would behave if p elements were to fail is only possible in a designated area or for a selection of those p elements.

Veeramany et al. (2018) illustrate how these approaches can identify opportunities for interventions with very high returns. They perform a network criticality analysis for seismic risks in the state of Washington in the U.S. Northwest. Working on a subset of the transmission network assumed to be vulnerable to seismic hazards, they consider 40 potential seismic events and run 200,000 scenarios to assess the behavior of the system during an earthquake. They are able to identify the most critical combination of assets, finding that hardening one asset or adding redundancy to "double" this asset would reduce risk by 88 percent.

Power transmission and distribution networks are built with some level of redundancy to allow them to cope with the disruption of one network element by rerouting power, thereby reducing the curtailment of plants and limiting disruptions to consumers. Such levels of redundancy are included in the planning and construction standards of most utilities. These standards are often more stringent at the transmission level than at the distribution level, because the risk of widespread outages is higher at the transmission level.

MAP 7.3 The strengthening of infrastructure assets in Mozambique is prioritized based on risk levels and criticality

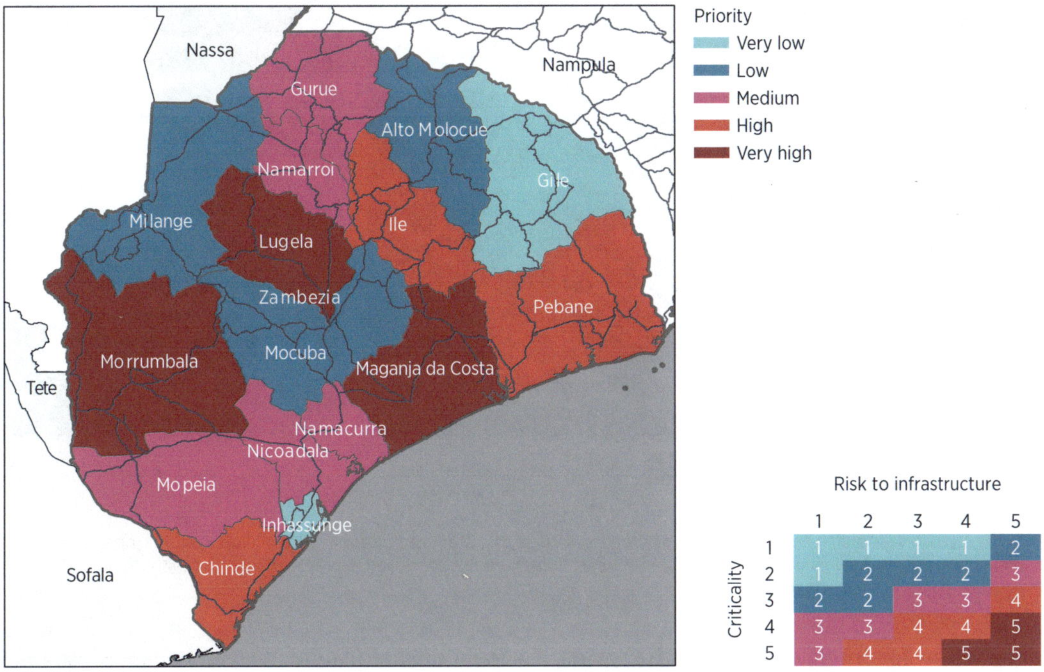

Source: Espinet Alegre et al. 2018.
Note: Criticality is defined as a combination of the poverty in the province served by the road, the agricultural potential of the province served by the road, and the loss of functionality if the road is removed.

Identifying critical assets via an $n-1$ or $n-2$ contingency analysis does not necessarily mean doubling or tripling key components of the network (for $n-1$ and $n-2$, respectively) or placing lines underground. A more effective approach is usually to create "ringed" or meshed networks that provide multiple supply points to various nodes in the grid (figure 7.3). A meshed network reduces the exposure to outages along corridors. It also enables networks to switch loads quickly between feeders or supply points. This approach is used more and more for distribution networks that used to be star-shaped (the traditional radial distribution) but are now becoming increasingly meshed, like most transmission networks.

Orion is one of the largest electricity distribution companies in New Zealand, providing power to remote rural areas, regional towns, and the city of Christchurch. Rather than operating a single line or cable into an area, Orion has multiple links, so that if one fails, an alternative power supply route is available. This spider's web approach greatly increased Orion's ability to restore power promptly after the 2010 and 2011 earthquakes. It meant that power stayed on unless all the multiple links into an area failed. If all of the links were damaged, Orion could fix the link that was the easiest and quickest to repair.

Water systems

In water systems, the typical methodology for assessing criticality in a network calls for carrying out a failure mode, effects, and criticality analysis (Stip et al. 2019). This analysis consists of mapping out all of the components of the network and assessing under which conditions they would fail, what the effects of that failure would be, and how they would affect service delivery. Based on the latter, the "criticality" of that component can be ranked and a rating

FIGURE 7.3 Network topology can improve grid resilience

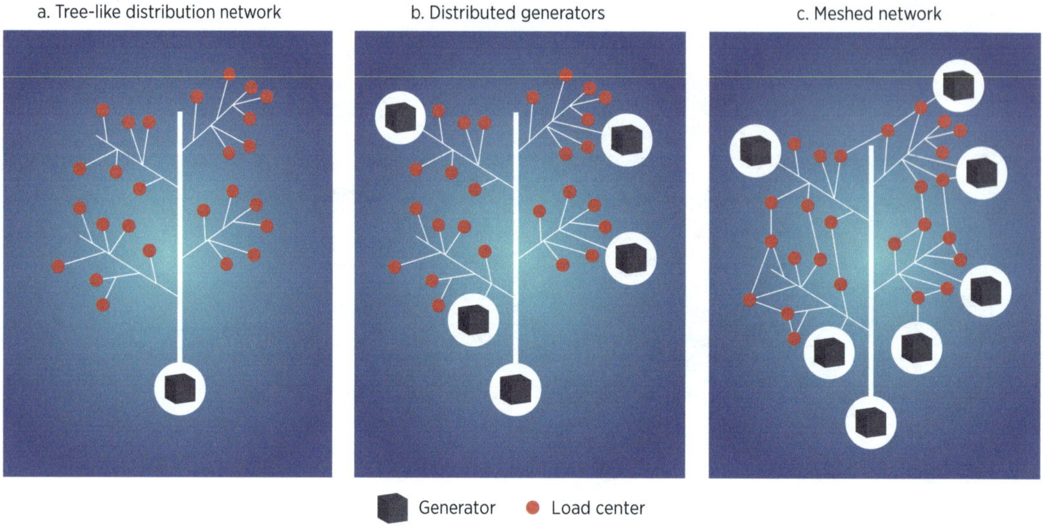

Source: Stöcker 2018.
Note: The meshed distribution network contains distribution feeders that are linked by open switches during normal operations to maintain the radial characteristic of the distribution network. These switches are closed to provide alternative paths for electricity when a distribution feeder is disconnected.

recorded accordingly. In the Netherlands, breakdowns are ranked by level: a level 1 breakdown should never occur because it would significantly disrupt service, a level 2 breakdown is allowed to occur every three years, and a level 3 breakdown can happen every year because it is not vital to operations (Wright-Contreras 2018). Based on this categorization, a regular maintenance regime can be implemented to check the elements linked to level 1 breakdowns, while spare parts can be stored for those elements in a level 3 breakdown, which is expected more often. These levels are also determined by whether the asset is essential to providing service to more than 1,000 households or to a hospital or providing other services such as firefighting.

In Cutzamala, Mexico, a sensitivity assessment that examined the city's water system for lack of maintenance of major system components identified elements that would have the severest negative impacts on maintaining acceptable performance of the system in different scenarios (Ray and Brown 2015). This knowledge could then be used to develop an optimized maintenance plan for a given budget constraint, prioritizing the most critical elements.

Japan and the Netherlands have built redundancy into their water distribution systems through "loops," so that if one element of the network breaks down, other elements of the system can always be reached via an alternate route (Wright-Contreras 2018). In the Netherlands, this redundancy is also found in storage systems and water treatment plants. For example, river intakes can be shut down if the water quality of the river worsens, and so the reservoir, because it has a storage supply of water for five to six months, will usually be able to "flush" the river water from that pollution event. Water treatment plants themselves are built with storage, which not only improves water quality at the inlet through sunlight and retention but also provides a water source for a given amount of time if the intake has to be closed or the plant malfunctions.

Telecommunications

Telecommunication networks can be designed to have high redundancy—physical and logical—that protects users against extreme events. The Great East Japan Earthquake in March 2011, measuring 9.0 on the Richter scale, and the resulting tsunami, damaged submarine cable systems along the Japanese coast. The effects of this disaster on Internet connectivity was, however, limited because the level of redundancy in Japan's international connectivity was adequate. Japan's diversity of submarine cable system routes ensured that the overall capacity landing in the country was not significantly curtailed. As a result, although there was some disruption from the cable breaks, international connectivity was remarkably robust considering the scale of the disaster. However, the right level of redundancy is hard to determine. In 2013 a diver intentionally cut the South East Asia–Middle East–Western Europe 4 (SE-ME-WE-4) cable system. The presence of eight submarine cables between the Arab Republic of Egypt and Europe meant that Egypt's Internet should not have been affected significantly. However, four cable systems reported faults or breaks during the same week, resulting in overloads and congestion on the active cable systems.[1] Internet speeds crashed by 60 percent, with impacts felt by all telecom operators in the country.

Commercial agreements between owners and users of telecommunications infrastructure allow for "logical redundancy" in networks, significantly reducing the risk and impact of damage to physical infrastructure. The industry has also adopted cost- and risk-sharing business models, where telecom-ready infrastructure—such as poles, underground ducts and channels, fiber-optic cables, and pylons—is shared between telecom operators and other sectors such as energy and transport. While these infrastructure-sharing models have enabled rapid and cost-efficient network roll-outs, the risk associated with aggregated infrastructure also increases. Therefore, there are trade-offs between cost sharing and adequate investment in the physical redundancy of networks, diversifying, decentralizing, and working across systems.

In addition to redundancy and strengthening of critical assets, other system-level interventions can be envisaged to increase the resilience of infrastructure services, ranging from diversification to decentralization and cross-system analyses.

DIVERSIFYING ASSETS TO INCREASE NETWORK RESILIENCE

The benefits of diversifying generation sources in the power sector were particularly evident in Texas following Hurricane Harvey. Nuclear power was able to operate at full capacity throughout the event. Wind farms were curtailed during the event, but most immediately came back online, compensating for much of the production deficit from reductions in the generation facilities located on the coast, which were affected by storm surges and flooding for longer time periods (Conca 2017). Schweikert et al. (2019) recommend a power mix that does not depend fully on water to reduce the risk of power shortages during droughts or extreme heat events (Alvaro 2018). Indeed, thermal generation facilities and nuclear power plants, which rely on water for cooling, often need to be curtailed or closed when intake water exceeds the permitted temperatures (approximately 24°C in most cases).

In transport, diversification is done through multimodal transport planning. Urban planning, for example, can include nonmotorized modes, such as walking and cycling, and mass transit. If transport planning is accompanied by policies that incentivize a higher urban density, this mode diversification can reduce traffic density and the need to build an increasingly large number of roads, thereby reducing obstacles to water flow and mitigating floods. In addition, by reducing the need to build more roads, urban planning can reduce the scale of the exposure and vulnerability of the transport sector to disasters. These alternative modes can also provide resilient forms of transport during an emergency (World Bank 2015).

DECENTRALIZING AND USING NEW TECHNOLOGIES

Distributed power systems that rely on solar energy and batteries can harden a grid and make it more resilient. Minigrids and microgrids, because they do not rely on long-distance transmission wires, can provide useful backup generation in case of grid failure. Indeed, most electricity outages result from damage to transmission lines and transformers rather than generation facilities. During Hurricane Sandy, the Co-Op City microgrid in New York successfully decoupled from the central grid and supported consumers during outages on the wider network (Strahl et al. 2016).

In the future, sensors will allow power distribution management systems to be programmed to reconfigure networks to distribute loads after isolating faulty segments of the network. Sensors within components of power systems will allow power plants and substations to communicate with one another as well as with the grid operator. The grid control system will take into account real-time conditions that affect the locational marginal price (changing the costs to operate and the congestion costs). Substations may communicate with control systems on the distribution end, sending signals about pricing to end-use customers' devices. Those signals may modulate and moderate customers' power demands accordingly—for example, by sending price signals to a building's air-conditioning system. The same types of sensors and optimizations could also function on a minigrid, perhaps even with more value because a minigrid's operation typically has fewer degrees of freedom than a central grid. The algorithms may help the minigrid operators to coordinate with the central grid (in cases where a connection is possible) and to decide whether the minigrid should supply power to help a central grid return from a forced outage and blackout or whether the minigrid should remain "islanded."

Rainwater harvesting and decentralized water treatment can contribute to more flexible hybrid water systems (Stip et al. 2019). New containerized treatment systems for wastewater treatment and for drinking water production, using ultrafiltration technology with low-fouling hollow-fiber membranes, can provide high-quality water effluent (Georges et al. 2018). The units, which are modular and plug and play, are easy to transport because they are installed in shipping containers. A basic decentralized rainwater harvesting system can provide nonpotable water for toilet flushing and other nonpotable requirements to reduce the demand for potable water. A more advanced system could collect harvested rainwater supplemented by rainwater harvesting and storage at the customer's property as well as use stormwater retention and treatment systems to supplement raw water resources. Such systems would increase resilience to droughts, bursts, and the pollution of raw water sources, and they would reduce the risk of urban flooding.

Container-based sanitation, in addition to providing low-cost sanitation services, is more resilient to floods and droughts than other solutions (Georges et al. 2018). In Haiti, users of container-based sanitation services reported that they were able to use their toilets during floods, whereas traditional latrines were unusable. In Nairobi, some service users found the waterless nature of Fresh Life toilets to be a distinct advantage. In that water-scarce environment, there is no piped water, and consequently water for household use is costly and has to be hauled over considerable distances—typically by women.

WORKING ACROSS SYSTEMS TO CAPTURE SYNERGIES

The criticality of an infrastructure asset also depends on complex interdependencies and possible cascading failures, including transboundary ones. Mapping interdependencies between critical infrastructure assets and sectors is increasingly important to understanding potential cascading consequences. Interdependencies between infrastructure sectors can be physical, cyber, geographical, or logical, and they can be between sectors or between assets.

All infrastructure sectors tend to be highly dependent on electricity. Contingency plans for water utilities should include ways to prevent or recover quickly from power outages at pumping stations, reservoirs, and storage tanks. Similarly, telephone, cellular, e-mail, or dedicated broadband networks cannot function without electricity, and so telecommunications facilities usually have reserve power—battery banks—for short-duration outages. In North America, these battery banks have power for three to eight hours, which is appropriate for frequent disruptions but perhaps insufficient for large-scale disasters. It is essential that key telecommunications facilities have a backup power generator and secure fuel storage arrangements for a prolonged power outage.

The power sector itself depends on other infrastructure sectors. Unpassable roads are one of the main obstacles that electric utilities face in repairing transmission lines. By working with road agencies, utilities can ensure that they have the right information on accessible routes. Such an arrangement would also ensure that the roads needed to repair the power system would receive priority for reopening. Generation technologies that require on-demand fuel delivery, such as natural gas, oil, and coal-fired systems, also rely heavily on the transport network. In Puerto Rico following Hurricanes Irma and Maria, port closures resulted in the loss of an estimated 1.2 million barrels of petroleum a day for 11 days, which directly affected the major generation stations that relied exclusively on imported fuel (U.S. Department of Energy 2018). Similar closures occurred in Texas in 2017, as well as in New Jersey and New York during Hurricane Sandy (U.S. Department of Energy 2018).

Managing services together or through effective collaboration platforms enhances efficiency and can generate cost savings, which can later be reinvested in the system. In Orange County, California, joint planning between the Orange County Water Department (in charge of the bulk water supply) and the Orange County Sanitation Department (in charge of sanitation) helped to identify wastewater reuse as a key cost saver for both the sanitation district (due to the avoided costs of seawater outfall) and the water district (by securing a new drought-proof source of water) (World Bank 2018). In general, a utility that manages both water supply and sanitation together may reduce the transaction costs associated with coordination, while being better placed to identify opportunities to close the water cycle.

Roads make a major imprint on hydrology by blocking and guiding water, concentrating runoff, interfering with subsurface flows, and changing flooding patterns. However, there is a beneficial connection between road planning and building and water management. Water is considered the prime enemy of road infrastructure and the single greatest factor in road damage. Therefore, a strong case can be made for managing water around roads better and for considering roads as an integral part of the watershed and landscape in which they are situated. Such an integrated approach will preserve road infrastructure and reduce the burden of maintenance, contributing to greater infrastructure productivity, while providing water supply and flood protection. Van Steenbergen et al. (2019) describe how the negative impact of roads on the surrounding landscape can be turned around and how roads can become instruments of beneficial water management. For example, in arid areas the water intercepted by road bodies can be guided to recharge areas or surface storage or applied directly on the land. On floodplains and in coastal areas, roads also play a role in flood protection. Roads can double as embankments and provide evacuation routes and flood shelters. In low-lying wetland areas and on floodplains, roads and bridges affect the shallow groundwater tables and have enormous consequences for land productivity. The way in which a road is built and, for example, the height of bridge sills and culverts will have considerable influence on the quality of the wetland on either side of the road (Van Steenbergen et al. 2019).

PROTECTING INFRASTRUCTURE SYSTEMS WITH DIKES IN DENSE AREAS

One option to reduce coastal and river flood risk is to protect infrastructure systems with dikes, which are part of water systems. Water systems act both as water service providers and as protection against water-related hazards. Dikes can be a cost-efficient strategy in high-density areas and would reduce the exposure of other infrastructure systems (Rozenberg and Fay 2019). However, dikes cannot protect against all possible events, and they need to be accompanied by clear communication campaigns on residual risk, as well as contingency plans in case of failure. While dikes can protect assets, appropriate early warning systems and evacuation plans remain important for managing the risk of large human losses in case of dike failure or overtopping.

Rozenberg and Fay (2019) assess the investment in coastal and river flood protection infrastructure (using dikes and storm surge barriers) needed to protect cities in low- and middle-income countries by 2030, under a range of socioeconomic and climate change scenarios. They find that, depending on acceptable risk levels and construction unit costs, total costs could go from $23 billion to $335 billion per year. Although these costs are again low compared with total infrastructure investment needs, and although dikes can generate high benefits, the development of appropriate institutions and governance mechanisms to deliver maintenance as well as the necessary funding streams is essential. Failure to do so would increase risk and could result in catastrophic failures, putting lives, not just assets, at risk. Absent a credible commitment to reliable maintenance, a combination of nature-based protection, land use planning, and retreat should be favored.

COMBINING INFRASTRUCTURE WITH NATURE-BASED SOLUTIONS TO REDUCE INVESTMENT NEEDS

Combining green and gray infrastructure can provide lower-cost, more resilient, and more sustainable infrastructure solutions (Browder et al. 2019). The filtration services provided by healthy forests saved Portland, Maine, between $97 million and $155 million over 20 years by canceling out the need for a water filtration plant (Gartner et al. 2013). In the Philippines, mangroves, reefs, and other natural systems prevent more than $1 billion in annual disaster losses (Tercek 2017). Meanwhile, 90 percent of New York City's water is provided by well-protected wilderness watersheds, so that New York's water treatment process is simpler than that of other U.S. cities (NRC 2000).

Good catchment management can increase the availability of freshwater and reduce the cost of treatment. Floating wetlands can be used for in situ treatment of elevated nutrient concentrations. And riparian planting can be used to lessen the rate of runoff, erosion, and nutrient reduction and to increase the quantity of water captured for use.

In Suva, Fiji, the RISE Program is working in communities exposed to tidal flooding and forced to rely on poor sanitation solutions that allow the spread of fecal contamination from latrines in each flooding event.[2] The proposed interventions would mix simplified sewerage to contain the waste, with wetlands and walkways that separate the community from flooding and filter the water as it flows in and out of the area.

Working with nature also means closing the water cycle. In 1968, faced with a severe drought, Windhoek, Namibia, became one of the first cities in the world to introduce full-scale wastewater reclamation for use as drinking water (World Bank 2018). The wastewater is treated to potable level and injected directly into the water supply, and it now provides 25 percent of Windhoek's water. The aquifer in Orange County, California, is also used as a buffer during dry conditions. Stormwater infiltration is promoted through canals and inflatable dams, while highly treated wastewater is injected to recharge the aquifer. This managed aquifer recharge increases the drinking water available to Orange County service providers, while also serving as a barrier to seawater intrusion.

A noteworthy example of such integration of the water cycle with city infrastructure is China's sponge cities (State Council of China 2015). Under this ambitious program, the country seeks to reduce the effects of flooding through a mix of low-impact development measures and urban greenery and drainage infrastructure, and to have 80 percent of urban areas reuse 70 percent of rainwater by 2020. This approach is similar to what Australia's Cooperative Research Centre for Water Sensitive Cities calls its vision of the "city as a water catchment."

Nature-based solutions are also used for flood protection, reducing the need for hard infrastructure like dikes. The fact that mangroves and coral reefs protect coastlines against floods and storm surges is well known. According to Beck et al. (2018), coral reefs halve the annual global damages from flooding and divide by three the costs from frequent storms. They estimate that the countries benefiting the most from reefs are Cuba, Indonesia, Malaysia, Mexico, and the Philippines, with annual expected flood savings of more than $400 million for each country. In Colombo, preserving the wetlands system proved to be a cost-effective solution to reduce flooding in the city, even when taking into account land development constraints (Browder et al. 2019)—see photo 7.1. Roads are especially vulnerable to landslides, and different forest management practices can have large implications for landslide susceptibility. According to Dhakal and Sidle (2003), partial cutting produces fewer landslides and lowers the volume of landslides by a factor of 1.5 compared with clear-cutting.

Power transmission lines are very vulnerable to falling trees during high wind events (see chapter 4). But by preventing certain high vegetation from encroaching on the rights-of-way alongside these lines, some utilities in the United States are encouraging native low-growth vegetation. The result is that, in some areas, the scrubby habitat under some transmission lines becomes the best place to find wild bees. As the scrub vegetation grows in, it excludes many taller trees, and over a few years, mowing costs drop dramatically. Such vegetation management thus comes at a lower

PHOTO 7.1 A wetland park in Colombo helps to mitigate flood risk and offers recreational opportunities, such as bird-watching towers

Photo credit: Matthew Simpson.

cost to the utilities and can create a network of wildlife corridors under transmission lines (Conniff 2014).

FAILING GRACEFULLY AND RECOVERING QUICKLY

It is sometimes more cost-effective to replace infrastructure after an event than to make it strong enough to resist everything, such as antennas in the telecommunications sector. Investing in the protection of these assets would not yield proportional returns, as opposed to investing in backups and restoration preparedness. In addition, no infrastructure asset or system can be designed to cope with all possible hazards. Because there is great uncertainty about the probability and intensity of the most extreme events, infrastructure systems should be stress-tested against events that go beyond the likely ones. Such a stress test would have two goals:

- Identify low-cost options that can reduce the vulnerability of infrastructure systems to extreme events, even if those events are considered extremely unlikely. For example, the Fukushima nuclear incident demonstrated that, even if large dikes are supposed to protect a nuclear power plant against all possible tsunamis, a "what-if" scenario exercise would be useful, considering the possibility that some unexpected event exceeds the level of protection. Such an exercise could produce additional vulnerability-reducing options, such as elevating a plant's backup generators in case flooding occurs despite the dikes.
- Understand the consequences of an unexpected failure to prepare for the required response—both in terms of management of the infrastructure system (such as how to recover from a major failure) and support for users (such as how to minimize impacts on hospitals). Running scenarios of failures is the first and most critical step in defining contingency plans.

Develop and update contingency plans

Contingency plans set out the measures to be taken by a service provider in the event of an emergency or unforeseen incident. Transport operators could, as part of their contingency plan, focus on restoring connections to critical nodes such as hospitals and ports (Benavidez and Mortlock 2018). Water utilities could have a standing contract with water tankers to provide water if the water system fails in an emergency situation. In the Philippines, after a typhoon, water tankers were contracted to ensure service continuity despite infrastructure damage.

In the power sector, contingency planning needs to be carried out more frequently to understand the extent of widespread blackouts, simulate various restoration procedures, and incorporate outputs into operational and training manuals for system operators. Contingency analysis could also be extended to include demand-side management. For example, predetermined loads could be disconnected to avoid a loss of grid stability and avert possible widespread outages (box 7.2).

New technologies can help to achieve quicker recovery in the power sector. Smart grids and advanced metering infrastructure (AMI) improve situational awareness and support rapid restoration after disasters. AMI is an integrated system of smart meters, communications networks, and data management systems that enables two-way communication between utilities and customers. This information is vital to system operators, who otherwise are blind to rapid changes in the energy system, and thus help to improve resilience in the grid (GridWise Alliance 2013; White House 2013). AMI was used after Hurricane Sandy by the Potomac Electric Power Company, which serves the Washington, DC, metropolitan area. The utility received "no power" signals from meters that enabled it to pinpoint outages and dispatch teams to specific areas instead of scouting wider areas to locate problems (Oguah and Khosla 2017).

BOX 7.2 Contingency planning for power utilities

Power utilities could recover quickly from disasters by taking the following specific steps:

- *Information gathering.* Once a disaster occurs, it is critical that utilities gather and share information in a timely manner. Crucial information includes (1) meteorological and terrestrial phenomena, (2) damage to power facilities, (3) blackouts, (4) affected staff, and (5) the traffic situation.
- *Information distribution.* To help users manage disruptions, it is important to publicize the information via television, radio, newspapers, and the Internet, especially information on blackouts and the restoration of power and further expected hazards.
- *Securing of staff.* Staff who are assigned to deal with disaster recovery should be present even during holidays and at nighttime. These staff oversee the disaster recovery operations and are responsible for deploying staff to the affected sites as well as for cooperating with external organizations until normal operations are restored.
- *Securing of materials and spare parts.* Utilities should confirm whether materials and spare parts are sufficient for recovery and, if insufficient, seek means to procure them, including from other utilities. Preselected vendors for cars, ships, and helicopters could be utilized to deliver materials and spare parts in a timely manner. Furthermore, staff should secure a place to store these materials, cooperating with municipalities if needed.
- *Cooperation with external institutions.* Cooperation with the central government and municipalities should include information sharing and staff deployment. The military may offer staff as well as the tools needed to restore affected facilities in the affected areas. Although utilities are often competitors, they frequently cooperate in disaster recovery periods by sharing staff, equipment, or spare parts. To ensure cooperation, utilities are increasingly entering into mutual aid agreements that describe possible ways of cooperation (Lindsey 2008).
- *Quick recovery tools for power facilities.* The resources required for the recovery period may include (1) alternate offices with appropriate access to information and communication; (2) special vehicles such as mobile substations and a generator vehicle; (3) alternative generation options (such as hydrogen, storage battery, co-generation, microgrids, or diesel emergency stations); and (4) helicopters for access to damaged assets if roads are closed.

In the telecommunications sector, as highlighted in chapter 4, natural shocks are likely to cause damage to exposed assets (such as towers and antennas) and underground assets (such as ducts and cables). Utility operators should be prepared and have the assets to restore services as soon as possible. As part of their contingency plans, they also need to ensure that the assets required to restore services are protected from hazards. For example, the 2011 earthquake and resulting tsunami in Japan that damaged submarine cable systems along Japan's coast also damaged most of the submarine cable repair vessels, rendering them unavailable in the immediate aftermath of the event and making recovery challenging.

In the water sector, so-called slow-onset events—hazards that happen over a long period—offer opportunities to react as the event unfolds. For example, in Spain the Aigües de Barcelona's Drought Management Plan tracks key indicators of water system performance and helps the service provider to respond through measures taken to guarantee drinking water supply and mitigate economic impacts (World Bank 2018). Based on surface storage levels, drought thresholds are established for the sources from which the utility will draw (figure 7.4). In a dry event, the more expensive sources (reuse and desalination) are used first, followed by strategic buffer sources (the aquifer). As a last resort, the city taps into water normally reserved for environmental flows to the water supply.

Build back better

Building back better is a central part of disaster recovery. Hurricane Sandy caused catastrophic damage in New York City, with kilometers of copper cables rendered useless. Verizon lost not only its carrier vaults in Manhattan (two vaults, each with a volume of more than 90,000 cubic feet) but also multiple manholes in the city. Estimating the loss at approximately $1 billion, Verizon did not see the value in repairing the existing network. Instead, it replaced the copper networks with fiber-optic cables, which are more resilient to water damage (Adams et al. 2014). Verizon also undertook other resilience-enhancing measures to protect its critical infrastructure. The carrier vaults, as well as fuel storage and pump rooms, were made watertight, with submarine doors to ensure continuity of operations.

In 2008 a major earthquake struck southwestern China. With more than 69,000 fatalities, 374,000 people injured, and about 18,000 missing, it was one of the deadliest earthquakes in recent history (Hallegatte, Rentschler, and Walsh 2018). In addition to the human toll, the disaster destroyed or severely damaged 34,000 kilometers of highways; thousands of schools, hospitals, and wastewater systems; and more than 4 million homes. In response to the disaster, the government of China adopted a build back stronger approach. It ensured that the reconstruction of affected infrastructure adhered to higher seismic standards and flood risk management codes, while ensuring a balance between reconstruction activities and laying a foundation for the longer-term sustainable economic recovery and development of the affected areas. Not only was the restored infrastructure built to be more resilient to natural hazards than before the disaster, but it also greatly enhanced the quality of services and access to essential public services (including water, sanitation, roads, health, and education). For example, 300 roads were rebuilt or renovated to new seismic standards and upgraded through the addition of modern traffic management and drainage systems.

Sometimes, the best approach is not to build

One way to reduce risk—or at least to minimize increases in risk—is to ensure that no new assets are located in at-risk areas. For example, to avoid the impact of heat waves on data center cooling, new large data centers are being built near the Arctic Circle to keep the servers as cool as possible, which in turn is reducing significantly the energy consumption for cooling and avoiding disruptions. Infrastructure can also guide households and firms toward low-risk areas if it is properly planned and future construction plans are communicated to the public (see chapter 8).

Sometimes, retreat is a better option than protection, especially considering long-term climate change trends and impacts on sea level or water scarcity. For instance, Nicholls et al. (2019) find that coastal protection against storm surges and sea-level rise would only make sense for about 22–32 percent of the world's coastlines throughout the 21st century, depending on assumptions about economic growth and sea-level rise. Thus, communities located adjacent to at least 68 percent of coastlines may have to retreat gradually or use low-cost ecosystem-based or nature-based approaches to coastal defense. These areas are mostly low-density areas with a small stock of assets, and the costs of protection are too high to be affordable. In those areas that cannot be realistically protected against long-term sea-level rise and coastal floods, not building new infrastructure may be the best approach to resilience. This approach should, however, be complemented by a consistent strategy to man-

FIGURE 7.4 Drought contingency plans in Spain use diverse water sources and are informed by historical drought threshold values

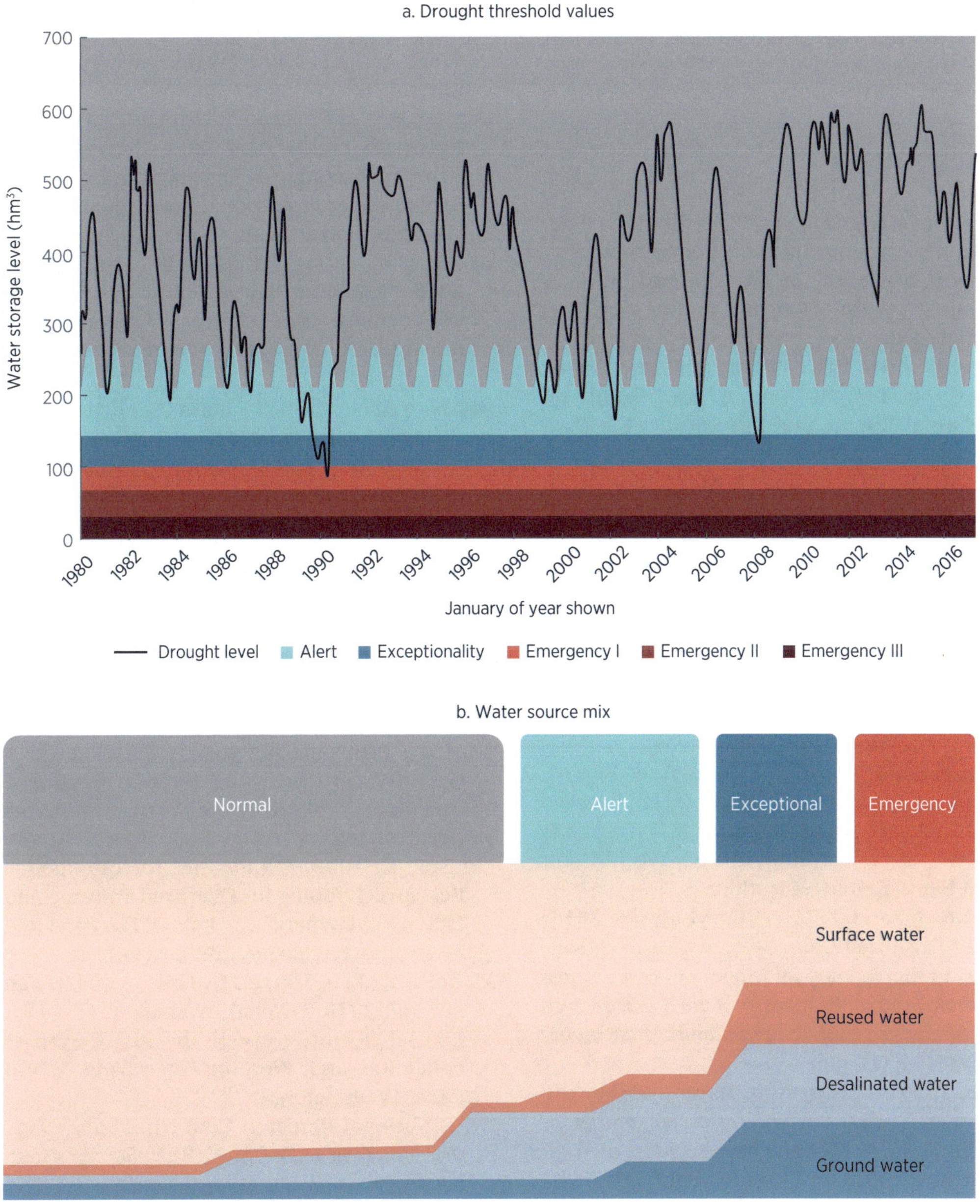

Source: World Bank 2018.

age retreat while maintaining livelihoods and community ties.

This chapter has highlighted how considering infrastructure *services*—instead of infrastructure *assets*—and looking at the system and network levels can offer opportunities to build resilience at a lower cost than strengthening assets. The next chapter brings users into the equation, because it is sometimes easier and cheaper to enable users to cope with infrastructure disruptions than it is to prevent all possible disruptions.

NOTES

1. "Undersea Cables Off Egypt Disrupted as Navy Arrests Three," *Guardian*, March 23, 2013. https://www.theguardian.com/technology/2013/mar/28/egypt-undersea-cable-arrests.
2. See https://www.rise-program.org/about.

REFERENCES

Adams, P., J. Steeves, B. Ashe, J. Firth, and B. Rabb. 2014. "Climate Risks Study for Telecommunications and Data Center Services." Report prepared for the General Services Administration, Riverside Technology, Fort Collins, CO.

Alvaro, L. 2018. "The Pitfalls of Hydroelectric Power in Drought-Prone Africa." Grantham Institute Climate and Environment at Peril (blog), August 21.

Beck, M. W., I. J. Losada, P. Menéndez, B. G. Reguero, P. Díaz-Simal, and F. Fernández. 2018. "The Global Flood Protection Savings Provided by Coral Reefs." *Nature Communications* 9 (2186): n.p.

Benavidez, M. J., and A. M. Mortlock. 2018. "Transport Sector Recovery: Opportunities to Build Resilience." GFDRR Guidance Note, Global Facility for Disaster Reduction and Recovery, Washington, DC, October.

Browder, G., S. Ozment, I. Rehberger Bescos, T. Gartner, and G.-M. Lange. 2019. *Integrating Green and Gray: Creating the Next Generation Infrastructure*. Washington, DC: World Bank and World Resources Institute.

Carlotto, T., and J. M. V. Grzybowski. 2014. "Self-Organized Criticality and Cascading Failures in the Topological Model of Power Grids: A Case Study." *Proceedings of the Brazilian Society of Applied and Computational Mathematics (SBMAC)* 2 (1): n.p.

Conca, J. 2017. "Hurricane Harvey Makes the Case for Nuclear Power." *Forbes*, September 1.

Conniff, R. 2014. "Electric Power Rights of Way: A New Frontier for Conservation." Yale Environment 360 (blog), October 16. https://e360.yale.edu/features/electric_power_rights_of_way_a_new_frontier_for_conservation.

Dhakal, A. S., and R. C. Sidle. 2003. "Long-Term Modelling of Landslides for Different Forest Management Practices." *Earth Surface Processes and Landforms* 28 (8): 853–68.

Espinet Alegre, X., J. Rozenberg, K. S. Rao, and S. Ogita. 2018. "Piloting the Use of Network Analysis and Decision-Making under Uncertainty in Transport Operations: Preparation and Appraisal of a Rural Roads Project in Mozambique under Changing Flood Risk and Other Deep Uncertainties." Policy Research Working Paper 8490, World Bank, Washington, DC.

Gartner, E. T., J. Mulligan, R. Schmidt, J. Gunn, A. Reference, and N. Price. 2013. "Natural Infrastructure Investing in Forested Landscapes for Source Water Protection in the United States." World Resources Institute, Washington, DC.

Georges, K., B. Hall, T. McNally, and B. Tam. 2018. "The Smart Water Utility: 21st Century Water Utility (Isles Utilities)." ICMA (International City/County Management Association) (blog), July 3.

GridWise Alliance. 2013. "Improving Electric Grid Reliability and Resilience: Lessons from Superstorm Sandy and Other Extreme Events." GridWise Alliance, Washington, DC, June 12.

Hallegatte, S., J. Rentschler, and B. Walsh. 2018. *Building Back Better: Achieving Resilience through Stronger, Faster, and More Inclusive Post-Disaster Reconstruction*. Washington, DC: World Bank. https://openknowledge.worldbank.org/handle/10986/29867.

Kwakkel, J., B. A. Jafino, A. Verbraeck, S. Eker, and J. Rozenberg. 2019. "Resilience of the Transport Network in Bangladesh: A Graph-Theoretical and Simulation-Based Approach." World Bank, Washington, DC (forthcoming).

Lindsey, K. 2008. "Guidelines for Emergency Resource Planning for Overhead Transmission Line Asset Owners." Institute of Electrical and Electronics Engineers (IEEE), New York.

Nicholls, R. J., J. Hinkel, D. Lincke, and T. van der Pol. 2019. "Global Investment Costs for Coastal Defense through the 21st Century." Policy Research Working Paper 8745, World Bank, Washington, DC.

NRC (National Research Council). 2000. *Watershed Management for Potable Water Supply: Assessing the New York City Strategy*. Washington, DC: National Academies Press.

Oguah, S., and S. Khosla. 2017. "Disaster Preparedness Offers Big Payoffs for Utilities." Live Wire 2017/84, World Bank, Washington, DC.

Ray, P. A., and C. M. Brown. 2015. *Including Climate Uncertainty in Water Resources Planning and Project Design: The Decision Tree Initiative*. Washington, DC: World Bank.

Rozenberg, J., C. Briceno-Garmendia, X. Lu, L. Bonzanigo, and H. Moroz. 2017. "Improving the Resilience of Peru's Road Network to Climate Events." Policy Research Working Paper 8013, World Bank, Washington, DC.

Rozenberg, J., and M. Fay. 2019. *Beyond the Gap: How Countries Can Afford the Infrastructure They Need While Protecting the Planet.* Washington, DC: World Bank.

Rozenberg, J., C. Fox, M. Tariverdi, E. Koks, and S. Hallegatte. 2019. "Road Show: Comparing Road Network Resilience around the World." Background paper for this report, World Bank, Washington, DC.

Schweikert, A. E., L. Nield, E. Otto, and M. Deinert. 2019. "Resilience and Critical Power System Infrastructure: Lessons Learned from Natural Disasters and Future Research Needs." Background paper for this report, World Bank, Washington, DC.

State Council of China. 2015. "Guideline to Promote Building Sponge Cities." State Council of China, Beijing.

Stip, C., Z. Mao, L. Bonzanigo, G. Browder, and J. Tracy. 2019. "The Resilience of Water Infrastructure: Examples from Dams, Wastewater Treatment Plants, and Water Supply and Sanitation Systems." Sector note for this report, World Bank, Washington, DC.

Stöcker, C. 2018. "Software Defined Digital Grid on a P2P Network: On Systems of Autonomous Energy Cells." Medium (blog), March 12.

Strahl, J., M. Bebrin, E. Paris, and D. Jones. 2016. "Beyond the Buzzwords: Making the Specific Case for Community Resilience Microgrids." Paper presented at the 2016 ACEEE Summer Study on Energy Efficiency in Buildings, American Council for an Energy-Efficient Economy, Pacific Grove, CA, August 21–26.

Tercek, M. 2017. "Mangroves: A Star Player in the Coastal Protection Game." Nature Conservancy (blog), August 7.

U.S. Department of Energy. 2018. "Hurricanes Nate, Maria, Irma, and Harvey Situation Reports." Office of Cybersecurity, Energy Security, and Emergency Response, U.S. Department of Energy, Washington, DC.

Van Steenbergen, F., T. Alemayehu, K. Woldearegay, and M. Agujetas Perez. 2019. *Guidelines: Green Roads for Water—Road Infrastructure in Support of Water Managements and Climate Resilience.* Hertogenbosch, the Netherlands: Meta Meta Research.

Veeramany, A., G. A. Coles, S. D. Unwin, T. B. Nguyen, and J. E. Dagle. 2018. "Trial Implementation of a Multihazard Risk Assessment Framework for High-Impact Low-Frequency Power Grid Events." *IEEE Systems Journal* 12 (4): 3807–15.

White House. 2013. "Economic Benefits of Increasing Electric Grid Resilience to Weather Outages." Executive Office of the President, Washington, DC.

World Bank. 2015. "Disaster Risk Management in the Transport Sector: A Review of Concepts and International Case Studies." Working Paper 98202, World Bank, Washington, DC.

———. 2018. *Water Scarce Cities: Thriving in a Finite World.* Washington, DC: World Bank.

Wright-Contreras, L. 2018. "VEI and Dawaco: Water Operators' Partnership Case Study." UN-Habitat, Nairobi.

From Resilient Infrastructure Services to Resilient Users

8

So far in part II, this report has shown how infrastructure networks could be made more resilient by employing a combination of interventions in assets (strengthening) and in networks (redundancy, diversification, and working across systems). These strategies offer the benefits of lower life-cycle costs of assets and more reliable services. Yet ultimately what matters is not the resilience of the supply of infrastructure services, but the resilience of the end users—the topic of this chapter.

After all, infrastructure disruptions can be catastrophic or more benign, depending on whether users—including people and supply chains—can cope with them. At this level, the benefit of more resilient infrastructure is a reduction in the total impact of natural hazards on people and economies. This chapter explores ways to reduce the vulnerability of users and to make supply chains more resilient.

REDUCING DEMAND FOR INFRASTRUCTURE SERVICES BY IMPROVING EFFICIENCY OFTEN BUILDS RESILIENCE

With growing populations and increasingly scarce—or fought-over—water resources, utilities must manage demand to reduce stress on their city's water supplies. A recent example is Cape Town, which had to take drastic measures to avoid reaching "Day 0"—the day the city would run out of water. After relying primarily on surface water resources for two centuries through an elaborate network of elevated lakes, the city was hit by three consecutive years of extremely low rainfall (1/590-year events) in 2014–16 and was forced to step back and take stock of its water situation. After much deliberation, Cape Town decided to focus initially on demand management (Kaiser 2018). The measures implemented reduced water usage by 400 million liters a day (40 percent of usage) between 2015 and 2018, making it possible to avoid a major socioeconomic crisis.

Las Vegas—by no means a low water consumer, at 284 net liters per capita per day—has managed to reduce its residential consumption by 40 percent since 2002 (World Bank 2018), despite its population growth and its 40 million visitors a year. At the other end of the spectrum, Zaragoza, with per capita consumption of 99 liters per person per day, one of the lowest in the country and worldwide, achieved a 30 percent decrease in consumption levels in the early 2000s, when the city launched ambitious efficiency improvement programs. This reduction was achieved through a combination of water pricing adjustment, network rehabilitation, and public outreach and education (World Bank 2018).

Demand management recognizes that service customers are at the center of efforts to build resilience in the water supply and sanitation system. In Belen, Costa Rica, customers of the water utility helped to identify low-cost demand reduction measures to be tested in a study (Datta et al. 2015). These focus group discussions revealed that customers generally agreed about the importance of conserving water but did not necessarily think that they themselves should reduce use and knew little about what high or low water consumption might be. Study results demonstrated that a descriptive social norm measure using a neighborhood comparison (through stickers on water bills) was most effective among high-consumption users and more effective than city-wide comparisons. Among low-consumption users, an intervention that gave customers the information they needed to devise their own water use reduction plan—with targets, measures, and milestones—was most effective. Including users in program design through both focus group and field testing yielded important findings that the Belen service provider could incorporate into future programming.

BOX 8.1 Building norms, urban forms, and behavioral changes can reduce energy demand during heat waves and prevent secondary impacts on power systems

Heat waves, which are becoming increasingly intense and frequent, can have severe effects on power systems. Urban forms and building characteristics can contribute to heat waves through the "urban heat island" (Lemonsu et al. 2013; Stone, Hess, and Frumkin 2010). Socioeconomic vulnerability and the vulnerability of power systems, therefore, depend on the choices made during urban planning.

Viguié et al. (2019) consider three broad categories of actions to reduce the vulnerability of cities to heat waves: (1) a large-scale urban reconfiguration policy, leading to the addition of many parks and green spaces; (2) a building-scale policy, in which strict building insulation rules and the use of reflective materials for walls and roofs might be applied to all buildings in urban areas except historical buildings; and (3) behavioral changes in the use of air-conditioning to maintain 28°C in residential buildings and 26°C in offices instead of 23°C in a reference scenario.

The addition of parks and green spaces across a city decreases air temperature mainly through evapotranspiration. However, this effect is not big enough to have a significant impact on electricity consumption for air-conditioning (−2 percent). Improvements in building insulation have a much greater impact on the use of energy for air-conditioning in buildings (−17 percent). Finally, behavioral change (increasing the thermostat setting) has the largest impact on energy consumption for air-conditioning (−43 percent). The higher effects of this action highlight the importance, beyond changes in infrastructure, of actions targeting behavioral change (figure B8.1.1).

FIGURE B8.1.1 Behavioral policies are the most efficient way to reduce energy consumption during heat waves

Numbers show reduced electricity consumption from air conditioning during a heat wave in Paris

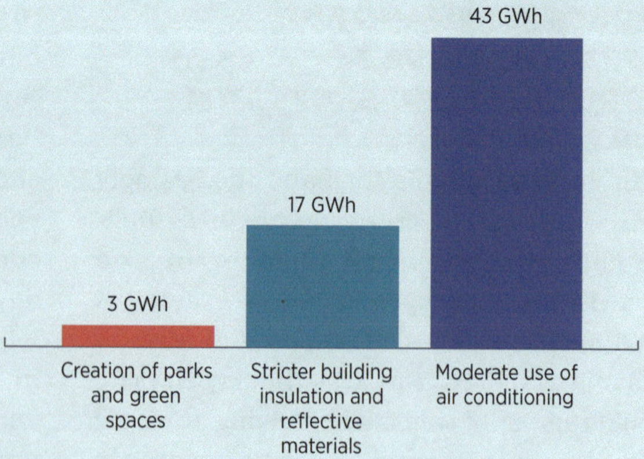

Source: Viguié et al. 2019.

Similar examples can be found in the power sector, where demand management can help in responding to crises (box 8.1). *Demand response* is defined by the U.S. Federal Energy Regulatory Commission as changes in customers' normal electricity consumption in response to changes in the price of electricity over time or to incentive payments designed to induce lower electricity use. This mechanism can be useful during disasters because it can help to reduce stress on the network. Indeed, Carlotto and Grzybowski (2014) show that the size and scope of blackouts in a network grow with its utilization rate, meaning that the closer a network is to its operational limit, the larger the blackouts.

Demand management was used in Texas in 2014 when two power plants went down because of the cold, suddenly forcing 1,800 megawatts offline. Because of the extreme weather, the grid was already under stress, so the Electric Reliability Council of Texas (ERCOT), the state's grid operator, had to call for a demand response across the state to avoid rolling blackouts. At the time, ERCOT relied predominantly on large industrial customers to reduce their consumption of electricity. Coupled with the use of all available power sources, the demand response proved to be the solution to the two power plant failures. Currently, automated demand response programs are being implemented in some countries. More traditional ways can also be used to implement this solution. Television, the Internet, radio, and newspapers, as well as automated phone or text messaging, can be used to let customers know when they need to reduce demand in the face of an extreme weather event (Brown, Prudent-Richard, and O'Mara 2016).

CRITICALITY DEPENDS ON THE END USER: SOME ASSETS ARE CRITICAL FOR FOOD SECURITY, OTHERS FOR COMPETITIVENESS

Understanding the needs and capacities of users helps utilities to target investments better and to identify the parts of the network to strengthen. The importance of a bridge or a power distribution line depends on who is using it. A power distribution line that connects a hospital or a flood shelter is likely more important during and after an emergency than the average distribution line in the country. A road or a bridge that is used by an on-demand supply chain with no inventory (such as for fresh food) cannot tolerate short disruptions, whereas industries with large inventories can tolerate long disruptions.

To investigate how criticality depends on users and supply chains, Colon, Hallegatte, and Rozenberg (2019) combine a transport and a supply chain model to investigate the criticality of the transport network in Tanzania. As expected, the most critical road segments depend on the types of products considered. Map 8.1 shows how a one-week disruption in certain roads in the Tanzanian transport network would affect four different users or supply chains: (1) the economy as a whole (panel a); (2) food supply chains only (panel b)—a food security issue; (3) the manufacturing sector (panel c); and (4) exports (panel d), which are important for trade competitiveness (and the profitability of the port).

Comparison of the maps reveals that investment priorities depend on policy objectives. For example, segments of the coastal trunk road located about 200 km south of Dar-es-Salaam are critical for food security but rather irrelevant for manufacturing and trade. For the latter purpose, improving the road east of Morogoro is a priority. This segment carries large freight flows moving between the port of Dar es Salaam and landlocked countries such as the Democratic Republic of Congo and Zambia.

END USERS NEED TO PREPARE FOR INFRASTRUCTURE DISRUPTIONS AND DESIGN MORE RESILIENT SUPPLY CHAINS

End users can take a range of measures to mitigate the adverse impacts of infrastructure

MAP 8.1 The criticality of a road depends on how it is used

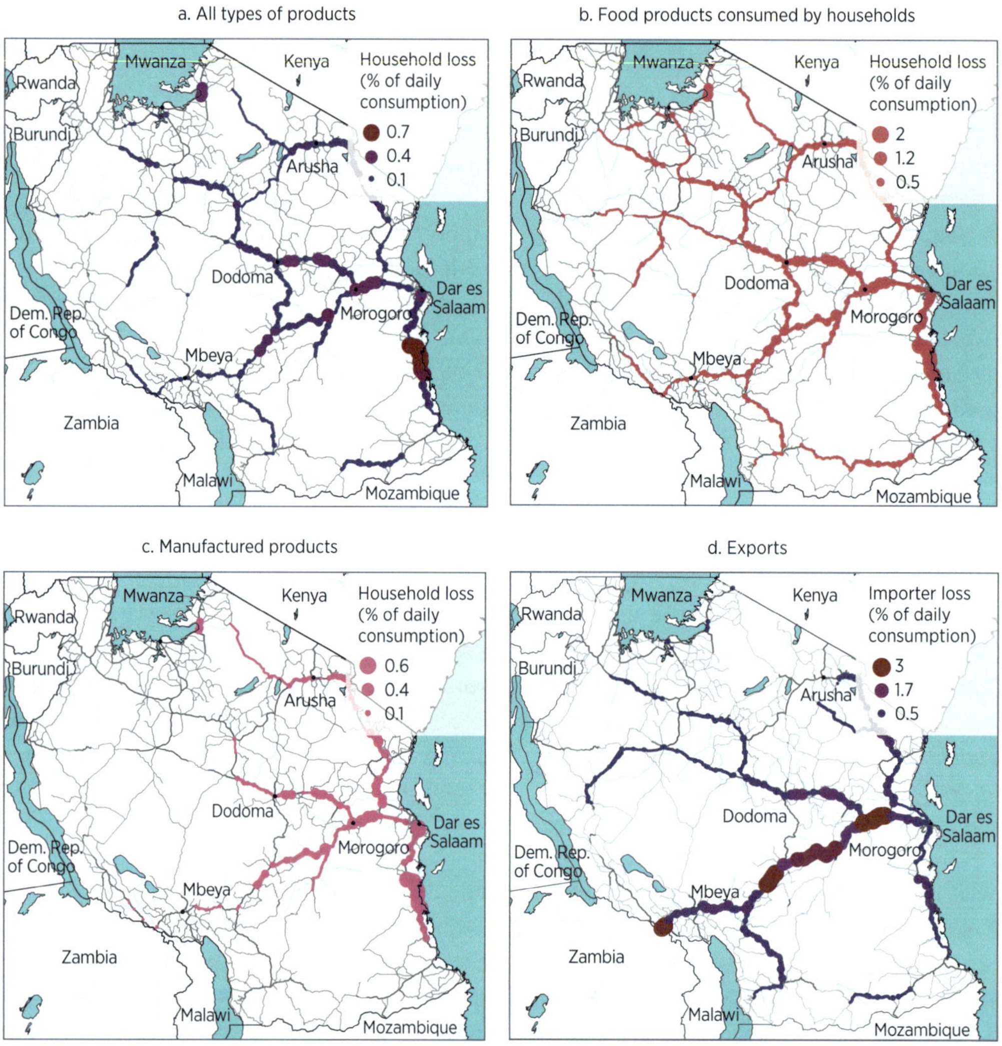

Source: Colon, Hallegatte, and Rozenberg 2019.
Note: In all four panels, the width of the line overlaying a given road is proportional to the impacts that a one-week disruption of the road would trigger. Impacts are measured in % of daily consumption in the considered sector. They represent exceptional expenditures due to costlier transport and missed consumption due to shortages. Panels a, b, and c depict the products used by Tanzanian households. Panel d depicts the exceptional expenditures and missed purchases from international buyers. These impacts relate specifically to exports and transit flows.

disruptions. Dormady et al. (2017) identify the coping measures that firms affected by Hurricane Sandy in the United States most commonly applied. The study uses survey data to estimate the costs and effectiveness of the measures. The most common coping measures can be summarized along the main components of a firm's production function—that is, they relate to a firm's decisions about its capital and assets and its labor, inputs, and production technology (figure 8.1). In practice, the measures applied by infrastructure

FIGURE 8.1 Firms have a wide range of coping measures that they can use to mitigate the adverse effects of infrastructure disruptions

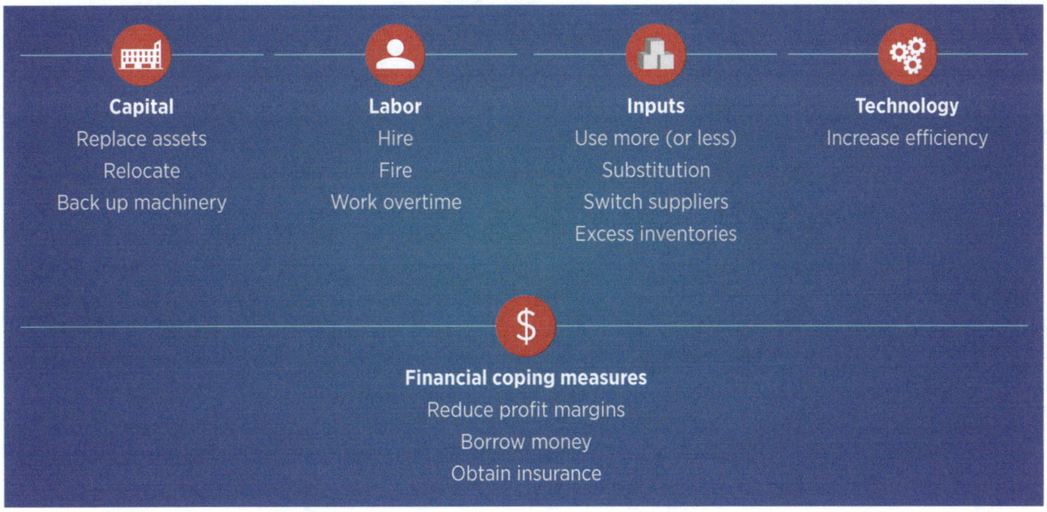

Source: Adapted from Dormady et al. 2017.

users depend on their local options and constraints.

In areas with frequent infrastructure service disruptions, end users can ramp up their own resilience by investing in backup resources such as generators or water and gas tanks. In addition, they can fill emergency generators with fuel and contact fuel suppliers with anticipated needs for deliveries after the storm has passed, as well as ensure that their business emergency supply kit is fully stocked. The U.S. Federal Emergency Management Agency has prepared comprehensive emergency preparedness materials for use in preparing for a disaster (FEMA 2014).

In Vietnam, a recent firm-level survey indicated that firms that purchase water equipment such as tanks or pumps in preparation for water outages face no impacts on production costs when water service is disrupted, compared with an increase in production costs of 8.24 percent otherwise (Hyland et al. 2019). However, unlike water tanks, an electricity backup capacity provided by diesel generators is associated with significant and additional operational cost, compared with the cost of electricity from the grid (box 8.2 discusses how Japanese firms have reduced these costs). These generators tend to be less affordable for smaller firms with limited cash reserves (see chapter 2).

Firms need to be prepared for shocks that affect them indirectly through supply chains

Firms also need to manage supply chain issues, which include not only transport disruptions but also problems with suppliers and clients. Indeed, a firm that is not affected by disasters directly or through disrupted infrastructure services may still be unable to produce because its suppliers cannot provide the required inputs, or because its clients are not able to continue buying. A broader view of the full supply chain is needed to assess disaster-related production risks.

Firms exposed to transport or supply chain disruptions tend to rely on large inventories for protection. In fact, firms in low- and middle-income countries have already adapted to poor

BOX 8.2 An energy management system to bridge power outages caused by disasters: The factory grid (F-grid) project in Ohira Industrial Park in Japan

Before the earthquake in eastern Japan in 2011, Toyota's automotive plant in Ohira village, Miyagi Prefecture, north of Fukushima, had relied entirely on the Tohoku Electric Power Company for energy. However, the earthquake shut down the power supply to the plant for two weeks, which led to considerable economic losses for Toyota and other companies in the surrounding industrial park as well as disruption of the supply chain. To avoid such losses in the future, companies in the industrial park sought to secure energy during power outages and shortages by building their own minigrid system with a comprehensive energy management system.

However, creating a backup power system to be used only during emergencies or a natural disaster is extremely costly. The companies thus recognized that they needed to build a power system that would be useful in both normal and disaster times. They also recognized that strong collaboration among firms to consolidate power demand within the industrial park would be critical to creating demand for minigrid power during normal operations.

In February 2013, nearly two years after the earthquake, Toyota, in partnership with 10 corporations and organizations located in the industrial park, established a limited liability partnership. The objective was to establish a comprehensive energy management system that contributes to improved energy efficiency in the industrial park during normal times, as well as serves as a backup power supply system during disaster times. Through the onsite generation of electricity and heat, as well as use of the community energy management system to balance the power supply optimally in the industrial park, F-grid achieved a 24 percent increase in energy efficiency and a 31 percent reduction in carbon dioxide emissions in 2016, compared with those of industrial parks similar in size. Overall, the F-grid system not only helps the industrial park to bridge power outages caused by natural disasters (or other reasons) but also helps to reduce energy costs thanks to increased efficiency.

Source: World Bank 2019.

infrastructure and tend to hold larger inventories than firms in high-income economies (Guasch and Kogan 2003). Simulations for Tanzania show that if firms maintain two weeks of inventories instead of one, the costs of disaster-related transport disruptions are reduced by 80 percent (Colon, Hallegatte, and Rozenberg 2019). In disaster-prone areas where transport disruptions are frequent but relatively short, holding larger inventories can be a cost-effective coping solution (Schmitt 2011). Firms with large inventories still suffer from higher transport costs due to disruptions, but they have to interrupt their own production processes only for long disruptions. However, excessive inventories are financial burdens—costly to maintain and, in some cases, such as perishable goods, a source of significant losses.

Maintaining a diversity of suppliers from both local and distant locations is another powerful safeguard, especially in long transport or supply chain disruptions. Relying on a single supplier is a critical vulnerability. For example, in 2011, many automakers used a paint pigment called Xirallic that was produced at only one factory in the world, the Onahama plant near the Fukushima-Daiichi nuclear power station in Japan.[1] When the factory was evacuated and closed after the earthquake, many automakers realized that they had no alternative suppliers and had to restrict sales of some colors. Maintaining a diversity of suppliers, if possible in different areas and using different delivery routes that cannot be simultaneously hit by a shock, strengthens supply chains. The total benefits of more diversity in suppliers could be large. For example, the modeling exercise described in this report suggests that for Tanzania sourcing critical inputs from two suppliers instead of one reduces the indirect costs of transport disruptions by about 70 percent. However, managing multiple suppliers creates significant transaction costs, which explains why recent supply chains have tended to reduce the number of suppliers (Bakos and Brynjolfsson 1993; Berger, Gerstenfeld, and Zeng 2004; Goffin, Szwejczewski, and New 1997). Thus, there is a trade-off between the efficiency of supply chains in normal times and their resilience to various shocks.

Local supply chains are more robust to transport disruption, but they are more vulnerable to direct shocks. Sourcing from local partners decreases the reliance on transportation and significantly reduces the risks of incurring the indirect damages of a distant disruption. In Tanzania, simulations suggest that having suppliers twice as close reduces impacts by 20 percent. At the same time, local supply chains are more often directly affected by a shock, which makes recovery more difficult. Maintaining relationships with distant partners helps firms to recover when their facilities and those of nearby partners are directly affected by a disaster (Kashiwagi, Todo, and Matous 2018; Todo, Nakajima, and Matous 2015). In this way, affected firms can receive support and help from their nonaffected clients and suppliers and do not suffer a disaster-related drop in demand that makes recovery more challenging. One extreme example of support to and from suppliers is Toyota, which in 2011 paid its employees to work at its suppliers so they could restore production as fast as possible. This type of support makes a large difference, especially for small and medium enterprises, which do not have the resources to prepare business continuity plans and have no specialist in recovery following a disaster.

A static supply chain cannot cope with a large-scale disaster and disruptions. Adaptability in supply chains is critical and should be embedded in business continuity plans. For this reason, a pillar of supply chain resilience is the development of organizational capacities to handle unexpected disruptions across firms (Blackhurst et al. 2005; Christopher and Peck 2004; Sheffi 2005). Decentralized decision making and increasing communication between firms are essential for resilience (Sheffi 2005). Specific actions include developing internal business continuity plans and rescue plans with suppliers and collocated companies. Since the 2011 earthquake in Japan, several firms have come together to redesign their evacuation protocols and emergency communication procedures and to develop new shared backup solutions for critical utilities (World Bank 2019).

Business continuity plans can also be calibrated by performing stress tests and exploring "what if" scenarios to identify bottlenecks and particularly vulnerable points (Chopra and Sodhi 2004). Such plans should be updated regularly, incorporating lessons from any new disruptions (Hamel and Välikangas 2003). And they should rely on sophisticated data management practices. After the 2011 earthquake in Japan, which caused large production disruptions, Toyota created a new database, Rescue, for the inventories held by 650,000 suppliers worldwide.[2] This information is being used to locate available resources more easily and to prevent bottlenecks in production processes.

Critical users during disasters: the special case of hospitals

Hospitals are both critical to the response to a disaster and highly vulnerable to its impacts (Tariverdi et al. 2019). A disaster in a heavily populated area can lead to a sudden surge in demand for regional health care services. Simultaneously, health care services may be diminished because of structural damage, loss of critical support systems such as power or water supply, or a reduced workforce because of transport network disruptions. Regional response planners need to ensure that the operations of critical support infrastructure are restored in a timely fashion.

Resilience-enhancing options can be divided into two main groups: health care alternative operations and infrastructure improvements. *Alternative operations* include (1) collaborative regional responses (such as transferring patients between hospitals) and individual hospital-based operational modifications (such as increasing bed capacity by using buffered capacity); (2) changing roles, such as nurses taking on roles ordinarily assigned to doctors; (3) increasing efficiency by speeding up patient care; and (4) applying alternative but lawful standards of care to the discharge and transfer of patients. These measures assume that hospitals take the necessary steps for preparedness, such as providing onsite family care to facilitate maintaining the required staff levels in a disaster event, establishing relationships across hospital units, and developing interhospital agreements.

Infrastructure improvement includes (1) potential mitigation, such as requesting that the poles of power lines to the hospital be strengthened; (2) redundancy in access to key health care facilities; (3) preparedness, such as prepositioning water reservoirs and generators and medical warehouse management; (4) repairs, such as reconstructing damaged facilities or lifelines; and (5) responses, such as refueling generators for an uninterrupted power supply.

INFRASTRUCTURE AFFECTS THE EXPOSURE OF USERS TO NATURAL HAZARDS

Because infrastructure localization decisions drive urbanization patterns and the exposure of populations and assets to risks, they should be coordinated with land use and urban plans. Baum-Snow (2007a, 2007b) provides both empirical and theoretical evidence that post–World War II suburbanization in the United States was driven largely by investments in highways that reduced travel times. Moreover, transit infrastructure investments can guide spatial development and influence land use, land use intensity, land values, and employment and population densities (map 8.2). Typically, transit-oriented development investments have a unique ability to influence the resilience of communities, because they inherently lead to concentrations of people and businesses around transit stops (Salat and Ollivier 2017). However, if these investments are not made strategically, taking into account information on the exposure of areas to natural hazards, the outcome could be an increase in vulnerability to disasters.

Infrastructure investments can be used to support the implementation of risk-informed land use and urbanization plans and to prevent unplanned developments. In cities in low- and middle-income countries, a large share—if not the vast majority—of households flock to informal settlements, often on the periphery of urban areas, because they are priced out of the narrow, formal housing market. Often these informal neighborhoods are located in disaster-prone areas, because that is where land tends to be available. For example, informal settlements on the outskirts of Dakar, grew when droughts in the 1970s sparked mass migration from rural areas. However, these land plots proved to be highly exposed to floods (a fact only obvious once the droughts had ended), with the result that between 100,000 and 300,000 people were affected by floods every rainy season, particularly during the destructive episodes in 2009 (World Bank 2016). In Conakry, Guinea's narrow peninsula capital, land is so scarce that many urban dwellers live in the lowest-lying areas, increasing their exposure to storm surges and floods, or directly in the mangroves, increasing the

MAP 8.2 The pattern of urbanization in Addis Ababa closely follows the major public transport lines

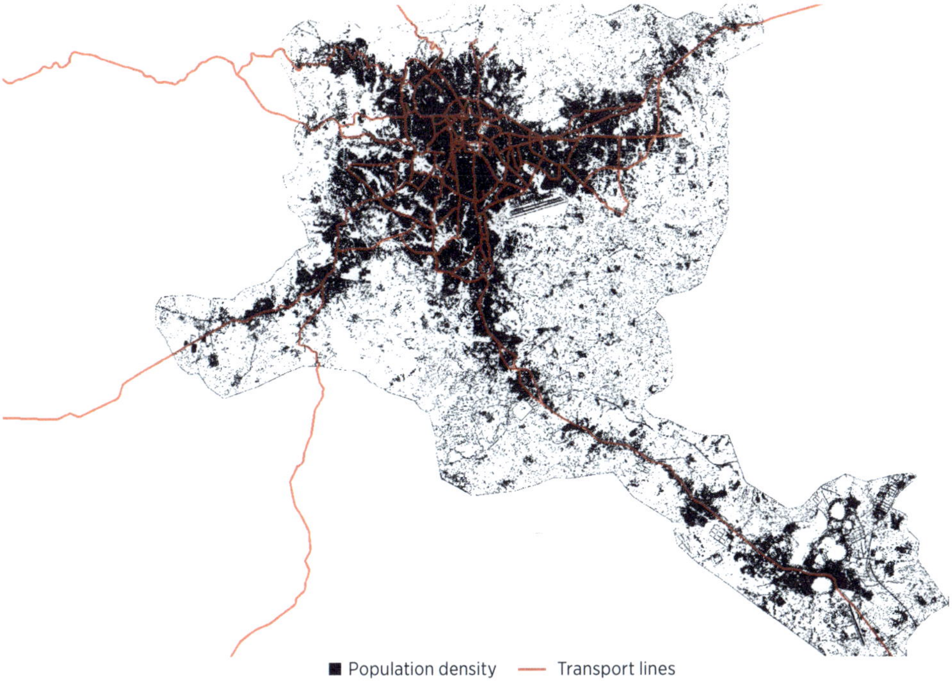

Source: World Bank staff.

city's exposure to floods in the process (World Bank, forthcoming). Once these neighborhoods have reached a critical mass, relocating households becomes very difficult. Similarly, retrofitting these neighborhoods with basic infrastructure and adapting them to the risk of natural hazards are expensive, lengthy, and sensitive processes.

A solution lies in equipping low-risk areas with basic infrastructure to guide the localization choices of people before they arrive. Such investments attract populations to areas that are relatively safe from natural hazards. Only the most basic infrastructure is needed in the early days to guide development while preserving the possibility of upscaling in the future, and it is essential at the outset to secure the rights of way for roads and sewage systems. This approach was followed in the Comás squatter community in Lima, where volunteer engineering students laid out the basic structure in the 1960s before the area was occupied. The layout of roads created small accessible blocks that would later be filled by residential structures. Today, a 160-square-meter house in this neighborhood (which was a slum not so long ago) costs $180,000 (Angel 2017). Similar models were applied to sites-and-services projects in India (Owens, Gulyani, and Rizvi 2018) and Tanzania (Michaels et al. 2017), consisting of the provision of basic infrastructure and services.

Areas to be given priority for infrastructure development can be identified using simple geographic information system approaches. The goal is to identify "good" land that is safe and close to opportunities, jobs, and the existing network infrastructure.

In Fiji, the city of Nadi sought to identify where future settlements and investment in infrastructure should be located to minimize exposure to natural risks and the cost of development (Government of Fiji and World Bank 2017). Nadi Town is the third-largest urban center in Fiji, with a population of around 52,800 (in 2016). The town is growing at the relatively fast rate of 2.5 percent a year, driven by tourism, transport, and high-value real estate developments. It is acting as an economic magnet, and in the absence of forward planning for low-income groups, informal settlements have mushroomed: 17 settlements (home to 18 percent of the town's population) are in unplanned areas, particularly in the urban boundary and periurban areas. The city is expected to maintain this growth into the next decade, and regularizing the existing unplanned settlements and planning for the absorption of future growth are an urban management and land use challenge.

Digital elevation models and flood maps are useful as a first screen for identifying areas that might be suitable for development. In map 8.3, the low-lying areas of Nadi that are highly exposed to coastal and river floods are indicated in red, blue, and orange. The areas that are considered at high or extreme risk of flood in a 100-year return flood risk map are purple, already-developed areas are gray, and areas with steep slopes are white.[3] The light pink areas are potentially suitable for future development, although further studies should be conducted to confirm this simple assessment, and more investment in drainage could make some of the flood-prone, low-lying areas suitable for development.

At this point, about 4.3 square kilometers are not developed within the town boundary (see

MAP 8.3 Risk-informed urbanization planning can help to accommodate the growing urban population of Fiji while limiting the increase in natural risks

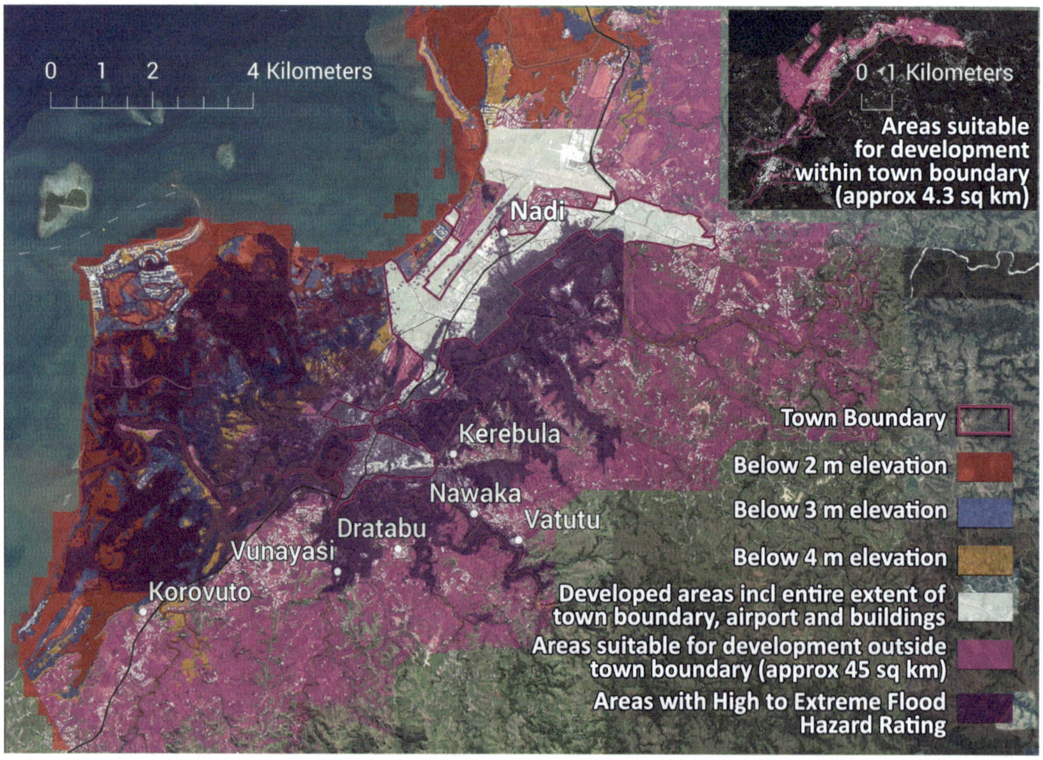

Sources: Government of Fiji and World Bank 2017.

inset). If additional investments were made to improve drainage in the area, this land could be a priority for future development. With future densities of between 10 dwellings per hectare (today's values) and 15 dwellings per hectare, the available area within the town boundary could host 4,300–6,500 households. In view of the current backlog of about 2,000 units in Nadi and 300 new households a year (2.5 percent growth rate), this land could accommodate Nadi's urban growth for 8–15 years.

Over the longer term, areas beyond the town boundary should be considered—possibly combined with an expansion of the boundary. More than 45 square kilometers are available close to Nadi, but outside the town boundary. That area could accommodate from 45,000 to almost 70,000 households—which is enough to manage rural-urban migration for several decades. Use of this land, however, would require addressing issues of land tenure and ownership and expanding networks, especially for water and sanitation.

Part II of this report has shown that building more resilient infrastructure assets is often costlier, but that the additional cost is small, especially if countries spend well, and the investment in more resilience is highly cost-effective. Building up the resilience of infrastructure services and users at a low cost is possible, provided the right interventions are implemented in the right places—for example, by targeting investments using hazards data and criticality analyses, by capturing synergies across sectors using smart and robust decision-making processes, by using nature-based solutions, and by capturing resilience benefits from diversification and decentralization. This part of the report has also shown that the benefits of resilient infrastructure systems can go beyond reliable infrastructure services; well-designed infrastructure system can reduce the exposure of populations and firms to natural hazards and increase their overall resilience without having to cost more.

These insights raise the question of *how* to implement these solutions. What concrete steps are necessary? What institutional systems and what types of incentives, capacities, and financial instruments are required to build more resilient infrastructure? These questions are the subject of the next part of this report.

NOTES

1. "Automakers Face a Paint Shortage after Japan Quake," Reuters, March 25, 2011. https://www.reuters.com/article/us-japan-pigment/automakers-face-paint-shortage-after-japan-quake-idUSTRE72P04B20110326.
2. "How Toyota Applied the Lessons of the 2011 Quake," *Automotive News*, April 25, 2016. https://www.autonews.com/article/20160425/OEM/304259956/how-toyota-applied-the-lessons-of-2011-quake.
3. The flood map is based on a flood risk assessment of Nadi, Fiji, by the Pacific Community and the National Institute of Water and Atmospheric Research.

REFERENCES

Angel, S. 2017. "Urban Forms and Future Cities: A Commentary." *Urban Planning* 2 (1). doi: http://dx.doi.org/10.17645/up.v2i1.863.

Bakos, J. Y., and E. Brynjolfsson. 1993. "Information Technology, Incentives, and the Optimal Number of Suppliers." *Journal of Management Information Systems* 10 (2): 37–53.

Baum-Snow, N. 2007a. "Did Highways Cause Suburbanization?" *Quarterly Journal of Economics* 122 (2): 775–805.

———. 2007b. "Suburbanization and Transportation in the Monocentric Model." *Journal of Urban Economics* 62 (3): 405–23.

Berger, P. D., A. Gerstenfeld, and A. Z. Zeng. 2004. "How Many Suppliers Are Best? A Decision-Analysis Approach." *Omega* 32 (1): 9–15.

Blackhurst, J., C. W. Craighead, D. Elkins, and R. B. Handfield. 2005. "An Empirically Derived Agenda of Critical Research Issues for Managing Supply-Chain Disruptions." *International Journal of Production Research* 43 (19): 4067–81.

Brown, R., G. Prudent Richard, and K. O'Mara. 2016. *Enhancing Power Sector Resilience: Emerging Practices to Manage Weather and Geological Risks.* Energy Sector Management Assistance Program. Washington, DC: World Bank Group.

Carlotto, T., and J. M. V. Grzybowski. 2014. "Self-Organized Criticality and Cascading Failures in the Topological Model of Power Grids: A Case Study." *Proceeding Series of the Brazilian Society of Applied and Computational Mathematics* 2 (1): n.p.

Chopra, S., and M. S. Sodhi. 2004. "Managing Risk to Avoid Supply-Chain Breakdown: By Understanding the Variety and Interconnectedness of Supply-Chain Risks, Managers Can Tailor Balanced, Effective Risk-Reduction Strategies for Their Companies." *MIT Sloan Management Review* 46 (Fall): 53–62.

Christopher, M., and H. Peck. 2004. "Building the Resilient Supply Chain." *International Journal of Logistics Management* 15 (2): 1–14.

Colon, C., S. Hallegatte, and J. Rozenberg. 2019. "Transportation and Supply Chain Resilience in the United Republic of Tanzania." Background paper for this report, World Bank, Washington, DC.

Datta, S., J. J. Miranda Montero, L. D. C. Zoratto, O. Calvo-Gonzalez, M. Darling, and K. J. O. Lorenzana. 2015. "A Behavioral Approach to Water Conservation: Evidence from Costa Rica." Policy Research Working Paper 7283, World Bank, Washington, DC.

Dormady, N., A. Rose, H. Rosoff, and A. Roa-Henriquez. 2017. "Estimating the Cost-Effectiveness of Resilience to Disasters: Survey Instrument Design and Refinement of Primary Data." In *Handbook on Resilience of Socio-Technical Systems*. Cheltenham: Edward Elgar.

FEMA (Federal Emergency Management Agency). 2014. "Every Business Should Have a Plan." FEMA, Washington, DC.

Goffin, K., M. Szwejczewski, and C. New. 1997. "Managing Suppliers: When Fewer Can Mean More." *International Journal of Physical Distribution and Logistics Management* 27 (7): 422–36.

Government of Fiji and World Bank. 2017. "Climate Vulnerability Assessment: Making Fiji Climate Resilient." World Bank, Washington, DC.

Guasch, J. L., and J. Kogan. 2003. "Just-in-Case Inventories: A Cross-Country Analysis." Policy Research Working Paper 3012, World Bank, Washington, DC.

Hamel, G., and L. Välikangas. 2003. "The Quest for Resilience." *Harvard Business Review* 81 (9): 52–56.

Hyland, M., J. Russ, R. Damania, and A. Khalil. 2019. "A Firm Commitment to Water Delivery in Vietnam: A View from the Private Sector." Policy Working Paper, World Bank, Washington, DC (forthcoming).

Kaiser, G. 2018. "Planning for Water Security in Cape Town." PowerPoint presentation, World Bank, Washington, DC.

Kashiwagi, Y., Y. Todo, and P. Matous. 2018. "International Propagation of Economic Shocks through Global Supply Chains." WINPEC Working Paper E1810, Waseda Institute of Political Economy, Waseda University, Tokyo.

Lemonsu, A., R. Kounkou-Arnaud, J. Desplat, J. L. Salagnac, and V. Masson. 2013. "Evolution of the Parisian Urban Climate under a Global Changing Climate." *Climatic Change* 116 (3-4): 679–92.

Michaels, G., D. Nigmatulina, F. Rauch, T. Regan, N. Baruah, and A. Dahlstrand-Rudin. 2017. "Planning Ahead for Better Neighborhoods: Long Run Evidence from Tanzania." CESifo Working Paper 6680, IFO Institute for Economic Research (CESifo), Munich.

Owens, K. E., S. Gulyani, and A. Rizvi. 2018. "Success When We Deemed It Failure? Revisiting Sites and Services Projects in Mumbai and Chennai 20 Years Later." *World Development* 106 (June): 260–72.

Salat, S., and G. P. Ollivier. 2017. *Transforming the Urban Space through Transit-Oriented Development: The 3V Approach*. Washington, DC: World Bank.

Schmitt, A. J. 2011. "Strategies for Customer Service Level Protection under Multi-Echelon Supply Chain Disruption Risk." *Transportation Research Part B: Methodological* 45 (8): 1266–83.

Sheffi, Y. 2005. *The Resilient Enterprise: Overcoming Vulnerability for Competitive Advantage*. Cambridge, MA: MIT Press.

Stone, B., J. J. Hess, and H. Frumkin. 2010. "Urban Form and Extreme Heat Events: Are Sprawling Cities More Vulnerable to Climate Change Than Compact Cities?" *Environmental Health Perspectives* 118 (10): 1425–28.

Tariverdi, M., H. Fotouhi, S. Moryadee, and E. Miller-Hooks. 2019. "Health Care System Disaster-Resilience Optimization Given Its Reliance on Interdependent Critical Lifelines." *Journal of Infrastructure Systems* 25 (1): 04018044.

Todo, Y., K. Nakajima, and P. Matous. 2015. "How Do Supply Chain Networks Affect the Resilience of Firms to Natural Disasters? Evidence from the Great East Japan Earthquake." *Journal of Regional Science* 55 (2): 209–29.

Viguié, V., A. Lemonsu, S. Hallegatte, A.-L. Beaulant, C. Marchadier, V. Masson, G. Pigeon, and J.-L. Salagnac. 2019. "Early Adaptation to Heat Waves and Future Reduction of Air-Conditioning Energy Use in Cities." Unpublished manuscript.

World Bank. 2016. *Perspectives urbaines: Villes emergentes pour un Sénégal emergent.* Washington, DC: World Bank.

———. 2018. *Water Scarce Cities: Thriving in a Finite World.* Washington, DC: World Bank.

———. 2019. *Resilient Industries: Ensuring Competitiveness in the Face of Natural Disasters.* Washington, DC: World Bank Group.

———. Forthcoming. "Republic of Guinea: Planning, Connecting, Financing in Conakry." World Bank, Washington, DC.

PART III

A Way Forward: Five Recommendations for More Resilient Infrastructure

So far, this report has shown that increasing the resilience of infrastructure services and users is possible, thanks to a set of cost-effective and readily available options—from using stronger materials to adopting redundancy or nature-based solutions. This raises the inevitable question of why these options are not always implemented in practice and why infrastructure systems so often are unable to cope with natural hazards.

Part III of this report explores the obstacles that prevent those who design, build, operate, and maintain infrastructure assets and systems from taking advantage of all available opportunities to boost resilience. It then identifies a set of five recommendations that can serve as a starting point from which to develop a country-specific strategy to enhance infrastructure resilience.

These obstacles differ in importance and relevance across countries: they depend on the level of income and wealth, the current extent and condition of the infrastructure systems in various sectors, and the institutional and technical capacity to design, build, and maintain infrastructure assets. To identify the appropriate recommendations in a country, decision makers need to account for the local context through a country-specific process. Nevertheless, the most common obstacles to resilient infrastructure can be identified (table PIII.1), and general recommendations to tackle these obstacles can be proposed. The first obstacle impairs infrastructure management in general, while the other four obstacles are about infrastructure resilience in particular.

The next five chapters consider these five obstacles and propose recommendations for actions to tackle them and to improve the resilience of infrastructure systems and users.

Chapter 9 starts from the fundamental challenge of infrastructure systems that are not resilient because they are poorly designed or mismanaged, such as when assets are not maintained adequately. It recommends that governments put in place some basic institutions, processes, and financing for managing infrastructure systems better—that is, that they "get the basics right." Better infrastructure governance is not only a prerequisite for functioning and reliable infrastructure systems, but also can help to increase the resilience of infrastructure systems and their ability to cope with, and recover from, shocks, regardless of their origin.

But while these basic principles of good infrastructure design and management are important, they are by no means sufficient to make infrastructure resilient—especially to rarer and higher-intensity events, such as hurricanes, earthquakes, and major floods. Moreover, good infrastructure management does not guarantee that climate change and other long-

TABLE PIII.1 Key obstacles to more resilient infrastructure services and examples of underlying causes

Obstacles to good infrastructure management	Obstacles to infrastructure resilience			
Poor design, operation, and maintenance of infrastructure systems	**Political economy challenges and coordination failures**	**Lack of incentives to increase resilience**	**Inadequate data, models, skills, or tools**	**Affordability and financing constraints**
• Absence of local standards, codes, and regulations (or lack of enforcement) • Underfinanced or understaffed regulators • Insufficient resources for the early-stage design of the infrastructure system and assets • Borrowing constraints and affordability issues • Lack of financing and capacity for asset maintenance	• Invisibility of resilience benefits • Interdependency of infrastructure systems • Synergies and trade-offs across different risks or infrastructure systems • Narrow mandates of institutions	• Infrastructure service providers not bearing the full cost of disruptions • Lack of incentives to protect or restore ecosystems	• Lack of data, methodologies, or technical skills • Designs often based on historical data and not on future hazards and climate change • Overconfidence in model results and historical data • Insufficient consideration of low-probability scenarios	• Lack of resources for risk-informed planning and risk assessment at early stages of project design • Lack of resources in postdisaster situations • Lack of information and transparency on infrastructure asset resilience

term environmental and socioeconomic trends will be planned for. To address these issues, decision makers need to tackle four more obstacles that are specific to resilience to natural hazards and climate change. These four obstacles lead to four additional recommendations.

Chapter 10 explores the challenges of political economy and the coordination failures that impede the creation of a resilient infrastructure ecosystem. It recommends creating a whole-of-government coordination mechanism for resilient infrastructure—along with identifying critical infrastructure, defining acceptable (and intolerable) risk levels, and ensuring equitable access to resilient infrastructure.

Chapter 11 examines why public and private decision makers often do not have sufficient incentives to create more resilient infrastructure systems. It recommends including resilience consideration in regulations and financial incentives to align the interest of infrastructure service providers with the public interest and updating them regularly to account for climate change and other long-term trends.

Chapter 12 focuses on the lack of data, models, and tools that make it difficult for infrastructure service providers to implement resilience-building solutions. It recommends investing in freely accessible data on natural hazards and climate change; improving decision making and minimizing the potential for catastrophic failures; and building the skills needed to use the data and models.

Chapter 13 examines affordability and financing issues for resilience. It recommends providing adequate funding to include risk assessments in master plans and early project design, developing government-wide financial protection strategies and contingency plans, and promoting transparency to better inform investors and decision makers.

These recommendations are not independent. They need to be coordinated and designed together. For example, a new institution in charge of infrastructure resilience needs to have appropriate incentives, capacity, and budget to be effective. And a financing initiative, such as a disaster risk financing strategy, can be used to create the right institutions or to build capacity. Thus, a comprehensive approach to these obstacles and recommendations is necessary.

The good news is that these measures would also contribute to better management of infrastructure systems in general and, therefore, do more than increase resilience. They would enhance the quality of infrastructure systems and make them more efficient and reliable.

The Foundation for Resilient Infrastructure 9

OBSTACLE	RECOMMENDATION	ACTIONS
Poor design, operation, and maintenance of infrastructure systems	Get the basics right	• 1.1: Introduce and enforce regulations, construction codes, and procurement rules • 1.2: Create systems for appropriate operation, maintenance, and postincident response • 1.3: Provide appropriate funding and financing for infrastructure planning, construction, and maintenance

THE OBSTACLE: MANY INFRASTRUCTURE SYSTEMS ARE POORLY DESIGNED, OPERATED, OR MAINTAINED

In some countries, infrastructure disruptions are chronic events: power outages occur every day, water supply is intermittent, and congestion makes travel slow and unpredictable. And in many places, a large fraction of these disruptions is not explained by any external factor like a natural hazard. Sometimes, infrastructure systems are simply insufficient to meet demand, leading to disruptions. This is the case when a lack of power generation forces utilities to shed load, which causes regular outages, or when a lack of public transit and transport infrastructure leads to massive congestion in fast-growing cities.

Sometimes, disruptions occur due to system failures that are the result of poor asset design or insufficient maintenance. For example, inadequate drainage infrastructure and clogging of existing systems by solid waste explain the regular occurrence of flooding in many large cities. This problem largely explains the recurrent transport disruptions in Dar es Salaam during the rainy season. Structural weaknesses sometimes cause bridges to collapse without any external shock, as happened in Genoa, in 2018. On August 14, 2003, a large blackout occurred in northeastern North America due to a combination of line contacts with overgrown trees and a technical failure of the alarm system in the utility control room (North American Electric Reliability Council 2004).

How can governments build more resilient infrastructure systems? The first step is to make them reliable in normal conditions by ensuring appropriate design, operation, and maintenance. A power system with tight capacity constraints and regular load shedding cannot be made resilient to storms or heat waves. Maintenance is particularly critical: culverts

FIGURE 9.1 Infrastructure quality correlates strongly with governance standards

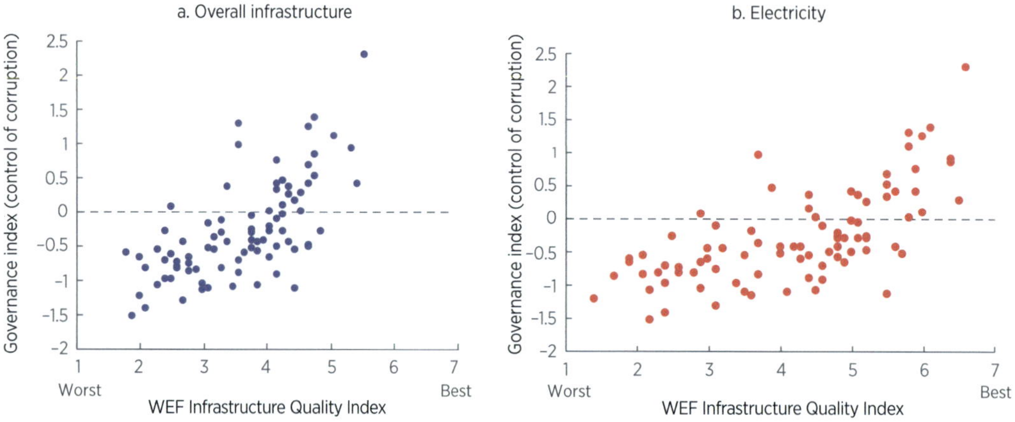

Source: Kornejew, Rentschler, and Hallegatte 2019.
Note: The World Economic Forum (WEF) Infrastructure Quality Index measures the quality of infrastructure services from 1 (extremely underdeveloped) to 7 (well developed and efficient by international standards). The *Worldwide Governance Indicators* report estimated governance standards for more than 200 countries and territories. For each country, these governance indicators reflect surveys of a large number of enterprises, citizens, and experts, based on more than 30 individual data sources. Control of corruption captures perceptions of the extent to which public power is exercised for private gain, including both petty and grand forms of corruption, as well as "capture" of the state by elites and private interests.

cannot protect a road if they are blocked by solid waste, transmission lines fail if nearby vegetation is not properly maintained, and leaking water pipes increase a water system's vulnerability to droughts.

But a government's ability to implement resilience-building options depends on whether it has effective systems in place to implement, finance, manage, and maintain infrastructure assets. Strong institutions, clear assignment of responsibilities, and transparent and reliable financing mechanisms are all essential to ensuring the effective provision of public services. In other words, good governance matters greatly for infrastructure quality.

Data show a clear correlation between governance and infrastructure quality. Figure 9.1 presents the relationship between the *Worldwide Governance Indicators* (WGI, World Bank, n.d.) subindex on corruption and the Infrastructure Quality Index of the *Global Competitiveness Report* (WEF 2018). Both panel a on infrastructure in general and panel b on the electricity sector show that as the quality of governance improves, so does the quality of infrastructure.[1] The same positive correlation between corruption and infrastructure quality exists for roads (Kornejew, Rentschler, and Hallegatte 2019). Similar patterns also appear for different WGI subindexes, such as for regulatory quality and government effectiveness.

Quality infrastructure does not have to be reserved for rich countries. The data behind figure 9.1 suggest significant differences in infrastructure quality for countries at the same income level. At low income levels, the difference is particularly large. For example, the reliability of electricity in Bhutan, whose gross domestic product (GDP) per capita is $2,500, is comparable to that of many middle- and high-income economies, whereas Nigeria, whose GDP per capita is $2,476, has some of the most frequent power outages of all countries.

This difference in governance and quality of investments may explain why infrastructure projects do not always deliver the intended benefits. For example, investments in electricity infrastructure have a mixed track record. Some studies show that electrification leads to a significant increase in school enrollment or years of schooling, while other studies estimate that it has no or few impacts on educational outcomes.[2] Regarding the impact on health, Brass et al. (2012) and Samad et al. (2013) find the same lack of conclusive evidence. Meanwhile, several impact assessments of electrification projects show significant increases in household income and female employment, while others do not.[3] Thus, simply spending money on infrastructure does not always yield benefits to users: investments need to be well designed and well implemented.

To explore the relationship between *spending more* and *spending better*, Kornejew, Rentschler, and Hallegatte (2019) explore the relationship between the reliability of and investment spending on transport infrastructure. Transport reliability is proxied by the timeliness subindicator of the Logistics Performance Index (LPI), and transport investment data are from the Organisation for Economic Co-operation and Development (OECD) (box 9.1).

The results show that when spending and governance improve together, higher spending significantly improves transport reliability (figure 9.2). In fact, doubling current spend-

BOX 9.1 Data on infrastructure spending are scarce and limited

Data on infrastructure investment and maintenance are rarely available (Fay et al. 2019). Few countries have common or harmonized public accounting standards, and the relevant expenditure items can be mixed in with other types of expenditures. Especially in low- and middle-income countries, the level of transparency varies, and so does the definition of infrastructure maintenance spending.

Moreover, disaggregating public spending data by sector is difficult because the organization of public budgets makes it difficult to distinguish public spending on water, electricity, and transport infrastructure. Rather than rely on nationally published budget figures, Kornejew, Rentschler, and Hallegatte (2019) use two main international sources of investment data, ensuring consistency and comparability.

The OECD International Transport Forum database provides transport infrastructure investment spending for 57 middle- and high-income countries, covering the years 1995–2016 (OECD 2018). These data are supplemented by public infrastructure investment data from the World Bank's BOOST Initiative, which are available through the Open Budgets portal (World Bank 2018b). Together, these data sources yield a panel of 603 individual country-year observations from 85 countries, covering all income groups. However, because of the OECD's focus on high-income countries, infrastructure spending data for low- and middle-income countries remain patchy. Fay et al. (2019) address this gap in an effort to estimate harmonized spending in low- and middle-income countries, although their estimates do not differentiate among infrastructure sectors.

Data on the performance and reliability of infrastructure services are also limited. The World Bank's Enterprise Surveys provide data on the total annual duration of blackouts and the total annual duration of water supply disruptions, as well as a subjective index (1–4) of the severity of transport problems in overall business operations (see chapter 2). No similar information is given on telecommunications disruptions.

In this chapter, transport reliability is measured using the LPI, which is a benchmarking tool created to help countries identify the challenges and opportunities they face in their performance on trade logistics (World Bank 2018a). LPI 2018 allows comparisons across 160 countries and offers country-specific scores along six dimensions: (1) customs, (2) infrastructure, (3) international shipments, (4) logistics competence, (5) tracking and tracing, and (6) timeliness. The infrastructure subindicator aggregates a quality scoring of ports, railroads, roads, and information technology. The timeliness subindicator measures reliability rather than quality per se. By scoring the timeliness of shipments in reaching their destination within the scheduled delivery time, this subindicator is a measure of unexpected transport disruptions rather than average performance. All LPI indicators are scored on a scale from 1 (worst) to 5 (best).

FIGURE 9.2 Spending more improves the reliability of the transport system, especially if governance also improves

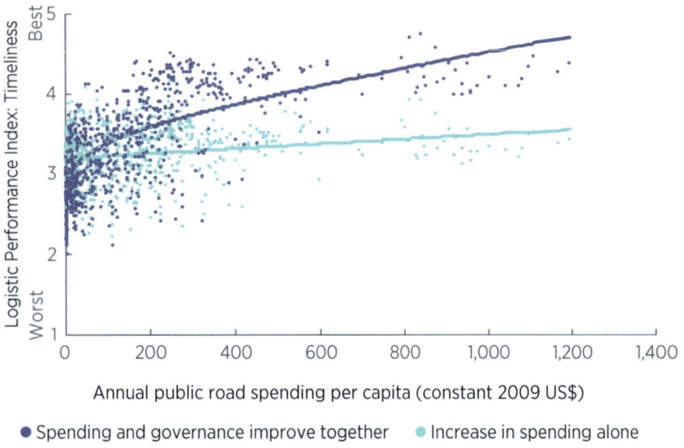

Source: Kornejew, Rentschler, and Hallegatte 2019.

ing levels is estimated to increase transport infrastructure performance (as measured by the LPI indicator for timeliness) by roughly 0.27 index points. For example, this improvement corresponds to improving Mozambique's transport service reliability to equal that of Cambodia.

But if governance quality is held constant, the impact of spending more is largely muted. With governance unchanged, the benefit of spending $1 on transport reliability remains larger than zero, but it is reduced by a factor of six. In other words, increasing spending and improving governance in parallel enhance transport system performance on average six times faster than increasing spending alone. Statistically, the results given in figure 9.2 suggest that only about 8 percent of the variation in transport reliability across countries can be explained by investment spending, whereas about 44 percent is explained by a country's governance quality.

Similar results can be found for energy and water. In the power sector, governance explains most of the difference in the annual duration of blackouts across countries, while public energy spending explains very little. But these results have to be considered cautiously, because of the small number of countries (only 33) for which data are available and the fact that public spending in the energy sector is an imperfect proxy for total (public and private) spending in the power sector. In the water sector, for the set of 32 countries for which data are available, the average daily hours of uninterrupted water supply are explained in part by governance indicators and, as in the power sector, public water spending does not seem to influence water outages.

What would be the benefits of improving the *quality* of infrastructure spending? Kornejew, Rentschler, and Hallegatte (2019) consider an ambitious but feasible governance reform. Under the WGI subindicator for government effectiveness, 10 percent of the sample's country-year observations achieved at least a 0.23 index point increase over a three-year period (for example, Ecuador between 2010 and 2013). By assuming the same ambitious governance improvement in every country, the model described in this report yields an estimate of how much transport infrastructure spending could be reduced without reducing the quality of transport service.[4]

The analysis suggests that the potential savings from improved governance could be substantial (figure 9.3). Specifically, such an ambitious but realistic governance reform could allow countries to cut their road expenditures by 30–90 percent over the long term without reducing the performance of their transport system. Relative savings are the highest for countries with poor governance quality but relatively high levels of per capita spending, such as Haiti and Sierra Leone. Savings are small in countries with good governance (such as New Zealand) and in countries with low spending on roads (such as Niger). These findings highlight the importance not only of spending enough on infrastructure but also of spending well to ensure that infrastructure services perform well.

FIGURE 9.3 Potential savings on road spending from governance reforms

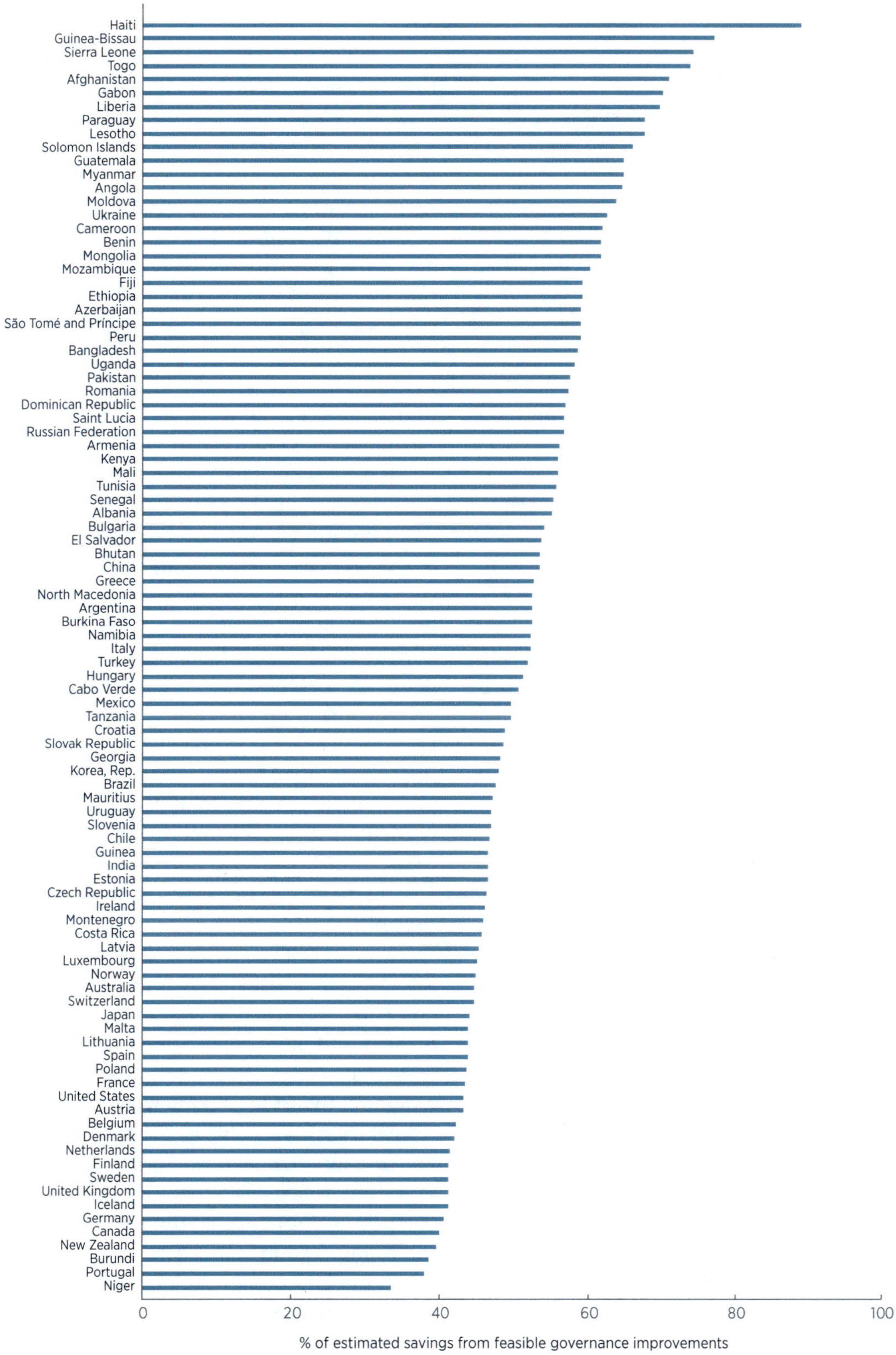

Source: Kornejew, Rentschler, and Hallegatte 2019.

RECOMMENDATION 1: GET THE BASICS RIGHT

What are the solutions for coping with these challenges for the design, operation, and maintenance of infrastructure? Beyond the usual recommendations on regulation and governance, which are well treated in other reports, this report identifies three basic actions that are essential for better managing infrastructure systems.

Action 1.1: Introduce and enforce regulations, construction codes, and procurement rules

Well-designed regulations, codes, and procurement rules are the simplest approach to enhancing the quality of infrastructure services, including their reliability and resilience. In the most widely applied solution, the government defines the level of service expected from public or private infrastructure providers and applies it through its procurement rules (when the asset is publicly owned—for example, roads), its market regulations (when private actors provide services such as electricity), or a contractual engagement (for example, through performance indicators for the procurement and monitoring of public-private partnerships). Regardless of the financial model, strong procurement rules and appropriate performance indicators in tender processes can ensure a minimum level of service and reliability.

Countries can define construction codes and regulations based on existing international standards. Organizations such as the International Organization for Standardization (ISO) and the American Society for Testing and Materials (ASTM) International are creating international standards for the components of infrastructure systems.[5] For example, a standard from the ASTM subcommittee on steel reinforcement (A01.05) provides a tool to promote the long-term strength of bridges and support the production of high-performance, corrosion-resistant steel (A1055/A1055M).

To make the best use of resources like these, countries should rely on local organizations to translate international standards into standards relevant for the country context. In particular, countries at different income levels—or with different preferences in terms of reliability—will want to design regulations and codes that are adapted to their needs. In the absence of a standardization body and centers of technical expertise, many low- and middle-income countries use standards from high-income countries, which do not take into account the local context. For example, Mozambique's National Administration of Roads designs and builds roads using the 2001 draft standards of the South African Transport and Communication Commission (SATCC) as a guide. The SATCC standard is in turn an adaptation of U.S. and European standards to the South African context. To adapt standards to their contexts, most countries have a standardization agency that is a member of the ISO. However, the capacity of these national agencies to adapt international standards and their scope of work vary widely, so they cannot always develop the local standards that are needed for the development of construction codes.

A particularly important issue is quality control and the enforcement of construction codes. In an analysis conducted for this report, Miyamoto International (2019) points out that enforcing construction codes and standards is costly and more challenging than defining them. Enforcement in the infrastructure sector requires a robust legal framework and strong regulatory agencies able to monitor construction and service quality and performance and to reward or penalize service providers based on their performance. Many regulators lack the resources and capacity to enforce existing construction codes. As a result, expensive infrastructure systems may be designed with inappropriate materials or technologies, leading to very high costs over the long term.

Action 1.2: Create systems for appropriate operation, maintenance, and postincident response

Operations and maintenance are critical to ensure the performance of infrastructure systems and to reduce investment costs (see part II of this report). Poor maintenance can increase infrastructure investment needs by 50 percent in the transport sector and by more than 60 percent in the water sector (Rozenberg and Fay 2019). And an analysis focusing on OECD countries performed for this report suggests that each additional $1 spent on road maintenance saves on average $1.50 in new investments, making better maintenance a very cost-effective option (Kornejew, Rentschler, and Hallegatte 2019).

How can proper maintenance be ensured? An important tool is the infrastructure asset management system, which utilities can use to better manage their operations. Such a system includes an inventory of all assets and their condition, as well as all of the strategic, financial, and technical aspects of the management of infrastructure assets across their life cycle. The objective is to move toward an evidence-based and preventive maintenance schedule and to move away from a reactive approach to maintenance.

A simple infrastructure asset management system focuses on each asset, independent of the system in which it functions. The system includes how much assets cost, who is responsible for maintaining them, their condition and functionality, and when they require rehabilitation. A more complex asset management system includes photographs and plans of all assets, their component parts, their maintenance schedules, and details of all actions involving the asset since it was designed. It includes an estimate of the life-cycle costs of the asset, the actual depreciation each year, amortization details, and possible development to better align the current components with the changing needs of users and their clients.

A complex asset management system also documents the functional context in which the infrastructure delivers its services. It identifies the related infrastructure systems that affect its ability to deliver the services required, the contact people, and the details of collaborative maintenance. Whatever form it takes, effective asset management relies on stakeholder commitment, effective institutions, and adequate resources.

One solution that is widely used for the maintenance of transport infrastructure, especially roads, is performance-based contracts (PBCs) (Iimi and Gericke 2017; Lancelot 2010). These contracts explicitly link payment of contractors to the performance of assets, providing a powerful incentive for the contractors maintaining or operating an asset to ensure that its reliability is accounted for in all decisions. However, designing and implementing PBCs requires capacity on behalf of both the government and contractor, and allocating too much risk to the contractor can have significant impacts on costs or place the PBC at risk of failure (Henning, Hughes, and Faiz 2018).

Even with preventive maintenance, the capacity to respond quickly to incidents and to dispatch teams and resources to repair damaged or failing assets is critical for a reliable infrastructure system. Chapter 7 describes in detail the need for emergency management or contingency plans for postdisaster situations, but these plans need to extend to smaller, isolated incidents that can easily propagate through an infrastructure network and have significant system-scale impacts. Thus, utilities and agencies need information-gathering systems and contingency plans, clear attribution of responsibility in case of incidents, and an appropriate stock of parts and emergency equipment. Countries that are unable to respond quickly to isolated system failures are obviously unable to deal with natural disasters, where the spatial scale of the damages is usually much larger.

Action 1.3: Provide appropriate funding and financing for infrastructure planning, construction, and maintenance

The quality of infrastructure services depends on many factors—from good planning to good maintenance—and each of these factors has a cost (figure 9.4). If resources are insufficient to meet the needs for any of these factors, the quality of infrastructure services is likely to suffer. Therefore, countries need to provide sufficient resources to meet their objectives in terms of infrastructure services and resilience, and they have to distribute these resources appropriately across the various needs. Even if total spending is appropriate, allocating insufficient resources for planning, designing, or maintaining assets would lead to low quality and reliability.

Underfunded and understaffed regulators or agencies are unlikely to design and enforce efficient regulations or create the master plans that maximize the reliability of infrastructure systems. Increasing the resources available for infrastructure regulators can therefore have transformational impacts. These impacts may include enhancing the regulation of energy and water utilities, boosting the capacity of road agencies, or creating open-data portals and asset management systems. Thus, appropriate funding of enforcement agencies is a priority.

Moreover, the design and preparation of infrastructure projects are very expensive. During the early stages of project preparation, mobilizing resources is particularly challenging. As a result, preparation budgets tend to be small, making it difficult to conduct the sophisticated analyses needed, even if they can generate massive savings over the lifetime of an infrastructure asset.

Funding of maintenance is also often challenging. Underinvestment in operation and maintenance is common, because it is generally easier to raise resources to finance new investments or a major rehabilitation than to cover continuous operation and maintenance costs. Maintenance is also less visible than new investments and can usually be delayed, which makes it an easy target for budget cuts (Briceno, Estache, and Shafik 2004; Regan 1989). Appropriate and reliable budgetary allocations—or the use of contracts that effectively precommit adequate maintenance expenditures, such as private-public partnerships and PBCs—are necessary to ensure that good maintenance can actually happen.

Financial constraints can push countries toward solutions that have lower up-front costs, even if these options have higher life-cycle costs or major social costs. Countries with fragile infrastructure systems often spend large amounts to repair and maintain this infrastructure, compounding the challenge of limited fis-

FIGURE 9.4 The full cost of infrastructure includes multiple cost components

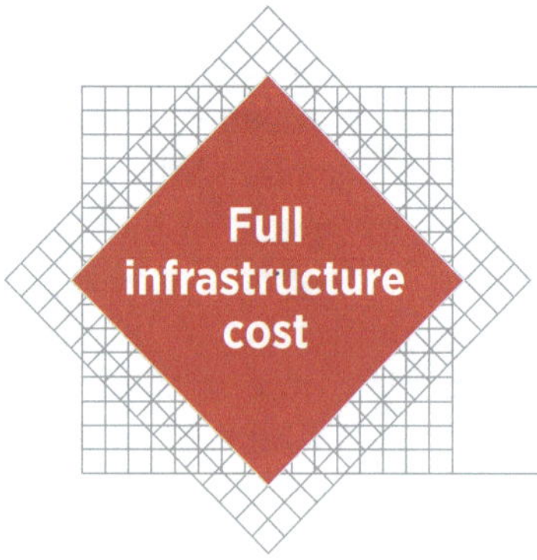

Cost to regulators and government

- Master planning, and regulation design and enforcement
- Data and model development, research, training, and education

Life-cycle cost to (public or private) infrastructure service providers

- Project design and preparation
- Up-front investment cost
- Operational, maintenance, and repair costs
- Decommissioning

cal space to finance an investment that could improve reliability and reduce vulnerability. Escaping this vicious circle of high fragility, high maintenance, and low investment requires a temporary increase in spending.

But governments in both low- and middle-income countries and high-income countries already struggle to finance the infrastructure investment needed to meet demand. Many infrastructure systems struggle to meet normal demand, with inadequate power generation capacity, unreliable Internet services, or highly congested public transit and urban roads, even in normal times. Systems that cannot satisfy normal demand are naturally highly vulnerable to any shock that reduces supply—for instance, the failure of one power plant or transmission line or the closure of a road.

Where governments struggle to raise finance for economically and financially viable investments in infrastructure, one option is to turn to the private sector. Private investors may raise finance on the basis of future cash flows generated by the asset itself (project finance) or, in the case of utility companies, their own balance sheet (corporate finance). Either approach reduces the burden on the government balance sheet—although not entirely, since almost all infrastructure investment creates contingent liabilities for the government where private investors cannot or will not bear the risks and maybe even direct liabilities where subsidies continue to be required. Moreover, attracting private investment—and making sure those investors are incentivized to deliver high-quality, efficient, and resilient infrastructure—also depends on the quality of the governance and regulatory environment.

Implementing these recommendations would improve infrastructure system design, management, and maintenance, and do much to improve the quality of infrastructure services and their resilience to frequent shocks. However, building resilience to more intense shocks and adapting infrastructure systems to changing climate conditions involve additional obstacles and require additional actions. They are the topic of the next four chapters.

NOTES

1. The *Worldwide Governance Indicators* report (World Bank, n.d.) estimates governance standards for more than 200 countries and territories along six dimensions: (1) voice and accountability, (2) political stability and absence of violence, (3) government effectiveness, (4) regulatory quality, (5) the rule of law, and (6) control of corruption. For each country, these governance indicators reflect surveys of a large number of enterprises, citizens, and experts, based on more than 30 individual data sources.
2. For details, see Bensch, Kluve, and Peters (2011); Khandker, Barnes, and Samad (2009); Kumar and Rauniyar (2011); and Lee, Miguel, and Wolfram (2016).
3. For details, see Dinkelman (2011); Grogan and Sadanand (2013); Lee, Miguel, and Wolfram (2016); Rud (2012); and van de Walle et al. (2017).
4. Specifically, the model described in the previous section is extended by interacting log per capita road spending with the subindicator for government effectiveness. This process is necessary to generate meaningful variation across countries—see Kornejew, Rentschler, and Hallegatte (2019) for details.
5. For an example for highways, see https://www.astm.org/ABOUT/OverviewsforWeb2015/HighwaysOvrvwApril2018.pdf.

REFERENCES

Bensch, G., J. Kluve, and J. Peters. 2011. "Impacts of Rural Electrification in Rwanda." *Journal of Development Effectiveness* 3 (4): 567–88. https://doi.org/10.1080/19439342.2011.621025.

Brass, J. N., S. Carley, L. M. MacLean, and E. Baldwin. 2012. "Power for Development: A Review of Distributed Generation Projects in the Developing World." *Annual Review of Environment and Resources* 37 (1): 107–36. https://doi.org/10.1146/annurev-environ-051112-111930.

Briceno, C., A. Estache, and N. T. Shafik. 2004. "Infrastructure Services in Developing Countries: Access, Quality, Costs, and Policy Reform." Policy Research Working Paper 3468, World Bank, Washington, DC. https://doi.org/10.1596/1813-9450-3468.

Dinkelman, T. 2011. "The Effects of Rural Electrification on Employment: New Evidence from South Africa." *American Economic Review* 101 (7): 3078–108.

Fay, M., S. Han, H. I. Lee, M. Mastruzzi, and M. Cho. 2019. "Hitting the Trillion Mark: A Look at How Much Countries Are Spending on Infrastructure." Policy Research Working Paper 8730, World Bank, Washington, DC.

Grogan, L., and A. Sadanand. 2013. "Rural Electrification and Employment in Poor Countries: Evidence from Nicaragua." *World Development* 43 (C): 252–65.

Henning, T. F. P., J. Hughes, and A. Faiz. 2018. "Incorporating Criticality and Resilience into Performance Based Contracts." Technical Report, World Bank, Washington, DC.

Iimi, A., and B. Gericke. 2017. "Output- and Performance-Based Road Contracts and Agricultural Production: Evidence from Zambia." Policy Research Working Paper 8201, World Bank, Washington, DC.

Khandker, S. R., D. F. Barnes, and H. A. Samad. 2009. "Welfare Impacts of Rural Electrification: A Case Study from Bangladesh." World Bank, Washington, DC. https://doi.org/10.1596/1813-9450-4859.

Kornejew, M., J. Rentschler, and S. Hallegatte. 2019. "Well Spent: How Governance Determines the Effectiveness of Infrastructure Investments." Background paper for this report, World Bank, Washington, DC.

Kumar, S., and G. Rauniyar. 2011. "Is Electrification Welfare Improving? Non-Experimental Evidence from Rural Bhutan." MPRA Paper 31482, Harvard University, Cambridge, MA; Asian Development Bank, Manila, February 20.

Lancelot, E. 2010. "Performance Based Contracts in the Road Sector: Towards Improved Efficiency in the Management of Maintenance and Rehabilitation—Brazil's Experience." Transport Paper TP-31, World Bank, Washington, DC.

Lee, K., E. Miguel, and C. Wolfram. 2016. "Experimental Evidence on the Demand for and Costs of Rural Electrification." NBER Working Paper 22292, National Bureau of Economic Research, Cambridge, MA.

Miyamoto International. 2019. "Overview of Engineering Options for Increasing Infrastructure Resilience." Background paper for this report, World Bank, Washington, DC.

North American Electric Reliability Council. 2004. "Technical Analysis of the August 14, 2003, Blackout: What Happened, Why, and What Did We Learn?" North American Electric Reliability Council, Princeton, NJ.

OECD (Organisation for Economic Co-operation and Development). 2018. "International Transport Forum—OECD.Stat." OECD, Paris.

Regan, E. V. 1989. "Holding Government Officials Accountable for Infrastructure Maintenance." *Proceedings of the Academy of Political Science* 37 (3): 180. https://doi.org/10.2307/1173761.

Rentschler, J., M. Kornejew, S. Hallegatte, M. Obolensky, and J. Braese. 2019. "Underutilized Potential: The Business Costs of Unreliable Infrastructure in Developing Countries." Background paper for this report, World Bank, Washington, DC.

Rozenberg, J., and M. Fay. 2019. *Beyond the Gap: How Countries Can Afford the Infrastructure They Need While Protecting the Planet.* Washington, DC: World Bank.

Rud, J. P. 2012. "Electricity Provision and Industrial Development: Evidence from India." *Journal of Development Economics* 97 (2): 352–67.

Samad, H. A., S. R. Khandker, M. Asaduzzaman, and M. Yunus. 2013. "The Benefits of Solar Home Systems: An Analysis from Bangladesh." Policy Research Working Paper 6724, World Bank, Washington, DC.

van de Walle, D., M. Ravallion, V. Mendiratta, and G. Koolwal. 2017. "Long-Term Gains from Electrification in Rural India." *World Bank Economic Review* 31 (2): 385–411.

WEF (World Economic Forum). 2018. *The Global Competitiveness Report 2017–2018.* Cologny: WEF.

World Bank. 2018a. Logistics Performance Index. Washington, DC: World Bank.

———. 2018b. "BOOST Initiative." Open Budgets portal, World Bank, Washington, DC. http://boost.worldbank.org/boost-initiative.

———. No date. *Worldwide Governance Indicators.* http://info.worldbank.org/governance/wgi.

Build Institutions for Resilience 10

OBSTACLE	RECOMMENDATION	ACTIONS
Political economy challenges and coordination failures	Build institutions for resilience	• 2.1: Implement a whole-of-government approach to resilient infrastructure, building on existing regulatory system • 2.2: Identify critical infrastructure and define acceptable and intolerable risk levels • 2.3: Ensure equitable access to resilient infrastructure

THE OBSTACLE: MULTIPLE POLITICAL ECONOMY CHALLENGES AND COORDINATION FAILURES IMPEDE PUBLIC ACTION ON RESILIENCE

Policy makers' incentives to invest in more resilient infrastructure systems are weakened by the asymmetry in the visibility of the costs and benefits of such investments. Catastrophes make headlines and produce in-depth analyses of what went wrong, but extreme natural events that lead to no or minor damage do not attract much interest. Understanding the benefits of adding resilience to infrastructure requires identifying the crises that are avoided (thanks to previous policies or measures), which is hard to do and even harder to communicate to the public. By contrast, the cost of making infrastructure more resilient is easy to identify and contest. In Finland, increased resilience in the power sector raised the distribution price of electricity by up to 30 percent in some regions, sparking strong public and political reactions and adjustment of the Electricity Market Act (OECD 2019).

Lack of coordination among actors is also a challenge. Coordination is needed to ensure that actions by stakeholders are consistent and synergetic. For example, a public-private insurance scheme regulated by the ministry of finance at the national level cannot be designed without considering risk reduction measures such as land use plans and building norms at the local level (tasks often led by local authorities). Power outages can have secondary effects on telecommunications, water treatment, and urban transit systems—and power generation utilities, especially coal power plants, can be dependent on the transport system for supplies. Kunreuther and Heal (2003) explore this inter-

BOX 10.1 A new hazard: Cyberdisasters and cyberattacks

Modern infrastructure systems are programmed and controlled by computer systems, making them vulnerable to cyberattacks. Take the case of Ukraine in December 2015, when a large-scale power grid hack left 230,000 people without power. In typical fashion, the hackers first gained access to control systems and then launched an attack and blocked attempts at quick fixes to reinstate services (Wagner 2016). In this attack, the hackers gained access to the business networks of the utilities using a phishing program. They eventually managed to obtain a worker's credentials for the control system, which enabled them to understand the programs that controlled the electricity networks. The next step was to overwrite operational programs with malicious versions that would stop operators from reclosing tripped circuit breakers. In this way, the hackers were able to manipulate multiple utilities and substations and then to trip all of the circuit breakers simultaneously (Zetter 2016).

Past cyberattacks have been limited mostly to attacks on power systems, which is why electricity systems are the focus of cybersecurity efforts. More and more Internet of Things devices (such as smart meters) and distributed energy resources (such as small-scale battery storage systems or photovoltaic systems) are being integrated into electric grids. Because all of these devices are active participants in grid operations, they open vulnerable new access points for cyberattacks on the grid (Cleveland and Lee 2013). The vulnerability of water and transport networks may also increase with the rise of smart transport solutions and the increasing digitization of infrastructure systems. For example, Zou, Choobchian, and Rozenberg (2019) warn that autonomous mobility systems, which move people and goods around using self-driving vehicles, are particularly vulnerable to cyberthreats.

Overall, it is important to weigh efficiency gains from smart systems against the vulnerabilities they may create. Smart grid and consumer demand response technologies may allow utilities to balance electrical loads more effectively, but these benefits should be weighed against the higher risk of cyberattacks on the grid. Even though a growing literature has investigated the vulnerability of smart grids to cyberattacks (Aloul et al. 2012), the trade-offs remain complex. The inadequacy of existing cybersecurity measures may mean that the efficiency gains from smart grid and consumer demand response systems are not fully justified because of the increase in risks from cyberattacks.

Source: Eugene Tan.

dependency theoretically, showing that, in the absence of cooperation mechanisms, individual actors may prefer not to invest in resilience.

One major challenge in risk management is to look across risks and threats, even beyond natural risks and climate change, to capture synergies and avoid instances in which reducing one vulnerability increases another. Many solutions seem attractive if one risk is considered, but then increase vulnerability to other risks. An example is the use of smart grids and consumer demand management to prevent power outages—both of which can increase vulnerability to cyberattacks (box 10.1). Even when considering a single risk, reducing the impact of a frequent occurrence can lead to an increase in vulnerability to rarer and more dangerous events. For example, when dikes prevent frequent floods, people wrongly assume that floods are now impossible. Such a wrong impression can lead to more investment in the protected area and greater vulnerability to floods that exceed the level of the dikes (Burby et al. 2001; Burby, Nelson, and Sanchez 2006).

An increase in protection can even lead to a net increase in average annual losses, because additional protection can lead to much larger investments in at-risk areas (Hallegatte 2017).

One particular trade-off between short-term and long-term risks is "maladaptation"—that is, measures that reduce the short-term level of risk but increase the longer-term vulnerability to climate change. Examples include the increased use of groundwater pumping and irrigation to manage droughts, which can lead to long-term vulnerabilities. *Uncharted Waters: The New Economics of Water Scarcity and Variability* (Damania et al. 2017) finds that in arid areas and in low-income countries, the presence of irrigation infrastructure can exacerbate the impact of shocks on agricultural yields because it encourages farmers to adopt more water-intensive crops that are even more vulnerable to droughts. Preventing maladaptation requires systematic exploration of the long-term implications of measures to reduce short-term risks.

RECOMMENDATION 2: BUILD INSTITUTIONS FOR RESILIENCE

What are the solutions for coping with these challenges of political economy and coordination? They include creating institutions to manage infrastructure resilience and defining the vision that can help actors to coordinate their actions.

Action 2.1: Implement a whole-of-government approach to infrastructure resilience, building on existing regulatory systems

Different countries take different approaches to infrastructure resilience, but common principles have been widely applied. These principles—discussed in detail in *Good Governance for Critical Infrastructure Resilience,* which was issued by the Organisation for Economic Co-operation and Development (OECD 2019)—are consistent with typical recommendations on the governance of risks.[1]

There is a consensus among experts that governments have a key role to play in ensuring the resilience of critical infrastructure and that they should adopt a whole-of-government approach. This approach involves the sectoral ministries and agencies overseeing infrastructure services delivery and regulation in multiple critical sectors, as well as those responsible for resilience to hazards and threats. It also involves local authorities, especially municipalities that, in many countries, are responsible for supplying drinking water and managing urban transit and transportation.

The most common solution for improving the coordination of risk management is to place an existing multiministry body (or, if necessary, a new body) in charge of the exchange of information, coordination, and perhaps the implementation of risk management measures. Many countries have agencies in charge of coordinating disaster risk management or national security issues, and these agencies can also tackle issues related to infrastructure resilience. For example, in France, the General Secretariat for Defense and National Security under the prime minister coordinates resilience policy for critical infrastructure across eight line ministries, using a multihazard approach.

The body in charge of critical infrastructure can be given special powers to collect information, perform assessments, and impose certain actions and ban others. For example, the recent Australian Security of Critical Infrastructure Act, which is aimed at protecting the country from sabotage and espionage, mandates the creation of a registry of critical infrastructure assets. It also gives the minister of the Department of Home Affairs the right to request information about these assets to determine whether any risk to national security is associated with an asset. The minister can impose or prohibit certain actions if there is "a risk of an act or omission that would be prejudicial to security."

A body in charge of infrastructure resilience needs to be appropriately staffed and funded.

However, it cannot, and should not, replace the regulatory bodies in charge of sectors, which should be a priority in low-capacity countries (see chapter 9). Various decisions or regulations need to be coordinated across sectors, but their design and practical implementation are better conducted by each sector regulator to ensure consistency with other regulations and to prevent conflicts. In practice, implementation will vary, depending on whether the regulation of an infrastructure sector is carried out directly by the government, by an independent agency, or through a contract (Eberhard 2007).

Action 2.2: Identify critical infrastructure and define acceptable and intolerable risk levels

The task of building infrastructure resilience at an acceptable cost begins with identifying the critical infrastructure—that is, the "systems, assets, facilities, and networks that provide essential services for the functioning of the economy and the well-being of the population" (OECD 2019, 47). This requires assessing the vulnerability of critical infrastructure assets and systems and the consequences of possible disruptions, so the government can prioritize actions. Chapter 7 illustrates the use of criticality analyses to identify the most important assets in an infrastructure network or to identify additional infrastructure that would do the most to build resilience of the network.

The United Kingdom and many other countries conduct regular national risk assessments (figure 10.1) to assess the main risks they face, regardless of the type and origin of risk (natural, technological, terrorist, or other). The assessments are based on similar approaches: identifying risks, generating scenarios, assessing the probability or plausibility and impacts of the risks, and enabling the construction of a national risk matrix.

A risk matrix summarizes the main risks and organizes them according to their likelihood and severity of impact. Regular national risk assessments can also be used to assess the quality of risk management of various agencies

FIGURE 10.1 U.K. national risk matrix

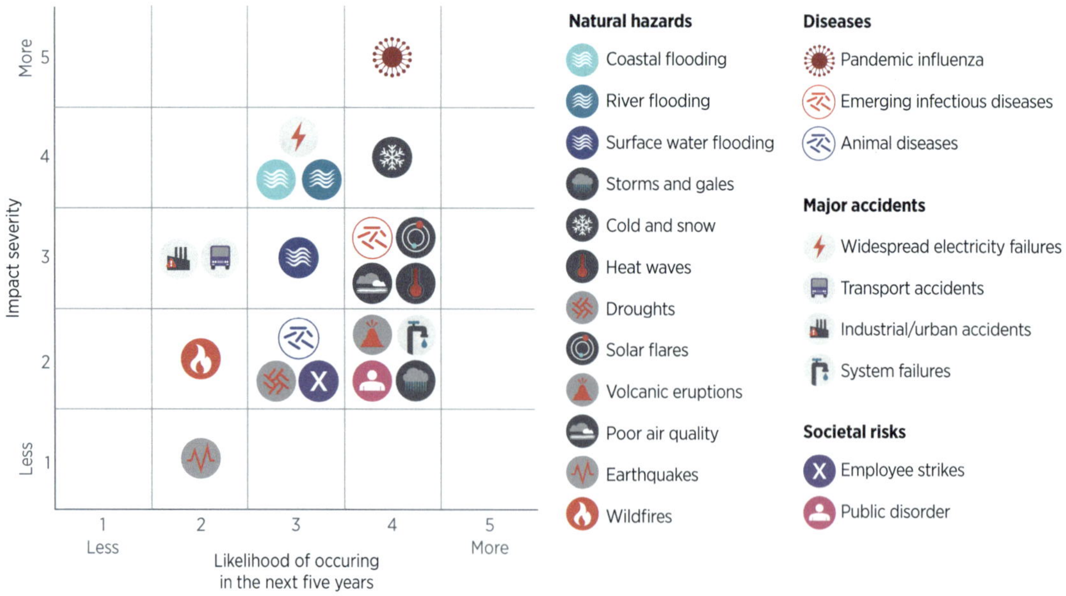

Source: U.K. Cabinet Office 2017.

and organizations (including local authorities and their land use plans) through risk audits and benchmarking. The results can be reported annually to the country's legislative body, raising policy makers' awareness of critical infrastructure issues.

Next, the government needs to define a shared vision of the level of risk that is considered acceptable, based on its potential impact and likelihood, and to identify the resources that are available for disaster risk management and infrastructure financing. Indeed, with the significant interdependencies across systems, applying a consistent level of resilience to various components of the infrastructure system is more cost-effective. It would not make sense for a government to invest major resources in making the power system highly resilient if the water supply or transport system cannot cope with frequent hazards. Instead, for systems that interact, it is more efficient to target a similar level of resilience. Using a target level of resilience is a more practical way of allocating investments efficiently across sectors than trying to equalize the rates of return of various investments.

Acceptable risks are usually those with consequences that can be managed or those that cannot be prevented at an affordable cost. When these risks materialize, it is expected that an infrastructure system will be damaged and its service disrupted, with consequences for the rest of the economy. For instance, significant residual risk often needs to be accepted for tertiary roads, especially in low-income countries, since their length would make it unaffordable to strengthen them beyond a certain point. The fact that these risks are acceptable does not mean that they can be ignored. Governments need to be prepared for the disasters and disruptions that cannot be avoided, including by having an emergency response and possibly financial support in place for infrastructure operators, households, and businesses.

In contrast, a risk is considered *intolerable* if its likelihood and potential impact are too high and the cost of prevention is affordable. For example, major transport infrastructure—such as a large bridge or tunnel—cannot be susceptible to failure and collapse from storms or moderate earthquakes because the human and economic impacts of such events would be unacceptable. If a major highway is forced to close several times a year because of local flooding, the disruptions would have a major economic impact. These unacceptable vulnerabilities can also be reframed as a *minimum expected level of service*.

The definitions of acceptable and intolerable risks for infrastructure systems need to adhere to four important principles.

First, the approach to defining these risks should be open and participatory, characterized by close cooperation between scientists, infrastructure service providers, infrastructure service users, and policy makers. Scientists and other experts alone cannot define what risks are acceptable; they lack the legitimacy to do so. Nor can policy makers; they usually lack the technical expertise. Relying on a participatory approach ensures that the appropriate data and concerns are given due consideration and helps to raise awareness of, and form a consensus on, the vision to anchor the decision making of various independent actors.

Second, risk taking sometimes yields benefits that justify the risk taken. Risk management should not become an obstacle to development (World Bank 2013). In some rural areas, proximity to water offers cheaper transport and regular floods increase agricultural productivity (Loayza et al. 2012). People may settle in risky coastal areas to benefit from job opportunities in industries driven by exports. Better jobs and services may attract people to cities, even if the cities are more exposed than rural areas to some threats. Innovation generates growth, but almost always involves risk. Risk taking is one of the drivers of economic growth and should not be suppressed indiscriminately (Hallegatte 2017).

Third, definitions of these risks should consider the local context and the cost of resilience—compared with the resources available. Countries at different income levels are unlikely to be able to afford the same level of resilience, and not all countries can aspire to the same level of resilience over the short term. Also, countries with different exposures may aim to achieve different resilience levels; a small island regularly affected by hurricanes is likely to dedicate a larger share of its resources to resilience than the average country. Highly exposed, wealthy countries like Japan and the Netherlands spend much larger amounts on flood protection and resilience-enhancing initiatives and regulations than other countries at the same income level.

Fourth, the definition of acceptable risk levels for infrastructure assets should look far into the future. With economic growth and technological change, resources, preferences, and standards will change, possibly leading to stronger demand for resilience and a lower risk of failure. These changes will be a challenge for the design of long-lived infrastructure. An acceptable level of risk at the time an infrastructure asset is designed and built may prove unacceptable 30 years later, when the asset will be only at its half-life. In the design of long-lived systems, the *potential for regret* is a critical metric and may justify fortifying an asset beyond the point the current situation would suggest.[2]

Action 2.3: Ensure equitable access to resilient infrastructure

Decisions on resilience cannot be driven by economic considerations alone. Indeed, economic losses are only one part of the many impacts of disasters, including infrastructure-mediated ones. Thus, the strengthening of infrastructure resilience should be guided by a more complete assessment of the potential risks and impacts of disruptions—especially for vulnerable and marginalized population groups.

First and foremost, the potential loss of life is important to include in any risk analysis. Of course, infrastructure disruptions can be life threatening for some people, such as for those who depend on electricity-powered medical devices or pregnant women who need urgent access to medically assisted delivery (see chapter 3). In the Netherlands, the Dutch Water Act of 2015, which sets out standards for flood defenses (along the coast, lakes, and rivers), explicitly considers loss of life. The starting point of the new flood defense standard is that every citizen should be able to rely on the same (minimum or basic) level of protection. This level of protection is expressed in the "local individual risk"—that is, the chance that an individual permanently present at a specific location will die as a result of flooding. The legal basis for considering these risks is in Article 21 of the Dutch Constitution, which imposes a duty on government "to ensure the habitability of the land and the protection and improvement of the environment."

Economic losses also hide the impact of disasters on poor people (Hallegatte et al. 2017). Because the wealthy have more assets and income to lose, their interests dominate in assessments of economic losses. If informed only by potential economic losses, decisions about the resilience of infrastructure or investments to reduce natural risks will tend to favor the richest areas of a country or a city. Although the poor often have very little to lose, they lack the resources and tools to smooth income shocks while maintaining consumption and coping with infrastructure disruptions. Thus, after disasters, they are more likely than the wealthy to forgo the consumption of food, health services, and education.

To ensure that resilience is distributed fairly across the population, one option is to measure the impacts of disasters and infrastructure disruptions using a metric that accounts for the

MAP 10.1 Different measures of natural risks in the Philippines highlight different priorities for interventions

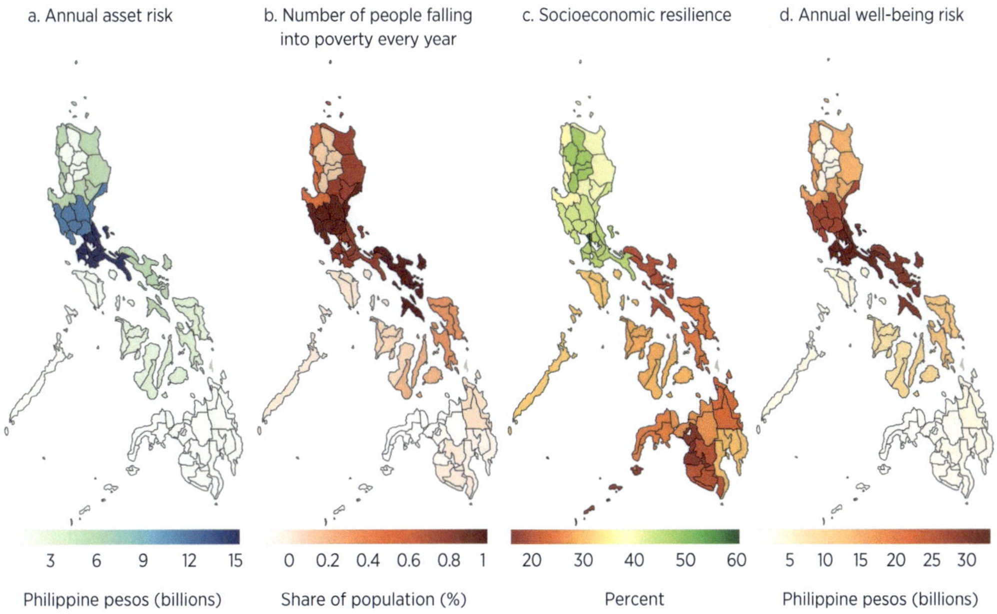

Source: Walsh and Hallegatte 2019.

socioeconomic status of the affected populations (Hallegatte et al. 2017). A recent analysis in the Philippines employed a multimetric assessment of disaster risks at the regional level using (1) traditional asset losses; (2) poverty-related measures such as the poverty headcount; (3) well-being losses for a balanced estimate of the impact on poor and rich households; and (4) socioeconomic resilience, an indicator that measures the ability of the population to cope with and recover from asset losses (Walsh and Hallegatte 2019).

Priority interventions—in both spatial terms (where to act?) and sectoral terms (how to act?)—are highly dependent on which metric for disaster severity is used (map 10.1). In the Philippines, the most important interventions will take place in the Manila area if asset losses are the main measure of disaster impacts. Other regions become priorities if the policy objectives are expressed in terms of poverty incidence and well-being losses. Assessments of national risk and identification of critical infrastructure need to account for multiple policy objectives and, therefore, use a set of metrics that goes beyond asset losses.

Affordability issues are a direct threat to universal access to infrastructure services and the achievement of the 2030 Sustainable Development Goals—and the higher costs arising from resilience-enhancing investments may negatively affect these important policy objectives. In some places, the retail price of electricity is already high, leaving some households connected to the grid but unable to afford electricity. In other places, infrastructure services are heavily subsidized to ensure affordability, but these subsidies can have unintended consequences for the ability of service providers to invest in new, and maintain existing, infrastructure assets. Any large increase in prices that would be triggered by regulations or financial incentives for more resilient infrastructure systems could magnify this problem

BOX 10.2 The structure of tariffs and targeted subsidies can help to ensure that the resilience of infrastructure services is not improved at the expense of access: The case of public transit

Public transit is a sector in which price subsidies are common, justified by the positive externality of increasing access to jobs and services and the benefits of public transit for congestion and air quality. In the United States, the median revenue from fares for major transit systems is approximately 35 percent of total expenses, meaning that the remaining 65 percent of operating expenses must be covered elsewhere.

Today, advanced targeted subsidy schemes can rely on modern electronic fare systems and sophisticated methodologies for defining and targeting beneficiary populations. In particular, the use of smart cards has allowed governments to structure subsidies that target demand rather than supply. Smart cards can be personalized, and subsidies delivered via smartcard can take on different structures. Examples are a flat rate or differential discounts, depending on the characteristics of individual trips such as time of day or type of route.

In February 2014, Bogotá rolled out a "pro-poor" transport subsidy program. The program builds on the progressive adoption of smart cards by Bogotá's public transit systems and on national experience with other poverty-targeting initiatives (such as conditional cash transfer programs) that use the country's poverty-targeting system and database (Sistema Nacional de Selección de Beneficiarios, or SISBEN). Beneficiaries defined as "SISBEN 1 and 2 users" can receive a public transit subsidy, effectively amounting to a 40 percent discounted fare capped at 21 trips a month. Well-targeted subsidies make it easier to fund urban transit with more cost recovery, without threatening access for the poorest.

Source: Mehndiratta, Rodriguez, and Ochoa 2014.

and potentially attract criticism and opposition. However, as discussed in part II of this report, the increase in infrastructure service costs to achieve higher resilience is expected to be limited and thus will not radically change the existing trade-off between affordability and cost recovery. As a result, the usual recommendations for managing this trade-off would apply, as in the case of public transit (box 10.2).

NOTES

1. See, for example, Renn (2008, 2017); Wiener and Rogers (2002); and World Bank (2013).
2. The use of *regret* as a decision-making criterion can help in planning for the future (see chapter 12).

REFERENCES

Aloul, F., A. R. Al-Ali, R. Al-Dalky, M. Al-Mardini, and W. El-Hajj. 2012. "Smart Grid Security: Threats, Vulnerabilities, and Solutions." *International Journal of Smart Grid and Clean Energy* 1 (1): 1–6.

Burby, R. J., A. C. Nelson, D. Parker, and J. Handmer. 2001. "Urban Containment Policy and Exposure to Natural Hazards: Is There a Connection?" *Journal of Environmental Planning and Management* 44 (4): 475–90. https://doi.org/10.1080/09640560120060911.

Burby, R. J., A. C. Nelson, and T. W. Sanchez. 2006. "The Problems of Containment and the Promise of Planning." In *Rebuilding Urban Places after Disaster: Lessons from Hurricane Katrina,* 47–65. Philadelphia: University of Pennsylvania Press.

Cleveland, F., and A. Lee. 2013. "Cyber Security for DER Systems." Electric Power Research Institute, National Electric Sector Cybersecurity Organization Resource, Palo Alto, CA.

Damania, R., S. Desbureaux, M. Hyland, A. Islam, S. Moore, A.-S. Rodella, J. Russ, and E. Zaveri. 2017. *Uncharted Waters: The New Economics of Water Scarcity and Variability.* Washington, DC: World Bank. https://doi.org/10.1596/978-1-4648-1179-1.

Eberhard, A. 2007. "Infrastructure Regulation in Developing Countries: An Exploration of Hybrid and Transitional Models." Working Paper 4,

World Bank, Washington, DC. http://documents.worldbank.org/curated/en/528801468176332574/Infrastructure-regulation-in-developing-countries-an-exploration-of-hybrid-and-transitional-models.

Hallegatte, S. 2017. "A Normative Exploration of the Link between Development, Economic Growth, and Natural Risk." *Economics of Disasters and Climate Change* 1 (1): 5–31. https://doi.org/10.1007/s41885-017-0006-1.

Hallegatte, S., A. Vogt-Schilb, M. Bangalore, and J. Rozenberg. 2017. *Unbreakable: Building the Resilience of the Poor in the Face of Natural Disasters.* Washington, DC: World Bank. https://doi.org/10.1596/978-1-4648-1003-9.

Kunreuther, H., and G. Heal. 2003. "Interdependent Security." *Journal of Risk and Uncertainty* 26 (2–3): 231–49. https://doi.org/10.1023/A:1024119208153.

Loayza, N. V., E. Olaberría, J. Rigolini, and L. Christiaensen. 2012. "Natural Disasters and Growth: Going beyond the Averages." *World Development* 40 (7): 1317–36. https://doi.org/10.1016/j.worlddev.2012.03.002.

Mehndiratta, S. R., C. Rodriguez, and C. Ochoa. 2014. "Targeted Subsidies in Public Transport: Combining Affordability with Financial Sustainability." World Bank, Washington, DC.

OECD (Organisation for Economic Co-operation and Development). 2019. *Good Governance for Critical Infrastructure Resilience.* OECD Review of Risk Management Practices. Paris: OECD.

Renn, O. 2008. "White Paper on Risk Governance: Toward an Integrative Framework." In *Global Risk Governance,* edited by O. Renn and K. D. Walker, 3–73. Stuttgart: Springer. http://link.springer.com/chapter/10.1007/978-1-4020-6799-0_1.

———. 2017. *Risk Governance: Coping with Uncertainty in a Complex World.* London: Routledge.

U.K. Cabinet Office. 2017. "U.K. National Risk Register of Civil Emergencies." U.K. Cabinet Office, London.

Wagner, D. 2016. "Threat of Cyber-Attacks on Critical Infrastructure." International Risk Management Institute, Dallas.

Walsh, B., and S. Hallegatte. 2019. "Measuring Natural Risks in the Philippines." Policy Research Working Paper 8723, World Bank, Washington, DC. https://doi.org/10.1596/1813-9450-8723.

Wiener, J. B., and M. D. Rogers. 2002. "Comparing Precaution in the United States and Europe." *Journal of Risk Research* 5 (4): 317–49. https://doi.org/10.1080/13669870210153684.

World Bank. 2013. *World Development Report 2014: Risk and Opportunity—Managing Risk for Development.* Washington, DC: World Bank. https://doi.org/10.1596/978-0-8213-9903-3.

Zetter, K. 2016. "Inside the Cunning, Unprecedented Hack of Ukraine's Power Grid." *Wired,* March 3.

Zou, B., P. Choobchian, and J. Rozenberg. 2019. "Autonomous Mobility Systems and Cyber Resilience: Threats, Vulnerabilities, and Possible Resilience-Enhancing Strategies." Background paper for this report, World Bank, Washington, DC.

Create Regulations and Incentives for Resilience 11

OBSTACLE	RECOMMENDATION	ACTIONS
Lack of incentives to increase resilience	Create regulations and incentives for resilience	• 3.1: Consider resilience objectives in master plans, standards, and regulations, and adjust them regularly to account for climate change • 3.2: Create financial incentives for service providers to promote resilient infrastructure services • 3.3: Ensure that infrastructure regulations are consistent with risk-informed land use plans and guide development toward safer areas

THE OBSTACLE: INFRASTRUCTURE PROVIDERS OFTEN LACK THE INCENTIVES TO AVOID DISRUPTIONS AND TO STRENGTHEN THE RESILIENCE OF USERS

Ideally, the providers of infrastructure services and the entities that design, build, operate, and maintain infrastructure assets would bear the full cost of infrastructure disruptions. This would include covering the cost of the repairs and additional maintenance needed after natural shocks, such as floods and storms, as well as the full cost of disruptions for the users of infrastructure services. Service providers would then have the incentives needed to minimize disruptions, including from natural hazards.

But the reality is different. Take the following cases, which highlight the existence of a gap between the full cost of infrastructure disruptions and the incentives that service providers face (table 11.1):

- For a road agency that operates with a fixed budget, there is an incentive to build roads in a way that minimizes the maintenance and repair costs, but no incentive to account for the full cost of transport disruptions, such as the impact on businesses and supply chains.
- For the operator of a toll road public-private partnership (PPP) or the owner of a private power generation plant, there are typically stronger incentives to incorporate resilience (although the ultimate decision will depend on the exact contractual structure). They want not only to minimize repair and maintenance costs but also to avoid revenue losses when the asset cannot be used. Even so, the cost borne is less than the real impact. For

TABLE 11.1 Examples of the presence (and absence) of incentives for resilience

	Resilience of infrastructure assets	Resilience of infrastructure services	Resilience of infrastructure users	
Costs that should be internalized in asset design, construction, maintenance, and operation	**Postdisaster repair costs (and increased maintenance costs) due to natural hazards**	**Loss of revenue during disruptions (when user fees are used to fund the asset)**	**Well-being or revenue losses for infrastructure users (or other infrastructure systems)**	**Impact of infrastructure assets on people's and firms' exposure to risk**
Rural road built and maintained by a public road agency	√	X	X	X
Toll road built and operated by a private actor through a public-private partnership	√	√	X	X
Solar power plan owned and operated by a private firm	√	√	X	X
Land that could be reforested to reduce landslide risks for nearby roads and water utilities downstream	X	X	X	X

Note: √ = presence; X = absence.

example, the social cost associated with a 1-kilowatt-hour power outage is at least 80 percent higher than the loss in revenue from an interruption (see chapter 3).

Making matters worse, there is no incentive for infrastructure owners or operators to account for how the infrastructure will affect the risk exposure of other people and firms or their ability to manage infrastructure disruptions (table 11.1). For example, a road agency may build a road on a floodplain, ensuring that the road can cope with floods, but not consider that the road will attract new settlements, businesses, and investments. Although the road itself may be resilient, it can still reduce the resilience of the community and those who build their livelihoods and economic activity around the new infrastructure. Without risk-informed land use planning, infrastructure providers are unlikely to recognize these risks. And even if they do, they are unlikely to bear the long-term costs of risky spatial development. Further, while nature-based solutions and green infrastructure can efficiently reduce the cost of infrastructure services and increase resilience, there is often little incentive to protect or restore ecosystems.

Another problem is that budgetary and contractual arrangements can further reduce the incentive to minimize life-cycle costs and disaster-related losses. For example, in a public road agency, the investment and maintenance budgets may be separate, making it difficult for lower maintenance and repair costs to compensate for higher investment costs. The usual budgeting processes are also an obstacle, because the benefits of lower maintenance and repair costs can take decades to materialize, well beyond the time horizon of even pluriannual budgeting. Another example is procurement and contracting models, in which the private contractor building or operating an asset does not own it and thus would not incur any repair costs resulting from a disaster. Such a situation could arise in standard procurement or in PPPs following the "build, transfer, operate" model. Even when the private contractor owns the asset (such as in "build, operate, transfer" models), the transfer of the asset to the government usually takes place long before the end of the asset's lifetime. And even when longer concessions are possible (for example, the Tours-Bordeaux high-speed rail line in France was built under a 50-year concession contract), the high discount rate observed in the private sector means that long-term natural hazard and climate change risks will have a minimal impact on decision making.

Further, the expectation that the government will provide ad hoc support if a disaster occurs can diminish the incentives to act. In the aftermath of a disaster, governments usually provide people, firms, and infrastructure owners and operators with support. But the mere possibility of public aid after disasters can create moral hazard, discouraging risk management and the purchase of insurance—and this moral hazard is simply unavoidable. Providing support during and after crises is one of the main missions of governments, and it is not realistic to expect them to withhold support from an area affected by a disaster just to avoid moral hazard, especially when basic services (such as electricity, water, and transport) are at stake. Governments will always support and facilitate the recovery of these infrastructure systems, and this fact needs to be acknowledged and taken into account in the design of regulations and incentives.

RECOMMENDATION 3: INCLUDE RESILIENCE IN REGULATIONS AND INCENTIVES

What are the solutions for coping with the challenges that arise from a lack of incentives to avoid disruptions and strengthen the resilience of users? The answer lies in governments designing a consistent set of regulations and financial incentives to align the interests of infrastructure service providers with the public interest, as illustrated in figure 11.1.

How is this done? First, for each hazard and infrastructure system, governments or regula-

FIGURE 11.1 Creating the right resilience incentives for infrastructure service providers requires a consistent set of regulations and financial incentives

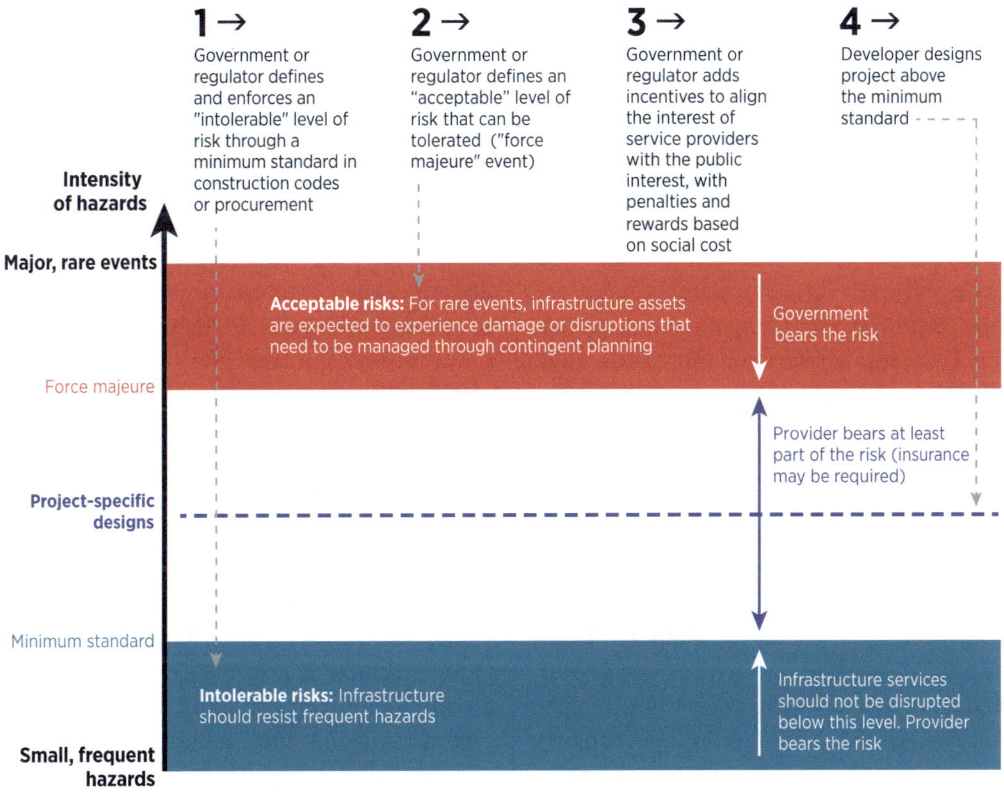

tors need to define a minimum standard of resistance—that is, a hazard intensity below which infrastructure assets should not suffer any damage or disruption. For example, all roads should be able to cope with a 20-year return period rainfall event. Second, they need to define the level of the force majeure or acceptable risk—that is, the level at which infrastructure failures have to be tolerated. Beyond this level, the risk from a natural hazard is usually supported by the public sector. Below this level, at least part of the risk is usually supported by the owner or operator of the infrastructure asset. Third, they need to create the right incentives to align the interest of the infrastructure asset owner or operator with the public interest. This can be achieved by penalizing an infrastructure operator for disruptions, for example, at an amount calibrated on the social cost of these disruptions. Based on these regulations, incentives, and risk allocations, project developers and asset owners can determine their strategy, the desired resilience level of their assets, and an appropriate design.

Action 3.1: Consider resilience objectives in master plans, standards, and regulations, and adjust them regularly to account for climate change

Agencies responsible for infrastructure services usually undertake regular master-planning exercises, typically on a five-year cycle, to formulate their investment program and financial needs. These master-planning exercises should explicitly consider the resilience of the plans and options available to reduce the vulnerability of their systems to various natural hazards and climate change.

Standards and regulations need to account for climate conditions, geophysical hazards, and climate change and other environmental and socioeconomic trends. Resilience-related standards can be expressed in many ways, with trade-offs between simplicity and enforceability, on the one hand, and specificity and adaptability, on the other. Very specific standards applied to infrastructure—such as the amount of rainfall (in millimeters) that road culverts should be able withstand are simple to apply and enforce, but they are not context specific and can be locally inappropriate. To ensure that infrastructure assets can cope with local hazards, standards can be developed for each region and for broad categories of assets—for example, primary versus secondary versus tertiary roads. All primary roads in a mountainous area could be required to be able to cope with a certain amount of rainfall. Even better, the standard could be asset and location specific. For example, roads could be required to withstand events of a certain return period, with the precise level based on the criticality of the road.

With climate change and other long-term environmental trends, standards and codes need to be revised regularly (box 11.1). According to Vallejo and Mullan (2017), approximately one-third of Organisation for Economic Co-operation and Development (OECD) countries are revising at least one mandatory national infrastructure standard to account for climate change adaptation, but similar processes are lacking in low- and middle-income countries. For instance, Sweden updated its road drainage standard in 2008, introducing a climate safety factor to cope with the anticipated increase in future rainfall due to climate change. Similarly, the European Commission mandated the Centre Européen de Normalisation to include climate change in the European civil engineering technical standards (the Eurocodes), especially for transport and energy infrastructure (European Commission 2014). Several national standards organizations have produced risk management guidelines that include climate change and resilience considerations for infrastructure (British Standards Institution 2011; Council of Standards Australia 2013; U.S. National Institute of Standards and Technology 2015). And

BOX 11.1 With climate change, when and where do standards need to be revised?

In the United States, stormwater infrastructure is designed using government documents on precipitation frequency, informed by states' department of transportation (DOT) guidelines that balance risks and costs. However, both the government precipitation documents and states' DOT guidelines are updated infrequently, which increases the risks in areas where patterns of precipitation have changed over time. Lopez-Cantu and Samaras (2018) review DOT design manuals for the 48 contiguous U.S. states and the District of Columbia and find wide variations in the design of return period standards recommended for similar roadways and types of infrastructure.

Patterns of precipitation and intensities used in various design manuals have been changing over time, indicating that stormwater infrastructure installed prior to the latest update of precipitation frequency documents could be underdesigned for present and future climate conditions. Comparing states' DOT design storm values for each roadway and type of infrastructure, Lopez-Cantu and Samaras (2018) develop an index for each climate region to assess the relative stringency of each state's requirements. Using these index values, the observed change in precipitation frequency estimates, and each state's design manual publication date, this research identifies the states that need to prioritize revision of their stormwater standards to maintain the originally intended design performance over time (see map B11.1.1 for the 25-year return period event). When considering all return periods, eight states are found to require an immediate revision of their stormwater standards. In addition, these states should assess whether the existing infrastructure requires additional adaptive capacity to manage observed precipitation increases.

Looking to 2050, under a scenario of climate change, the priority for such a revision becomes more urgent for all states. Although local assessments comparing the infrastructure cost of increasing the stringency of standards with the expected cost of future damages remain necessary, revising stormwater standards to incorporate observed precipitation increases is a no-regret option.

MAP B11.1.1 In some U.S. states, revising stormwater infrastructure standards is urgent

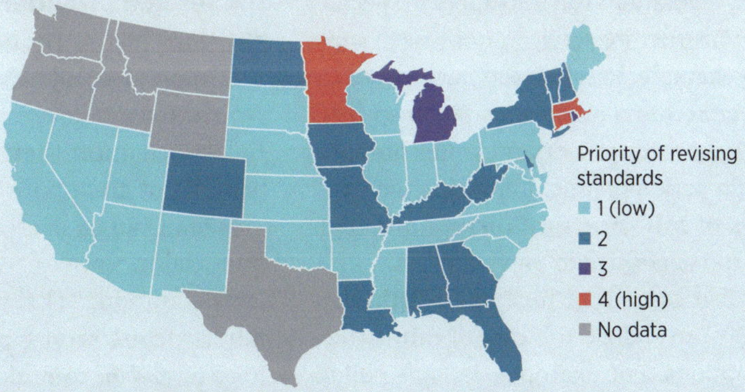

Source: Lopez-Cantu and Samaras 2018.
Note: Map shows priority (1 lowest, 4 highest) assigned to each state to revise stormwater infrastructure standards, according to the observed changes in 25-year return period. As of January 2018, states in gray remain uncovered by the National Oceanic and Atmospheric Organization's Atlas 14 of precipitation frequency and thus are not included in the analysis.

in 2015, the International Standards Organisation (ISO) created the Adaptation Task Force to develop standards for vulnerability assessment, adaptation planning, and adaptation monitoring and evaluation (ISO 2015).

Resilience-related regulations can also be based on outcome indicators, using observed performance. For example, electricity utilities can be required to limit power outages to below a certain number of hours a year. In France, the electricity distribution company is committed to limiting power outages to below an average of one long outage (longer than three minutes) and five short outages a year. The main advantage of outcome-based regulations is that they outsource the risk assessment to infrastructure operators and should automatically adjust for climate change. However, such observed outcomes cannot be applied to rare shocks—such as a 100-year return period hurricane—because such an event cannot be regularly observed. Input-based or process-based approaches founded on construction codes are the only ones that can be applied to exceptional events.

It is sometimes easier to enable the users of infrastructure services to manage disruptions than to prevent all disruptions (see chapter 8). As a result, regulations can also apply to specific users of infrastructure services, not just to suppliers. For example, hospitals can be required to invest in generators and water tanks so that they can cope with power and water outages for a certain period of time, mitigating the consequences of infrastructure disruptions that would be too expensive to prevent.

Firms also can adopt business continuity plans (BCPs) to reduce the cost of infrastructure disruptions. For example, Japan's policy and institutional framework for industry resilience, the Basic Disaster Response Plan, requires companies to recognize the role that they are expected to play when disaster strikes, to understand their own risk from a natural disaster, and to implement risk management and develop a BCP to minimize the consequences of shocks. The 2012 Japan Revitalization Strategy sets BCP establishment targets for 100 percent of large firms and 50 percent of small and medium enterprises by 2020.

Households can do much to be better prepared to cope with infrastructure disruptions. Basic disaster supply kits are widely available, and most disaster management agencies and organizations, such as the Red Cross, provide guidance.[1] Traditional recommendations include having 72-hour reserves of emergency supplies, such as water, canned food (with a manual can opener), extra batteries, candles, pet supplies, and copies of important personal documents (like passports, land titles, bank account information, and insurance contracts). Vulnerable people and groups (like people with disabilities or chronic diseases, the elderly, and young children) have specific needs that should also be accounted for (including prescription medicines and baby formula and diapers). Well-equipped households provide more room for utilities, agencies, and governments to restore services, while avoiding the worst impact on people's health and well-being.

Action 3.2: Create financial incentives for service providers to promote resilient infrastructure services

A common limit of codes and regulations is that regulators and governments may not have all the information they need on the costs and benefits of all options for building resilience. This limit can be overcome with economic and financial incentives. Two options are particularly common: (1) rewards and penalties for infrastructure service providers, pushing them to *go beyond the code* and capture further opportunities to build resilience, and (2) payment for ecosystem service schemes to promote nature-based solutions.

Rewards and penalties can motivate service providers to implement cost-effective solutions to improve resilience beyond the mandatory

(Pardina and Schiro 2018). The Australian Energy Regulator established the Service Target Performance Incentive Scheme (STPIS) to incentivize electricity providers to improve the quality of their services, including their reliability and resilience (Pardina and Schiro 2018). The goal of STPIS is to prevent providers from achieving cost reductions at the expense of service quality. Penalties and rewards distributed by STPIS are calibrated according to how willing consumers are to pay for improved service. This arrangement aligns distributors' incentives for efficient price and nonprice outcomes with the long-term interests of consumers (Australian Energy Regulator 2014).

Similarly, in Finland, the 2013 revision of the Electricity Market Act sets compulsory resilience targets for weather hazards with which operators must comply by the end of 2028 (OECD 2019). It specifies that the longest acceptable interruption time is six hours in urban areas and 36 hours in rural areas. Enforcement is ensured by economic incentives that also encourage service providers to reach higher than minimum levels of security of supply. The compensation paid by electricity distribution operators to their customers in the event of a long outage reaches up to 200 percent of the yearly average electricity fee—up to a maximum of €2,000—when the disruption exceeds 12 days. The new scheme was first activated during the January 2018 winter storm that left 40,000 people in northern Finland without electricity, some of them for up to a week. As a result, 10,000 customers received compensation totaling €5 million.

But financial incentives are challenging to implement (see box 11.2 regarding PPPs). First, calibrating the value of the reward or penalty can be difficult due to a lack of data, even though a financial incentive for resilience does not need to be precisely calibrated to improve the situation. Second, such instruments will be effective only if the infrastructure operators have the capacity to respond (see chapter 12). In the many countries where the power sector is not financially viable (Kojima and Trimble 2016), for instance, financial penalties may exacerbate existing challenges for utilities and may not support better design or maintenance of infrastructure systems.

Another instrument is payment for ecosystem services (PES) schemes, which can be used to create an incentive to promote nature-based solutions to increasing resilience. These schemes entail a user fee that those who benefit from ecosystem services pay for protection or restoration of the ecosystem (Browder et al. 2019). And the fee can be applied to nature-based solutions that reduce the cost or increase the resilience of infrastructure services, with payment originating from dedicated service fees, government revenues, or specialized funds.

Infrastructure service providers can, with the approval of regulators, create a distinct fee to support nature-based solutions. Some U.S. water utilities have "watershed protection fees" that are reinvested in watershed protection measures. In Brazil, water users pay a federally mandated fee to the local water company that local watershed committees use for watershed maintenance and reforestation.

If a specific fee is not possible, government revenues (or the reallocation of other subsidies) can be earmarked to fund nature-based solutions. In the 1990s, the power supply of Costa Rica was threatened by unsustainable farming practices that accelerated the siltation of hydropower reservoirs. Using revenues from fuel and water taxes and grants and loans from multilateral donors, the government created a PES program that gives landowners incentives to restore and conserve forestland (Blackman and Woodward 2010). As a result, siltation is being reduced, helping to preserve the country's electrical power generation infrastructure.

In addition, nature-based solutions can be encouraged by removing some of the obstacles to their implementation. One obstacle is the fact that the mandate of most infrastructure

BOX 11.2 Public-private partnerships and their force majeure clauses

Governments should develop a legal framework and institutional structure to ensure that disaster resilience is incorporated into PPP projects. Many governments have a disaster risk framework and a PPP framework, but the two frameworks rarely interact. Even in Japan, where PPPs are well developed and natural hazards are well managed, guidelines for including resilience in PPPs exist, but they are not mandatory.

The incentives for operators to incorporate resilience in their assets depend on the type of contract, with "build, operate, transfer" models creating a stronger incentive than "build, transfer, operate" models. However, contracts can be weakened by excessively broad force majeure clauses, which transfer the risks from the private to the public sector. When they are too broad, force majeure clauses reduce the incentives for actors to build and operate an infrastructure asset in a way that accounts for low-probability risks. For example, many force majeure clauses include "acts of God (such as fires, explosions, earthquakes, droughts, tidal waves, and floods)."

Force majeure clauses are essential for establishing PPPs at a reasonable cost, and they can be designed to minimize the negative impact on incentives for resilience. One solution is for a contract to include a *quantified* definition of the force majeure for each event category and to define force majeure as applicable only in extreme cases. Ideally, a third party would decide after an event whether the return period or intensity of the event was sufficient to trigger the force majeure clause. The contract can then determine the allocation of risk in terms of both missed revenues and restoration costs, ensuring that the private operator always bears a significant share of the cost. Mandatory or voluntary insurance could also ensure the sustainability of the infrastructure services—protecting the private operator against losses, while minimizing the cost for the public sector and maintaining the incentive to build more resilient assets and systems.

However, the design of PPPs needs to account for many context-specific factors, including the maturity of the PPP market, the risk tolerance of private sector players, and other risk factors such as vulnerability to commodity price shocks. These factors will determine how much risk can be transferred to private operators, creating trade-offs for governments between incentivizing resilience and mobilizing private sector finance. When the private sector is unable to bear the risks from natural hazards, it becomes even more important to use alternative tools, such as strong construction codes and procurement rules.

Source: World Bank 2019.

service regulators and operators often includes hard infrastructure systems, but not the environment and ecosystems that support these systems. For example, water utilities are usually responsible for the systems of pipes, pumps, and treatment stations needed to provide households and firms with high-quality, reliable water, but they have no mandate to act on the upstream ecosystems that are so essential to the provision of quality water. A second obstacle is that the incentives to preserve and protect ecosystems and the services they provide are often reduced by subsidies in the water, agriculture, energy, or housing sectors. For example, some agricultural subsidies favor the extension of farming at the expense of forests and wetlands. And tax incentives for construction, intended to improve housing affordability or create economic activity and jobs, can similarly lead to urban sprawl at the expense of the natural areas that play a key role in mitigating floods (Brueckner and Kim 2003).

Action 3.3: Ensure that infrastructure regulations are consistent with risk-informed land use plans and guide development toward safer areas

Infrastructure regulators or operators have little incentive to account for the effects of their actions on the resilience of users. To ensure that new infrastructure does not increase exposure and vulnerability to natural hazards, infrastructure regulations should be aligned with risk-informed land use and urbanization plans. Infrastructure localization choices need to account for the public and private investments that a new infrastructure asset will attract and their implications for resilience. For example, a new road on a floodplain may be a bad idea if it attracts people to this flood-prone area who will not be able to build resilient housing, even if the road itself is designed to cope with all possible natural disasters. To prevent such outcomes, infrastructure risk assessments have to consider induced investments, not just the infrastructure asset itself.

Even better, infrastructure localization choices can be used to implement land use planning and promote low-risk spatial development. Indeed, infrastructure investments can actively guide the development of evolving spatial patterns, and thus they should be embedded in land use and regional planning. Take the case of Nadi, Fiji, where land that is safe and well connected to jobs and services can be given priority for future development (see chapter 8). People and developers can be attracted to this priority land by means of early investments in transport, water and sanitation, and electricity infrastructure. Simple communication can then help to drive urbanization toward safer areas. In Tunis, the wide dissemination of simple plans indicating where the government was planning infrastructure extensions helped to guide urban development (Lozano-Gracia and Garcia Lozano 2018).

Because infrastructure investments make land more attractive by improving its accessibility or the amenities it includes, they also lead to an increase in land values. This increase can be "captured" through tax instruments or specific fees and used for infrastructure development. *Land value capture* finance is a process whereby part or all of the value created through public interventions or investments and accruing to private agents is recuperated by the public sector and used to finance public goods (Huxley 2009). Such financing can fund resilience-enhancing infrastructure systems, creating an incentive for infrastructure service providers to build the resilience of the community.

NOTE

1. See, for instance, the Red Cross emergency supply kit at https://www.redcross.org/get-help/how-to-prepare-for-emergencies/survival-kit-supplies.html.

REFERENCES

Australian Energy Regulator. 2014. "Overview of the Better Regulation Reform Package." Australian Energy Regulator, Melbourne. https://www.aer.gov.au.

Blackman, A., and R. T. Woodward. 2010. "User Financing in a National Payments for Environmental Services Program: Costa Rican Hydropower." *Ecological Economics* 69 (8): 1626–38.

British Standards Institution. 2011. "Climate Change Adaptation—Adapting to Climate Risks Using ISO 9001, ISO 14001, BS 25999, and BS 31100." British Standards Institution, London.

Browder, G., S. Ozment, I. Rehberger Bescos, T. Gartner, and G.-M. Lange. 2019. *Integrating Green and Gray: Creating Next Generation Infrastructure.* Washington, DC: World Bank and World Resources Institute.

Brueckner, J. K., and H.-A. Kim. 2003. "Urban Sprawl and the Property Tax." *International Tax and Public Finance* 10 (1): 5–23. https://doi.org/10.1023/A:1022260512147.

Council of Standards Australia. 2013. "Australian Standards: Climate Change Adaptation for Settlements and Infrastructure: A Risk Based

Approach." AS 5334—2013, Council of Standards Australia, Sydney. https://infostore.saiglobal.com/store/details.aspx?ProductID=1631218.

European Commission. 2014. "Commission Implementing Decision of 28.5.2014 on Deciding to Make a Standardisation Request to the European Standardisation Organisations." European Commission, Brussels. www.etsi.org/images/files/ECMandates/M526.pdf.

Huxley, J. 2009. "Value Capture Finance: Making Urban Development Pay Its Way." Urban Land Institute, Washington, DC.

ISO (International Standards Organisation). 2015. "Practical Tools for Addressing Climate Change." ISO, Geneva. www.iso.org/iso/climatechange_2015.pdf.

Kojima, M., and C. Trimble. 2016. "Making Power Affordable for Africa and Viable for Its Utilities." World Bank, Washington, DC. https://openknowledge.worldbank.org/handle/10986/25091.

Lopez-Cantu, T., and C. Samaras. 2018. "Temporal and Spatial Evaluation of Stormwater Engineering Standards Reveals Risks and Priorities across the United States." *Environmental Research Letters* 13 (7): 074006. https://doi.org/10.1088/1748-9326/aac696.

Lozano-Gracia, N., and M. Garcia Lozano. 2018. "Haitian Cities: Actions for Today with an Eye on Tomorrow." World Bank, Washington, DC.

OECD (Organisation for Economic Co-operation and Development). 2019. *Good Governance for Critical Infrastructure Resilience.* OECD Review of Risk Management Practices. Paris: OECD.

Pardina, M. R., and J. Schiro. 2018. "Taking Stock of Economic Regulation of Power Utilities in the Developing World: A Literature Review." Policy Research Working Paper 8461, World Bank, Washington, DC. https://doi.org/10.1596/1813-9450-8461.

U.S. National Institute of Standards and Technology. 2015. *Community Resilience Planning Guide for Buildings and Infrastructure Systems.* Vols. I and II. Washington, DC: U.S. Department of Commerce. www.nist.gov/el/resilience/guide.cfm.

Vallejo, L. and M. Mullan. 2017. "Climate-Resilient Infrastructure: Getting the Policies Right." OECD Environment Working Paper 121, OECD Publishing, Paris. http://dx.doi.org/10.1787/02f74d61-en.

World Bank. 2019. "Technical Brief on Resilient Infrastructure Public-Private Partnerships (PPPs)—Contracts and Procurement." World Bank, Washington, DC.

Improve Decision Making 12

OBSTACLE	RECOMMENDATION	ACTIONS
Insufficient consideration of natural hazards and climate change	Improve decision making	• 4.1: Invest in freely accessible natural hazard and climate change data • 4.2: Make robust decisions and minimize the potential for regret and catastrophic failure • 4.3: Build the skills needed to use data and models and mobilize the know-how of the private sector

THE OBSTACLE: PUBLIC AND PRIVATE ACTORS OFTEN LACK DATA, MODELS, AND CAPACITY

So far, the three recommendations given in part III of this report have stressed the need for standards and regulations, plans, and financial incentives to build the resilience of infrastructure systems (see chapters 9–11). But a major challenge is to include natural hazards and climate change in these regulations, plans, and incentives. And in the absence of natural hazard and climate change data and models, well-meaning operators are unable to improve resilience, and regulators are unable to create smart, efficient regulations and incentives. Thus, a package of resilient infrastructure policies should include investments to ensure that stakeholders have access to the right data and tools and to support improvements in how decisions are made.

Major "data bottlenecks" impair the design of more resilient infrastructure. One example is the high-resolution digital elevation model (DEM), a data set that provides the topography of a given area. Such data are the basis for many hazard models and assessments, including hydrological and flood models and landslide susceptibility analysis. These data are frequently generated using a LIDAR installed on a plane. Recent DEMs have been generated at a lower cost using drones—for example, in Dar es Salam, through collaboration between the World Bank and the Red Cross—but this approach has its limits when a large area needs to be mapped.[1] Although a DEM is generally available for all urbanized areas in high-income countries, such data are often unavailable in low- and middle-income countries, making it impossible to create the required flood and landslide hazard maps. Investing a few million dollars in a DEM would help to improve the design of billions of dollars of resilient infrastructure.

Another example of a data bottleneck is the lack of long time series of hydrometeorological data. These data are needed to design infrastructure, but they may not be available because the data have never been collected, or because they have never been digitized, or because they are accessible only at a prohibitive price. Remote sensing using satellites, drones, and progress in computing has made it easier and cheaper to monitor and model environmental conditions. However, these new tools cannot fully replace the networks of well-maintained weather- and water-monitoring stations and data processing that are still missing in many low-income countries. This situation stems in part from the low capacity and lack of resources of national hydrometeorological services in most of the world (Rogers and Tsirkunov 2013).

Because of climate change and other long-term trends—from land use artificialization to soil degradation—historical data are now insufficient predictors of future risks. Many studies have shown that infrastructure design and management cannot assume that the future will resemble the past (McCarl, Villavicencio, and Wu 2008; Milly et al. 2008). Today, proper risk assessment should include the effects of climate change, using the many climate models now available. However, outputs of climate models are very different from observations of the historical climate (Hallegatte 2009; Kalra et al. 2014), and using them requires accounting for the uncertainty in these results.

Data on natural hazards and climate change are not enough. Also needed are data on how users are managing disruptions. The minimum level of resilience that can be set in construction codes and standards, for example, depends on what the users of infrastructure services can easily handle. The introduction of compensation systems for power or water outages (such as in Finland, where power distribution companies have to compensate users for outages) requires an estimate of the economic cost of these outages. This information relies, in turn, on collecting data from infrastructure users as well as understanding how disruptions affect households' daily lives and the productivity and effectiveness of businesses. However, this knowledge is very patchy, especially in low- and middle-income countries, and far more systematic household and business surveys are needed to better map and understand users' needs (see chapter 2 and 3).

RECOMMENDATION 4: IMPROVE DECISION MAKING

What are the solutions for coping with these challenges of insufficient data, models, skills, and competencies, which result in insufficient consideration of natural hazards and climate change? Besides investing in freely accessible data on these issues—aided by new technologies—it is important to make an appropriate use of these data, identify robust decisions in the face of great uncertainties, and minimize the potential for regret and catastrophic failures. At the same time, governments should build the skills needed to create and use the data and models and mobilize the know-how of the private sector.

Action 4.1: Invest in freely accessible natural hazard and climate change data

Investments in data and models can provide extremely high returns on investments by improving the design of billions of dollars of long-lived infrastructure assets. The scenarios developed in chapter 6 suggest that strengthening infrastructure is much cheaper if investment is targeted to the most exposed and most critical assets. The ability to target investments is estimated to divide the cost by 10, reducing it from between $120 billion and $670 billion to between $11 billion and $65 billion. This finding suggests that the value of precise hazard information is orders of magnitude higher than the cost of generating these data and modeling results. Other studies have concluded that investing in hazard data and forecasting capacities is very cost-effective (Hallegatte 2012; Rogers and Tsirkunov 2013; WMO et al. 2015).

Specific investments in data bottlenecks could be transformational and generate large benefits. For instance, producing a DEM would cost between $120 and $200 per square kilometer with a plane-installed LIDAR, with other options (such as stereo photography) ranging between $30 to $100 per square kilometer. Producing DEM for all urban areas in low- and middle-income countries would cost between $50 million and $400 million in total—making it possible to perform an in-depth risk assessment for all new infrastructure assets and, in the process, inform hundreds of billions in investment per year. In addition to better-designed infrastructure systems, these data would allow risk-informed land use and urbanization planning, which would also generate large benefits. And if the data were available for free, one could expect private sector actors to use them in innovative ways to improve risk management for the whole economy. Overall, the benefits would be at least an order of magnitude larger than the cost of generating and distributing these data, which is also continuously declining, thanks to new technology to collect and process data (box 12.1).

To improve data availability, some organizations have undertaken "data rescue"—in particular, digitizing the paper-based records of hydrometeorological data (WMO 2016). In addition to historical data, weather forecasting and early warning systems can play a key role in anticipating extreme weather events and mitigating their impacts on infrastructure systems. For example, power plants are usually curtailed before the arrival of a hurricane to minimize the potential for damage and cascading events. Before Hurricane Sandy hit New York City in 2012, the Metropolitan Transit Authority moved its trains out of flood-prone areas, minimizing the impact on its equipment and allowing it to restore services relatively rapidly after the storm.

To be useful, data need to be available to those making decisions. Multiple initiatives to improve access to hazard and risk data contribute to improved decision making—such as the Global Facility for Disaster Reduction and Recovery (GFDRR) ThinkHazard! platform, which provides a simple estimate of hazard exposure everywhere on the globe and a link to the underlying data necessary to conduct more in-depth assessments.

Also, there are increasing calls to adopt open-data policies across government and academic research to ensure that these data generate as much benefit as possible. Open-data licensing supports transparency, efficiency, and participation in government; peer review of science; and more widespread and effective use of data for decision making in general. The Open Data for Resilience Initiative (OpenDRI) of the GFDRR has been working on these issues in relation to disaster and climate risk assessment since 2011. OpenDRI has partnered with national governments, universities, and community-based organizations to launch data-sharing platforms, such as the Sri Lanka Disaster Risk Information Platform. The goal is to support community-mapping projects for disaster risk assessment and to build tools for communicating complex risk information to diverse stakeholders. GFDRR (2016) has compiled a list of key principles to use in applying open-data approaches to disaster risk management.

To make sure that these data influence and support decision making, the asset management systems that are so useful to improve the design and maintenance of infrastructure

BOX 12.1 New technologies make data collection and processing easier

Satellite images and image processing. Today, urban development, transport networks, and power generation plants can be mapped through the post-treatment of satellite images. For example, Graesser et al. (2012) have used satellite images and machine learning to map informal settlements in Caracas, Kabul, Kandahar, and La Paz, helping to identify areas with poor infrastructure services and supporting the prioritization of investments. However, difficult challenges remain, as illustrated by the relatively low performance of algorithms for mapping the electric grid.[a] In postdisaster situations, aerial and satellite images can also be used to assess the damage rapidly and to prioritize emergency actions (GFDRR 2019).

Crowdsourcing. This term describes the ways in which the Internet and mobile telephones facilitate outsourcing data collection tasks to the public. Crowdsourcing can be used to collect large amounts of data in real time at potentially lower costs than traditional approaches (UNISDR 2017). OpenStreetMap, which has been used extensively in the risk assessments discussed in parts I and II of this report, is one of the best-known examples of an open database built by crowdsourcing, but it is not the only one. In Dar es Salam, the Ramani Huria community maps identify flood-prone areas. The project, initiated in 2015, trains students and community members to create detailed flood maps of each community and publishes an atlas that includes community maps of the 21 most flood-prone wards (World Bank 2018).

Social network analyses. Social media data include a wealth of information, but the challenge here is to manage the huge volume of data and extract what is useful for decision making. For example, FloodTags uses Twitter information, natural language processing, and mapping tools to support postflood emergency management by identifying the location of flood emergencies. This tool has been piloted in the Philippines by the Red Cross. Although these approaches will not replace direct data collection, they provide useful complementary insights into a crisis and help to guide action.

Traditional surveys. These surveys continue to play an important role in collecting data and understanding the importance of infrastructure services and their disruptions. Part I of this report gives multiple examples of business or household surveys that provide information on the cost of infrastructure disruptions. These surveys support design of the right incentives for infrastructure service providers. For example, they help to determine the appropriate magnitude of penalties when service disruptions exceed regulations, or rewards when performance goes beyond the construction code.

a. See https://code.fb.com/connectivity/electrical-grid-mapping/.

assets (see chapter 9) can easily be upgraded to incorporate climate change and natural disaster risks into decision-making processes. In particular, the data recorded can include the exposure of each asset to various hazards, which would inform the prioritization of maintenance actions. For instance, keeping the culverts exposed to frequent floods free of waste can be prioritized, reducing their vulnerability and eventually the repair costs after heavy rainfall.

Making data broadly available faces important challenges. One is that the collection of data on the individual users of infrastructure services may pose privacy issues. As data collection increases its spatial resolution and devices such as smartphones collect individual data, it becomes possible to link risk information to specific individuals. Concerns include the use of these data for purposes beyond risk management (for example, to target advertising). Moreover, flood exposure data can also create issues, as households often fear expropriation without due process and compensation if their home is in a flood zone. The trade-off between the efficiency of risk management and privacy concerns needs to be taken seriously, and any data collection and distribution should come with clear and well-enforced regulations regarding how the data can be used.

Another challenge is the need to balance access to data with security considerations. The data needed to identify critical infrastructure and the priorities for strengthening networks are the same data needed to plan the most damaging attacks on these networks. Since the 9/11 attacks in the United States, these considerations have led to the removal of much data from the public domain in many countries. One of the roles of the public agencies in charge of risk management and critical infrastructure is to determine which data can be made publicly available, which data can be shared among infrastructure service providers with some conditions on their use and dissemination, and which data should be considered too sensitive to be shared beyond specialized agencies. Although these considerations are legitimate and create real trade-offs, national security should not be used as a blanket excuse to restrict access to data. Best practices suggest making open access to data the default situation and creating strict processes to restrict access for data proven to be too sensitive.

Action 4.2: Make robust decisions and minimize the potential for regret and catastrophic failures

Regardless of the quality of the data and models available, the long lifetime of assets and deep uncertainty about the future exacerbate the challenges of sound decision making in infrastructure risk management.[2] Past evidence and current research suggest that any ability to predict the future is limited at best (Kahneman 2011; Silver 2012). Compounding the problem, parties to a decision often have competing priorities, beliefs, and preferences. These conditions create deep uncertainty, which occurs when parties to a decision do not know or cannot agree on (1) the models that describe the key processes that shape the future; (2) the probability distribution of key variables and parameters in these models; or (3) the value of alternative outcomes (Lempert, Popper, and Bankes 2003).

What is certain is that a cascade of uncertainties plague climate change, and these uncertainties preclude prediction of the precise nature, timing, frequency, intensity, and location of climate change impacts. Uncertainty about the future rise in sea levels and about temperature, precipitation, and other climate factors has tremendous implications for the near-term choices of decision makers. Examples are where to locate key infrastructure such as airports, how to protect coastal areas from flooding, and how to ensure water security.

But climate-related uncertainty is not the only issue; socioeconomic changes, political factors, disruptive new technologies, and behavioral changes also create major uncertainties that affect infrastructure-related decision making. For example, the future performance and cost of electric cars or the availability of self-driving vehicles could significantly affect how cities develop. Because the potential of these technologies is still being debated, urban planners and developers face these uncertainties as well.

In the presence of such deep uncertainty, traditional methods—such as least-cost approaches or cost-benefit analyses—are unable to point to the preferred infrastructure design. Traditional methods tend to search for an optimum, which requires considering all possible scenarios and knowing their probability. In situations of deep uncertainty, the probabilities of future scenarios are difficult to estimate, and this difficulty often leads to disagreement. Faced with disagreement and deep uncertainty, traditional decision-making approaches are vulnerable to bias and gridlock. They are also vulnerable to reaching brittle decisions—ones that are optimal for a particular set of assumptions but that perform poorly, or even disastrously, under other assumptions.

An alternative to seeking the "optimal" solution is to look for a robust decision—one that performs well across a wide range of futures, preferences, and worldviews, although it may not be optimal in any particular one. New methods such as robust decision making, decision trees, and adaptive pathways have been developed in the search for more robust options (Haasnoot et al. 2013; Lempert and Groves 2010; Ray and Brown 2015). These methods are sometimes also called "context-first" (Ranger et al. 2010) or "agree-on-decisions" (Kalra et al. 2014).

These methods begin by stress-testing the available options under a wide range of plausible conditions, without requiring a decision or agreement on which conditions are more or less likely. They evaluate the decision options repeatedly, under many different sets of assumptions, including low-likelihood but high-consequence events.

This process promotes consensus around decisions and can help in the management of deep uncertainty. Analyses performed in this way help decision makers to debate important questions:

- Are the conditions under which an option performs poorly likely enough to result in the choice of a different option?
- What trade-offs should be made between robustness and, for example, cost?
- Is it possible to add safety margins to a project to hedge against surprises?
- Which options offer the most flexibility for responding to unexpected changes in the future?
- What is the potential for regret in the future?
- What should be done in case of failure?

Selecting robust solutions can usually be achieved by selecting options that minimize the potential for regret. Here, regret is defined as the difference between what a given decision would achieve—for instance, in terms of financial performance—and what the best decision could have achieved. For instance, there is regret from having strengthened a bridge to resist a strong earthquake, if no such strong earthquake occurs during the lifetime of the bridge. Similarly, there is regret from not having strengthened the bridge if a strong earthquake does happen and the bridge is destroyed.

This metric and approach are used in chapter 6, where an exploration of the uncertainty regarding the costs and benefits of strengthening infrastructure assets shows that such strengthening is a robust action that is highly unlikely to lead to significant regret. This approach has also been applied to efforts to identify the best design for future investments in hydropower in Africa (Cervigni et al. 2015) and to assess the effort to preserve wetlands in Colombo (box 12.2). In addition, the results of stress tests can be used to create "failure scenarios" that can serve as a starting point for preparing for disruptions and creating contingency plans.

Action 4.3: Build the skills needed to use data and models and mobilize the know-how of the private sector

Even if all actors have access to data and models, using them appropriately requires skills and competencies that are not always available. For a government, utility, or agency, outsourcing the production of hazard and climate change data without building the skills to use these data appropriately in a robust decision-making framework is unlikely to lead to significant improvements in resilience.

BOX 12.2 Preserving wetlands in Colombo minimizes the risk of regret

A study of Colombo's floods, conducted amid large uncertainties about climate change and urban development, evaluates various choices for the preservation of wetlands (Browder et al. 2019). The study looks specifically at how much regret decision makers would experience in 2030, comparing the realized level of risk and the best possible outcome.

The study finds that all conservation levels could lead to zero regret. In other words, for each conservation level measured on a scale of between 0 and 100 percent, there is at least one scenario in which the level is optimal (figure B12.2.1). But if a small share of the wetlands is preserved and the rest is developed, the potential for regret is high: in scenarios with a major increase in rainfall and river runoff, high population growth, and high building vulnerability, the development of wetlands would lead to substantial flood losses. And because wetlands are difficult and costly to recreate, these losses would be largely irreversible, resulting in high regret. By contrast, the conservation of wetlands cannot lead to high regret because the main cost of this option is the opportunity cost of not developing the wetland areas, which is less uncertain than the cost of floods. Because conserving wetlands is a reversible solution, if decision makers want to avoid experiencing regret by 2030, they may prefer to conserve Colombo's urban wetlands for now, wait for more information on how climate and urbanization will evolve, and reconsider their position in a decade or two.

FIGURE B12.2.1 Preserving a large share of Colombo's wetlands minimizes the potential for regret in 2030

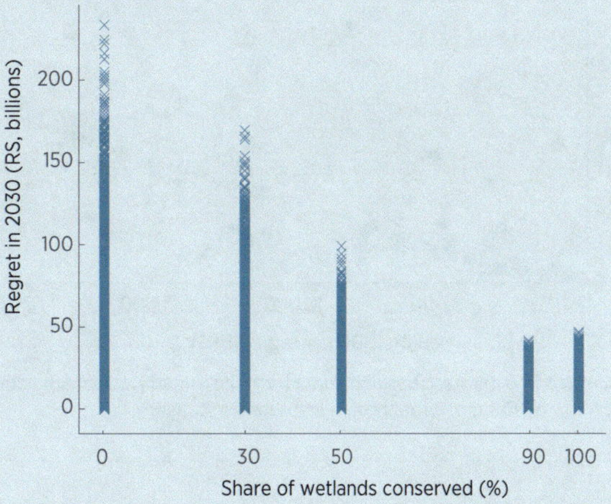

Source: Browder et al. 2019.

This is a major challenge in a low-income, low-capacity environment in which skilled engineers are scarce (figure 12.1). But it is also a common challenge in local authorities and municipalities, which are often in charge of managing water or transport infrastructure. Small cities, even in rich countries, do not have the resources to hire specialized staff and need to rely on external advisers and service providers or on support from national or regional agencies.

Infrastructure sectors at all scales benefit from the support and expertise of local consulting and engineering firms and other expertise centers based in universities, think tanks, and research centers. Universities and research centers can play an important role, training people in the right skills, developing new methodologies or adapting them to the local context, and advising policy and decision makers. This support is required not only for suppliers of infrastructure services, but also for users who can prepare for infrastructure disruptions and minimize their costs—for example, with business continuity plans.

When public sector expertise is insufficient, bringing in the private sector—as advisers or through direct procurement or public-private partnerships (PPPs)—can be a solution. Both domestic or international firms may have the capacity and know-how to implement innovative solutions. This capacity is particularly

FIGURE 12.1 Many low- and middle-income countries need to increase their enrollment in technical tertiary education

Share of students in tertiary education enrolled in engineering, manufacturing, and construction in 2016

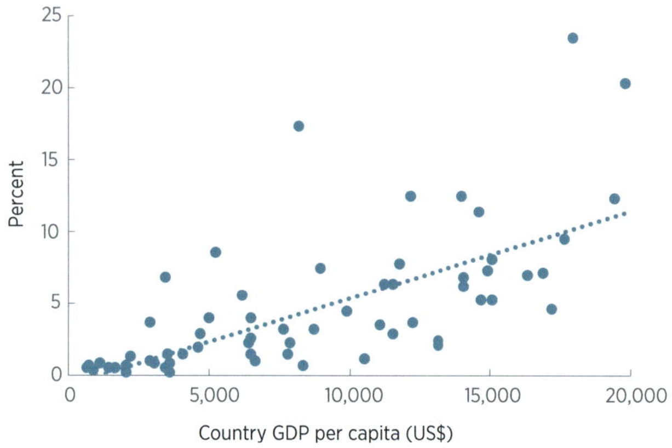

Source: World Bank staff, based on data from the United Nations Educational, Scientific, and Cultural Organization Institute for Statistics.

important in mobilizing the new technologies that are mostly developed in, and implemented by, the private sector—for example, those related to finance, telecommunications, and cybersecurity. However, cooperation between the public and private sectors is often difficult to establish because of differences in culture and work habits, issues related to privacy and commercial secrecy, and the risks of capture and rent-seeking behaviors from private actors, especially where public agencies have limited capacity.

Experts supporting long-term planning would benefit from the introduction of labels and certifications. In the areas of climate change and resilience to low-probability events, customers and users cannot easily observe the performance of various engineering and consulting firms. The effectiveness of a recommendation on climate change adaptation (for example, for the construction of a road) will not be evident until decades after the asset is built. The resilience of infrastructure cannot be observed until it is tested by severe weather or an earthquake. The fact that a bridge performs as expected for decades does not mean that a design flaw will not lead to its collapse during a stronger storm.

Where performance cannot be easily measured and verified, labels and certifications can provide the clients of a particular industry with some level of protection. Such labels can be provided through self-regulation (such as when professional organizations create the label) or assigned by the public sector (such as when the ministry of construction certifies private companies as capable of performing certain tasks). Designing such certification is tricky, however. If too strict, a certification process can easily slow down innovation, create barriers to entry for new players, and reduce competition. If too lax, a label or certification can help low-quality players—or even crooks—to enter the game.

NOTES

1. See https://drones.fsd.ch/wp-content/uploads/2016/03/Case-Studies-Dar-es-Salaam-Final2-1617045.pdf.
2. This section is adapted from Kalra et al. (2014).

REFERENCES

Browder, G., S. Ozment, I. Rehberger Bescos, T. Gartner, and G.-M. Lange. 2019. *Integrating Green and Gray: Creating Next Generation Infrastructure.* Washington, DC: World Bank and World Resources Institute.

Cervigni, R., R. Liden, J. E. Neumann, and K. M. Strzepek, eds. 2015. *Enhancing Climate Resilience of Africa's Infrastructure: The Power and Water Sectors.* Washington, DC: World Bank. https://doi.org/10.1596/978-1-4648-0466-3.

GFDRR (Global Facility for Disaster Reduction and Recovery). 2016. "Open Data for Resilience Initiative." GFDRR, Washington, DC.

———. 2019. "Machine Learning for Disaster Risk Management." GFDRR, Washington, DC.

Graesser, J., A. Cheriyadat, R. R. Vatsavai, V. Chandola, J. Long, and E. Bright. 2012. "Image Based Characterization of Formal and Informal Neighborhoods in an Urban Landscape." *IEEE Journal of Selected Topics in Applied Earth Observations and Remote Sensing* 5 (4): 1164–76.

Haasnoot, M., J. H. Kwakkel, W. E. Walker, and J. ter Maat. 2013. "Dynamic Adaptive Policy

Pathways: A Method for Crafting Robust Decisions for a Deeply Uncertain World." *Global Environmental Change* 23 (2): 485–98.

Hallegatte, S. 2009. "Strategies to Adapt to an Uncertain Climate Change." *Global Environmental Change* 19 (2): 240–47. https://doi.org/10.1016/j.gloenvcha.2008.12.003.

———. 2012. "A Cost-Effective Solution to Reduce Disaster Losses in Developing Countries: Hydro-Meteorological Services, Early Warning, and Evacuation." Policy Research Working Paper 6058, World Bank, Washington, DC. https://doi.org/10.1596/1813-9450-6058.

Kahneman, D. 2011. *Thinking, Fast and Slow*. New York: Farrar, Strauss and Giroux.

Kalra, N., S. Hallegatte, R. Lempert, C. Brown, A. Fozzard, S. Gill, and A. Shah. 2014. "Agreeing on Robust Decisions: New Processes for Decision Making under Deep Uncertainty." Policy Research Working Paper 6906, World Bank, Washington, DC. https://doi.org/doi:10.1596/1813-9450-6906.

Lempert, R. J., and D. G. Groves. 2010. "Identifying and Evaluating Robust Adaptive Policy Responses to Climate Change for Water Management Agencies in the American West." *Technological Forecasting and Social Change* 77 (6): 960–74.

Lempert, R. J., S. W. Popper, and S. C. Bankes. 2003. *Shaping the Next One Hundred Years: New Methods for Quantitative, Long-Term Policy Analysis*. Santa Monica, CA: RAND Corporation.

McCarl, B. A., X. Villavicencio, and X. Wu. 2008. "Climate Change and Future Analysis: Is Stationarity Dying?" *American Journal of Agricultural Economics* 90 (5): 1241–47. https://doi.org/10.1111/j.1467-8276.2008.01211.x.

Milly, P. C. D., J. Betancourt, M. Falkenmark, R. M. Hirsch, Z. W. Kundzewicz, D. P. Lettenmaier, and R. J. Stouffer. 2008. "Stationarity Is Dead: Whither Water Management?" *Science* 319 (5863): 573–74. https://doi.org/10.1126/science.1151915.

Ranger, N., A. Milner, S. Dietz, S. Frankhauser, A. Lopez, and G. Ruta. 2010. "Adaptation in the UK: A Decision-Making Process." Centre for Climate Change Economics and Policy, University of Leeds; Grantham Research Institute on Climate Change and the Environment, London.

Ray, P. A., and C. M. Brown. 2015. *Confronting Climate Uncertainty in Water Resources Planning and Project Design: The Decision Tree Framework*. Washington, DC: World Bank. https://doi.org/10.1596/978-1-4648-0477-9.

Rogers, D., and V. Tsirkunov. 2013. *Weather and Climate Resilience: Effective Preparedness through National Meteorological and Hydrological Services*. Vol. 62. Washington, DC: World Bank. https://doi.org/10.1596/978-1-4648-0026-9.

Silver, N. 2012. *The Signal and the Noise: Why So Many Predictions Fail—but Some Don't*. New York: Penguin Press.

UNISDR (United Nations Office for Disaster Risk Reduction). 2017. "Words into Action Guidelines: National Disaster Risk Assessment—UNISDR." UNISDR, Geneva. https://www.unisdr.org/we/inform/publications/52828.

WMO (World Meteorological Organization). 2016. "Guidelines on Best Practices for Climate Data Rescue." WHO, Geneva. https://public.wmo.int/en/resources/library/guidelines-best-practices-climate-data-rescue.

WMO (World Meteorological Organization), World Bank Group, GFDRR (Global Framework for Disaster Reduction and Recovery), and USAID (U.S. Agency for International Development). 2015. "Valuing Weather and Climate: Economic Assessment of Meteorological and Hydrological Services." WMO, Geneva. https://public.wmo.int/en/resources/library/valuing-weather-and-climate-economic-assessment-of-meteorological-and-hydrological.

World Bank. 2018. "Ramani Huria: The Atlas of Flood Resilience in Dar es Salaam." Working Paper 125586, World Bank, Washington, DC. http://documents.worldbank.org/curated/en/200421524092301920/Ramani-Huria-the-atlas-of-flood-resilience-in-Dar-es-Salaam.

Provide Financing 13

OBSTACLE	RECOMMENDATION	ACTIONS
Affordability and financing constraints	Provide financing	• 5.1: Provide adequate funding to include risk assessments in master plans and early project design • 5.2: Develop a government-wide financial protection strategy and contingency plans • 5.3: Promote transparency to better inform investors and decision makers

THE OBSTACLE: THE INFRASTRUCTURE SECTOR FACES AFFORDABILITY AND FINANCING CONSTRAINTS

Efforts to increase the resilience of infrastructure can increase various components of its full cost, including the cost borne by the government or regulators or the cost borne by the providers of infrastructure services (see figure 9.4).

In some cases, making an infrastructure asset more resilient leads to an absolute increase in its life-cycle cost and thus to *affordability* challenges. For example, when structural reinforcements of schools are needed to prevent the loss of life during an earthquake, solutions might include either an increase in funding (such as from higher taxes, higher user fees, or larger regional or international transfers) or a trade-off between the resilience and quantity of infrastructure services (such as fewer but stronger schools).

More often, however, making a project more resilient does not increase its life-cycle cost, but will increase its design cost, construction cost, or maintenance cost, linking the challenge to *financing*. If the life-cycle cost is manageable within the available resources, then the challenge is to allocate resources toward the early project stages to ensure good design, toward the substantial up-front investments required for resilient infrastructure, and toward a regular flow of resources to ensure good maintenance.

RECOMMENDATION 5: ENSURE FINANCING

What are the required measures that can help to address affordability challenges and financing constraints? This section highlights three key actions: the need for adequate funding to include risk assessments in master plans and early project design; the need for a government-wide financial protection strategy to aid recovery from disasters that cannot be prevented; and the need for greater transparency of infrastructure investments to ensure that investors and decision makers have the information they need to select the best, and most resilient, projects.

Action 5.1: Provide adequate funding to include risk assessments in master plans and early project design

Regulators often have limited budgets, thus making it difficult for them to design the right codes and regulations or to enforce them (see chapter 9). Further, master-planning exercises are critical to capture the system-level options for resilience (see chapter 7), but these exercises often lack the resources to conduct a full-fledged risk assessment.

Similarly, budgets tend to be small at the early stage of preparation of an infrastructure asset project, making it difficult to conduct the sophisticated risk and resilience analyses needed (such as those recommended in chapter 12)—even if they can generate massive savings over the lifetime of an infrastructure asset. When projects are more mature and financing is easier to access, more resources become available. However, at this stage most strategic decisions already have been made, and most low-cost options to increase resilience are no longer available, including, for example, changing the location of an asset or even the nature of a project. Providing the financing and technical support needed to include risk analysis at the early stages of project design can, therefore, be extremely cost-effective.

Governments or international organizations can achieve a transformational impact, with relatively limited resources, by financing the generation of appropriate data and dedicated risk assessment to inform master-planning exercises and early infrastructure project development. For this reason, disaster and climate risk assessment is one of the areas that has been identified as a priority for the use of climate finance (World Bank 2018) and one of the main focuses of the 2018–21 strategy of the Global Facility for Disaster Reduction and Recovery (GFDRR).

Dedicated organizations and project preparation facilities can support the inclusion of risk assessment in master planning, regulation design, and early stages of infrastructure projects. For example, the Global Infrastructure Facility—a partnership of governments, multilateral development banks, private sector investors, and financiers—supports the preparation, structuring, and implementation of complex infrastructure projects. In particular, it supports preliminary work to prioritize investments and test a project concept through "prefeasibility" analysis. It also supports, if needed, the legal, regulatory, and institutional reforms required to enable the successful development or participation of long-term private capital in the financial structure of a project. These interventions could easily have some resilience-related aspects, such as considering resilience in a prefeasibility study or developing the legal and regulatory environment to ensure that climate and disaster risk are considered in the development of public-private partnerships.

Action 5.2: Develop a government-wide financial protection strategy and contingency plans for natural hazards

This report has identified the need for infrastructure asset operators to have the capacity to respond quickly to incidents, so that incidents that cannot be avoided can be managed (see chapter 9). However, disruptions caused by natural hazards have specific characteristics: they tend to be larger, last longer, and be costlier than those caused by system failure. For instance, hazard-related power outages in

Europe last four times longer than those due to nonnatural causes. And while Bangladesh experiences almost daily power outages, a tropical cyclone caused the largest outage in the country, during which all 26 power plants stopped operating. Similarly, while congestion linked to car accidents is a daily occurrence in all countries in the world, an earthquake can damage hundreds of bridges at once.

To manage hazard-related asset losses and disruptions, countries need additional instruments, with specific contingency plans and a financial protection strategy. Resources to help countries to build such a strategy can make countries more resilient—a topic generating increasing interest from the international community. For instance, the Global Risk Financing Facility (GRiF) is a recently established financing mechanism that supports the development of risk-informed financial planning across different sectors and the continuity of critical public services (such as electricity, transport, and water).

When a disaster damages infrastructure, resources are needed to manage the disruptions both on the supply side (to recover, repair, and reconstruct) and on the demand side (to help users to manage the disruptions). Postdisaster needs usually have two phases: recovery and reconstruction. The recovery phase refers to the weeks and months following a disaster, during which relatively limited resources are urgently required. In this phase, timeliness is critical. The reconstruction phase refers to the longer period, during which infrastructure and buildings are repaired or rebuilt. This phase often involves massive funding and financing needs, but with less urgency so that traditional funding and financing mechanisms can be mobilized.

But the availability of financial resources is only half of the story. The capacity of a government to support postdisaster recovery and reconstruction depends greatly on its ability to deliver these resources to where they are needed. Doing so requires that governments be prepared before a disaster hits, with the right instruments, institutions, and capacities in place. The measures that can ensure rapid recovery and reconstruction include (1) contingency plans to ensure that the coordination of recovery and reconstruction efforts is effective and that responsibilities are clearly allocated among government agencies; (2) contingent financial arrangements—such as contingent credit lines or insurance products—to ensure that financing is immediately available and not delayed by budgetary procedures; (3) prearranged contracts to accelerate procurement—for example, ensuring that debris can be removed as soon as possible to facilitate reconstruction; and (4) international cooperation to share the cost of the staff and equipment needed for the recovery and reconstruction.

Governments usually finance most infrastructure recovery and reconstruction. They can ensure liquidity during these phases in three ways: (1) maintaining sufficient reserve funds, (2) arranging for contingent credit facilities, or (3) using insurance schemes or transferring risk. Governments can structure these financial instruments along "risk layers," with different instruments covering different types of risks (figure 13.1). By using a layered disaster risk financing strategy, countries such as Mexico and the Philippines have prepared themselves for a wide range of contingencies. Reserve funds are used to manage low-cost, high-probability events, whereas contingent financing and sovereign risk transfer instruments are used for high-cost, low-probability events (Ghesquiere and Mahul 2007; Mahul and Ghesquiere 2010; World Bank 2017).

Sometimes, infrastructure assets can be insured directly by their owners or operators, whether private or public entities. For example, the Kenyan government has implemented requirements for mandatory disaster risk insurance coverage in power purchase agreements. Insurance helps to finance repairs and recon-

FIGURE 13.1 Countries need a layered risk financing strategy

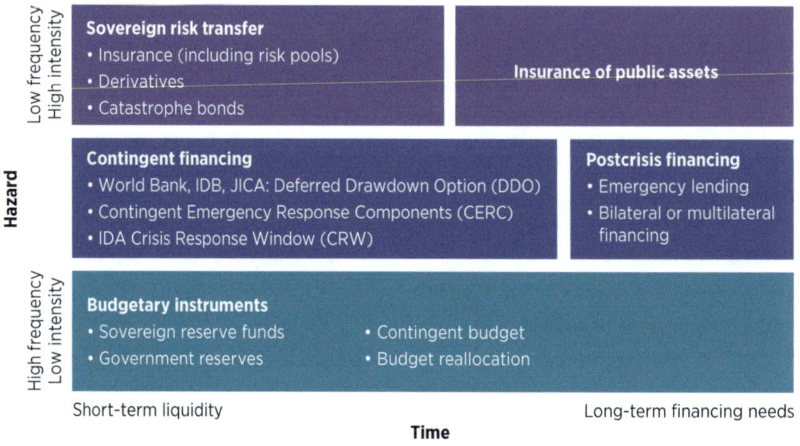

Source: World Bank 2017.
Note: IDB = Inter-American Development Bank; JICA = Japan International Cooperation Agency; IDA = International Development Association.

struction after a shock and also creates a powerful incentive for infrastructure asset owners and operators to reduce risks in order to pay a lower premium for more resilient assets. Usually, an insurance policy requires appropriate maintenance as a condition of the insurance payment, which should incentivize governments to maintain infrastructure properly and to mitigate disaster risks. The feasibility and desirability of insurance depend on the maturity of the domestic insurance markets, the feasibility of accessing the global reinsurance markets or other capital market instruments, and cost considerations.

The choice of financial instruments is determined not only by their functionality but also by their cost and speed of disbursement. Table 13.1 provides an indicative cost multiplier for different financial risk instruments. The cost multiplier is defined as the ratio of the cost of a financial product (such as the premium of an insurance product or the expected net present value of the cost of a contingent debt facility) to the expected payout over its lifetime. A ratio of 2 indicates that the overall cost of the financial product is likely to be twice the amount of the expected payout over a long period of time. The speed at which funds can be obtained is determined by the underlying legal and administrative processes (Mahul and Ghesquiere 2010). However, the cost multipliers and speed of fund disbursement may vary on a case-by-case basis, depending on the type of hazard, the frequency of the payout, or the institutional and management capacity in the country.

Other important considerations include the transparency and predictability of the resources (Clarke and Dercon 2016). Rule-based instruments—such as index insurance products and risk transfer mechanisms based on measurable indicators—provide governments, technical agencies, local authorities, and firms and households with a predictable amount of support and enable them to design their own response (such as taking out their own insurance contract). From a government perspective, rule-based instruments also help to build discipline regarding how postdisaster resources are mobilized and used.

Contingent financing can also help users to cope with, and recover from, infrastructure disruptions. Indeed, as emphasized in this report, reconstruction costs make up only a

TABLE 13.1 Cost multipliers vary across financial instruments for risk management

Instrument	Indicative cost multiplier	Disbursement (months)	Amount of funds potentially available
	Ex post financing		
Donor support (humanitarian relief)	0–1	1–6	Uncertain
Donor support (recovery and reconstruction)	0–2	4–9	Uncertain
Budget reallocations	1–2	0–9	Small
Domestic credit (bond issues)	1–2	3–9	Medium
External credit (e.g., emergency loans, bond issue)	1–2	3–6	Large
	Ex ante financing		
Budget contingencies	1–2	0–2	Small
Reserves	1–2	0–1	Small
Contingent credit	1–2	0–1	Medium
Parametric insurance	1.3 and up	0–2	Large
Alternative risk transfer (for example, cat bonds, weather derivatives)	1.5 and up	1–6	Large
Traditional (indemnity-based) insurance	1.5 and up	2–12	Large

Source: Mahul and Ghesquiere 2010.

fraction of the full cost of a lack of resilience. After major disruptions, small firms will have lost clients and sales, and households will have had to spend more to buy bottled water and batteries or will have lost income after members are unable to go to work. And the firms and households that are affected by infrastructure disruptions can be located far from the areas directly hit by natural hazards, and the distribution of postdisaster support may have to cover a much larger spatial area than the disaster itself (Colon, Hallegatte, and Rozenberg 2019; Rentschler et al. 2019).

In some countries, the regulations governing infrastructure services call for compensating users affected by outages—especially those in the power, telecommunications, and water sectors. In the absence of a compensation system, government may want to help firms and households to manage infrastructure disruptions in the same way that it helps them to manage the reconstruction of dwellings and replacement of assets. Typical instruments for households (and households' individual enterprises) include an adaptive social protection system, supplemented by ad hoc postdisaster transfers for people who are not covered by existing systems (Hallegatte et al. 2017). Firms in the formal sectors can usually be supported through tax breaks, ad hoc transfers, or subsidized loans. For example, in 2007 the Shizuoka Prefecture Credit Guarantee Association in Japan developed a postdisaster guarantee program for small and medium enterprises. Through the program, small and medium firms with business continuity plans can submit preapplications for a postdisaster credit guarantee, and the guarantee fee is waived if a business borrows after a disaster. Often, small businesses in the informal sector are the most difficult to support in the face of legal and technical obstacles, and ad hoc action may sometimes be necessary.

Action 5.3: Promote transparency to better inform investors and decision makers

One way to ensure that financing is directed to more resilient infrastructure projects is to ensure that investors are informed about the risks attached to projects. They may, then, prefer the more resilient ones. Such an approach requires transparency on every project's exposure and vulnerability to various hazards in a way that is currently not available.

Multiple international, regional, and national initiatives have been designed to increase the transparency of the physical risks attached to investments in assets. Examples include the Task Force for Climate-Related Financial Disclosure (TCFD), which recommends that businesses (and the financial actors that invest in them) report physical risks and how they are managed. Recognizing the challenges of standardizing the disclosure of physical risks, the European Bank for Reconstruction and Development and the Global Centre of Excellence on Climate Adaptation launched a study that highlights the need to perform forward-looking assessments of climate-related risks using various scenarios. Titled "Advancing TCFD Guidance on Physical Climate Risk and Opportunities," it recommends that firms and financial institutions report on the exposure of their assets to natural hazards and provide qualitative information on how they manage them, thereby facilitating assessment of the impacts of climate risk on corporate performance and credit risks.

The decision making of infrastructure investors is increasingly including consideration of environmental sustainability (Bennon and Sharma 2018), mainly through the adoption of environmental, social, and governance (ESG) principles or a responsible investment approach. The United Nations–supported Principles for Responsible Investment Program has been endorsed by more than 2,000 organizations (including asset owners, investment managers, and other financial service providers). And although infrastructure equity investments have led the way in taking ESG principles into consideration, the fixed-income space is also beginning to include ESG principles—for example, green bonds and social bonds. The number of U.S. institutional investors considering ESG factors in their decisions almost doubled between 2013 and 2018, from 22 to 40 percent, according to the Callan Institute, but the inclusion of resilience within ESG considerations remains limited.

There are many indicators for measuring the sustainability of infrastructure, using an ESG lens (box 13.1). However, resilience is also a key driver of performance. One challenge for the tools that inform investors and decision makers is how to identify the performance dimension (how will natural risks and climate change affect the return on a financial product?) and the ESG dimensions (how will a financial product contribute to economic, social, and environmental sustainability?).

To identify these dimensions and complement the existing measurement systems, the World Bank Group is committed to developing a *resilience rating system*, which would aim at better informing investors and decision makers on the resilience characteristics of their projects. This rating system would not create new information or data. Instead, it would translate the highly technical information already existing in project documents into a simple rating that can be of use to people without an engineering background. It will rate projects along two dimensions of resilience:

- *Dimension 1: resilience of investments and projects.* This dimension measures the extent to which a project has taken climate and disaster risks into consideration. The rating, expressed in grades from A+ to D, characterizes the confidence in a project's ability to avoid financial, environmental, and social underperformance. A high rating, for example, denotes higher confidence that the expected rate of return of an investment accounts for the possible negative impacts of natural hazards or climate change on the investment. With a low rating and everything else being equal, the expected rate of return is unlikely to be achieved and would

BOX 13.1 Many indicators have been developed to measure the sustainability of infrastructure

Today, various sets of standards for sustainable infrastructure are including considerations of resilience or at least governance dimensions related to resilience. What follows is a summary of five of these standards:

- *Standard for Sustainable and Resilient Infrastructure (SuRe),* a project certification standard developed by the Global Infrastructure Basel Foundation in Switzerland, in collaboration with Natixis, a French investment bank:
  - SuRe's cost for certification is between $30,000 and $60,000, depending on the size of the project and its stage of development.
  - The certification applies 61 criteria across 14 themes. The criterion dedicated to "resilience planning" requires that a vulnerability assessment be conducted for the project's life cycle, that resilience measures be reported, and that a risk-monitoring system be included in the project. It also includes components regarding emergency response preparedness and supply chain vulnerabilities.

- *Envision,* a rating system developed jointly by the Institute for Sustainable Infrastructure and the Zofnass Program for Sustainable Infrastructure at Harvard University:
  - Projects can opt for verification, with fees ranging from $11,000 to $56,000.
  - The rating system includes 60 sustainability criteria, or credits, in five categories: quality of life, leadership, resource allocation, natural world, and climate and risk.
  - The climate and risk category includes many subindicators related to resilience: the development of a comprehensive impact assessment and adaptation plans; consideration of long-term trends such as climate change; preparation for long-term adaptability; and the management of short-term threats and heat island effects.

- *Civil Engineering Environmental Quality Assessment and Awards (CEEQUAL) scheme,* an assessment scheme launched in 2003, with fees ranging from less than $6,500 for very small projects to more than $58,000 for large projects:
  - The scheme assesses nine categories of a project's environmental management and impacts.
  - Each category consists of a series of point-scored questions that can be applied to different management practices and performance indicators.
  - The scheme includes simple questions related to the consideration of and response to expected changes in climate conditions.

- *International Finance Corporation (IFC) Performance Standards (and Equator Principles),* a methodology with eight performance standards for projects financed by the IFC, derived from the World Bank Group's environmental, health, and safety project guidelines:
  - The first standard relates to the "Assessment and Management of Environmental and Social Risks and Impacts" and includes requirements for emergency management.
  - Performance standards focus on the risk created by the project without in-depth exploration of the risks to the project.

- *GRESB (ESG Benchmark for Real Assets) Infrastructure,* a project-level and a portfolio-level assessment tool for asset owners, fund managers, contractors, and asset managers:
  - Data collected include management practice indicators regarding sustainability planning, eight categories of environmental performance indicators, and project performance metrics.
  - A resilience module focuses on preparation for disruptive events and long-term trends such as climate change.

Source: Bennon and Sharma 2018.

need to be adjusted to account for disasters and climate change. This metric provides information not on whether the project is likely to fail, but on whether the risk of failure (which can be low or high, depending on the case) is considered in the economic or financial analysis that justifies the project. As a result, a project with a high risk of failure can be highly rated, provided this risk is accounted for in the analysis. The project may in fact be attractive in spite of this risk, if the potential returns in the absence of failure are extremely high.

- *Dimension 2: resilience building through investments and projects.* Targeted investments, or specific components of investments, are often designed with the objective of building the resilience of beneficiaries. Examples of this are a seawall or a drainage system needed to manage storm surges or heavy precipitation in cities or a new road that connects an isolated village to markets, building food security. Such investments thus support moving toward greater resilience against current and future risks. The distinction between this dimension and the first is important: although all projects should be resilient, not all projects seek to improve the resilience of the broader community or country. Thus, the second dimension helps to prioritize and promote those investments that are key to climate-resilient development and longer-term resilience development pathways. The rating conditions for this category—also expressed with letter grades—are by necessity less technical than those of the first, and they depend, other things being equal, on beneficiaries and related vulnerabilities.

The objective of this two-dimensional rating system is to ensure that each and every investment made by the private or the public sector gives due consideration to natural disaster and climate change risks, examining its own resilience and ability to deliver the expected benefits and profits. It also accounts for the broader impacts on communities and economies. This tool aims to help investors select the best projects and contribute to a more productive and resilient future.

If such a resilient rating system becomes common practice, it could allow investors to impose a minimum standard in terms of how new infrastructure projects account for natural hazards and climate change. It would help to translate high-level commitments to support more resilient societies into changes in practices and designs in the real economy. And if such a system becomes embedded in government budgetary processes, it could also influence public spending—which represents the large majority of investments in infrastructure—and support a broad transition toward more resilient infrastructure systems.

More transparency regarding the resilience of private and public investments would also provide a strong incentive for implementation of the other recommendations presented in this report and help to manage the political economy challenges highlighted earlier. Today, there is little immediate reward for a government that provides the right hazards and climate change data to its infrastructure operators or that regularly updates its construction codes and infrastructure sector regulations. More transparency on the resilience of infrastructure projects would give visibility to these actions, by improving the rating of the investments taking place in a country. If aggregated, it could even help to build a country-level measure of the resilience of new investments.

These synergies are only a fraction of the many synergies that exist between the recommendations made in this report. Indeed, no single intervention can make all infrastructure systems resilient. Instead, governments will need to define and implement a consistent strategy—in partnership with all stakeholders such as utilities, investors, business associations, and citizen organizations—to tackle the many obstacles to more resilient infrastructure systems. And while doing so will be challenging and take time, this report highlights the potential benefits of doing so and of doing it without delay. According to the analysis presented in this report, each decade of inaction may cost the world trillions of dollars.

REFERENCES

Bennon, M., and R. Sharma. 2018. "State of the Practice: Sustainability Standards for Infrastructure Investors." *SSRN Electronic Journal*, October. https://doi.org/10.2139/ssrn.3292469.

Clarke, D. J., and S. Dercon. 2016. "Dull Disasters? How Planning Ahead Will Make a Difference." World Bank, Washington, DC. https://doi.org/10.1017/CBO9781107415324.004.

Colon, C., S. Hallegatte, and J. Rozenberg. 2019. "Transportation and Supply Chain Resilience in the United Republic of Tanzania." Background paper for this report, World Bank, Washington, DC.

Ghesquiere, F., and O. Mahul. 2007. "Sovereign Natural Disaster Insurance for Developing Countries: A Paradigm Shift in Catastrophe Risk Financing." Policy Research Working Paper 4345, World Bank, Washington, DC. https://doi.org/10.1596/1813-9450-4345.

Hallegatte, S., A. Vogt-Schilb, M. Bangalore, and J. Rozenberg. 2017. *Unbreakable: Building the Resilience of the Poor in the Face of Natural Disasters*. Washington, DC: World Bank. https://doi.org/10.1596/978-1-4648-1003-9.

Mahul, O., and F. Ghesquiere. 2010. "Financial Protection of the State against Natural Disasters: A Primer." Policy Research Working Paper 5429, World Bank, Washington, DC. https://doi.org/10.1596/1813-9450-5429.

Rentschler, J., M. Kornejew, S. Hallegatte, M. Obolensky, and J. Braese. 2019. "Underutilized Potential: The Business Costs of Unreliable Infrastructure in Developing Countries." Background paper for this report, World Bank, Washington, DC.

World Bank. 2017. *Sovereign Catastrophe Risk Pools*. Washington, DC: World Bank. https://openknowledge.worldbank.org/handle/10986/28311.

———. 2018. *Strategic Use of Climate Finance to Maximize Climate Action*. World Bank, Washington, DC. https://openknowledge.worldbank.org/handle/10986/30475.

APPENDIX A

Engineering Options to Increase the Resilience of Infrastructure Assets

The tables in this appendix are adapted from Miyamoto International (2019), which provides more information on each of the options, including sources for the estimates provided. The data in many of the cells rely on past experience and engineering judgment. The data are intended to be a representative sample. The actual improvements, benefits from such improvements, and the costs of such improvements depend on specific applications, site conditions, and other variables. Unless stated otherwise, the improvement costs are typically for enhancements implemented during the construction of new units. For most applications, the costs of retrofitting improvements are similar. For more details, see Miyamoto International (2019).

TABLE A.1 Engineering options to improve infrastructure asset resilience in the power sector

Type	Natural hazard: Hazard	Natural hazard: Intensity	Component	Critical system/component: Engineering improvement	Critical system/component: Quality improvement	Damage probability: Baseline	Damage probability: Improved	Incremental cost (including quality control)
Thermal power plants (coal, natural gas, oil)	EQ motion	Mw 7 PGA 0.4g	Items and their attachments	Seismic component and anchorage	Construction inspection, testing	0.25	0.02	0.20
	Liquefaction	ND	Substrate	Soil improvement Deep foundation	Geotechnical report and testing	0.30	NS	0.20
	Wind	100 mph	Building structures stacks	Stiff braced structures Helical strake	Welding quality control, inspection, testing	0.40	0.1	0.10
	Flood	2- to 3-ft. inundation	Entire facility	Floodwall, sheet piling	Ensure watertight construction, inspection	0.05	NS	0.02
Hydropower plants	EQ motion	Mw 7 PGA 0.4g	Gateway, lift joints, intake towers	Design for stronger events, use proper anchorage and seismic components	Inspection during construction, periodic inspection	0.7	0.4	0.2
	Liquefaction				N/A			
	Wind				N/A			
	Flood	Large rainstorms, 200- to 500-year flood	Spillways, dam crest overtopping	Increased spillway capacity	Proper drenching, underwater inspection	0.1	0.05	0.03
Solar farms	EQ motion	Mw 7 PGA 0.4g	Support structure	Adequate anchorage, proper design and bracing	Inspection, maintenance	0.1	0.02	0.05
	Liquefaction				N/A			
	Wind	100 mph	Uplift support	Proper anchorage support for platform	Ensure tested components use, perform random sampling	0.2	0.08	0.15
	Flood	ND	Pole foundation	If scour concern, use riprap	Periodic maintenance	NS	NS	NS
Wind farms	EQ motion	PGA 1.0g (large event)	Monopole	Use seismically robust unit	Maintenance, obtain manufacturer testing and certificates	0.1	0.08	0.05
	Liquefaction	ND	Monopole foundation	Use deep foundations	Inspection during installation	0.2	NS	0.3
	Wind	Design wind 70 to 100 mph	Blade	Optimize blade configuration Use material with higher fatigue life Conservatism in design	Periodic inspection, report any crack initiation on blades or connections	0.2	0.1	0.05
	Flood	N/A						

(Table continues next page)

TABLE A.1 Engineering options to improve infrastructure asset resilience in the power sector *(continued)*

	Natural hazard			Critical system/component		Damage probability		Incremental cost (including quality control)
Type	**Hazard**	**Intensity**	**Component**	**Engineering improvement**	**Quality improvement**	**Baseline**	**Improved**	
Nuclear power plants	EQ motion	Large events	Main structures, interior components	Seismic isolation of main building, Flexible connections Seismically rated components; pipes, cable racks, etc.	Testing, inspection, construction documentation	0.3	0.02	0.05
	Liquefaction				NA			
	Wind				NA			
	Flood	Large events	Reactor ground, cooling towers, buildings	Improved dike construction, extreme event flood design	Shutdown drills, document review, including geotechnical, hydrological, and construction documents	0.1	0.07	0.05
Substations	EQ motion	Mw 7 PGA 0.4g	Bushings, switches, circuit breakers	Component anchorage, use of seismic components	Review all test documents, ensure redundancy, spares	0.8	0.3	0.1
	Liquefaction	Mw 7 PGD 300 mm	Switches, elevated components	Deep foundation	Geotechnical report, pile load testing	0.6	NS	0.2
	Wind	Design wind 70 to 100 mph	Elevated components	More robust components	Testing, inspection	0.3	0.1	0.2
	Flood	2- to 3-ft. inundation	Transformers, buildings, ground-mounted equipment	Elevate components	Review construction reports, inspections	0.1	NS	0.1
Transmission and distribution lines	EQ motion	Mw 7 PGA 0.4g	T&D systems	Use seismic components	Periodic inspection	0.02	0.01	0.02
	Liquefaction	ND	Lattice support	Use deep foundation	Construction inspection	0.2	NS	0.15
	Wind	Design wind 70 to 100 mph	Tower	Use steel, concrete, or composite towers Use vibration dampers	Construction inspection, Use tested components	0.3	0.07	0.2
	Flood				N/A			

TABLE A.2 Engineering options to improve infrastructure asset resilience in the water sector

	Natural hazard			Critical system/component		Damage probability		Incremental cost (including quality control)
Type	**Hazard**	**Intensity**	**Component**	**Engineering improvement**	**Quality improvement**	**Baseline**	**Improved**	
Reservoirs (impounding)	EQ motion	PGA 0.6g	Embankment	Design for higher seismic design forces	Drenching, maintenance	0.15	0.05	0.05
	Liquefaction	ND	Embankment	Restressed concrete piling	Geotechnical report, inspection during construction and pile driving	0.2	0.02	0.20
	Wind				N/A			
	Flood	Large event	Embankment crest	Design for higher freeboard (taller structure)	Maintenance, drenching	0.2	0.05	0.05
Reservoirs (storage tanks)	EQ motion	Mw 7 PGA 0.4g	Tank elevated support	Thicker tanks (ground) Perform seismic design and use larger members and adequate connections (elevated)	Construction inspection, random testing during erection	0.2	0.02	0.05
	Liquefaction	ND	Tank support	Use pile foundation	Geotechnical testing and pile inspection	0.4	0.1	0.5
	Wind	Large events	Elevated tank	Design for higher wind force	Keep tank full during storms	0.2	0.05	0.1
	Flood				N/A			
Water and wastewater treatment plants	EQ motion	Mw 7 PGA 0.4g	Pumping system	Higher threshold seismic design	Improving anchoring system and introducing seismic protective devices	0.7	0.4	0.15
	Liquefaction	ND	Sewage system	Higher threshold for permanent ground displacement	Improving the backfilling	0.7	0.4	0.2
	Wind				N/A			
	Flood	Large event	Pumping system	Elevating	Improve construction quality	0.5	0.2	0.05
Distribution pipes	EQ motion	Mw 7 PGA 0.4g	Joints	Higher threshold in seismic design	Replace joints with flexible joints with higher displacement and rotation capacities	0.7	0.4	0.2
	Liquefaction	Large event	Joints and sections	Higher threshold for permanent ground displacement	Replace the sections and joints to accommodate very large differential displacement and rotation demand	0.7	0.4	0.55
	Wind				N/A			
	Flood	Large event	Pipelines	Higher threshold for large pipe displacement	Keep the pipes filled with water to mitigate buoyancy effects	0.2	0.1	0.02

(Table continues next page)

TABLE A.2 Engineering options to improve infrastructure asset resilience in the water sector *(continued)*

Type	Natural hazard		Critical system/component			Damage probability		Incremental cost (including quality control)
	Hazard	Intensity	Component	Engineering improvement	Quality improvement	Baseline	Improved	
Sewage network emissaries	EQ motion	MMI VII to VIII (equiv. PGA = 0.3g)	Pumping station	Equipment anchorage retrofit	Apply higher level of quality assurance	0.56	0.39	0.25
	Liquefaction	PGD	Buried pipe	Soil improvement/ compaction	Apply higher level of quality assurance	NA	NA	0.55
	Wind	PGWS = 90 mph	WTP building	Roof-wall connection retrofit and Bldg. envelopes replacement	Apply higher level of quality assurance	0.04	0.03	0.15
	Flood	FID = 3.3 ft.	Pumping station	Elevation and watertight barrier installation	Apply higher level of quality assurance	0.08	0.01	0.40
Water conveyance systems (canals)	EQ motion	PGV 0.5 m/ sec PGD 0.15 m	Canal walls	Use reinforced concrete liner	Construction inspection, cylinder testing, rebar placement	0.2	0.05	0.2
	Liquefaction	Based on small segment of long canal	Canal wall and base	Geomembrane liners, soil densification	Construction inspection, geotechnical testing	0.2	0.01	0.03
	Wind	N/A						
	Flood	Large events	Gates and locks	Use proper gates, dry channels adjacent	Periodic maintenance, construction inspection	0.1	0.02	0.15
Drainage systems	EQ motion	MMI VII to VIII (PGA or PGV)	Drainpipe	Drainpipe replacement	Apply higher level of quality assurance	NA	NA	1.05
	Liquefaction	PGD	Drainpipe	Soil improvement/ compaction	Apply higher level of quality assurance	NA	NA	0.55
	Wind	N/A						
	Flood	N/A						

TABLE A.3 Engineering options to improve infrastructure asset resilience in the railways sector

Type	Natural hazard		Critical system/component			Damage probability		Incremental cost (including quality control)
	Hazard	Intensity	Component	Engineering improvement	Quality improvement	Baseline	Improved	
Railways (diesel and electric)	EQ motion	MMI VII to VIII (equiv. PGA = 0.3g)	Bridge pier	Pier jacketing retrofit	Apply higher level of quality assurance	0.12	0.05	0.25
	Liquefaction	PGD = 12 in.	Tracks/ roadbeds	French drainage and drainpipe installation	Apply higher level of quality assurance	0.16	0.01	0.45
	Wind	PGWS = 90 mph	Railway stations	Roof-wall connection retrofit and building envelopes replacement	Apply higher level of quality assurance	0.04	0.03	0.15
	Flood	FID = 3.3 ft.	Fuel/DC substations	Elevation and watertight barrier installation	Apply higher level of quality assurance	0.03	0.01	0.50

TABLE A.4 Engineering options to improve infrastructure asset resilience in the roadway sector

	Natural hazard			Critical system/component		Damage probability		Incremental cost (including quality control)
Type	Hazard	Intensity	Component	Engineering improvement	Quality improvement	Baseline	Improved	
Highways (on grade)	EQ motion	PGD 0.5 m	Embankment	Provide geogrid reinforcement	Construction inspection, use of approved material	0.1	0.05	0.1
	Liquefaction	ND	Embankment	Soil improvement	Geotechnical testing, construction inspection and testing	0.1	0.05	0.05
	Wind				N/A			
	Flood				N/A			
	Landslide	ND	Road surface	Add retaining wall, stabilize sloe, shotcrete, soil nails	Construction monitoring	0.2	0.02	0.1
Highway bridges	EQ motion	Mw 7 PGA 0.4g	Bridge superstructure, column, foundation	Use CA or Japan seismic design, columns as fuse	Construction inspection, testing, qualify contractors	0.4	0.05	0.1
	Liquefaction	PGD 250 mm	Bridge foundation	Use pile foundation	Geotechnical testing, construction inspection	0.3	0.05	0.2
	Wind	Small events	Steel bridge members and connections	Use details with longer fatigue life during bridge design life	Inspection of welded connections, reduce section loss by corrosion prevention	0.05	0.01	0.05
	Flood	Large floods	Bridge foundation	Use riprap	Hydrological report, construction inspections	0.05	0.02	0.05
	Landslide	PGD = 14 in., 7 in.	Bridge foundation	Soil improvement	Apply higher level of quality assurance	0.5	0.16	0.15
Secondary urban roads (on grade)	EQ motion	Mw 7 PGA 0.4g	Road surface and underlying material	Provide seismic reinforcement, compact the underlying material	Use earthquake resistance foundations	0.1	0.05	0.05
	Liquefaction	Large PGD: more than 0.3 m	Road surface and underlying material	Provide reinforcement against large ground displacement	Soil improvement, avoid areas subjected vulnerable to liquefaction	0.1	0.05	0.05
	Wind	N/A						
	Flood	Large floods	Road surface	Provide barriers, improve drainage	Construction inspection, testing, qualify contractors	0.1	0.05	0.03
	Landslide	N/A						

(Table continues next page)

TABLE A.4 Engineering options to improve infrastructure asset resilience in the roadway sector *(continued)*

	Natural hazard			Critical system/component		Damage probability		Incremental cost (including quality control)
Type	**Hazard**	**Intensity**	**Component**	**Engineering improvement**	**Quality improvement**	**Baseline**	**Improved**	
Urban (roadway) bridges	EQ motion	Mw 7 PGA 0.4g	Bridge superstructure, abutments, footings	Use CA or Japan seismic design, columns as fuse	Construction inspection, testing, qualify contractors	0.35	0.04	0.2
	Liquefaction	PGD 250 mm	Bridge foundation	H pile or prestressed pile foundation	Geotechnical testing, construction inspection	0.4	0.1	0.3
	Wind	Small events	Connection of diaphragms to steel girders	Reduce dissertation-induced fatigue cracking, redundant nonfracture critical design	Inspection of welded connections, reduce section loss by corrosion prevention	0.1	0.03	0.05
	Flood	Large events	Pier and abutment foundations	Mitigation of local scour, use rocks or pier walls	Regular inspection, construction quality control	0.03	0.02	0.01
	Landslide	N/A						
Unpaved tertiary roads	EQ motion	Mw 7 PGA 0.4g	Road surface and underlying material	Provide seismic reinforcement, compact the underlying material	Use earthquake-resistant foundations	0.1	0.05	0.1
	Liquefaction	Large PGD: more than 0.3 m	Road surface and underlying material	Provide reinforcement against large ground displacement	Soil improvement, avoid areas vulnerable to liquefaction	0.1	0.05	0.05
	Wind	N/A						
	Flood	Large floods	Road surface	Provide barriers, improve drainage	Maintain the roads	0.1	0.05	0.03
	Landslide	ND	Road surface	Add retaining wall, stabilize slope, shotcrete, soil nails	Construction monitoring	0.2	0.02	0.05
Wooden bridges	EQ motion	Accelera-tion = 0.4g	Wood bridge trusses	Truss strengthening and connection retrofit	Apply higher level of quality assurance	0.35	0.03	0.20
	Liquefaction	PGD = 10 in.	Bridge foundation	Pile addition (foundation retrofit)	Apply higher level of quality assurance	0.44	0.13	0.30
	Wind	Connection fatigue category	Truss connections	Connection retrofit/ replacement	Apply higher level of quality assurance	0.15	0.05	0.10
	Flood	Flood return period (1,000 to 100 yr.)	Foundation ground	Scour mitigation by ground strengthening (riprap, rock, etc.)	Apply higher level of quality assurance	0.06	0.02	0.03
	Landslide	PGD = 14 in., 7 in.	Bridge foundation	Soil improvement	Apply higher level of quality assurance	0.63	0.25	0.25

Source: Miyamoto International 2019.
Note: FID = flood inundation depth; N/A = denotes hazards that are not considered critical for the given infrastructure; ND = designates hazard for which intensity is not defined explicitly; NS = designates small or negligible; NA = specific damage probability is not available; Mw = moment magnitude scale; PGA = peak ground acceleration; PGD = permanent ground deformation.

Made in the USA
Monee, IL
17 September 2026

63484150R00122